2

TOSHIHIKO KOBAYASHI

Translated and adapted by David Ury

Lettered by Foltz Design

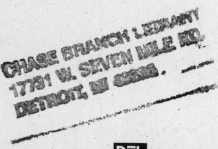
DEL
REY

BALLANTINE BOOKS • NEW YORK

Pastel, volume 2 is a work of fiction. Names, characters, places, and incidents are the products of the author's imagination or are used fictitiously. Any resemblance to actual events, locales, or persons, living or dead, is entirely coincidental.

A Del Rey Trade Paperback Original

Published in the United States by Del Rey Books, an imprint of The Random House Publishing Group, a division of Random House, Inc., New York.

DEL REY is a registered trademark and the Del Rey colophon is a trademark of Random House, Inc.

Publication rights arranged through Kodansha Ltd.

First published in Japan in 2002 by Kodansha Ltd., Tokyo

Library of Congress Control Number: 2005932019

ISBN 0-345-48628-5

Printed in the United States of America

www.delreymanga.com

1 2 3 4 5 6 7 8 9

Translator and Adapter—David Ury
Lettering—Foltz Design

Pastel

CONTENTS

A Note from the Author

KOBAYSHI, WHO FOR SOME REASON CAN NEVER REMEMBER GARY OLDMAN'S NAME.

EVER SINCE I STARTED DOING A WEEKLY SERIES, MY MEMORY HAS BEEN GETTING WORSE AND WORSE. I KNOW I'VE GOT A BIG BRAIN...BUT I'VE ALWAYS HEARD THAT HUMANS ONLY USE A VERY SMALL PORTION OF THEIR BRAINS. IF ONLY I COULD LEARN TO USE THE WHOLE THING. THEN I'D NOT ONLY BE ABLE TO REMEMBER THINGS AGAIN, I'D PROBABLY EVEN BE ABLE TO DRAW SOME REALLY AMAZING MANGA...

Honorifics Explained

Throughout the Del Rey Manga books, you will find Japanese honorifics left intact in the translations. For those not familiar with how the Japanese use honorifics, and, more important, how they differ from American honorifics, we present this brief overview.

Politeness has always been a critical facet of Japanese culture. Ever since the feudal era, when Japan was a highly stratified society, use of honorifics–which can be defined as polite speech that indicates relationship or status–has played an essential role in the Japanese language. When addressing someone in Japanese, an honorific usually takes the form of a suffix attached to one's name (example: "Asuna-san"), as a title at the end of one's name, or in place of the name itself (example: "Negi-sensei" or simply "Sensei!").

Honorifics can be expressions of respect or endearment. In the context of manga and anime, honorifics give insight into the nature of the relationship between characters. Many translations into English leave out these important honorifics, and therefore distort the feel of the original Japanese. Because Japanese honorifics contain nuances that English honorifics lack, it is our policy at Del Rey not to translate them. Here, instead, is a guide to some of the honorifics you may encounter in Del Rey Manga.

-san: This is the most common honorific and is equivalent to Mr., Miss, Ms., Mrs., etc. It is the all-purpose honorific and can be used in any situation where politeness is required.

-sama: This is one level higher than "-san." It is used to confer great respect.

-dono: This comes from the word "tono," which means "lord." It is an even higher level than "-sama" and confers utmost respect.

-kun: This suffix is used at the end of boys' names to express familiarity or endearment. It is also sometimes used by men among friends, or when addressing someone younger or of a lower station.

-chan: This is used to express endearment, mostly toward girls. It is also used for little boys, pets, and between lovers. It gives a sense of childish cuteness.

Bozu: This is an informal way to refer to a boy, similar to the English terms "kid" or "squirt."

Sempai/

Senpai: This title suggests that the addressee is one's senior in a group or organization. It is most often used in a school setting, where underclassmen refer to their upperclassmen as "sempai." It can also be used in the workplace, such as when a newer employee addresses an employee who has seniority in the company.

Kohai: This is the opposite of "-sempai," and is used toward underclassmen in school or newcomers in the workplace. It connotes that the addressee is of a lower station.

Sensei: Literally meaning "one who has come before," this title is used for teachers, doctors, or masters of any profession or art.

-[blank]: This is usually forgotten in these lists, but is perhaps the most significant difference between Japanese and English. The lack of honorific means that the speaker has permission to address the person in a very intimate way. Usually, only family, spouses, or very close friends have this kind of license. Known as *yobisute*, it can be gratifying when someone who has earned the intimacy starts to call one by one's name without an honorific. But when that intimacy hasn't been earned, it can also be insulting.

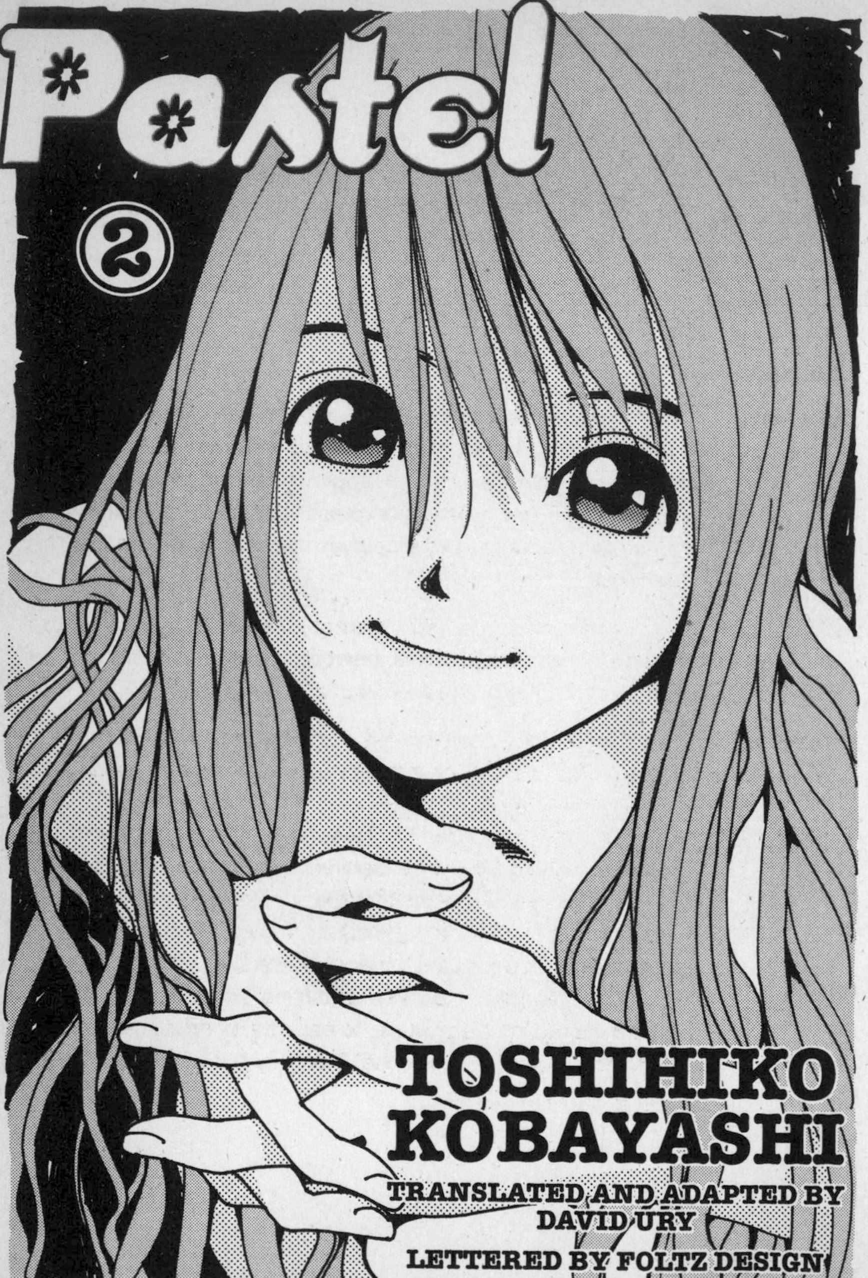
Pastel
2
TOSHIHIKO KOBAYASHI
TRANSLATED AND ADAPTED BY DAVID URY
LETTERED BY FOLTZ DESIGN

Pastel

CONTENTS

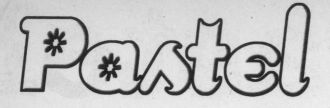

Pastel

MIRACLE 5: THE LONG DAY

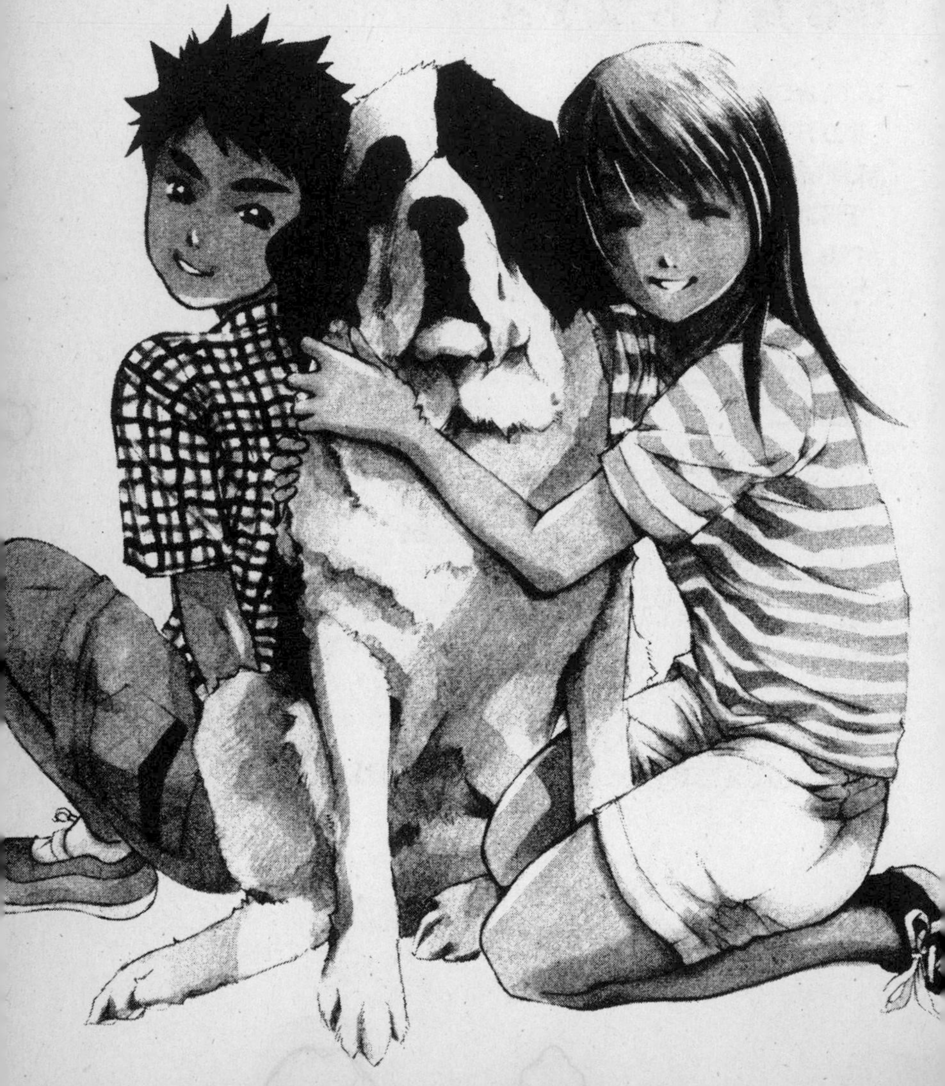

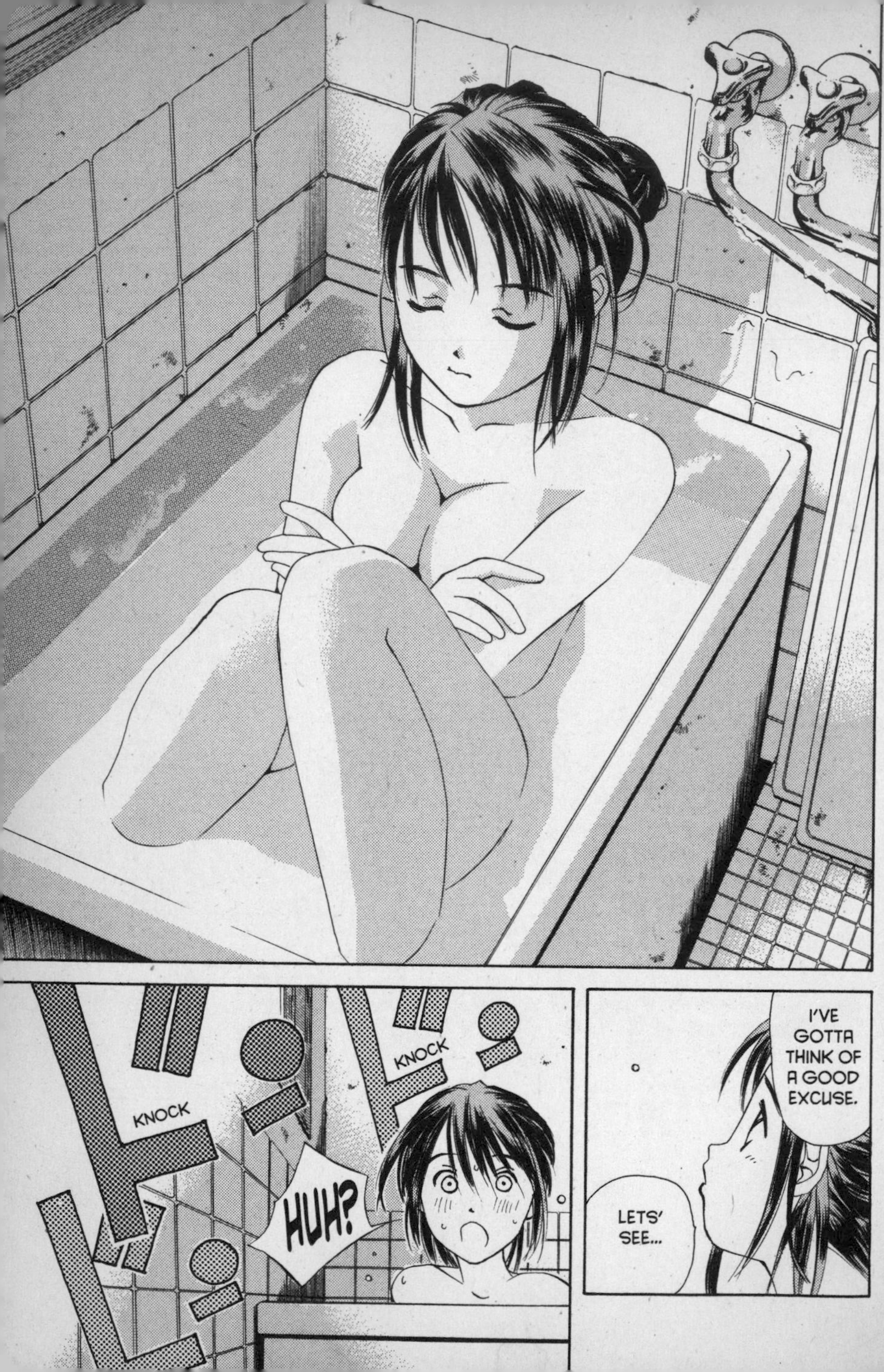
I'VE GOTTA THINK OF A GOOD EXCUSE.
LETS' SEE...
KNOCK
KNOCK
HUH?

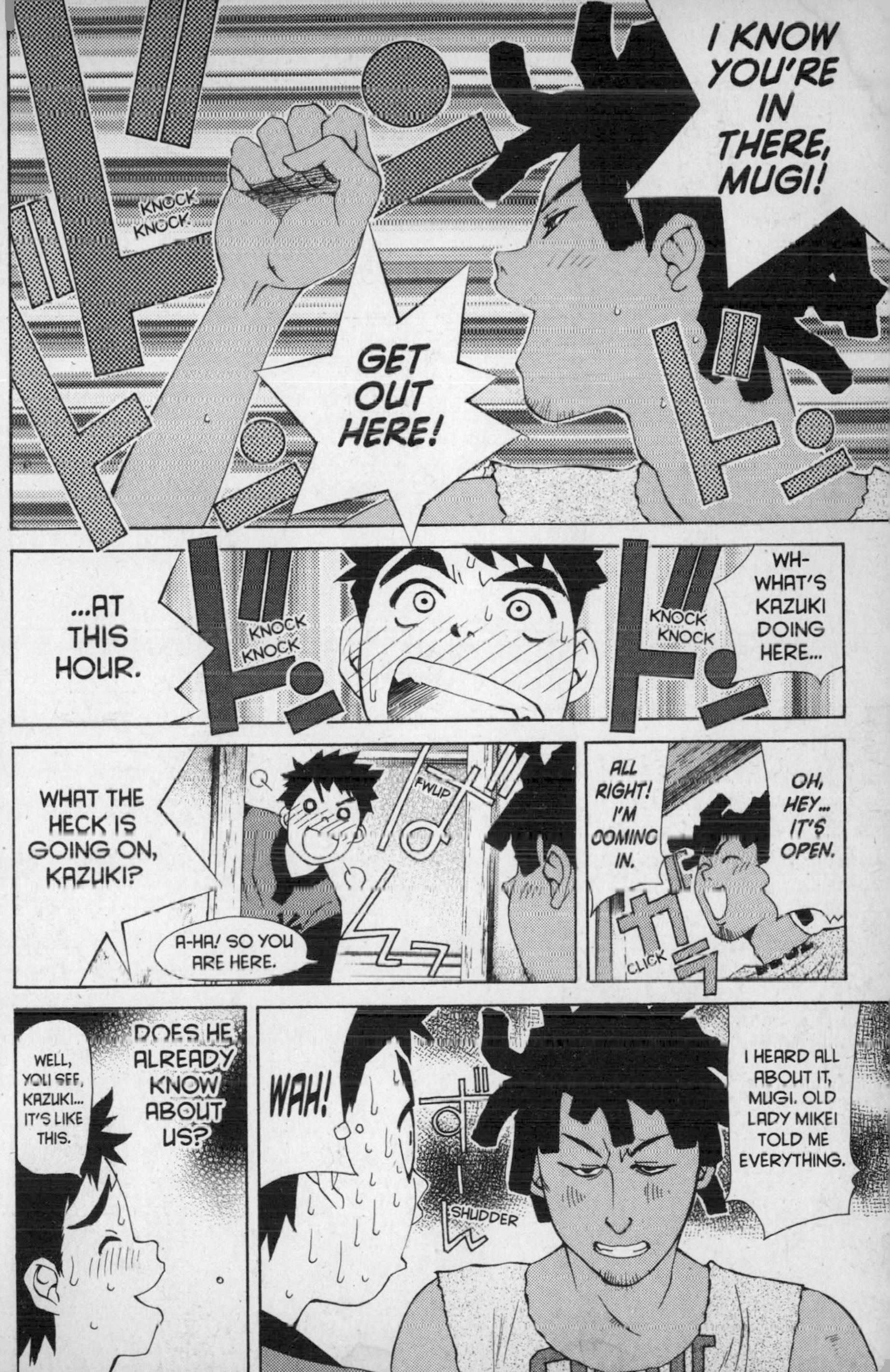
I KNOW YOU'RE IN THERE, MUGI!
KNOCK KNOCK
GET OUT HERE!
WH-WHAT'S KAZUKI DOING HERE...
KNOCK KNOCK
KNOCK KNOCK
...AT THIS HOUR.
OH, HEY... IT'S OPEN.
ALL RIGHT! I'M COMING IN.
CLICK
FWUP
WHAT THE HECK IS GOING ON, KAZUKI?
A-HA! SO YOU ARE HERE.
I HEARD ALL ABOUT IT, MUGI. OLD LADY MIKEI TOLD ME EVERYTHING.
WAH!
SHUDDER
DOES HE ALREADY KNOW ABOUT US?
WELL, YOU SEE, KAZUKI... IT'S LIKE THIS.

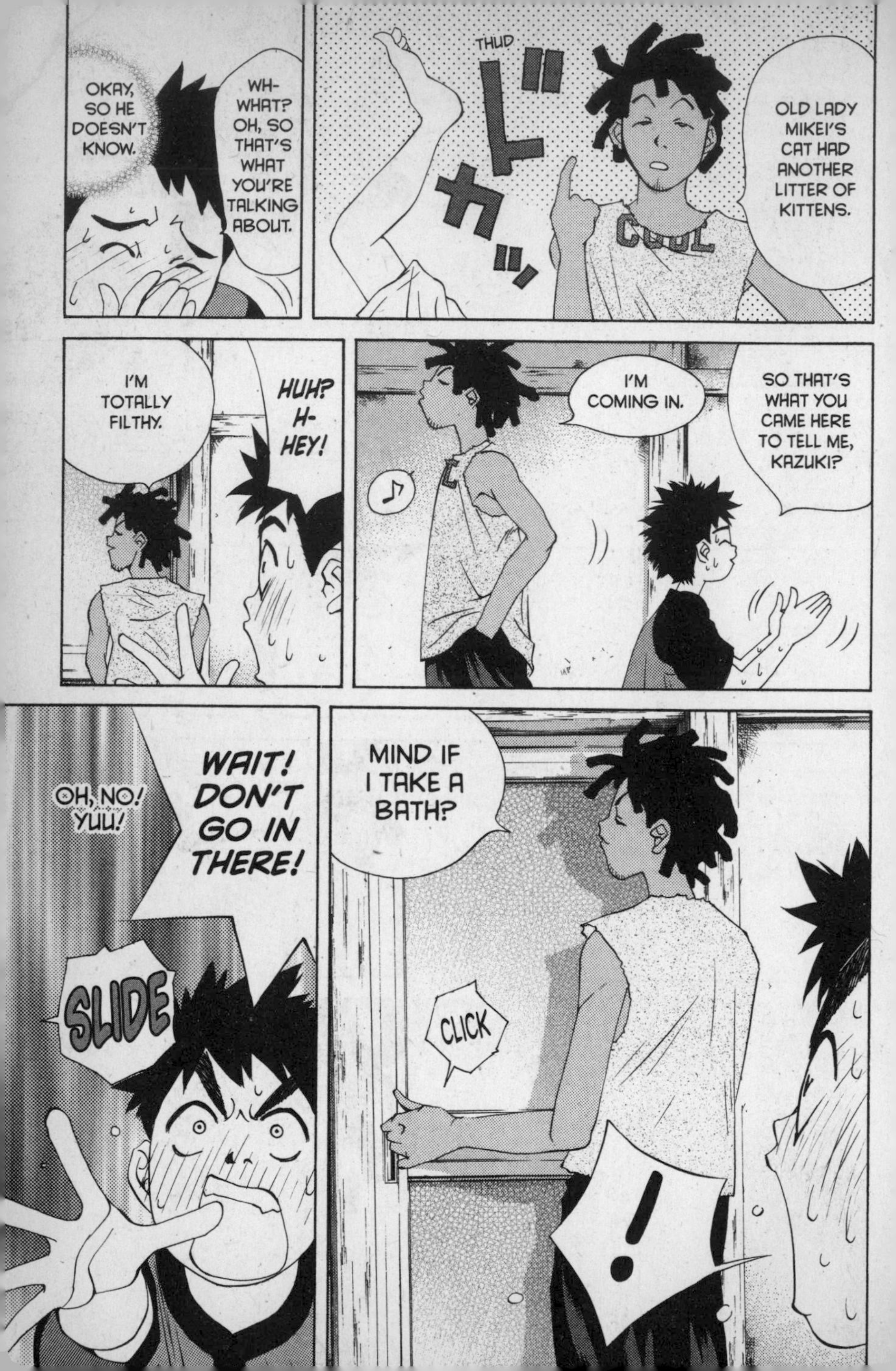
THUD
ドカッ
OLD LADY MIKEI'S CAT HAD ANOTHER LITTER OF KITTENS.
WH- WHAT? OH, SO THAT'S WHAT YOU'RE TALKING ABOUT.
OKAY, SO HE DOESN'T KNOW.
SO THAT'S WHAT YOU CAME HERE TO TELL ME, KAZUKI?
I'M COMING IN.
♪
HUH? H-HEY!
I'M TOTALLY FILTHY.
MIND IF I TAKE A BATH?
CLICK
!
WAIT! DON'T GO IN THERE!
OH, NO! YUU!
SLIDE

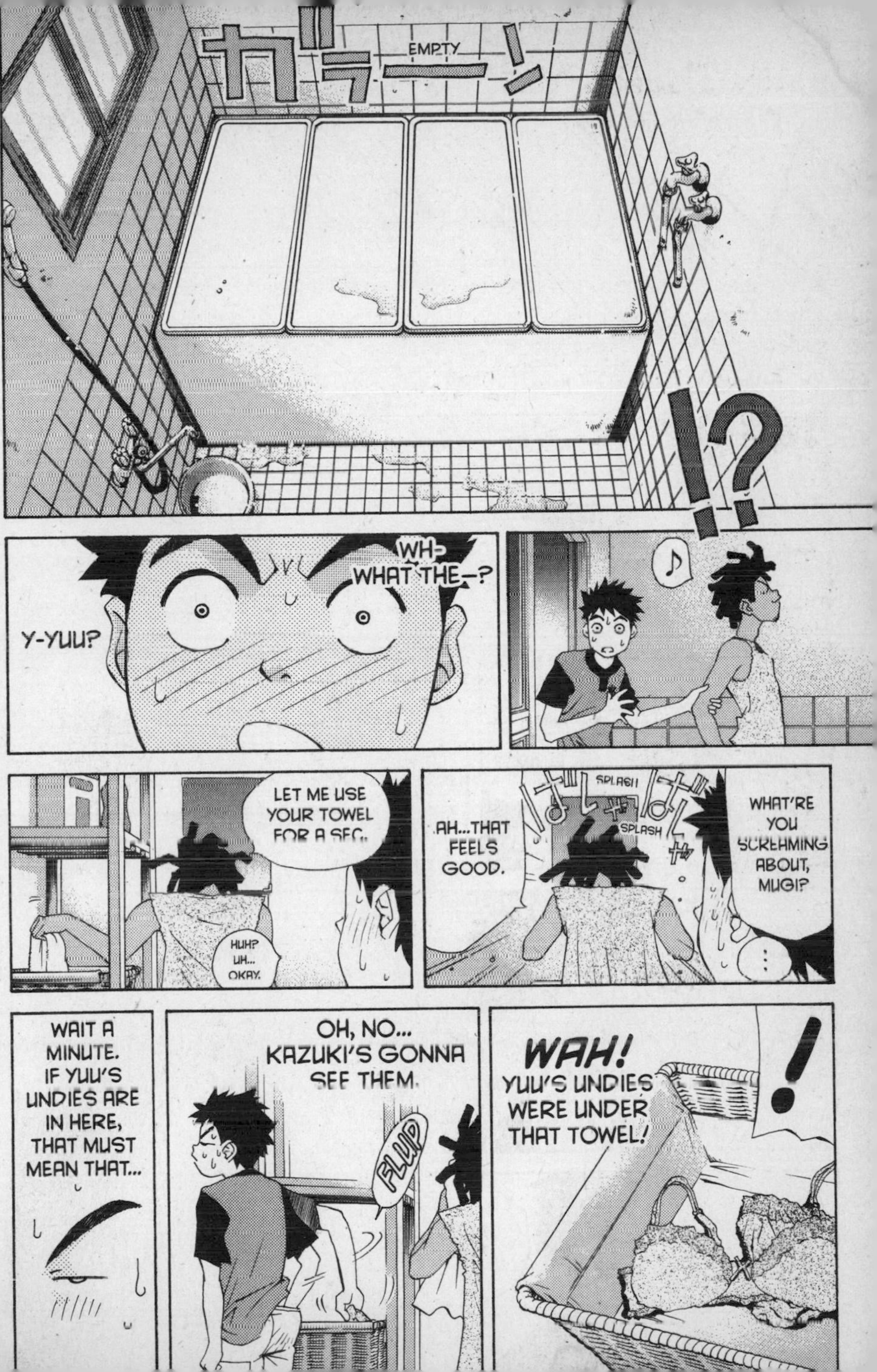
EMPTY
!?
♪
WH- WHAT THE–?
Y-YUU?
SPLASH
SPLASH
WHAT'RE YOU SCREAMING ABOUT, MUGI?
AH...THAT FEELS GOOD.
...
LET ME USE YOUR TOWEL FOR A SEC.
HUH? UH... OKAY.
!
WAH! YUU'S UNDIES WERE UNDER THAT TOWEL!
OH, NO... KAZUKI'S GONNA SEE THEM.
FLUP
WAIT A MINUTE. IF YUU'S UNDIES ARE IN HERE, THAT MUST MEAN THAT...

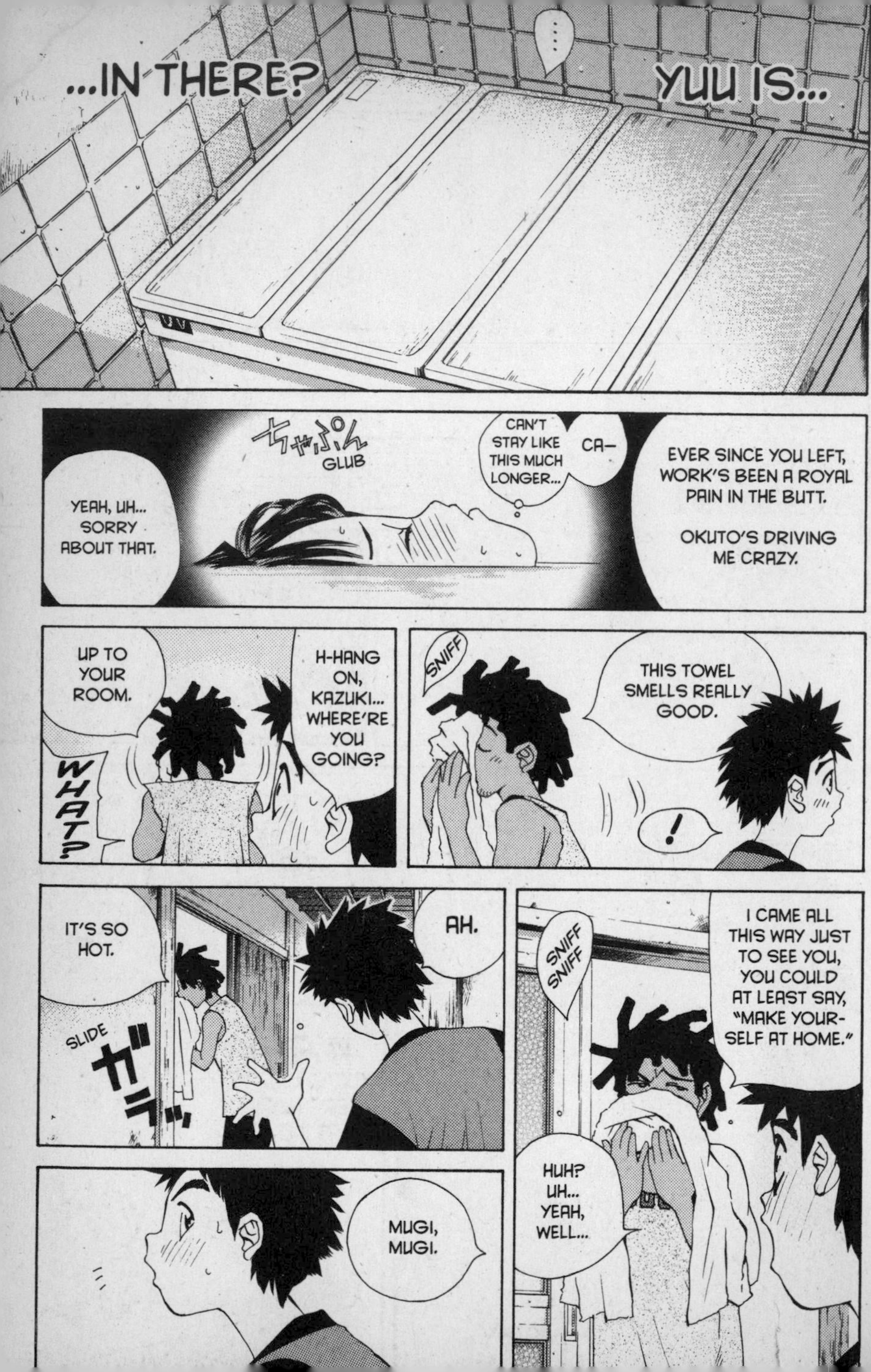
YUU IS...
...
...IN THERE?
EVER SINCE YOU LEFT, WORK'S BEEN A ROYAL PAIN IN THE BUTT.
OKUTO'S DRIVING ME CRAZY.
CA—
CAN'T STAY LIKE THIS MUCH LONGER...
ちゃぷん
GLUB
YEAH, UH... SORRY ABOUT THAT.
THIS TOWEL SMELLS REALLY GOOD.
SNIFF
!
H-HANG ON, KAZUKI... WHERE'RE YOU GOING?
UP TO YOUR ROOM.
WHAT?
I CAME ALL THIS WAY JUST TO SEE YOU, YOU COULD AT LEAST SAY, "MAKE YOUR-SELF AT HOME."
SNIFF SNIFF
HUH? UH... YEAH, WELL...
AH.
IT'S SO HOT.
SLIDE
ガラッ
MUGI, MUGI.

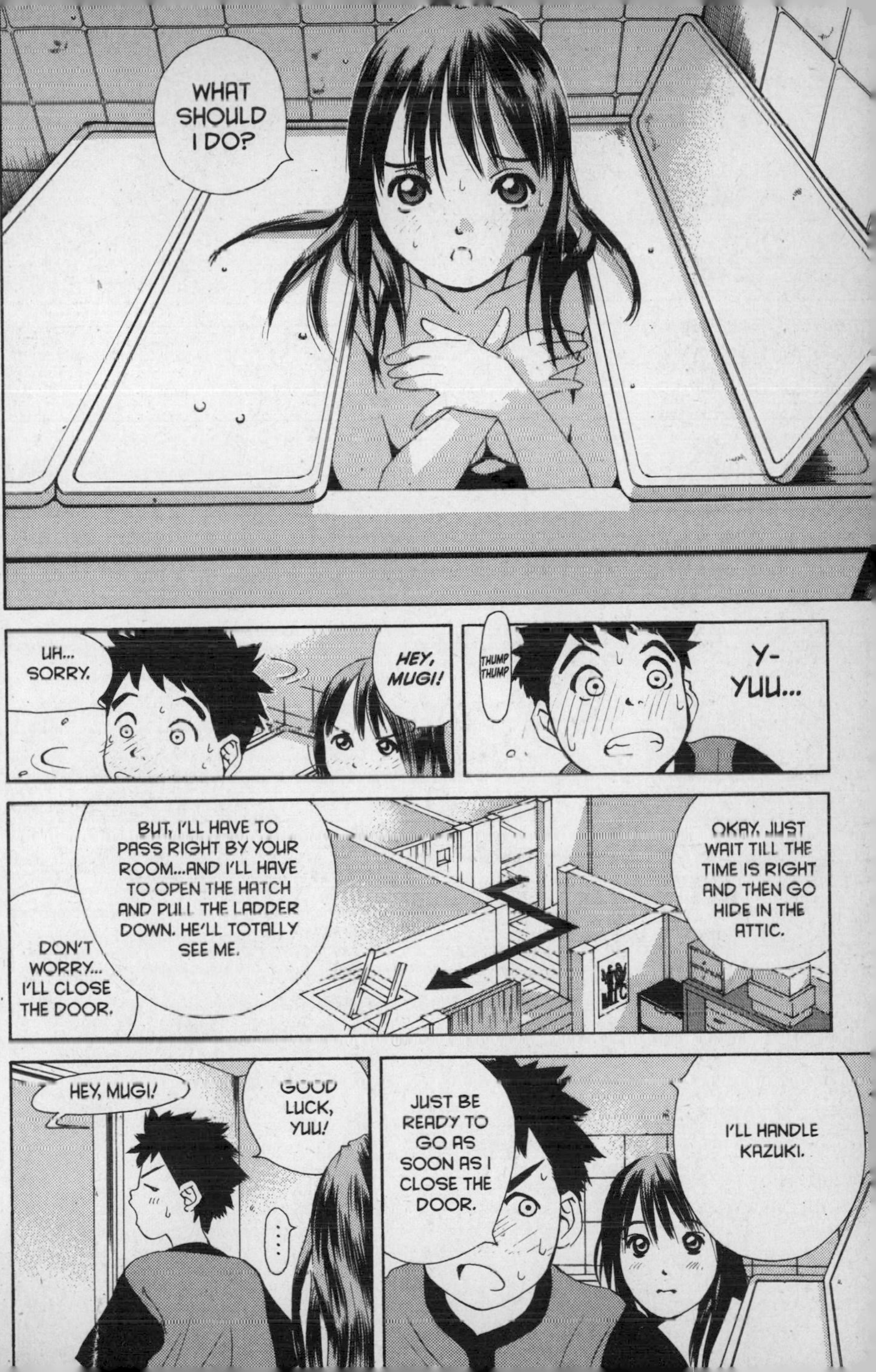
WHAT SHOULD I DO?
Y- YUU...
THUMP THUMP
HEY, MUGI!
UH... SORRY.
OKAY, JUST WAIT TILL THE TIME IS RIGHT AND THEN GO HIDE IN THE ATTIC.
BUT, I'LL HAVE TO PASS RIGHT BY YOUR ROOM...AND I'LL HAVE TO OPEN THE HATCH AND PULL THE LADDER DOWN. HE'LL TOTALLY SEE ME.
DON'T WORRY... I'LL CLOSE THE DOOR.
I'LL HANDLE KAZUKI.
JUST BE READY TO GO AS SOON AS I CLOSE THE DOOR.
GOOD LUCK, YUU!
....
HEY, MUGI!

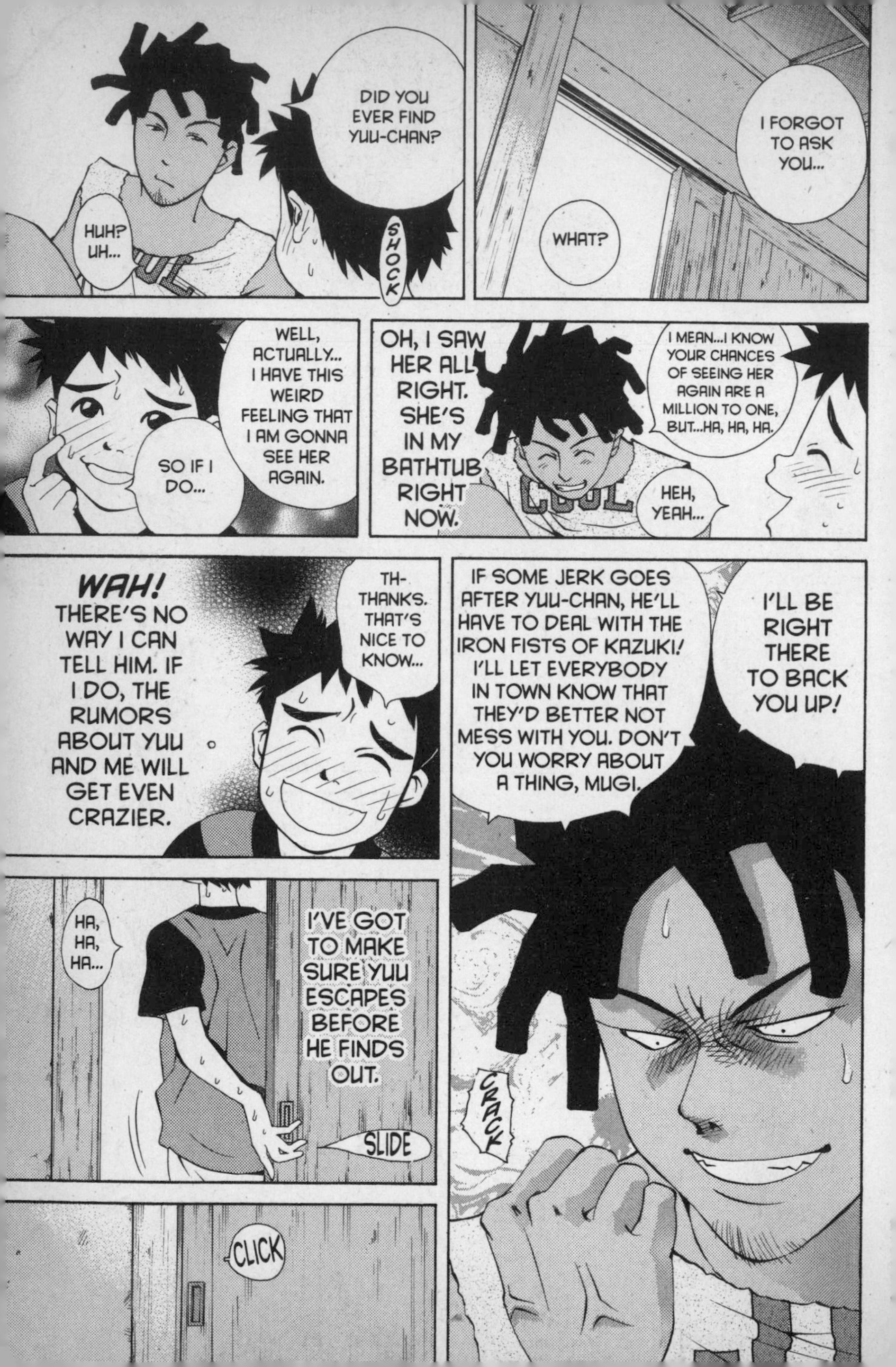
I FORGOT TO ASK YOU...
WHAT?
DID YOU EVER FIND YUU-CHAN?
SHOCK
HUH? UH...
I MEAN...I KNOW YOUR CHANCES OF SEEING HER AGAIN ARE A MILLION TO ONE, BUT...HA, HA, HA.
HEH, YEAH...
OH, I SAW HER ALL RIGHT. SHE'S IN MY BATHTUB RIGHT NOW.
WELL, ACTUALLY... I HAVE THIS WEIRD FEELING THAT I AM GONNA SEE HER AGAIN.
SO IF I DO...
I'LL BE RIGHT THERE TO BACK YOU UP!
IF SOME JERK GOES AFTER YUU-CHAN, HE'LL HAVE TO DEAL WITH THE IRON FISTS OF KAZUKI! I'LL LET EVERYBODY IN TOWN KNOW THAT THEY'D BETTER NOT MESS WITH YOU. DON'T YOU WORRY ABOUT A THING, MUGI.
CRACK
TH-THANKS. THAT'S NICE TO KNOW...
WAH! THERE'S NO WAY I CAN TELL HIM. IF I DO, THE RUMORS ABOUT YUU AND ME WILL GET EVEN CRAZIER.
I'VE GOT TO MAKE SURE YUU ESCAPES BEFORE HE FINDS OUT.
HA, HA, HA...
SLIDE
CLICK

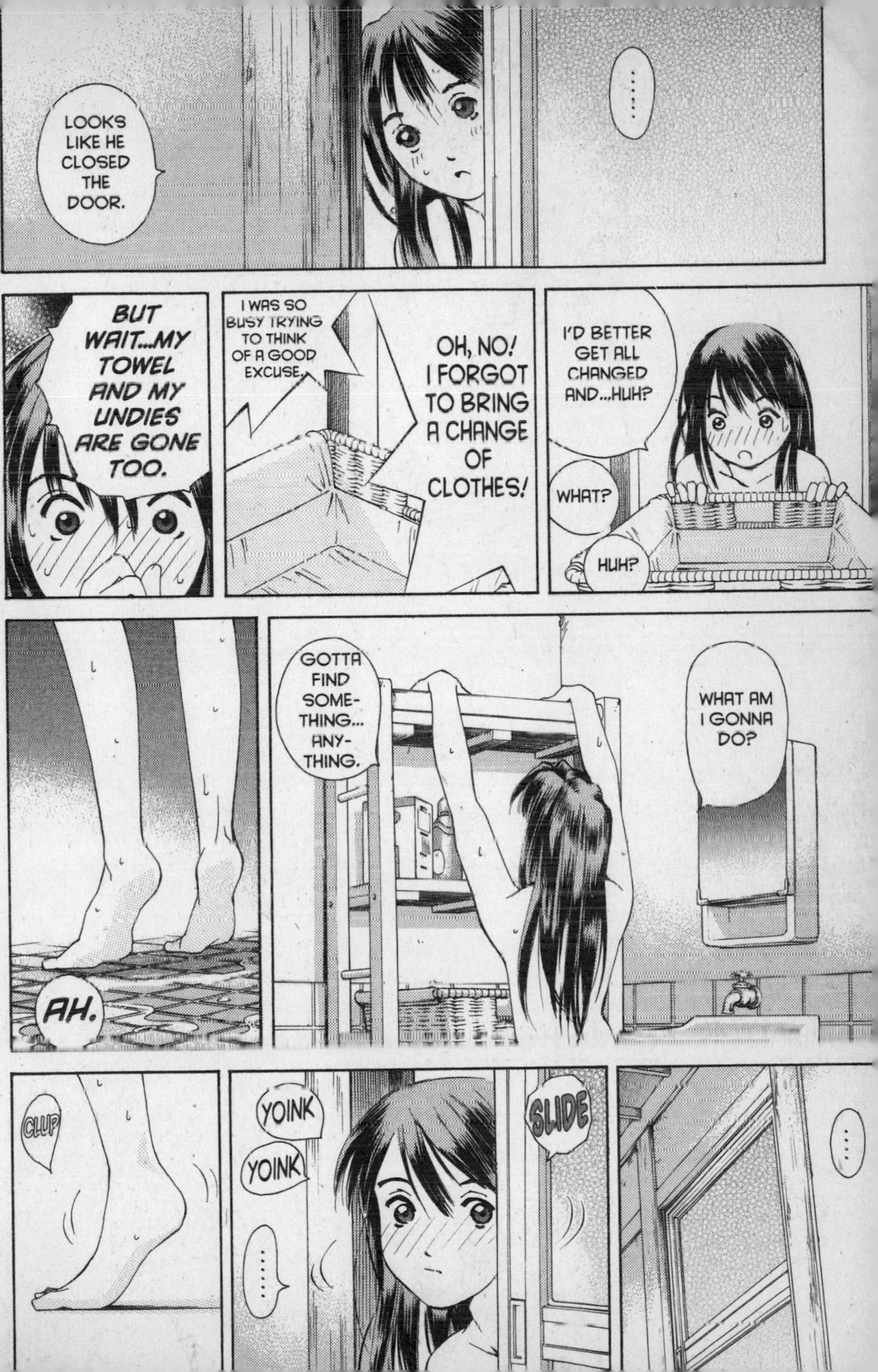
……
LOOKS LIKE HE CLOSED THE DOOR.
I'D BETTER GET ALL CHANGED AND...HUH?
WHAT?
HUH?
OH, NO! I FORGOT TO BRING A CHANGE OF CLOTHES!
I WAS SO BUSY TRYING TO THINK OF A GOOD EXCUSE,
BUT WAIT...MY TOWEL AND MY UNDIES ARE GONE TOO.
WHAT AM I GONNA DO?
GOTTA FIND SOME-THING... ANY-THING.
AH.
……
SLIDE
YOINK
YOINK
……
CLUP

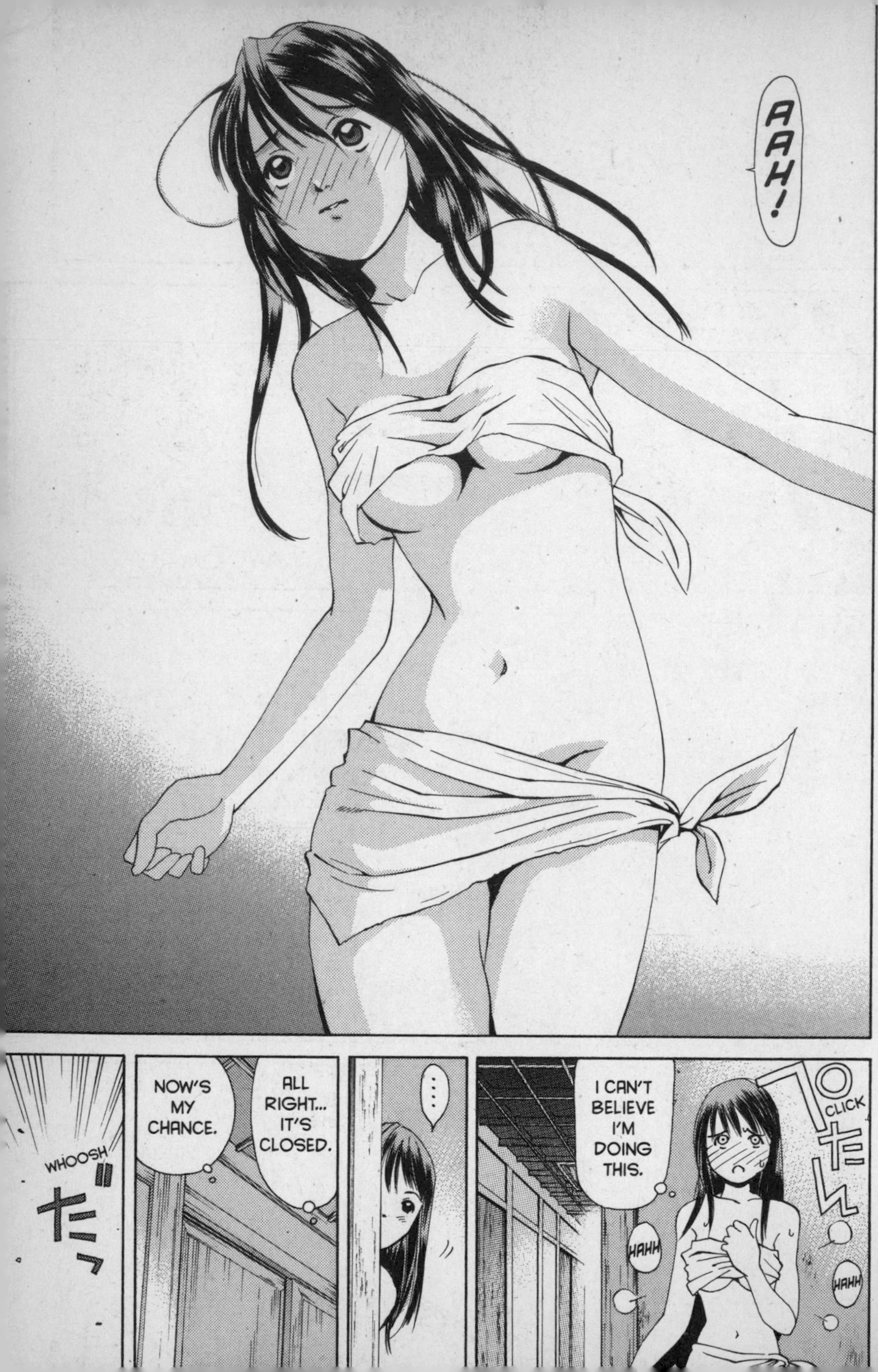
AAAH!
I CAN'T BELIEVE I'M DOING THIS.
CLICK
HAHH
HAHH
....
ALL RIGHT... IT'S CLOSED.
NOW'S MY CHANCE.
WHOOSH

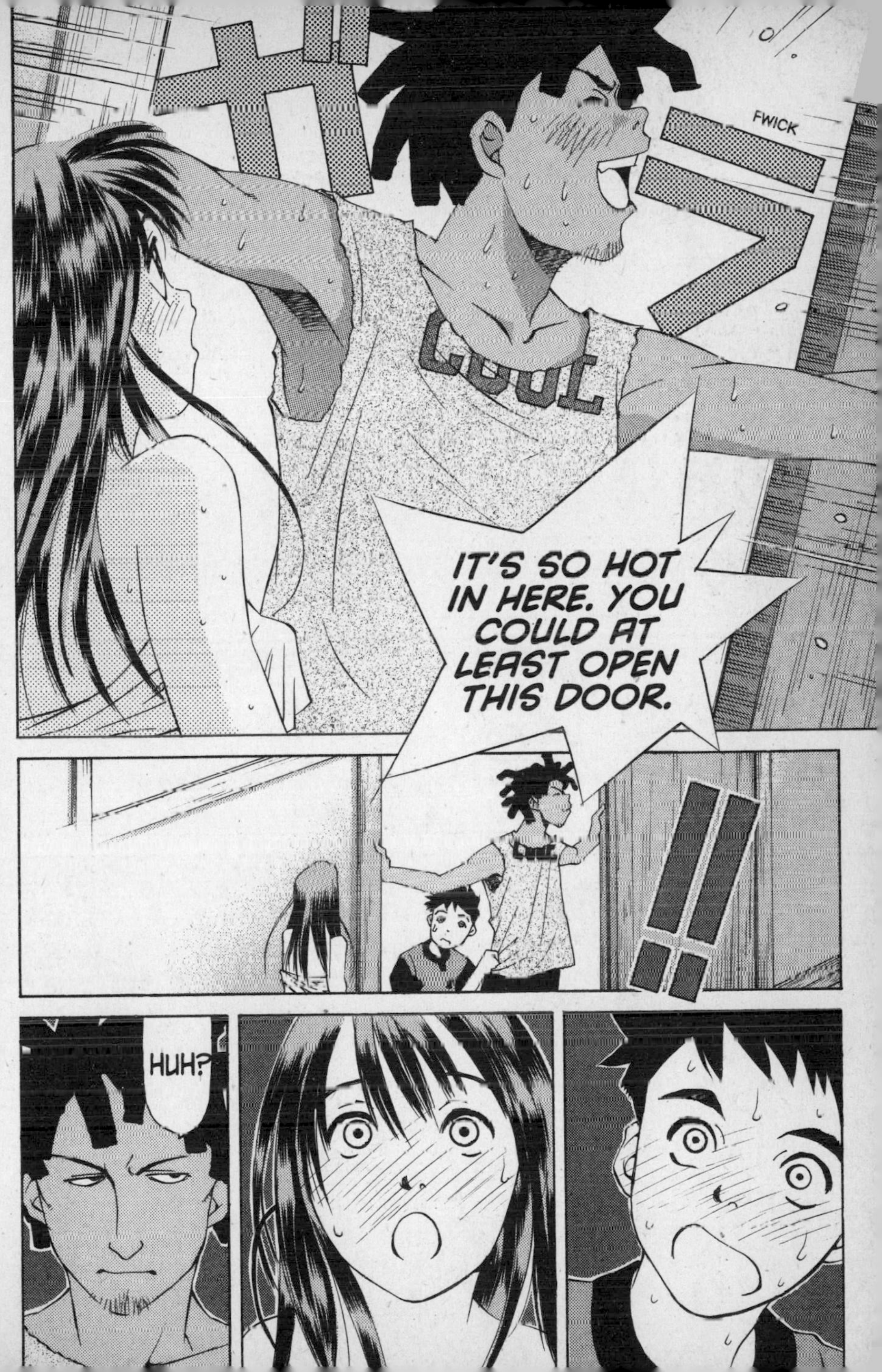
FWICK
IT'S SO HOT IN HERE. YOU COULD AT LEAST OPEN THIS DOOR.
!!
HUH?

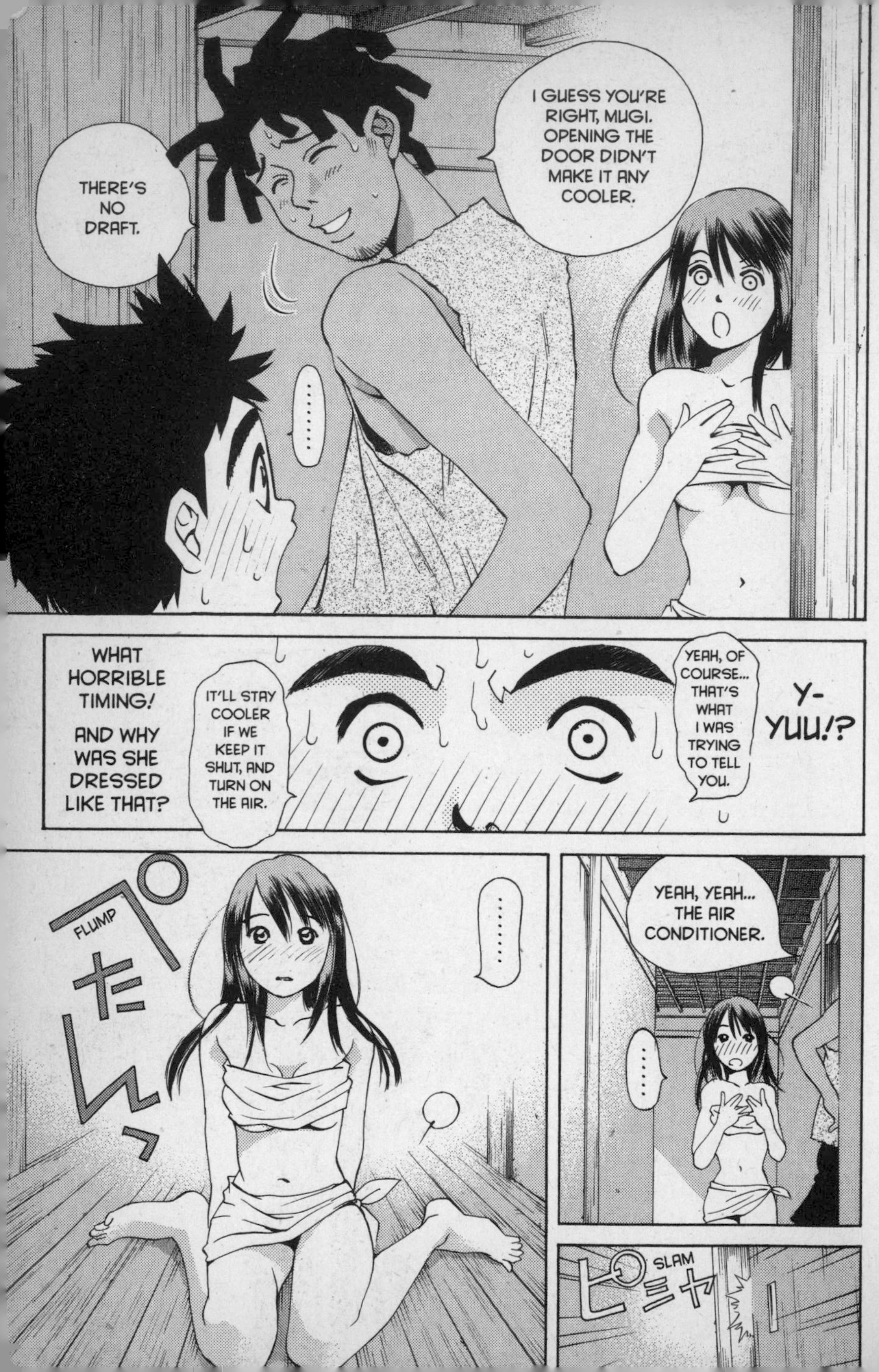
I GUESS YOU'RE RIGHT, MUGI. OPENING THE DOOR DIDN'T MAKE IT ANY COOLER.
THERE'S NO DRAFT.
......
Y-YUU!?
YEAH, OF COURSE... THAT'S WHAT I WAS TRYING TO TELL YOU.
IT'LL STAY COOLER IF WE KEEP IT SHUT, AND TURN ON THE AIR.
WHAT HORRIBLE TIMING!
AND WHY WAS SHE DRESSED LIKE THAT?
YEAH, YEAH... THE AIR CONDITIONER.
......
ピシャー
SLAM
......
ぺたんっ
FLUMP

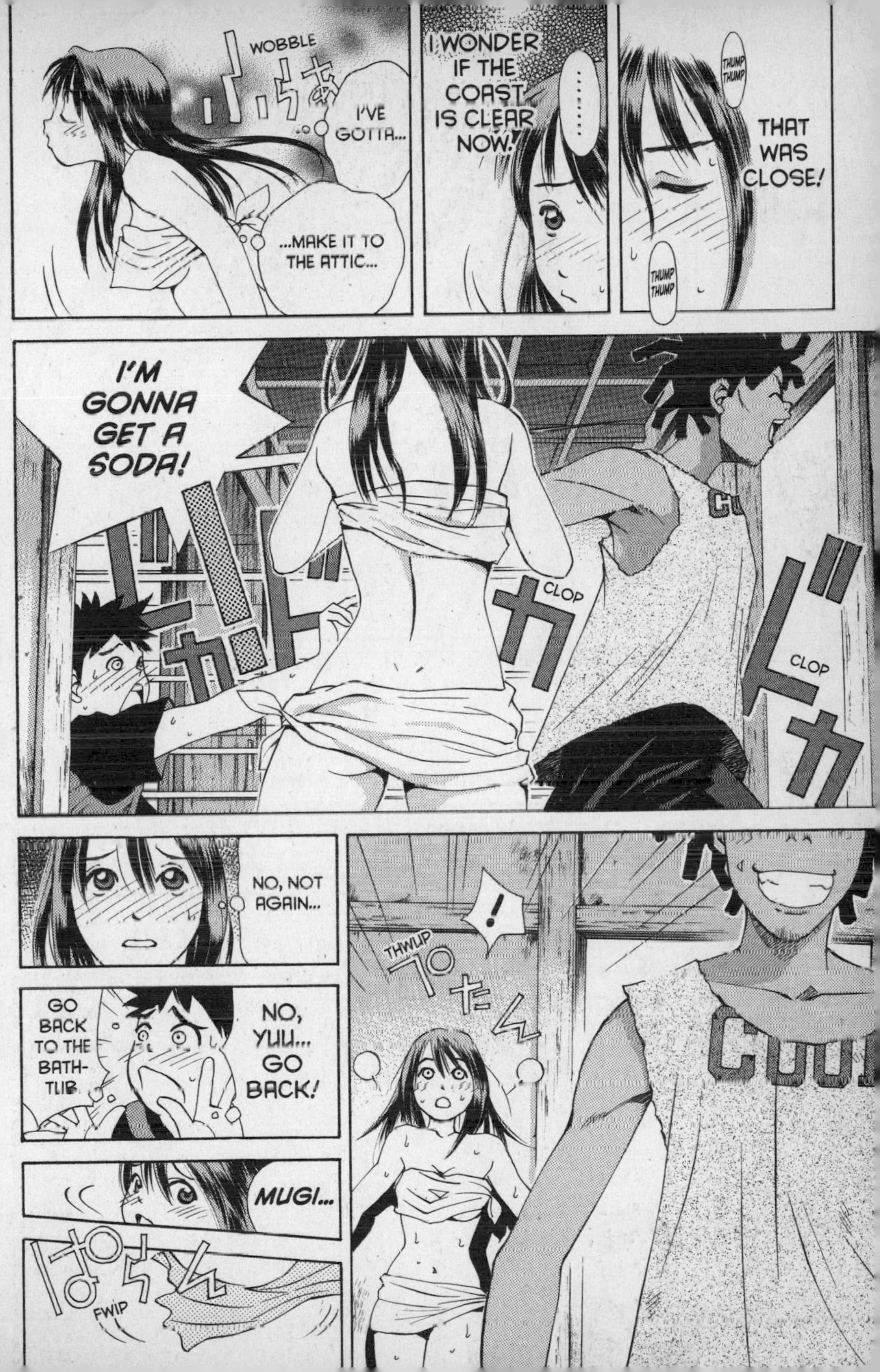
THUMP THUMP
THAT WAS CLOSE!
THUMP THUMP
I WONDER IF THE COAST IS CLEAR NOW!
......
WOBBLE
I'VE GOTTA...
...MAKE IT TO THE ATTIC...
I'M GONNA GET A SODA!
CLOP
CLOP
!
THWUP
NO, NOT AGAIN...
NO, YUU... GO BACK!
GO BACK TO THE BATH-TUB
MUGI...
FWIP

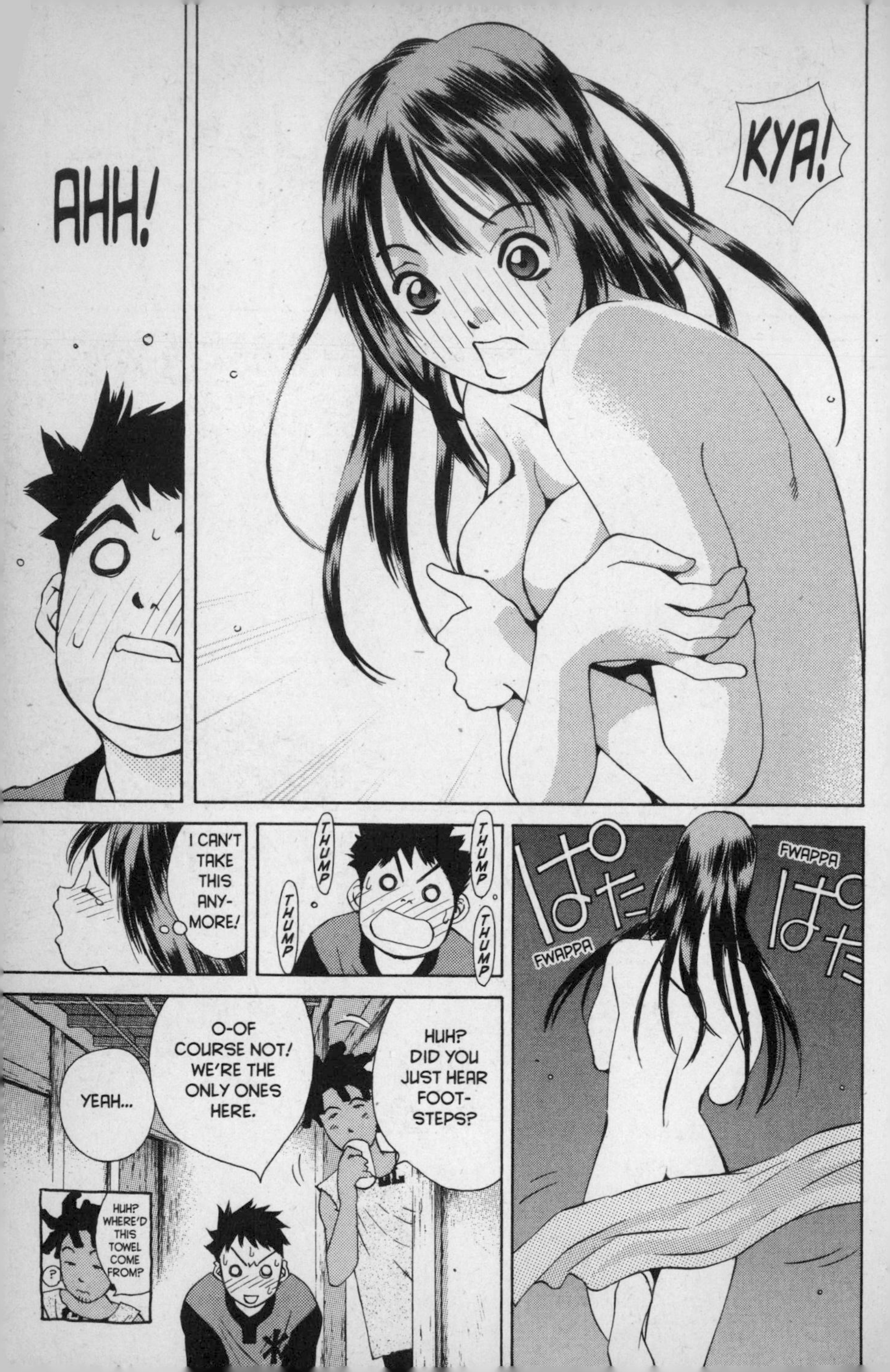

KYA!
AHH!
FWAPPA
ぱた
ぱた
FWAPPA
THUMP
THUMP
THUMP
THUMP
I CAN'T TAKE THIS ANYMORE!
HUH? DID YOU JUST HEAR FOOT-STEPS?
O-OF COURSE NOT! WE'RE THE ONLY ONES HERE.
YEAH...
HUH? WHERE'D THIS TOWEL COME FROM?
?

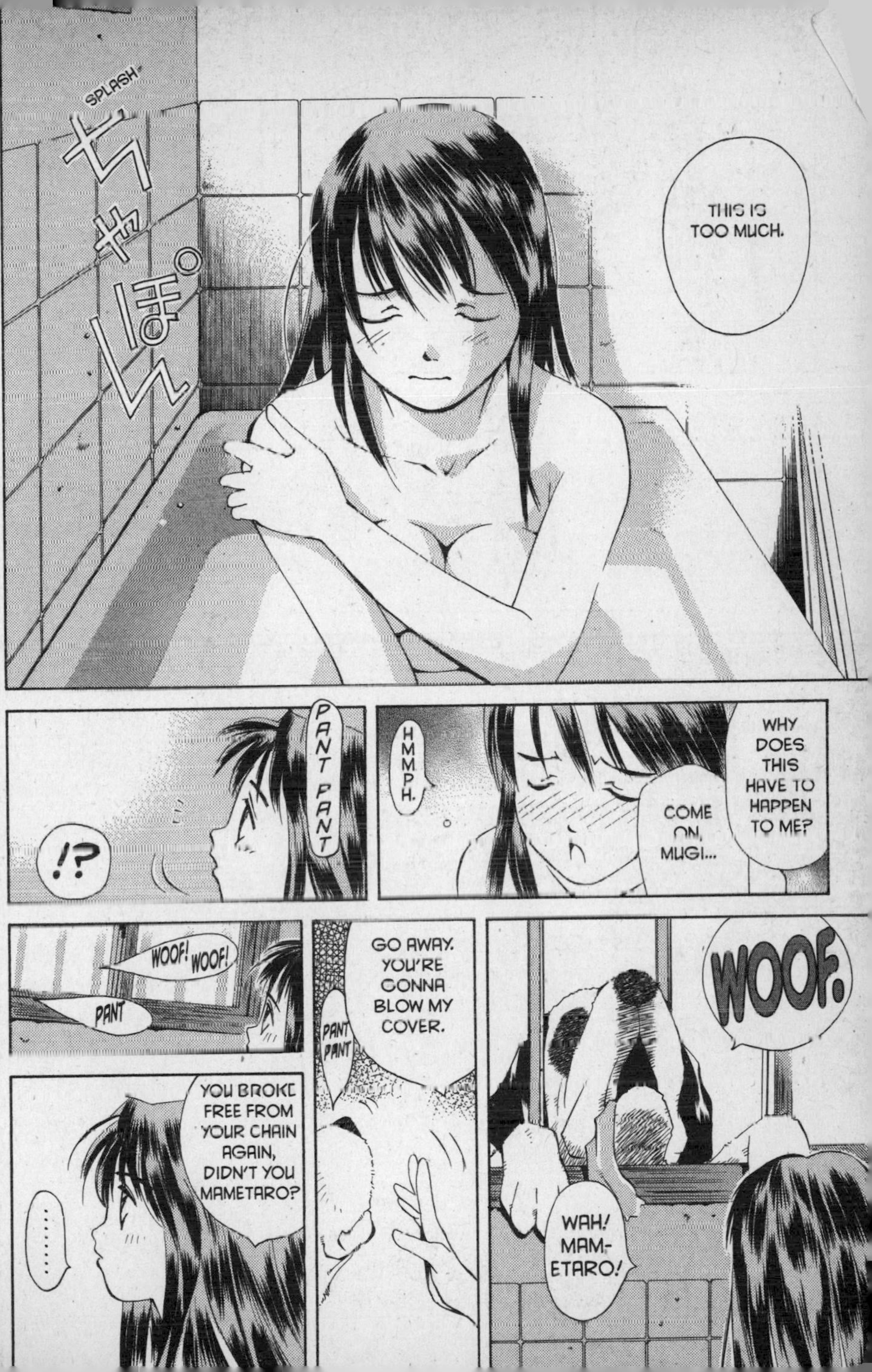
ちゃぽん
SPLASH
THIS IS TOO MUCH.
WHY DOES THIS HAVE TO HAPPEN TO ME?
COME ON, MUGI...
HMMPH.
PANT PANT
!?
WOOF.
WAH! MAM-ETARO!
GO AWAY. YOU'RE GONNA BLOW MY COVER.
PANT PANT
WOOF! WOOF!
PANT
YOU BROKE FREE FROM YOUR CHAIN AGAIN, DIDN'T YOU MAMETARO?
......

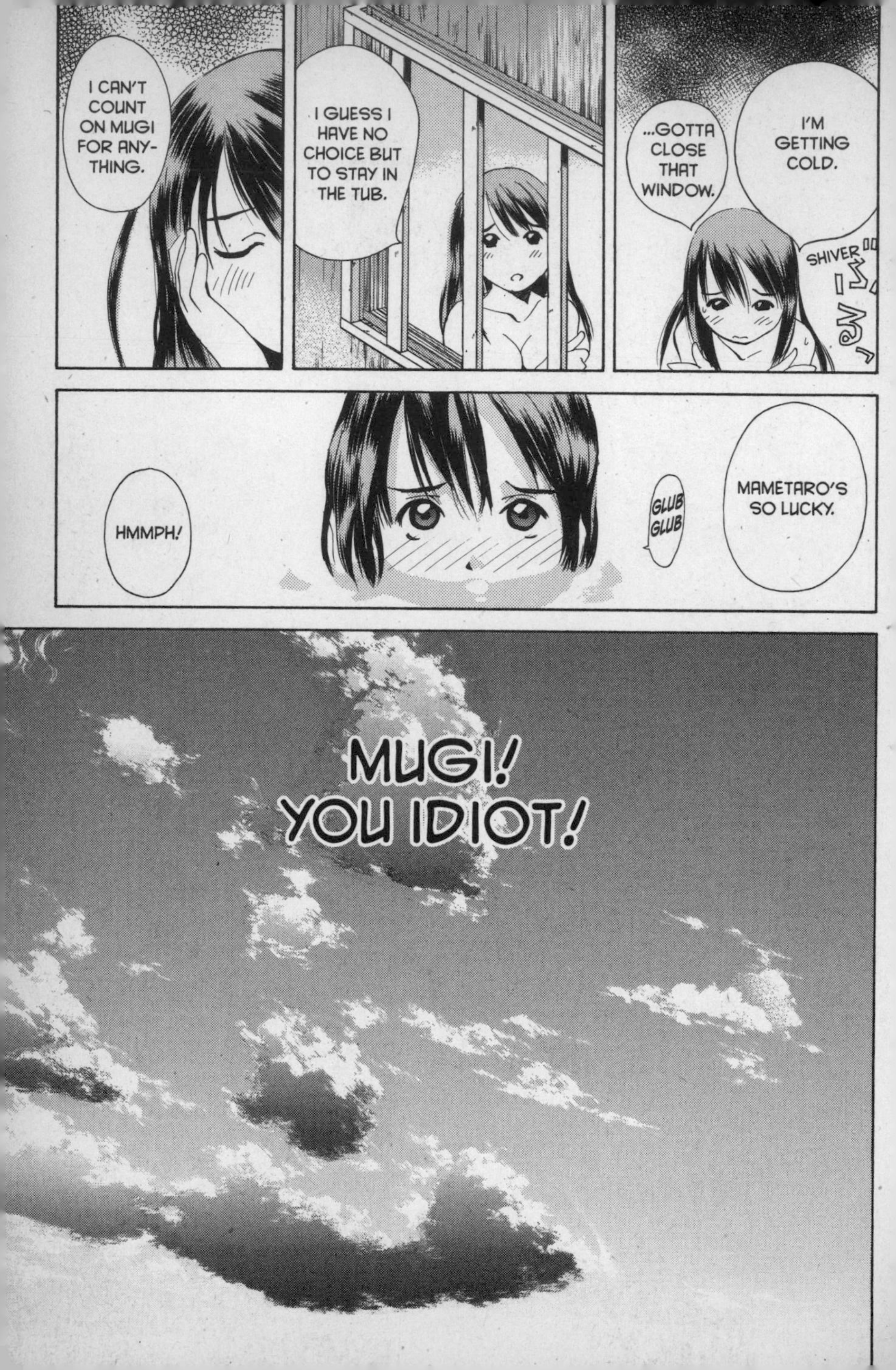
I'M GETTING COLD.
...GOTTA CLOSE THAT WINDOW.
SHIVER
I GUESS I HAVE NO CHOICE BUT TO STAY IN THE TUB.
I CAN'T COUNT ON MUGI FOR ANY-THING.
MAMETARO'S SO LUCKY.
GLUB GLUB
HMMPH!
MUGI! YOU IDIOT!

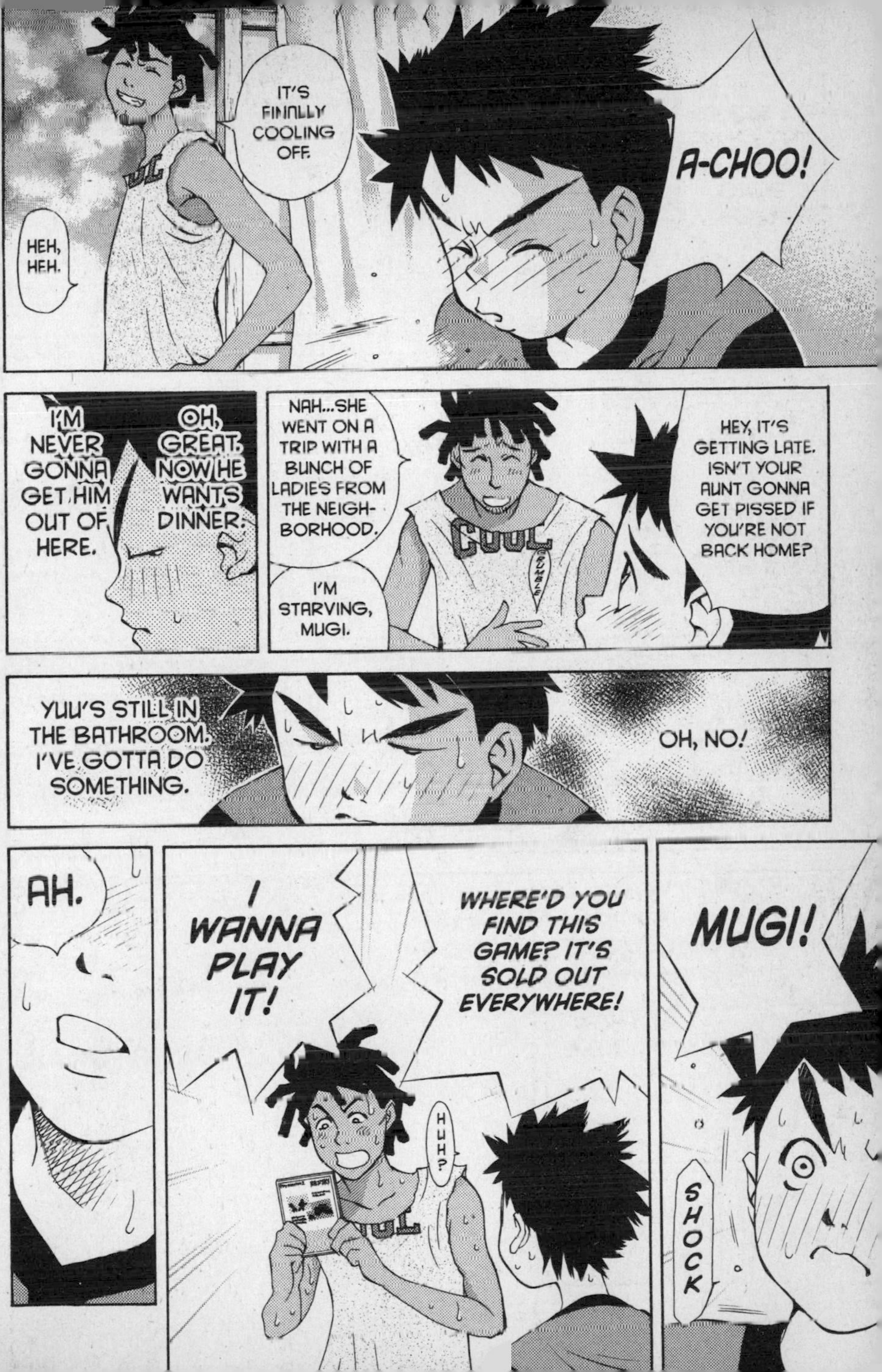
A-CHOO!
IT'S FINALLY COOLING OFF.
HEH, HEH.
HEY, IT'S GETTING LATE. ISN'T YOUR AUNT GONNA GET PISSED IF YOU'RE NOT BACK HOME?
NAH...SHE WENT ON A TRIP WITH A BUNCH OF LADIES FROM THE NEIGHBORHOOD.
GRUMBLE
I'M STARVING, MUGI.
OH, GREAT. NOW HE WANTS DINNER.
I'M NEVER GONNA GET HIM OUT OF HERE.
OH, NO!
YUU'S STILL IN THE BATHROOM. I'VE GOTTA DO SOMETHING.
MUGI!
SHOCK
WHERE'D YOU FIND THIS GAME? IT'S SOLD OUT EVERYWHERE!
I WANNA PLAY IT!
HUH?
AH.

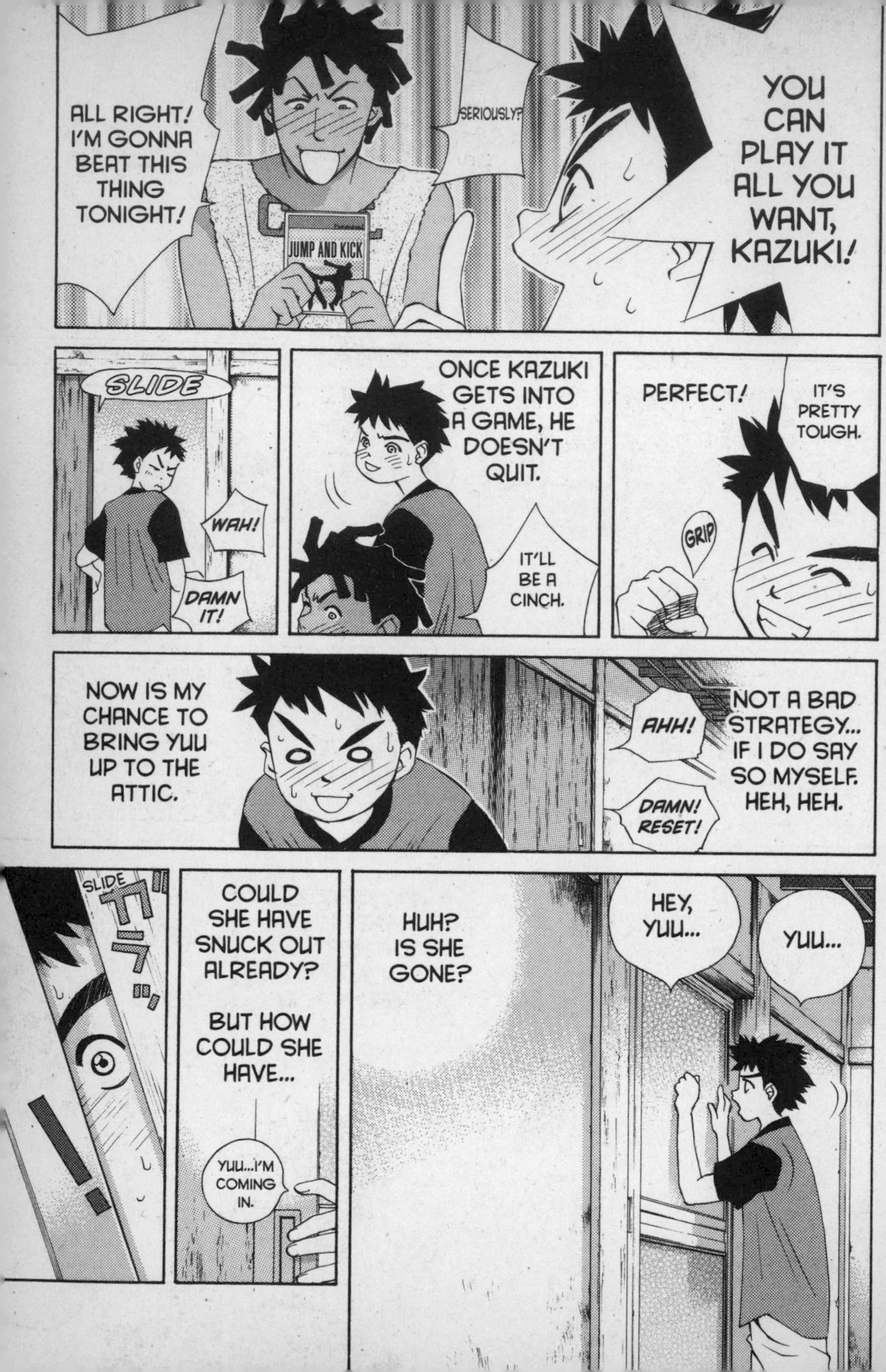
YOU CAN PLAY IT ALL YOU WANT, KAZUKI!
SERIOUSLY?
ALL RIGHT! I'M GONNA BEAT THIS THING TONIGHT!
JUMP AND KICK
IT'S PRETTY TOUGH.
PERFECT!
GRIP
ONCE KAZUKI GETS INTO A GAME, HE DOESN'T QUIT.
IT'LL BE A CINCH.
SLIDE
WAH!
DAMN IT!
NOT A BAD STRATEGY... IF I DO SAY SO MYSELF. HEH, HEH.
AHH!
DAMN! RESET!
NOW IS MY CHANCE TO BRING YUU UP TO THE ATTIC.
YUU...
HEY, YUU...
HUH? IS SHE GONE?
COULD SHE HAVE SNUCK OUT ALREADY?
BUT HOW COULD SHE HAVE...
YUU...I'M COMING IN.
SLIDE
!

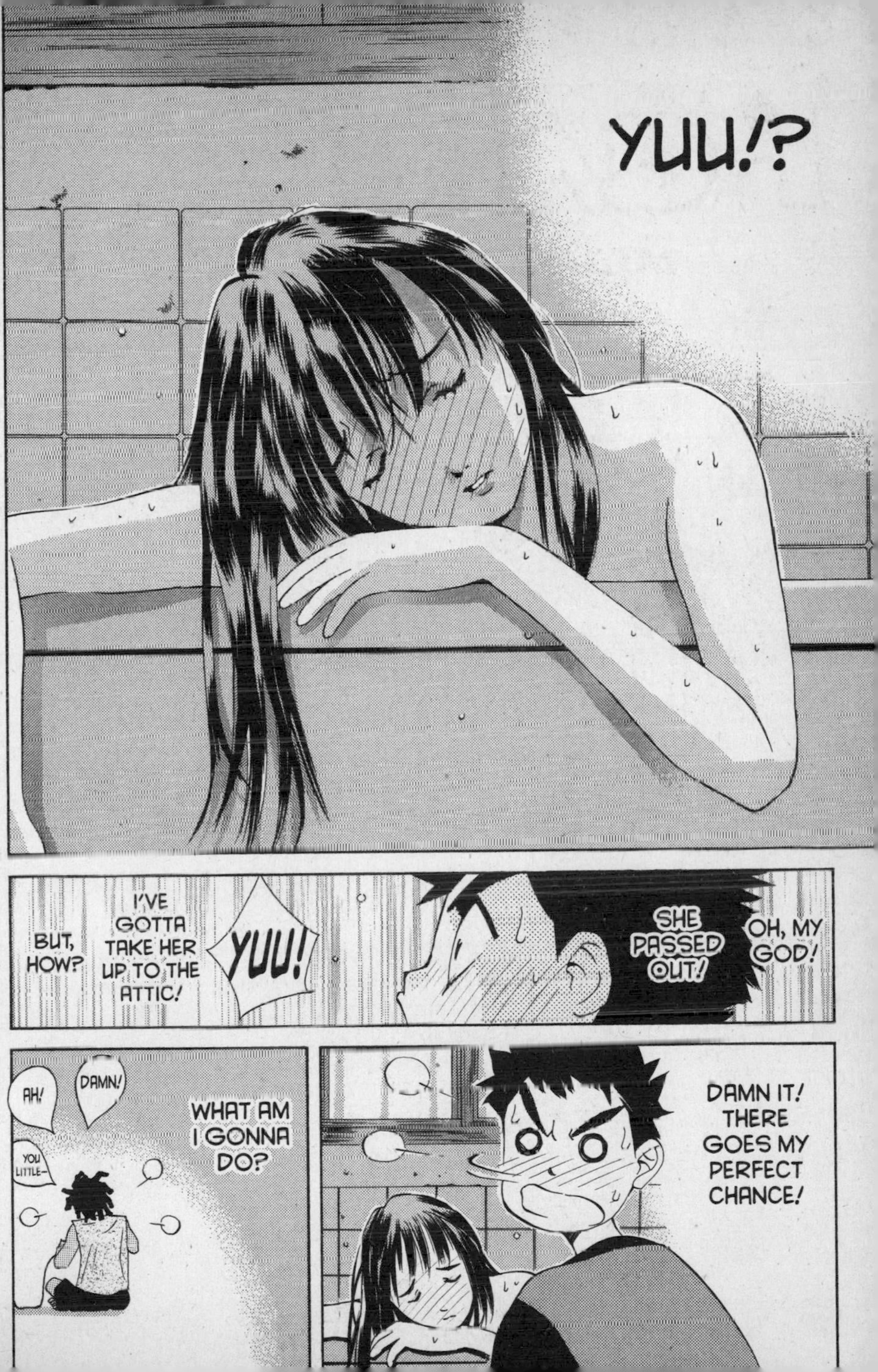
YUU!?
OH, MY GOD!
SHE PASSED OUT!
YUU!
I'VE GOTTA TAKE HER UP TO THE ATTIC!
BUT, HOW?
DAMN IT! THERE GOES MY PERFECT CHANCE!
WHAT AM I GONNA DO?
DAMN!
AH!
YOU LITTLE–

Pastel

MIRACLE 6: THE SECRET PAIR

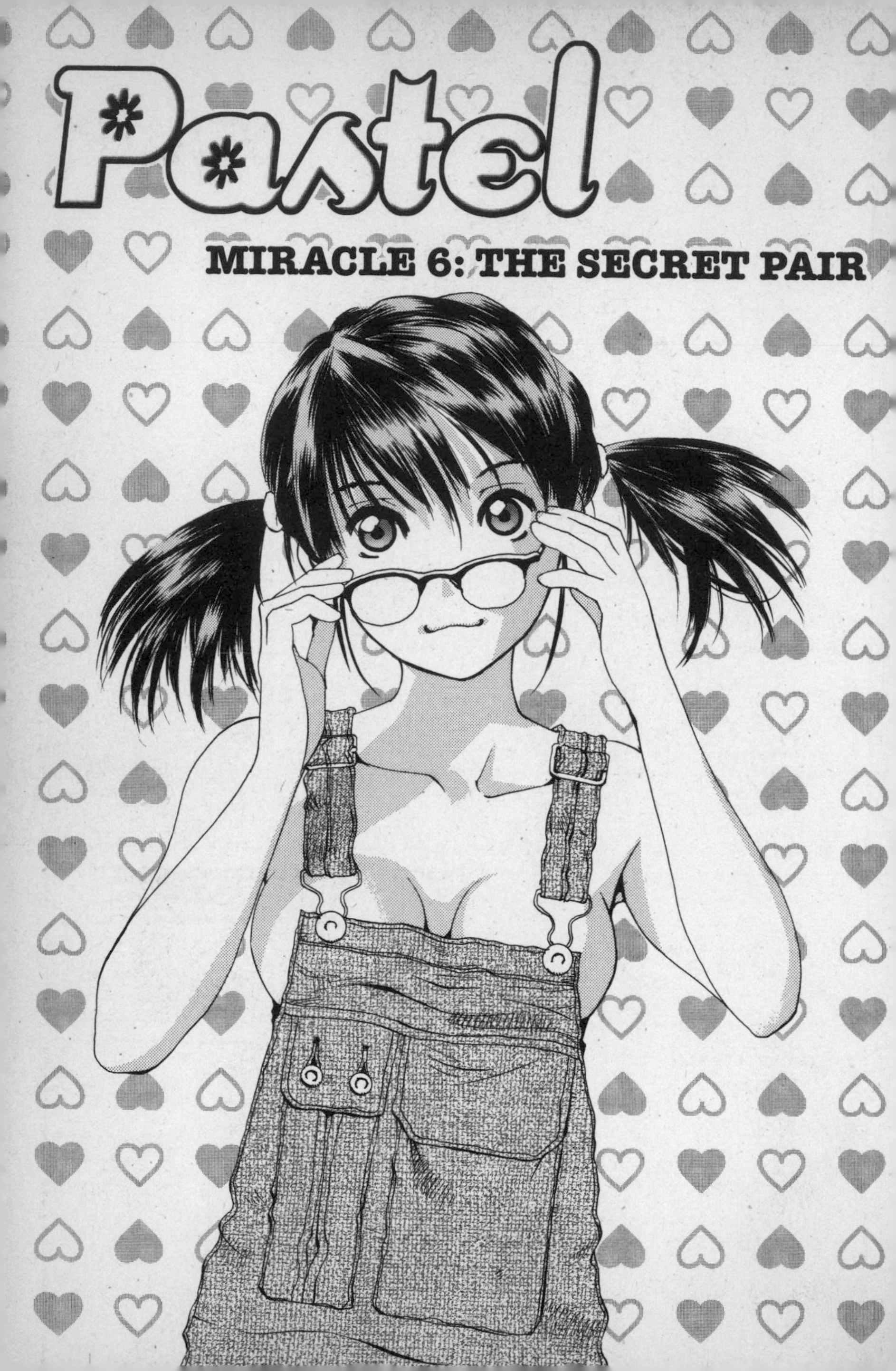

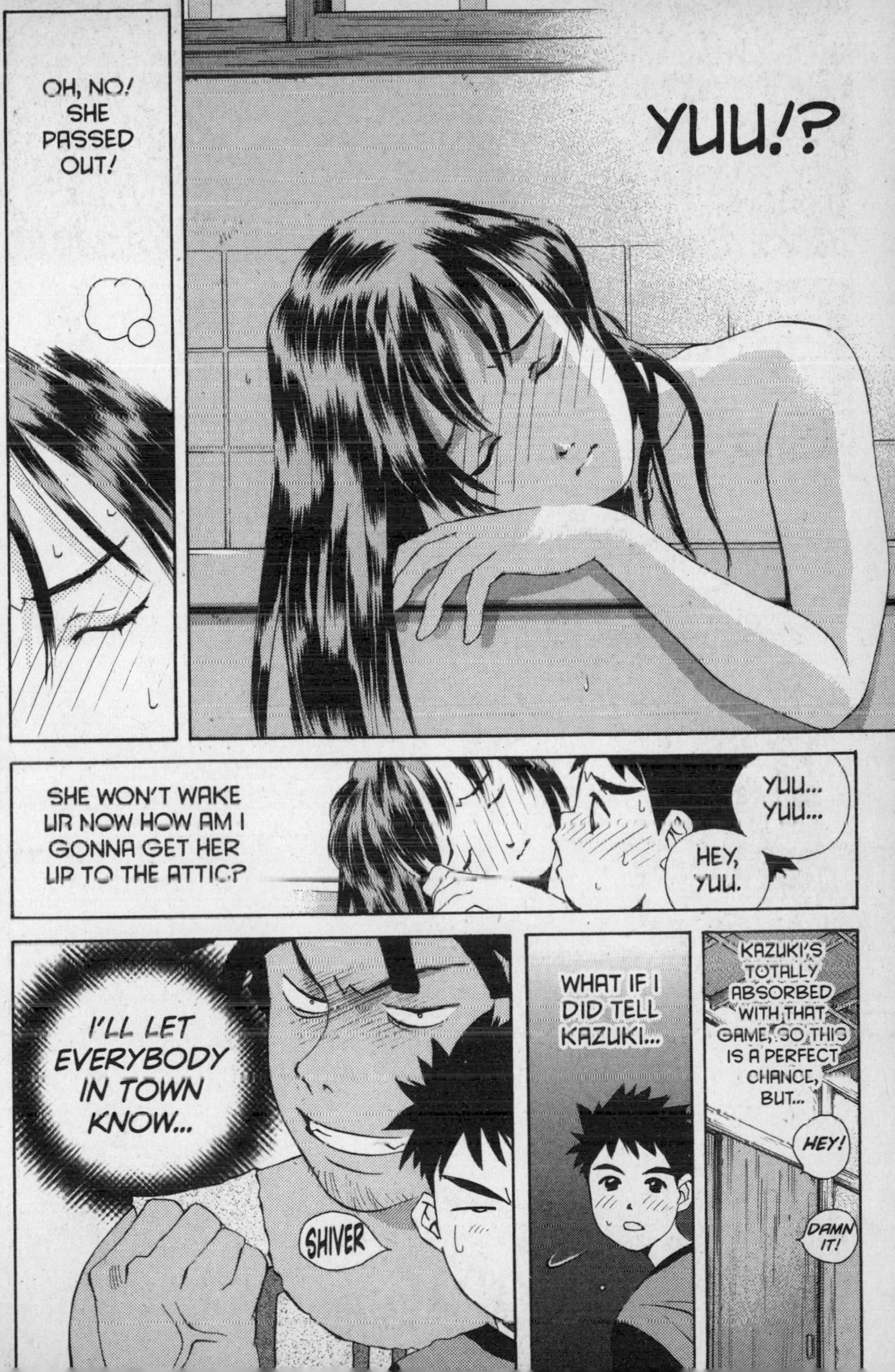
YUU!?
OH, NO! SHE PASSED OUT!
YUU... YUU...
HEY, YUU.
SHE WON'T WAKE UP NOW HOW AM I GONNA GET HER UP TO THE ATTIC?
KAZUKI'S TOTALLY ABSORBED WITH THAT GAME, SO THIS IS A PERFECT CHANCE, BUT...
HEY!
DAMN IT!
WHAT IF I DID TELL KAZUKI...
I'LL LET EVERYBODY IN TOWN KNOW...
SHIVER

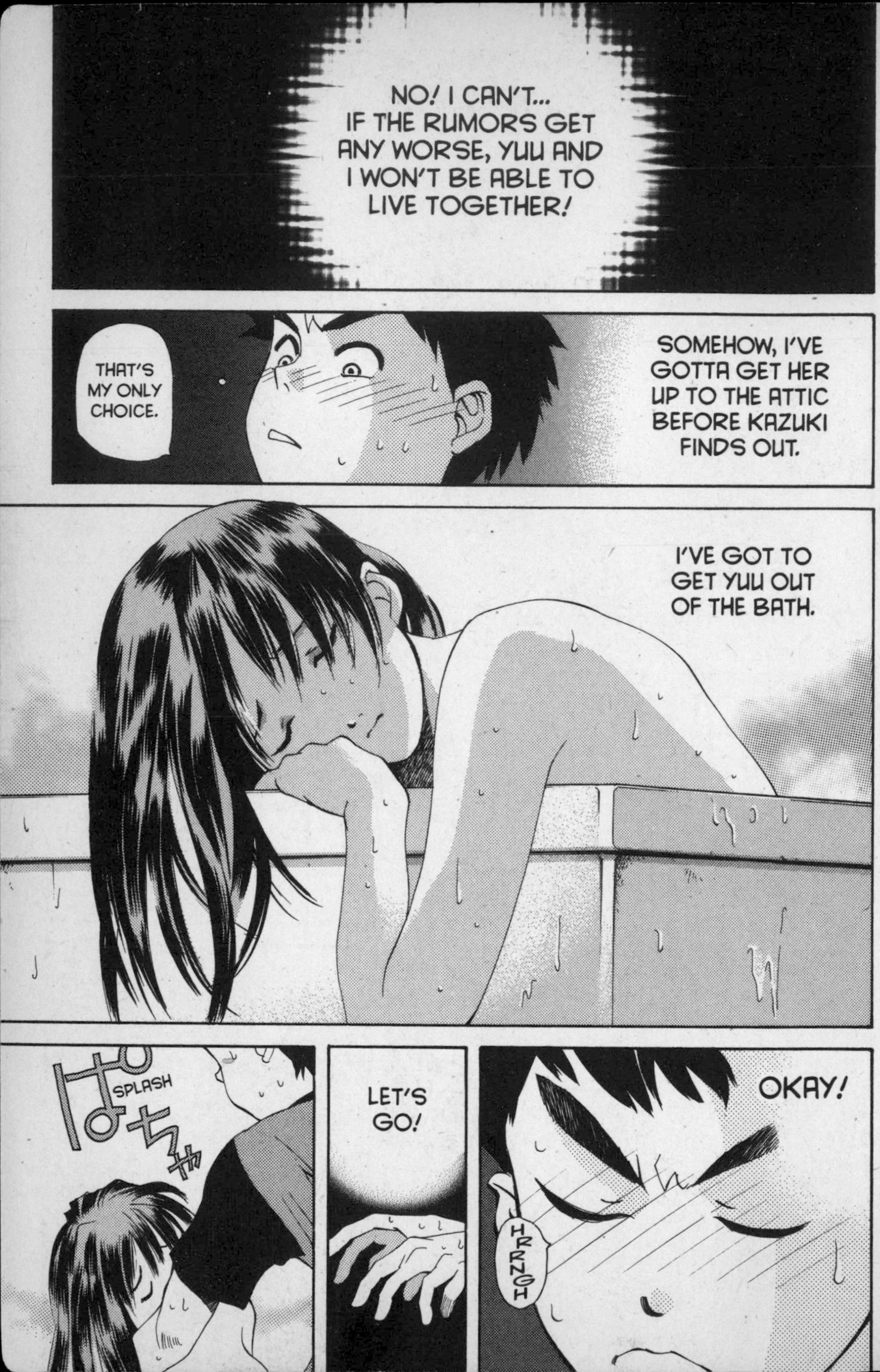
NO! I CAN'T... IF THE RUMORS GET ANY WORSE, YUU AND I WON'T BE ABLE TO LIVE TOGETHER!
SOMEHOW, I'VE GOTTA GET HER UP TO THE ATTIC BEFORE KAZUKI FINDS OUT.
THAT'S MY ONLY CHOICE.
I'VE GOT TO GET YUU OUT OF THE BATH.
OKAY!
HRRNGH
LET'S GO!
SPLASH

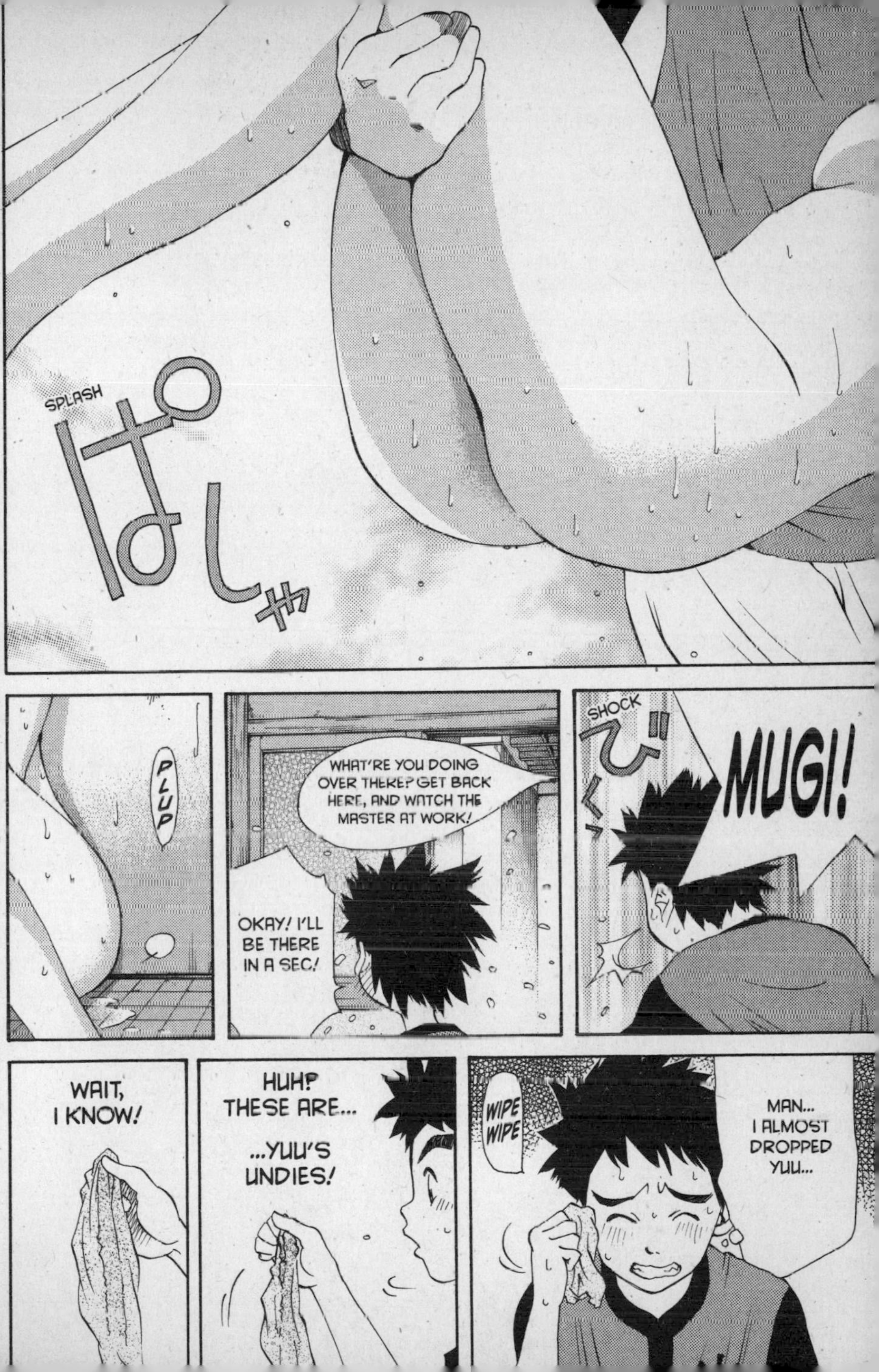
SPLASH
ぱしゃ
SHOCK
びくっ
MUGI!
WHAT'RE YOU DOING OVER THERE? GET BACK HERE, AND WATCH THE MASTER AT WORK!
OKAY! I'LL BE THERE IN A SEC!
PLUP
MAN... I ALMOST DROPPED YUU...
WIPE WIPE
HUH? THESE ARE...
...YUU'S UNDIES!
WAIT, I KNOW!

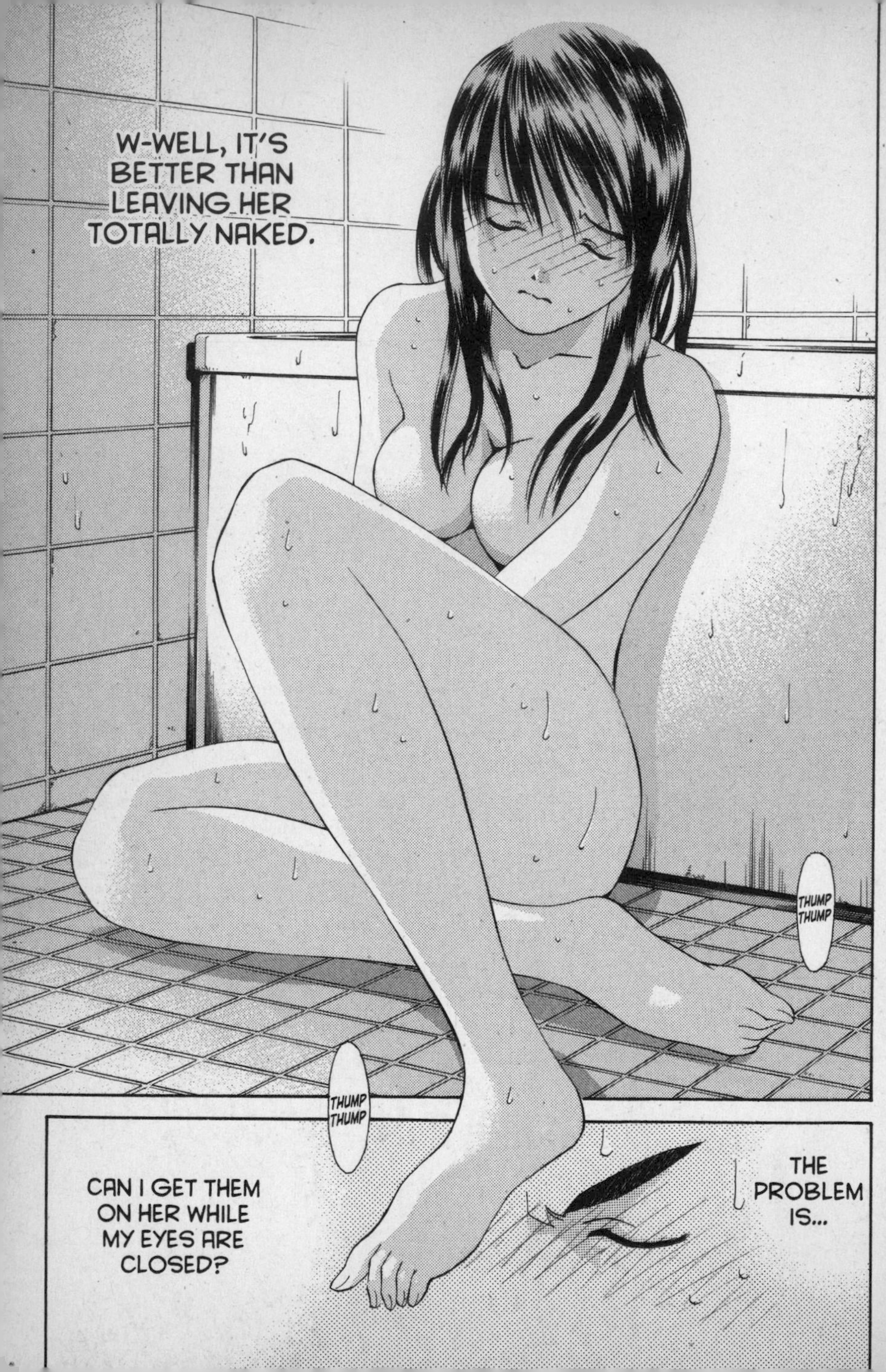
W-WELL, IT'S BETTER THAN LEAVING HER TOTALLY NAKED.
THUMP THUMP
THUMP THUMP
THE PROBLEM IS...
CAN I GET THEM ON HER WHILE MY EYES ARE CLOSED?

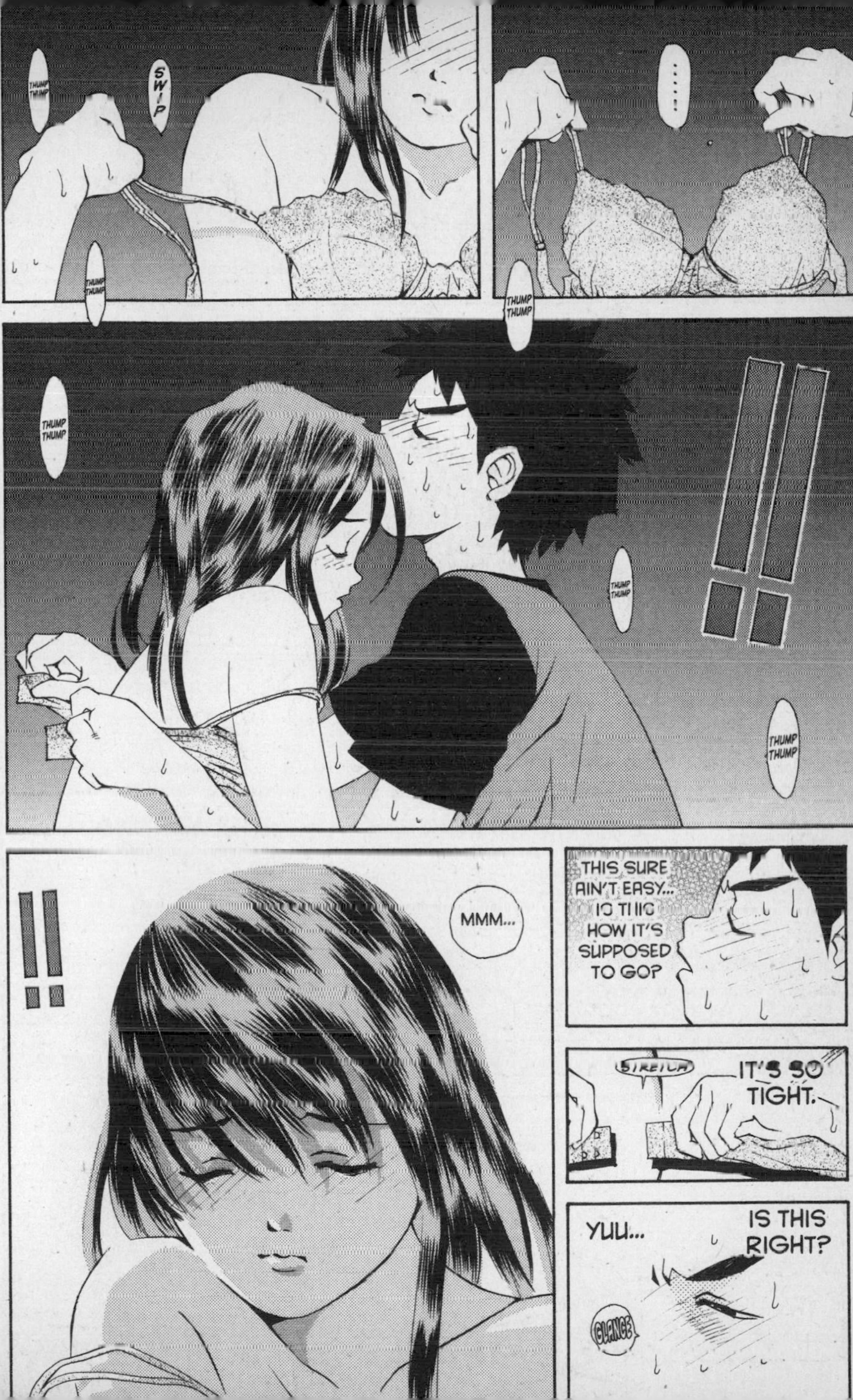

...!
THUMP THUMP
THUMP THUMP
SWIP
THUMP THUMP
THUMP THUMP
THUMP THUMP
THUMP THUMP
THUMP THUMP
THIS SURE AIN'T EASY... IS THIS HOW IT'S SUPPOSED TO GO?
STRETCH
IT'S SO TIGHT.
YUU... IS THIS RIGHT?
GLANCE
MMM...

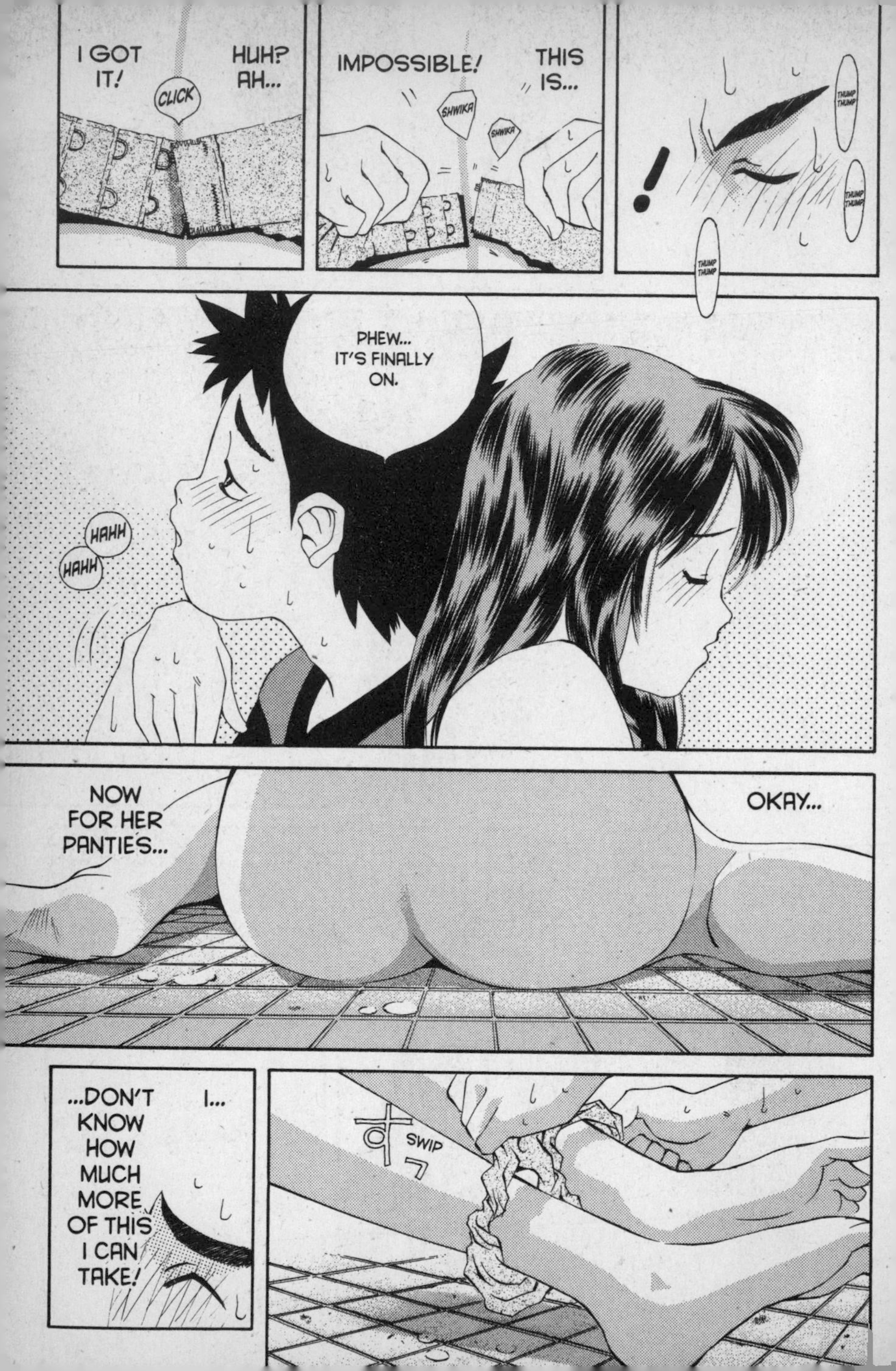

THUMP THUMP
THUMP THUMP
THUMP THUMP
!
THIS IS...
IMPOSSIBLE!
SHWIKA
SHWIKA
HUH? AH...
CLICK
I GOT IT!
PHEW... IT'S FINALLY ON.
HAHH
HAHH
OKAY...
NOW FOR HER PANTIES...
す
SWIP
I...
...DON'T KNOW HOW MUCH MORE OF THIS I CAN TAKE!

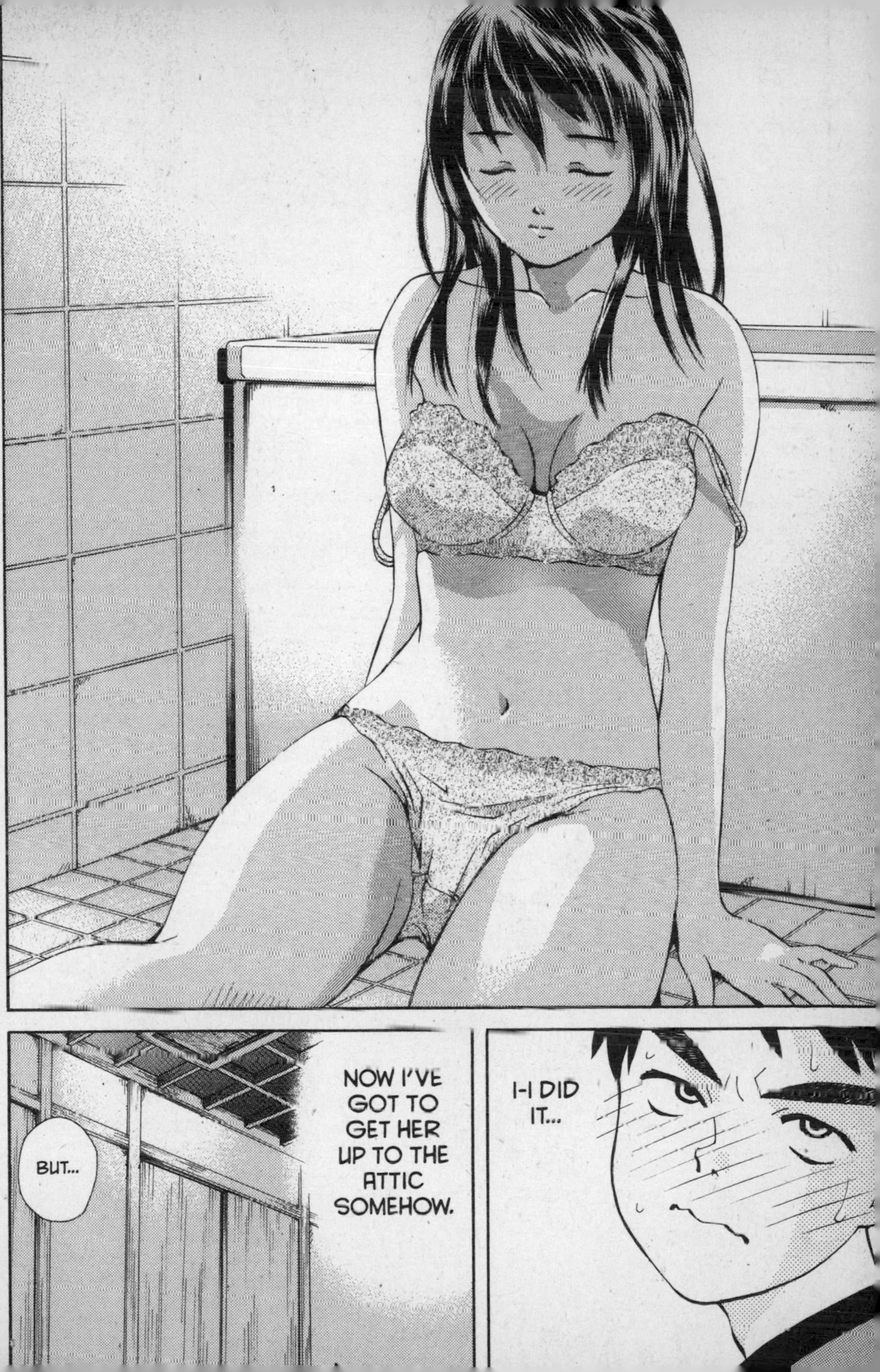
I-I DID IT...
NOW I'VE GOT TO GET HER UP TO THE ATTIC SOMEHOW.
BUT...

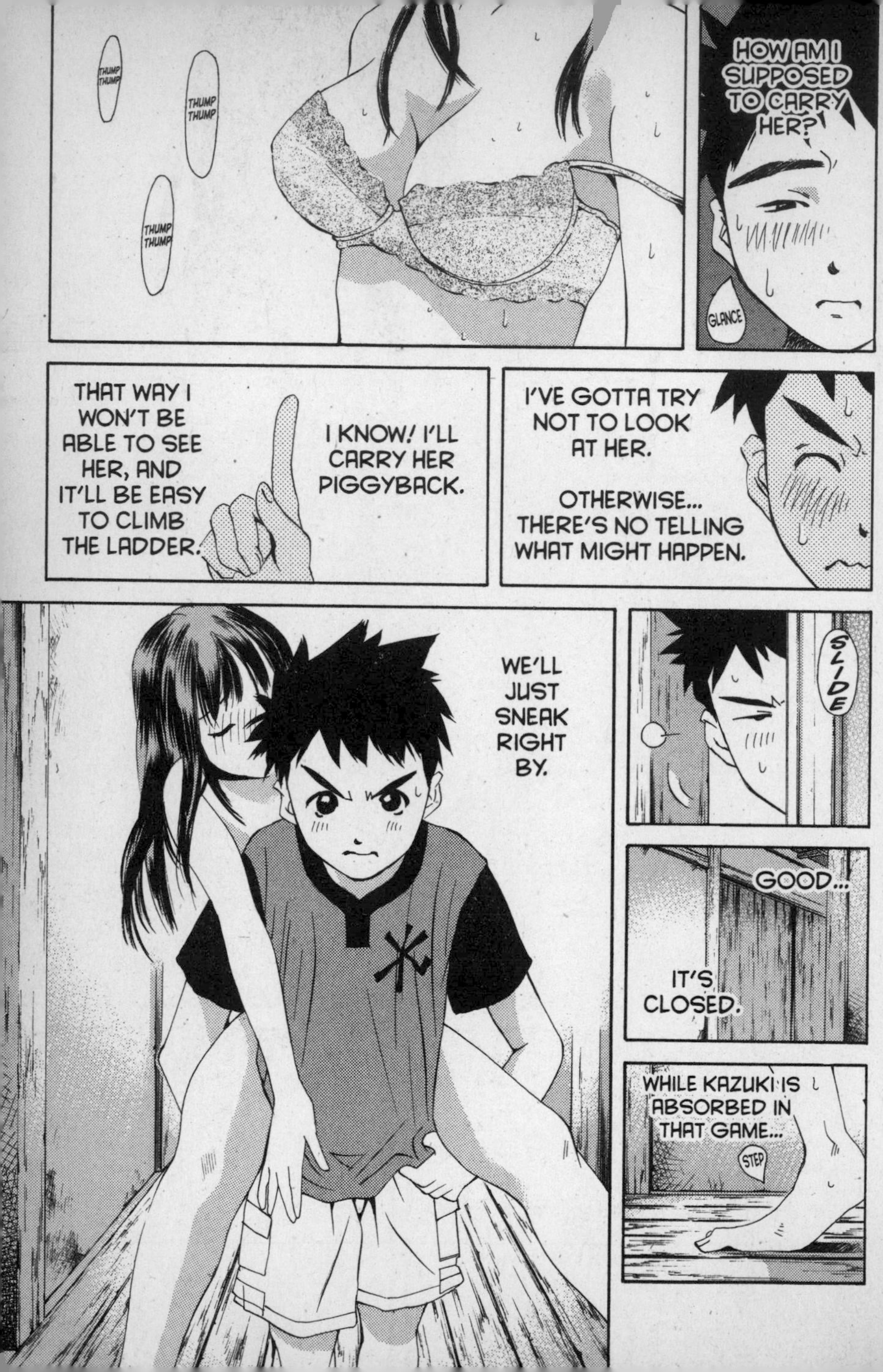
HOW AM I SUPPOSED TO CARRY HER?
GLANCE
THUMP THUMP
THUMP THUMP
THUMP THUMP
I'VE GOTTA TRY NOT TO LOOK AT HER.
OTHERWISE... THERE'S NO TELLING WHAT MIGHT HAPPEN.
I KNOW! I'LL CARRY HER PIGGYBACK.
THAT WAY I WON'T BE ABLE TO SEE HER, AND IT'LL BE EASY TO CLIMB THE LADDER.
SLIDE
GOOD...
IT'S CLOSED.
WHILE KAZUKI IS ABSORBED IN THAT GAME...
STEP
WE'LL JUST SNEAK RIGHT BY.

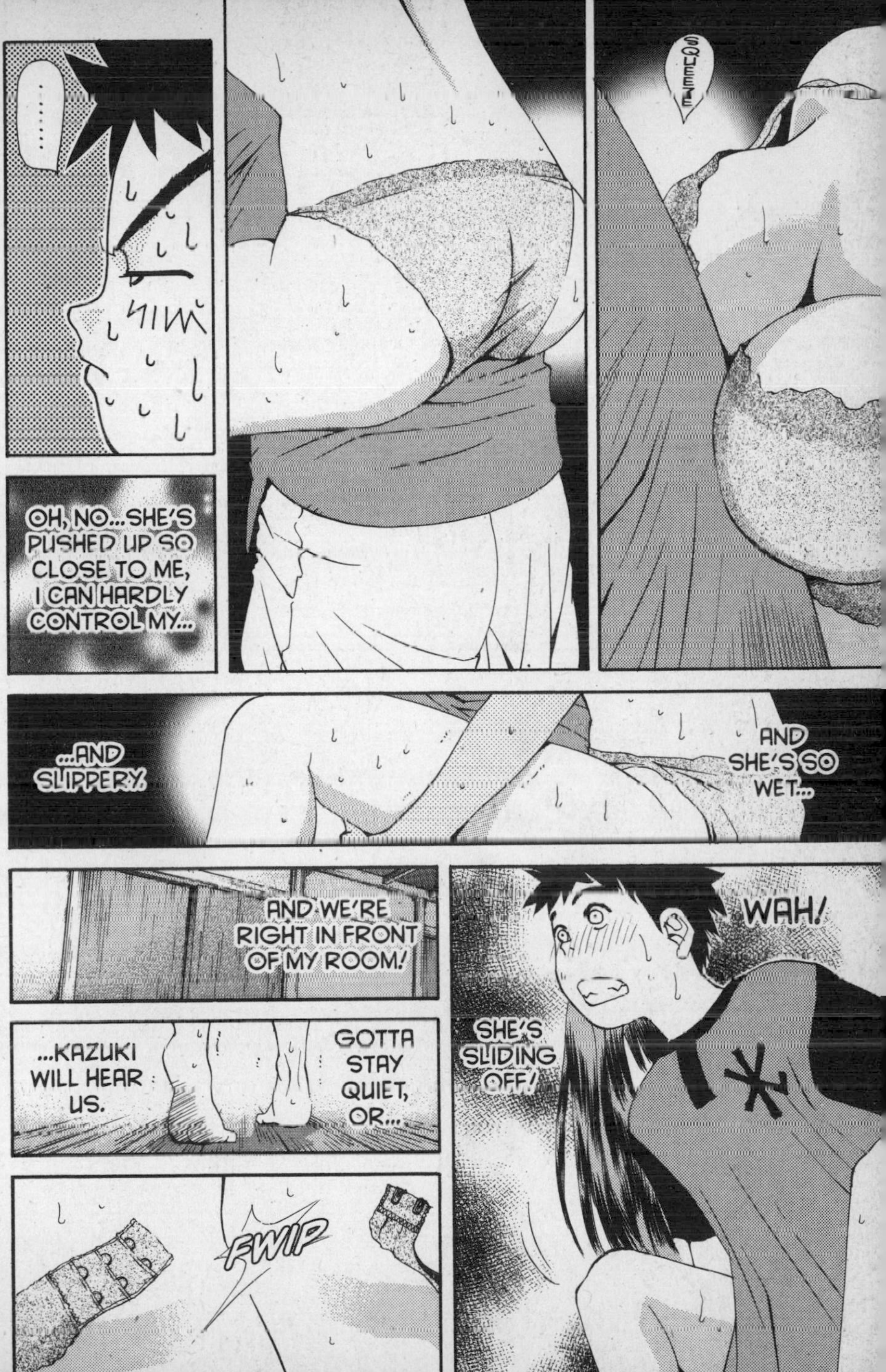
SQUEEZE
......
OH, NO...SHE'S PUSHED UP SO CLOSE TO ME, I CAN HARDLY CONTROL MY...
AND SHE'S SO WET...
...AND SLIPPERY.
WAH!
SHE'S SLIDING OFF!
AND WE'RE RIGHT IN FRONT OF MY ROOM!
GOTTA STAY QUIET, OR...
...KAZUKI WILL HEAR US.
FWIP

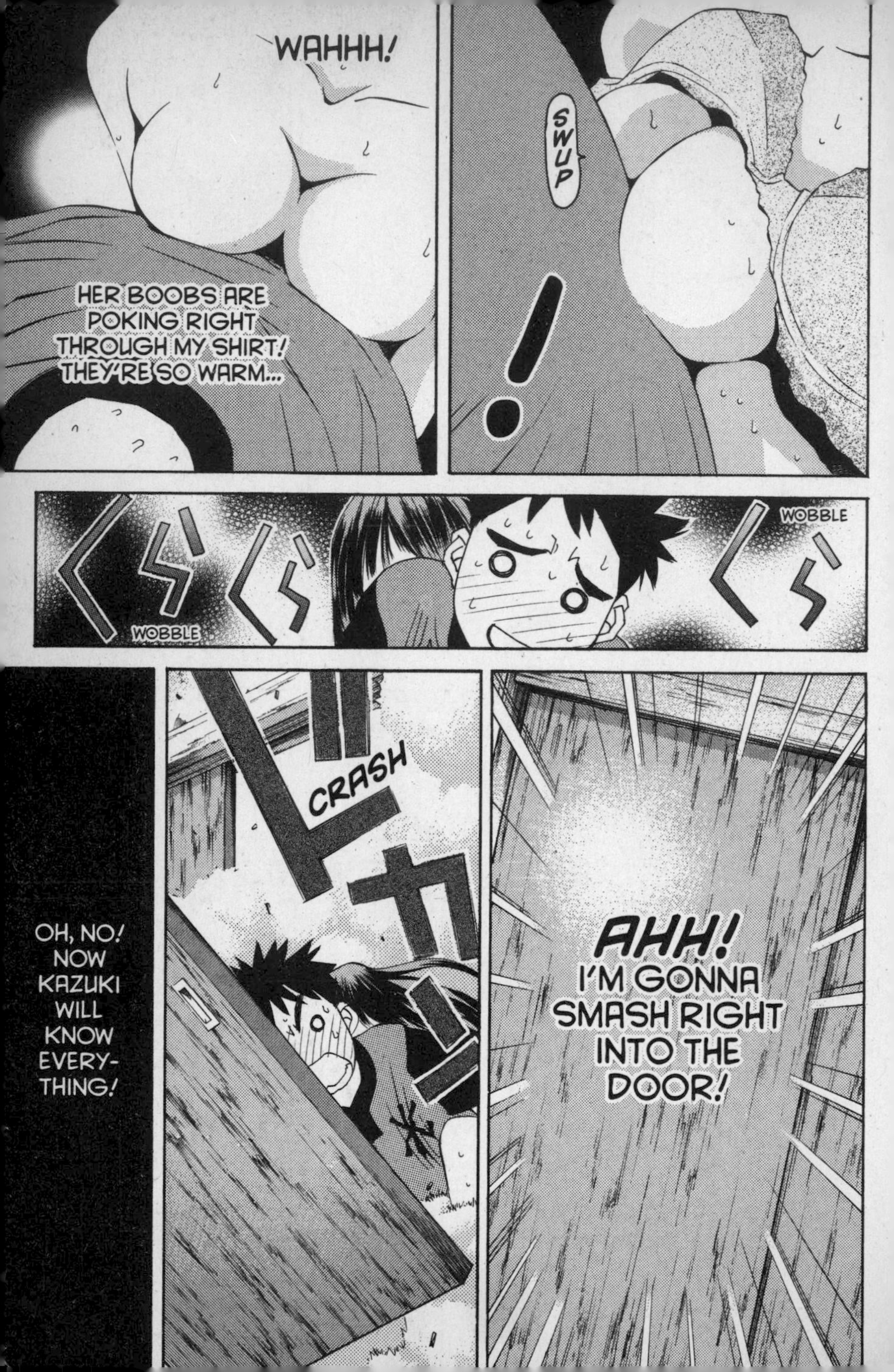
SWUP
!
WAHHH!
HER BOOBS ARE POKING RIGHT THROUGH MY SHIRT! THEY'RE SO WARM...
WOBBLE
WOBBLE
AHH! I'M GONNA SMASH RIGHT INTO THE DOOR!
CRASH
OH, NO! NOW KAZUKI WILL KNOW EVERY-THING!

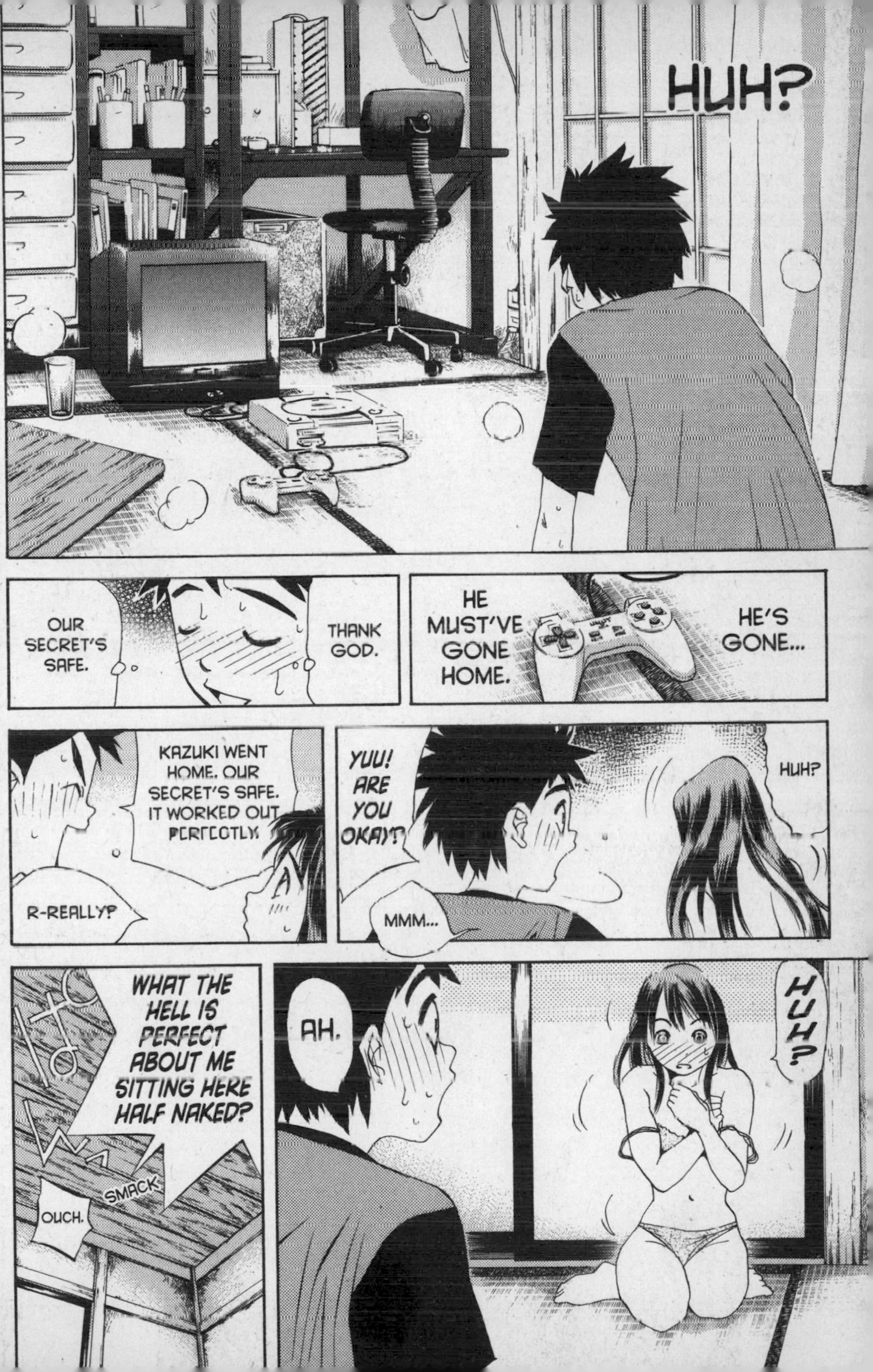
HUH?
HE'S GONE...
HE MUST'VE GONE HOME.
THANK GOD.
OUR SECRET'S SAFE.
HUH?
YUU! ARE YOU OKAY?
MMM...
KAZUKI WENT HOME. OUR SECRET'S SAFE. IT WORKED OUT PERFECTLY.
R-REALLY?
HUH?
AH.
WHAT THE HELL IS PERFECT ABOUT ME SITTING HERE HALF NAKED?
SMACK
OUCH.

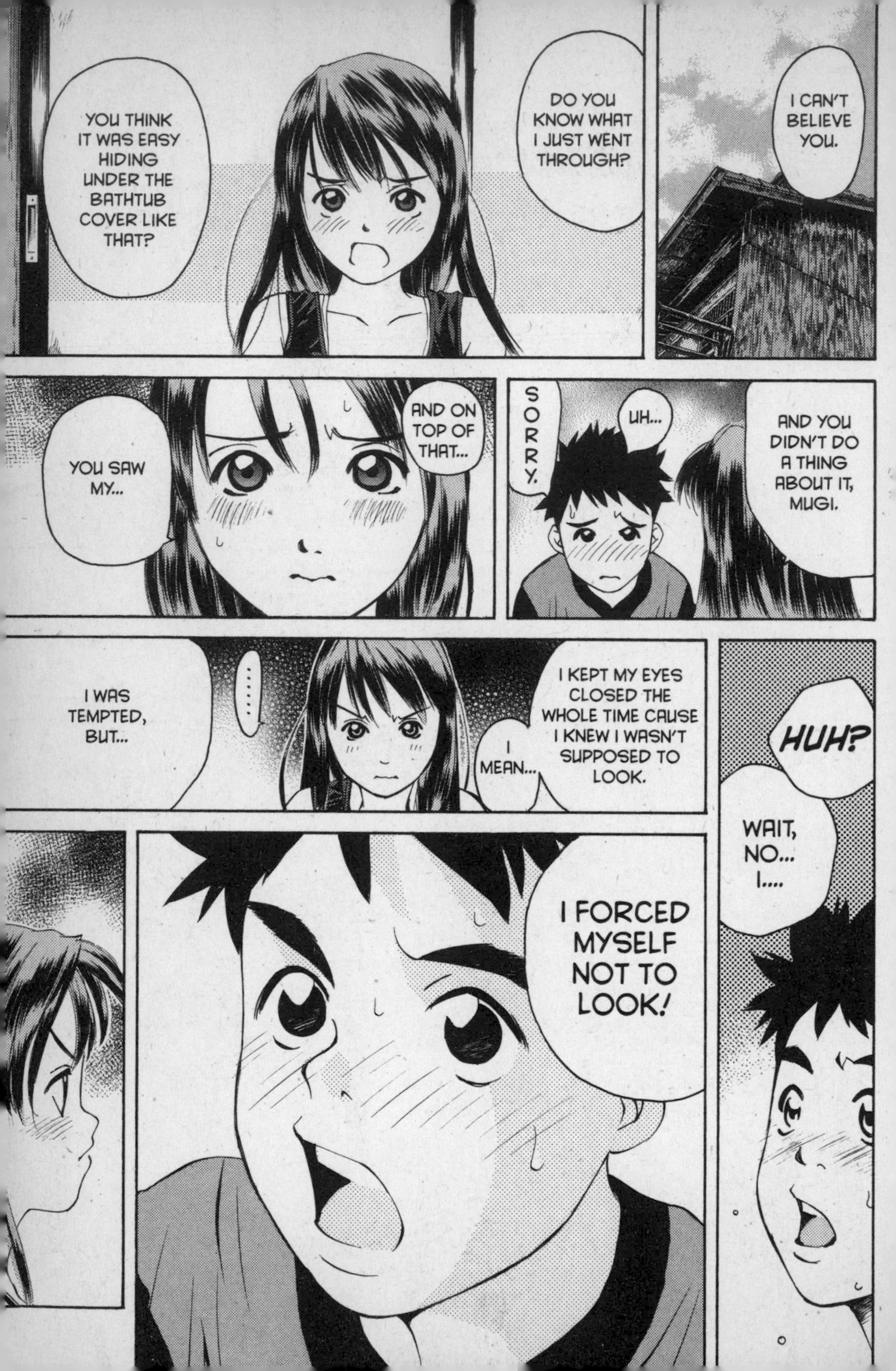
I CAN'T BELIEVE YOU.
DO YOU KNOW WHAT I JUST WENT THROUGH?
YOU THINK IT WAS EASY HIDING UNDER THE BATHTUB COVER LIKE THAT?
AND YOU DIDN'T DO A THING ABOUT IT, MUGI.
UH...
SORRY.
AND ON TOP OF THAT...
YOU SAW MY...
HUH?
WAIT, NO... I....
I KEPT MY EYES CLOSED THE WHOLE TIME CAUSE I KNEW I WASN'T SUPPOSED TO LOOK.
I MEAN...
......
I WAS TEMPTED, BUT...
I FORCED MYSELF NOT TO LOOK!

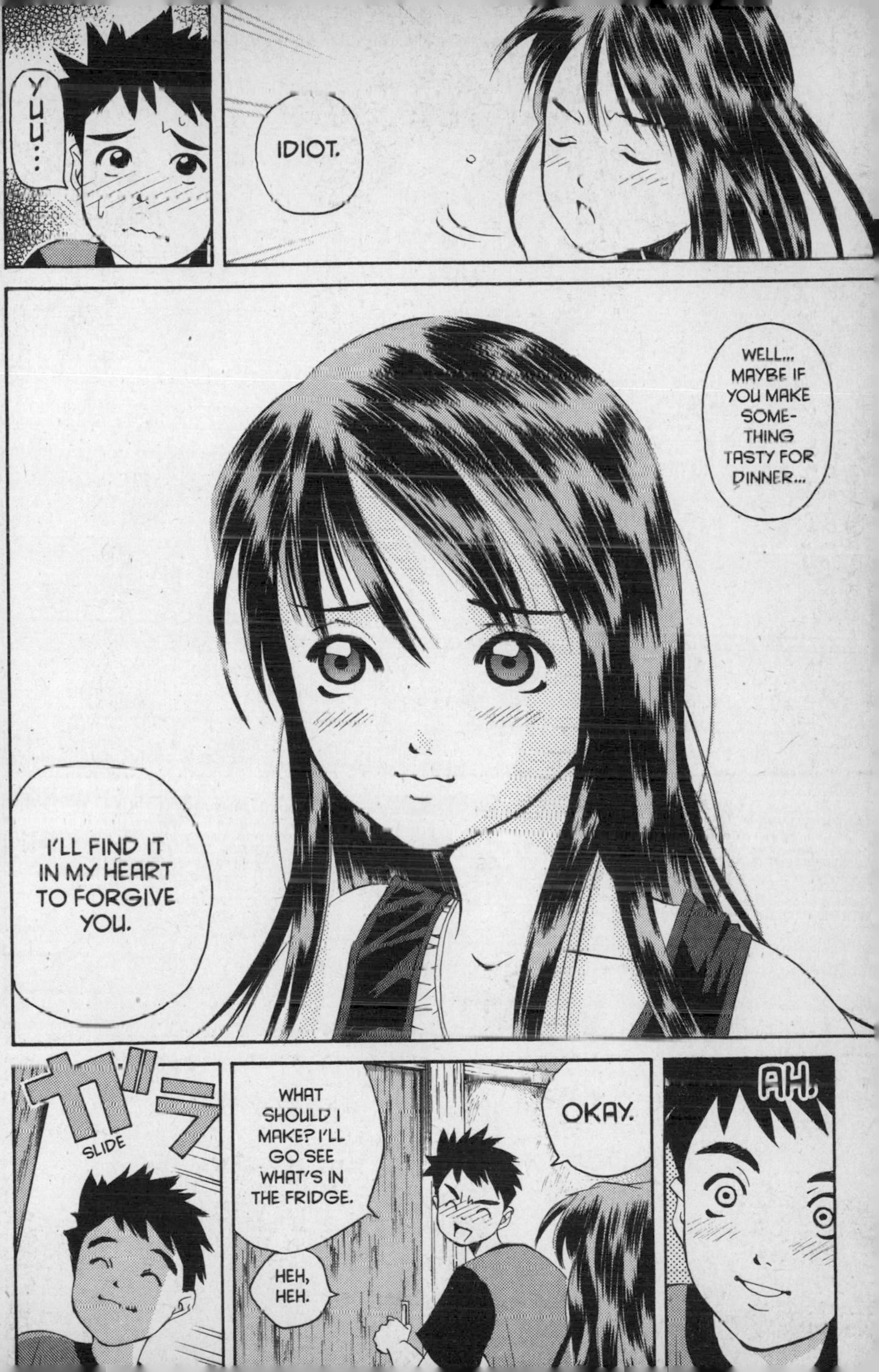
IDIOT.
YUU...
WELL... MAYBE IF YOU MAKE SOME-THING TASTY FOR DINNER...
I'LL FIND IT IN MY HEART TO FORGIVE YOU.
AH.
OKAY.
WHAT SHOULD I MAKE? I'LL GO SEE WHAT'S IN THE FRIDGE.
HEH, HEH.
ガラ
SLIDE

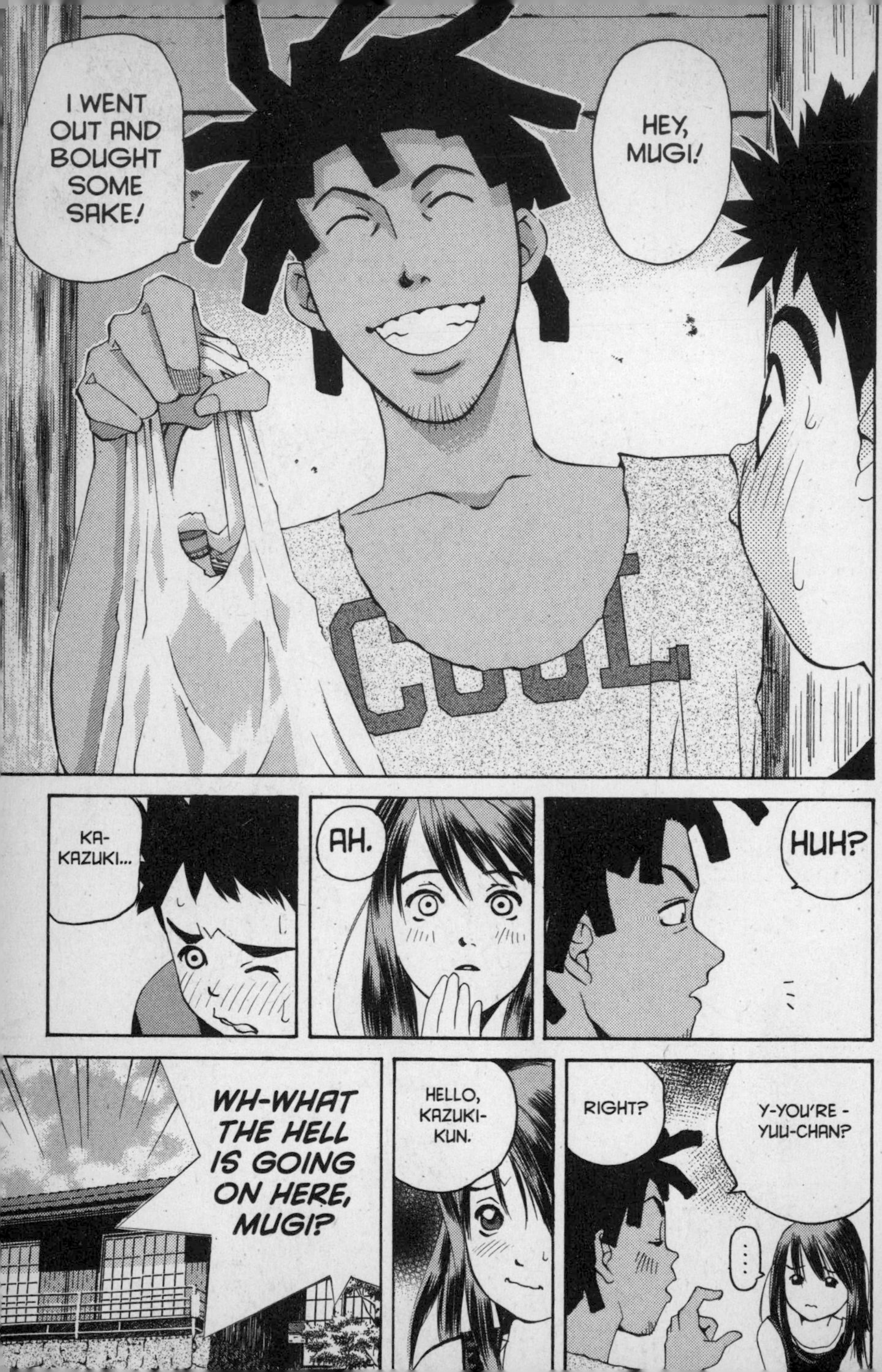
HEY, MUGI!
I WENT OUT AND BOUGHT SOME SAKE!
HUH?
AH.
KA-KAZUKI...
Y-YOU'RE - YUU-CHAN?
RIGHT?
....
HELLO, KAZUKI-KUN.
WH-WHAT THE HELL IS GOING ON HERE, MUGI?

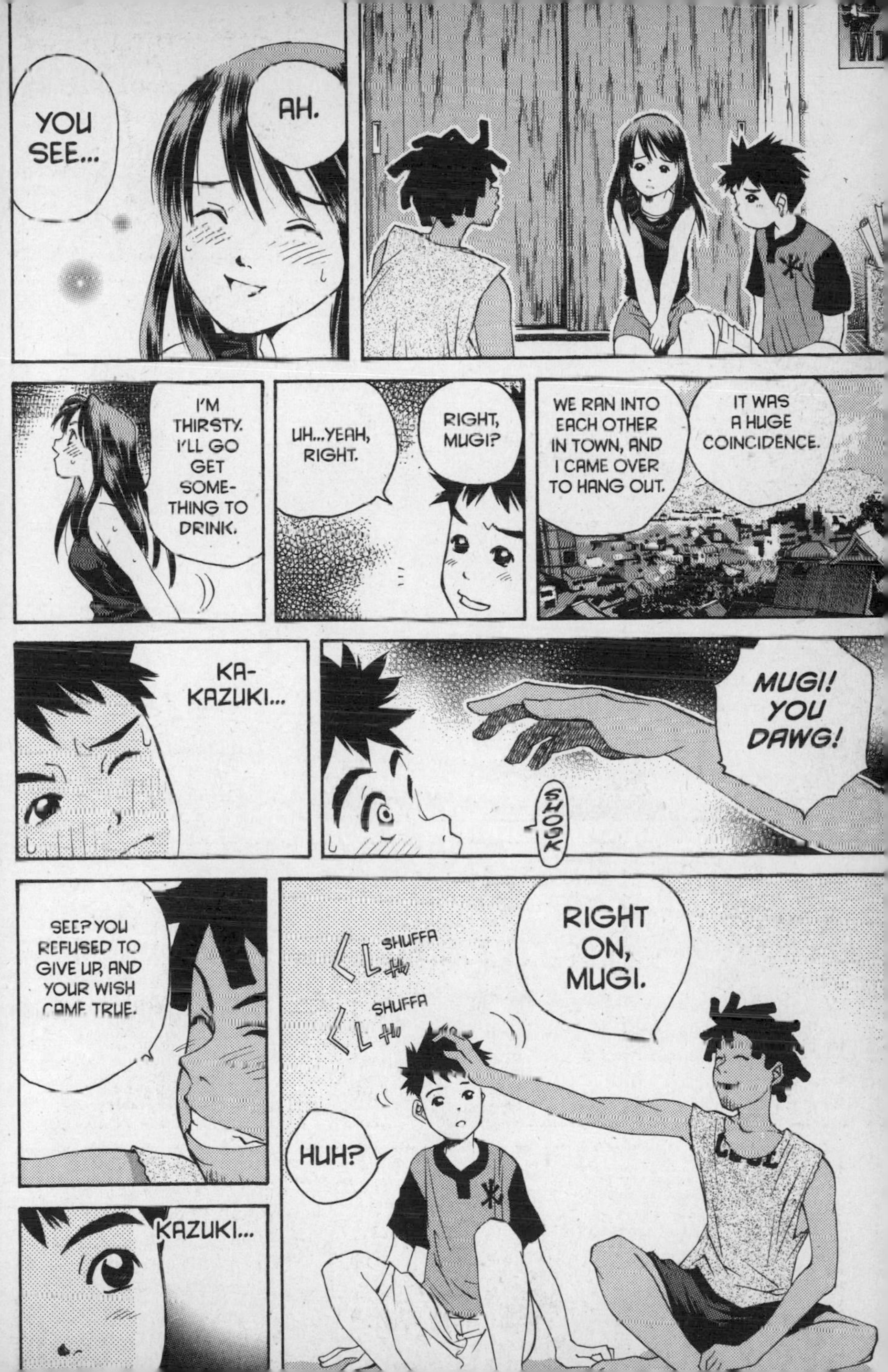
AH.
YOU SEE...
IT WAS A HUGE COINCIDENCE.
WE RAN INTO EACH OTHER IN TOWN, AND I CAME OVER TO HANG OUT.
RIGHT, MUGI?
UH...YEAH, RIGHT.
I'M THIRSTY. I'LL GO GET SOME-THING TO DRINK.
MUGI! YOU DAWG!
SHOCK
KA-KAZUKI...
RIGHT ON, MUGI.
SHUFFA
SHUFFA
HUH?
SEE? YOU REFUSED TO GIVE UP, AND YOUR WISH CAME TRUE.
KAZUKI...

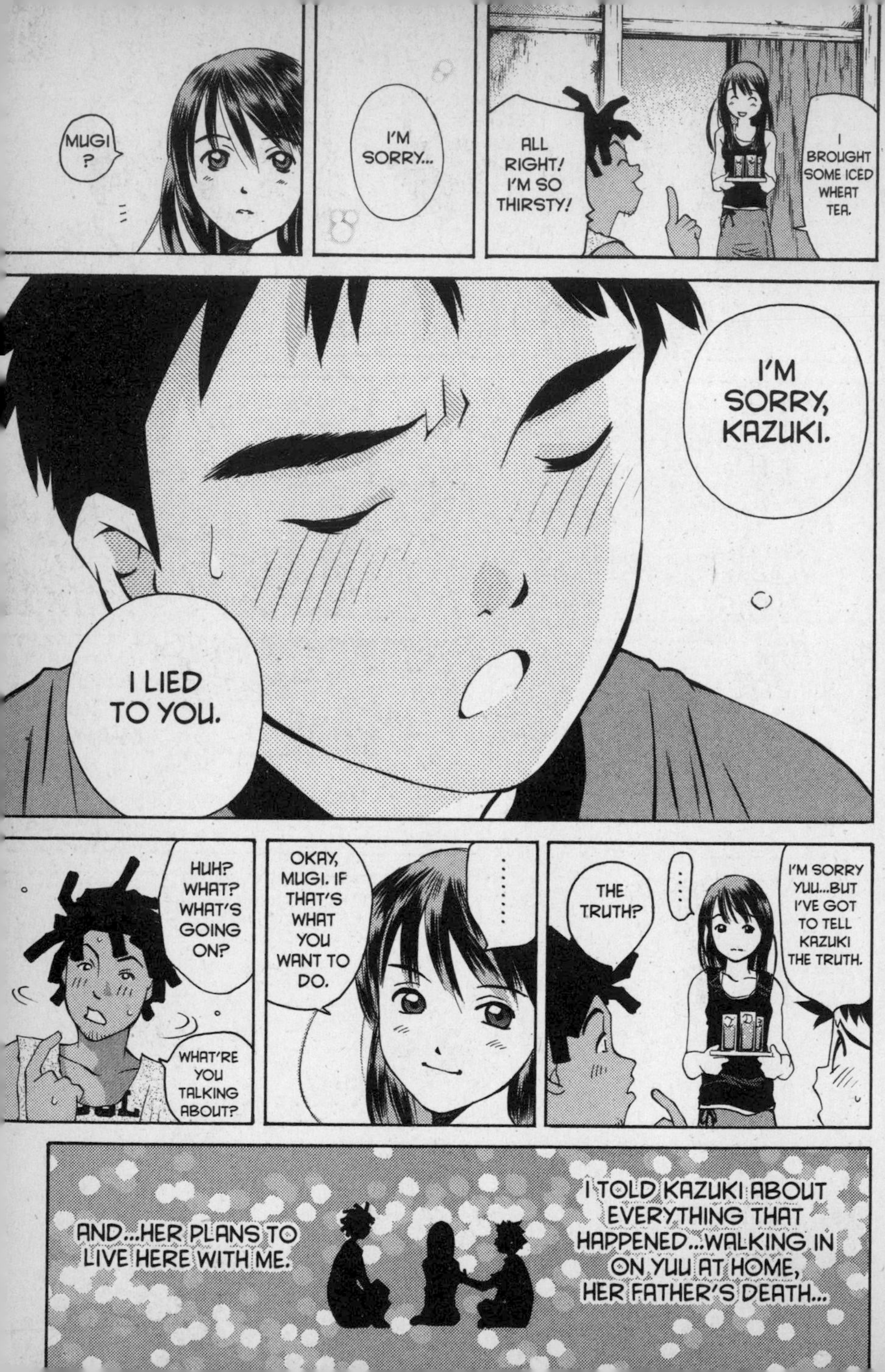
I BROUGHT SOME ICED WHEAT TEA.
ALL RIGHT! I'M SO THIRSTY!
I'M SORRY...
MUGI ?
I'M SORRY, KAZUKI.
I LIED TO YOU.
I'M SORRY YUU...BUT I'VE GOT TO TELL KAZUKI THE TRUTH.
.....
THE TRUTH?
....
OKAY, MUGI. IF THAT'S WHAT YOU WANT TO DO.
HUH? WHAT? WHAT'S GOING ON?
WHAT'RE YOU TALKING ABOUT?
I TOLD KAZUKI ABOUT EVERYTHING THAT HAPPENED...WALKING IN ON YUU AT HOME, HER FATHER'S DEATH...
AND...HER PLANS TO LIVE HERE WITH ME.

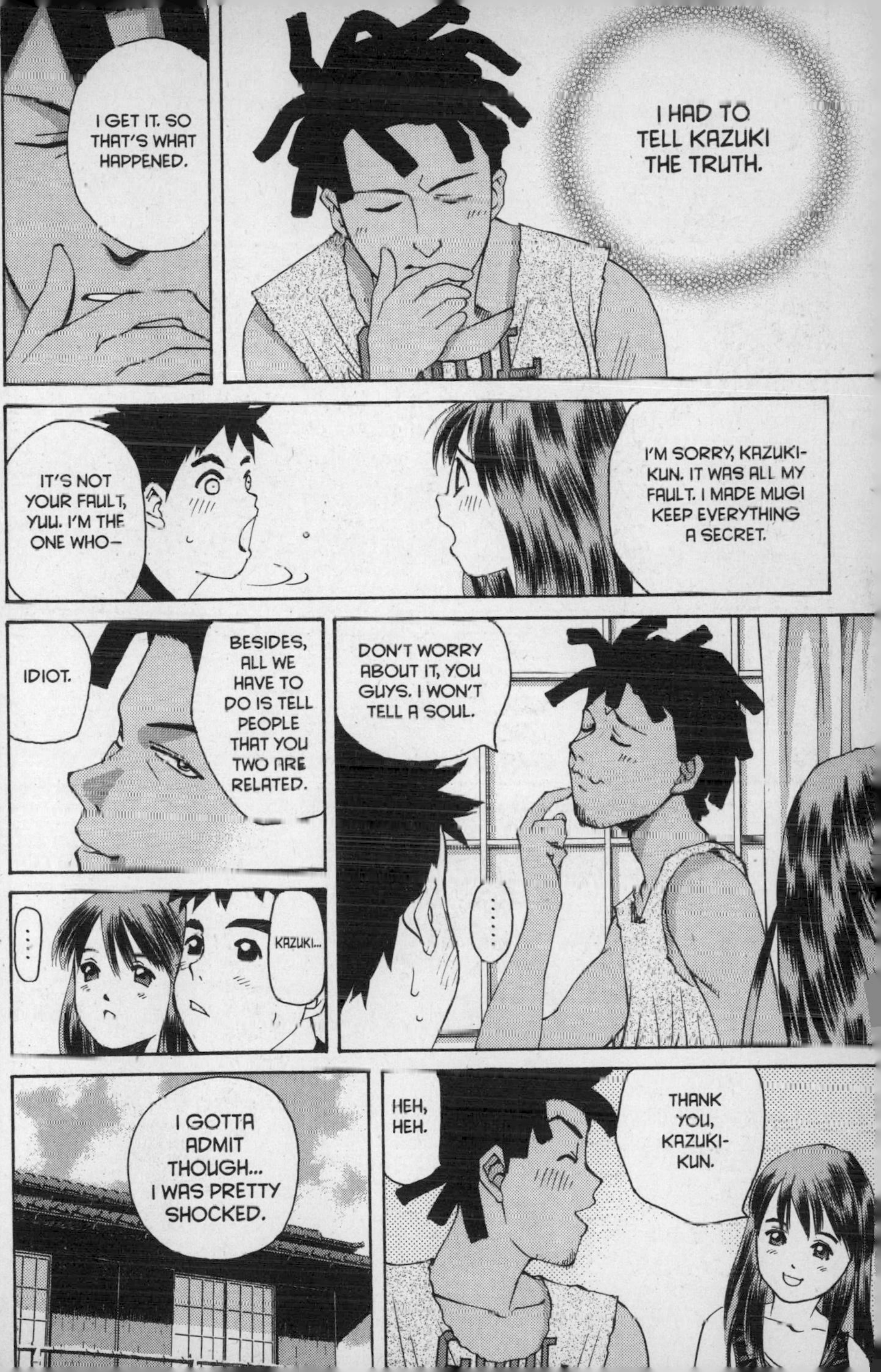

I HAD TO TELL KAZUKI THE TRUTH.
I GET IT. SO THAT'S WHAT HAPPENED.
I'M SORRY, KAZUKI-KUN. IT WAS ALL MY FAULT. I MADE MUGI KEEP EVERYTHING A SECRET.
IT'S NOT YOUR FAULT, YUU. I'M THE ONE WHO—
DON'T WORRY ABOUT IT, YOU GUYS. I WON'T TELL A SOUL.
.....
BESIDES, ALL WE HAVE TO DO IS TELL PEOPLE THAT YOU TWO ARE RELATED.
IDIOT.
KAZUKI...
....
THANK YOU, KAZUKI-KUN.
HEH, HEH.
I GOTTA ADMIT THOUGH... I WAS PRETTY SHOCKED.

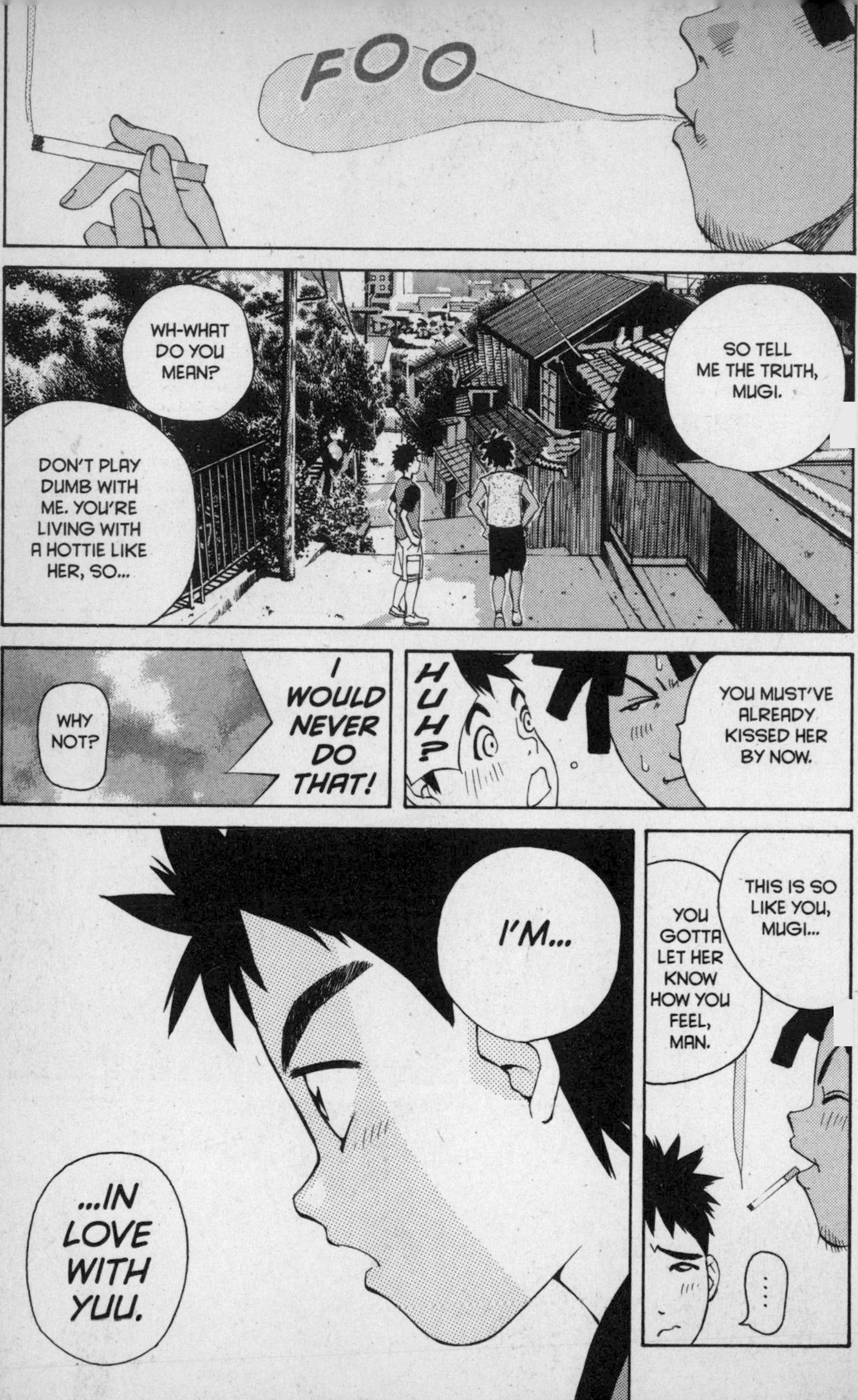
FOO
SO TELL ME THE TRUTH, MUGI.
WH-WHAT DO YOU MEAN?
DON'T PLAY DUMB WITH ME. YOU'RE LIVING WITH A HOTTIE LIKE HER, SO...
YOU MUST'VE ALREADY KISSED HER BY NOW.
HUH?
I WOULD NEVER DO THAT!
WHY NOT?
THIS IS SO LIKE YOU, MUGI...
YOU GOTTA LET HER KNOW HOW YOU FEEL, MAN.
....
I'M...
...IN LOVE WITH YUU.

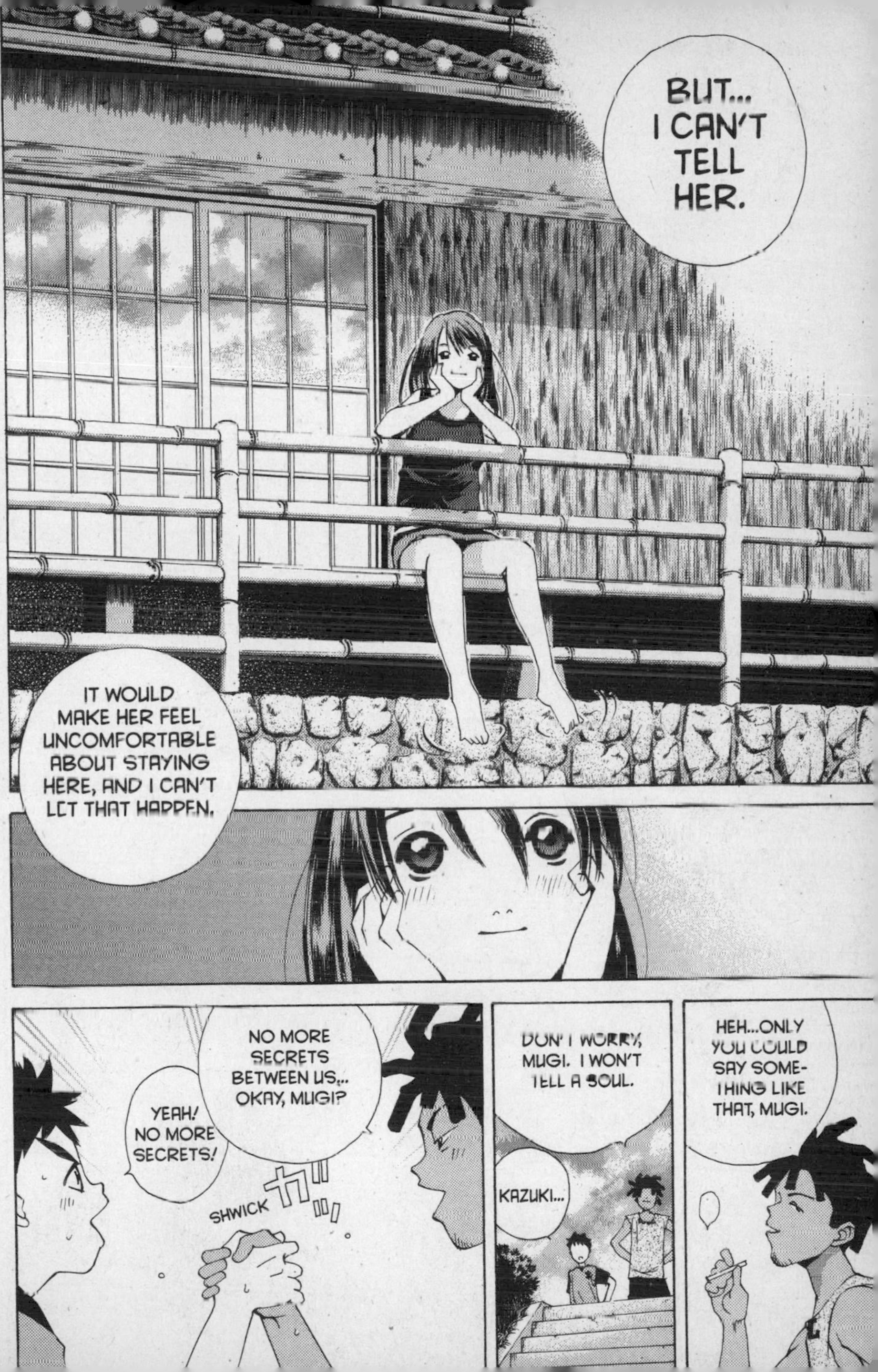
BUT... I CAN'T TELL HER.
IT WOULD MAKE HER FEEL UNCOMFORTABLE ABOUT STAYING HERE, AND I CAN'T LET THAT HAPPEN.
HEH...ONLY YOU COULD SAY SOME-THING LIKE THAT, MUGI.
DON'T WORRY, MUGI. I WON'T TELL A SOUL.
KAZUKI...
NO MORE SECRETS BETWEEN US... OKAY, MUGI?
YEAH! NO MORE SECRETS!
SHWICK

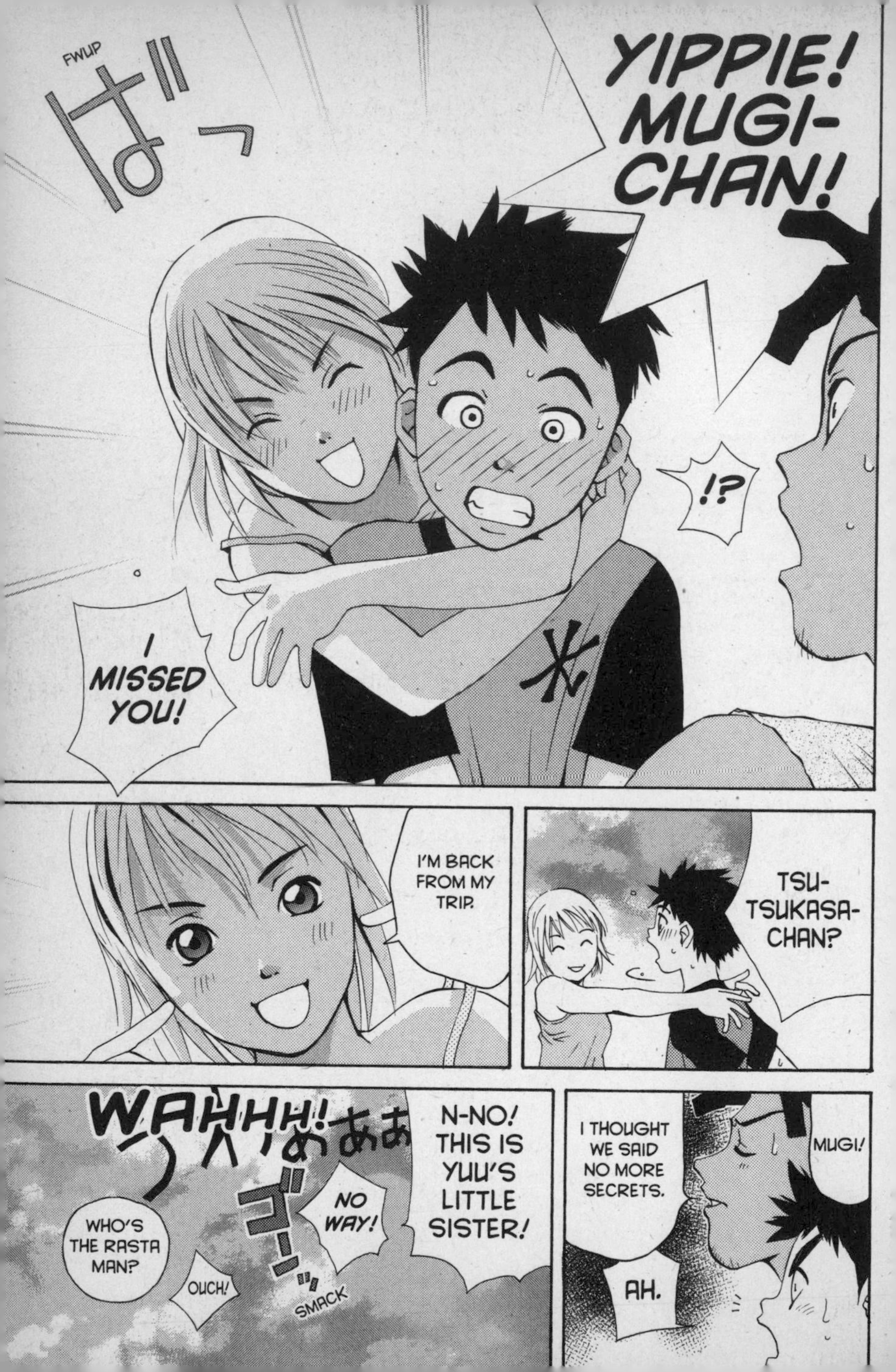
YIPPIE! MUGI-CHAN!
FWUP
はっ
!?
I MISSED YOU!
TSU-TSUKASA-CHAN?
I'M BACK FROM MY TRIP.
MUGI!
I THOUGHT WE SAID NO MORE SECRETS.
AH.
N-NO! THIS IS YUU'S LITTLE SISTER!
NO WAY!
WAHHH!
WHO'S THE RASTA MAN?
OUCH!
SMACK

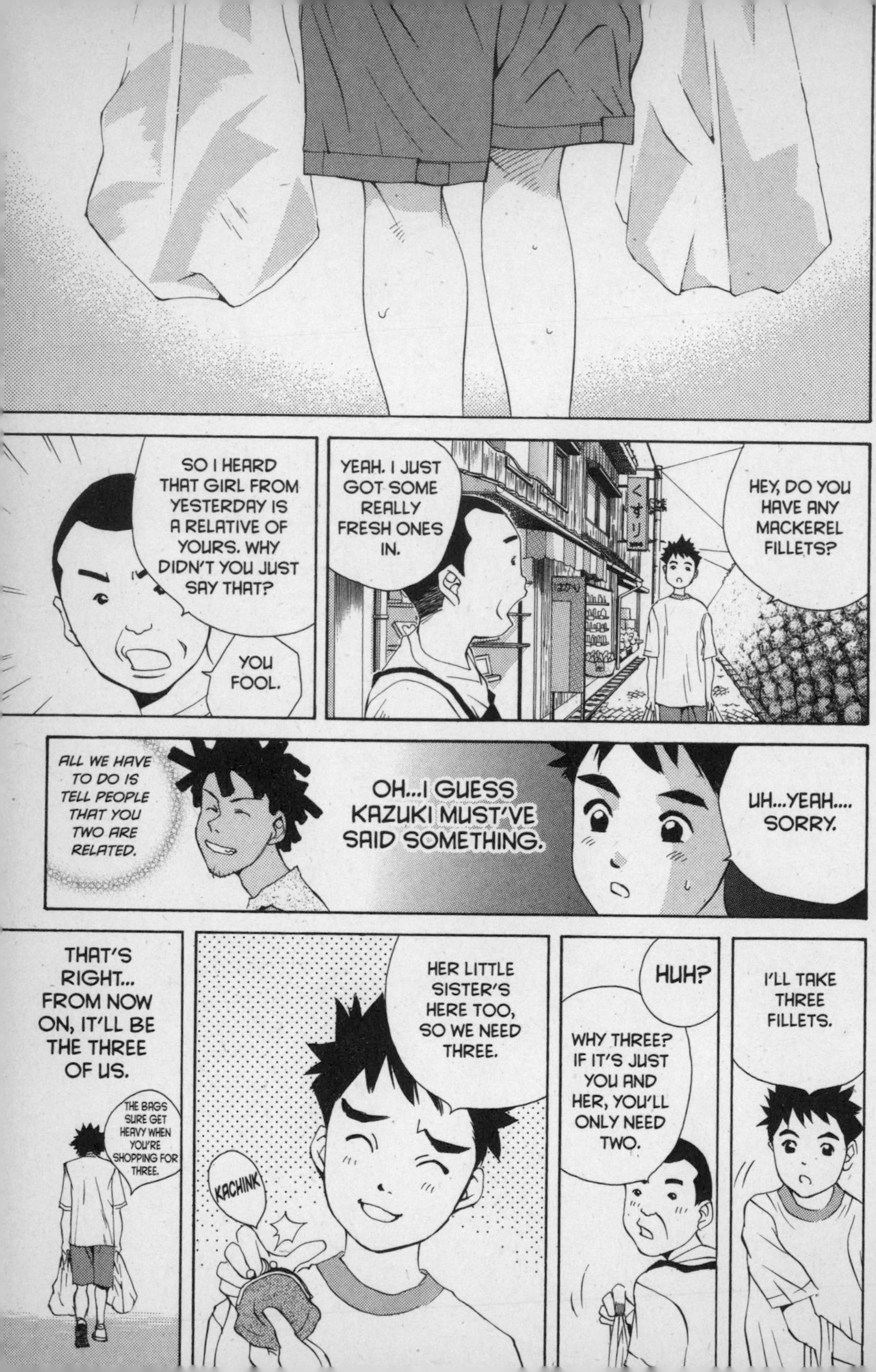
HEY, DO YOU HAVE ANY MACKEREL FILLETS?
くすり
YEAH. I JUST GOT SOME REALLY FRESH ONES IN.
SO I HEARD THAT GIRL FROM YESTERDAY IS A RELATIVE OF YOURS. WHY DIDN'T YOU JUST SAY THAT?
YOU FOOL.
UH...YEAH.... SORRY.
OH...I GUESS KAZUKI MUST'VE SAID SOMETHING.
ALL WE HAVE TO DO IS TELL PEOPLE THAT YOU TWO ARE RELATED.
I'LL TAKE THREE FILLETS.
HUH?
WHY THREE? IF IT'S JUST YOU AND HER, YOU'LL ONLY NEED TWO.
HER LITTLE SISTER'S HERE TOO, SO WE NEED THREE.
KACHINK
THAT'S RIGHT... FROM NOW ON, IT'LL BE THE THREE OF US.
THE BAGS SURE GET HEAVY WHEN YOU'RE SHOPPING FOR THREE.

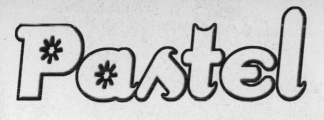

Pastel

MIRACLE 7: THREE KIDS, ONE ROOF

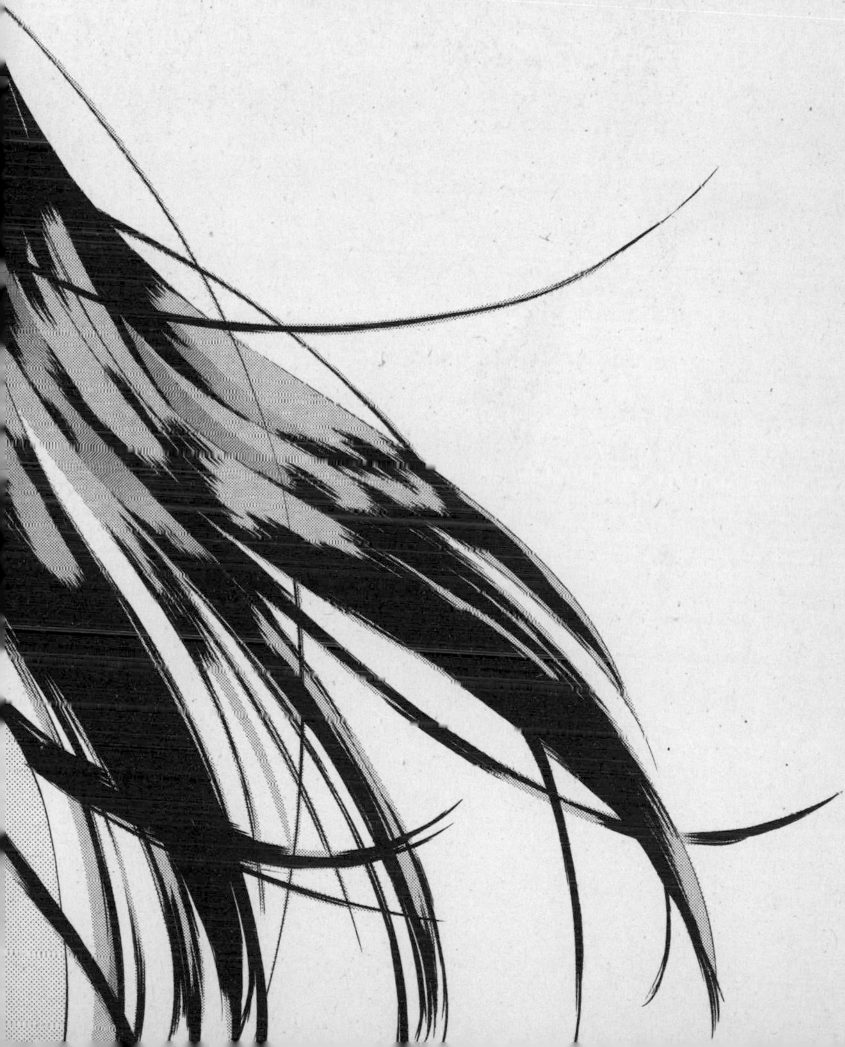

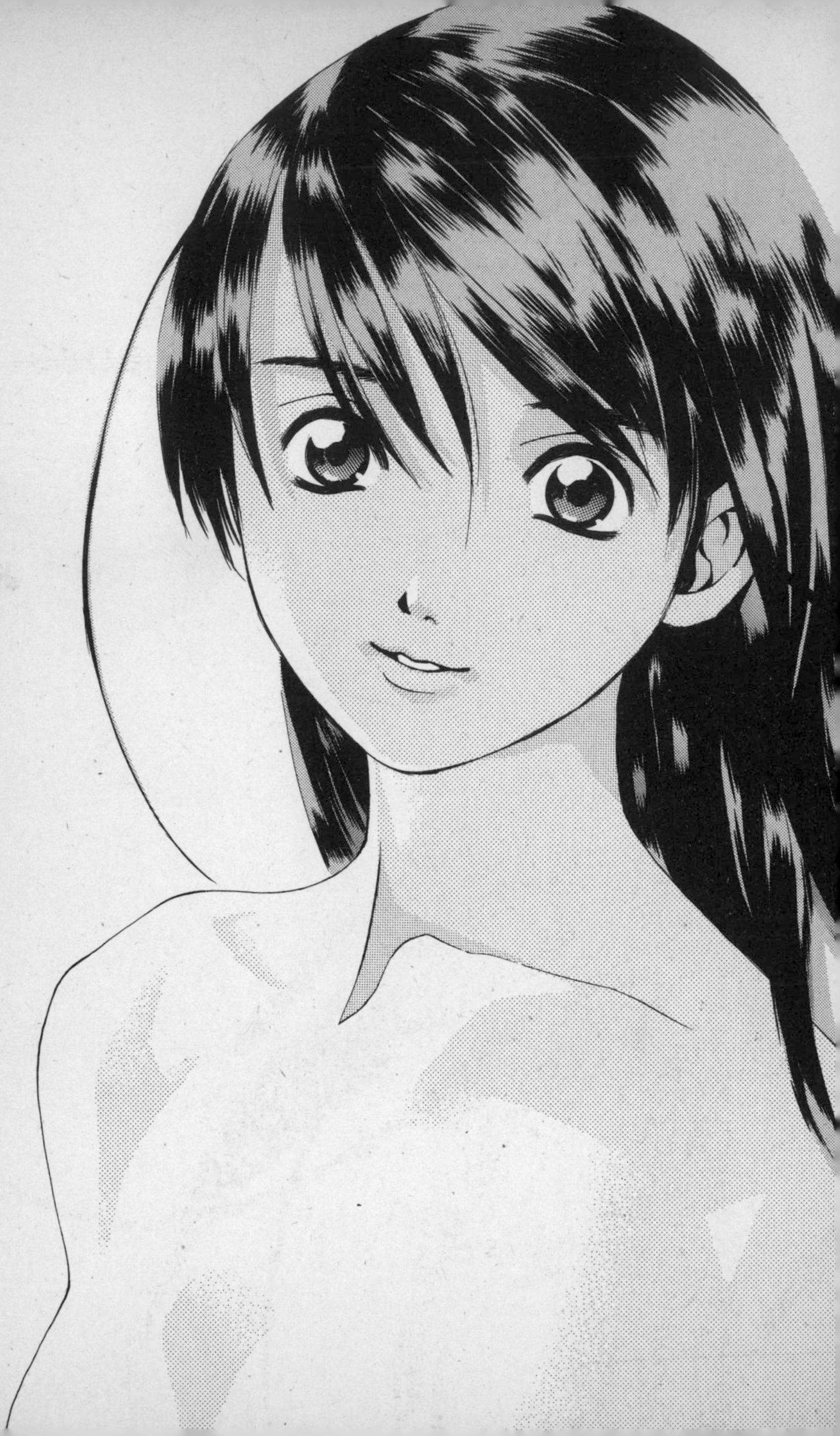

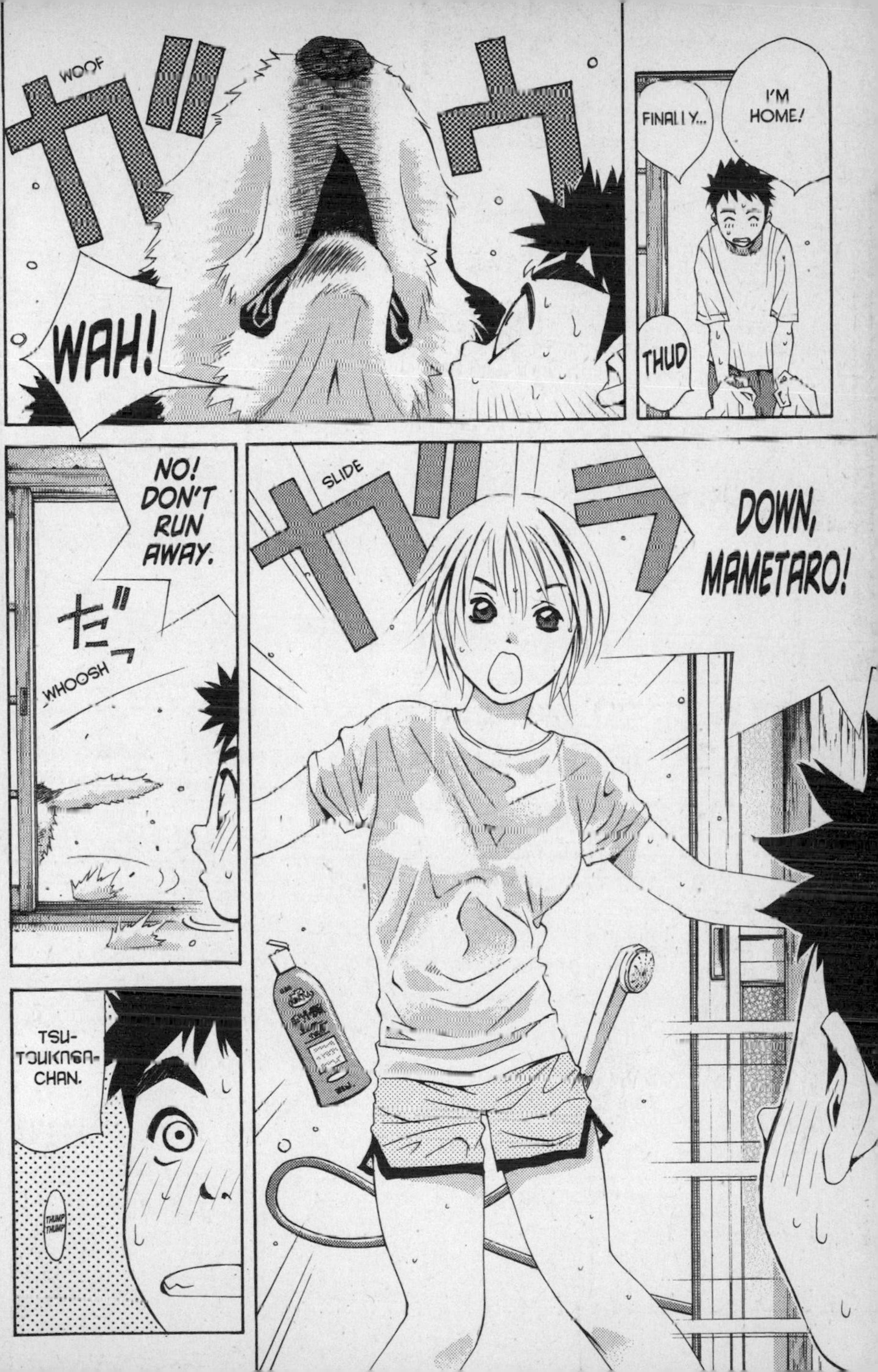

I'M HOME!
FINALLY...
THUD
ガウ
WOOF
WAH!
ガラ
SLIDE
DOWN, MAMETARO!
NO! DON'T RUN AWAY.
だっ
WHOOSH
TSU-TSUKASA-CHAN.
THUMP THUMP

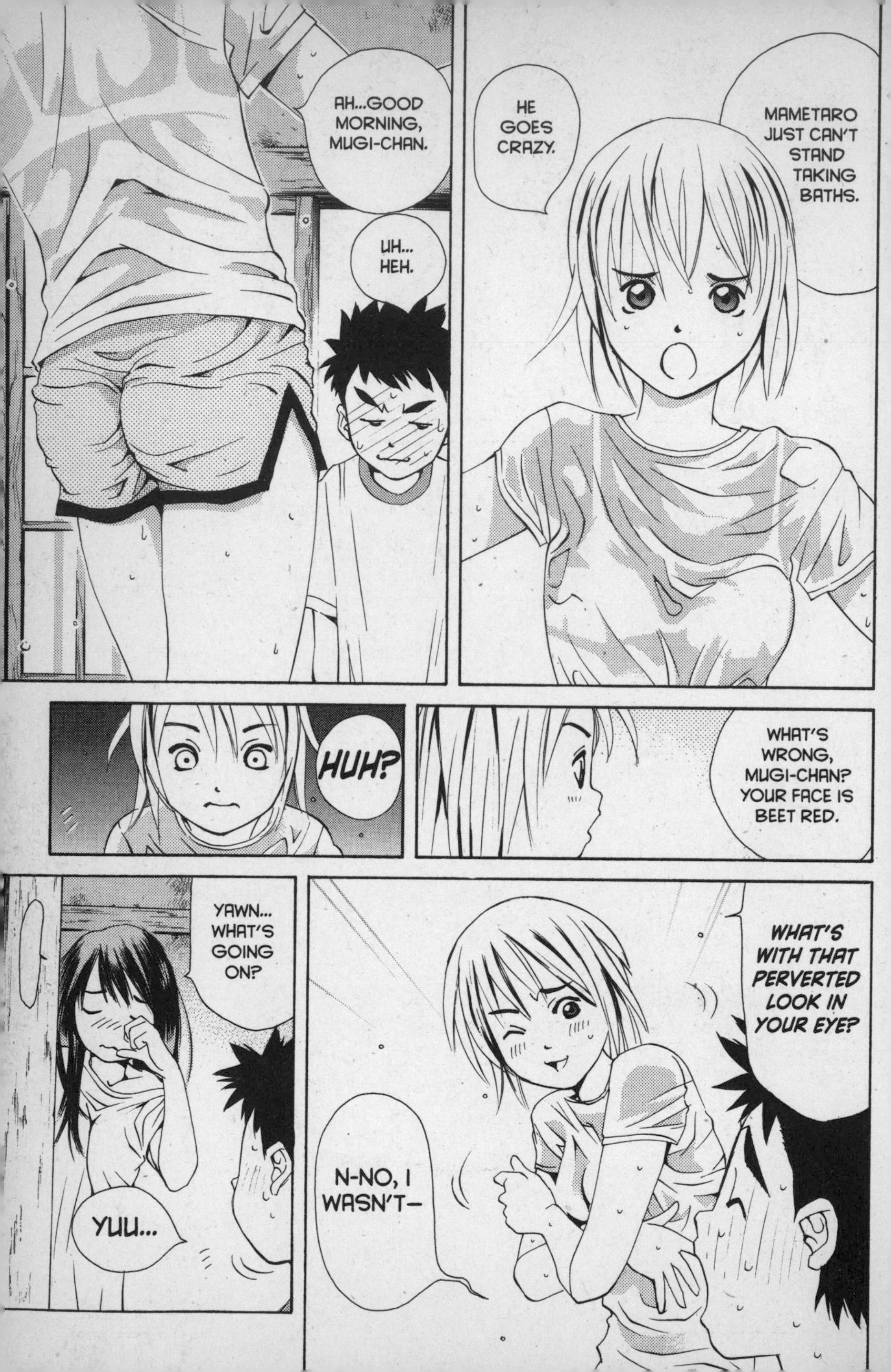
MAMETARO JUST CAN'T STAND TAKING BATHS.
HE GOES CRAZY.
AH...GOOD MORNING, MUGI-CHAN.
UH... HEH.
WHAT'S WRONG, MUGI-CHAN? YOUR FACE IS BEET RED.
HUH?
WHAT'S WITH THAT PERVERTED LOOK IN YOUR EYE?
N-NO, I WASN'T—
YAWN... WHAT'S GOING ON?
YUU...

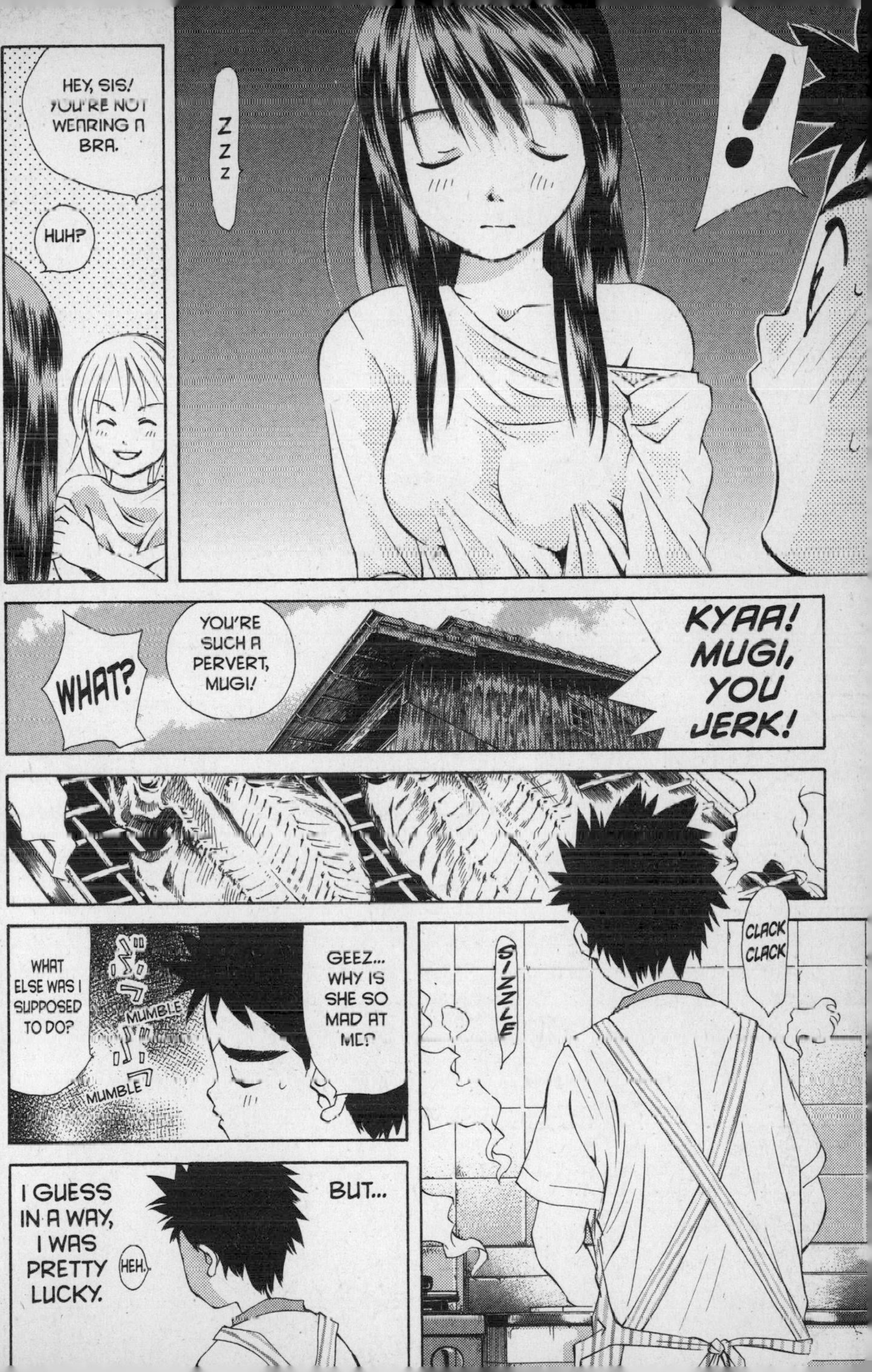
!
ZZZ
HEY, SIS! YOU'RE NOT WEARING A BRA.
HUH?
KYAA! MUGI, YOU JERK!
YOU'RE SUCH A PERVERT, MUGI!
WHAT?
CLACK CLACK
SIZZLE
GEEZ... WHY IS SHE SO MAD AT ME?
MUMBLE
MUMBLE
WHAT ELSE WAS I SUPPOSED TO DO?
BUT...
I GUESS IN A WAY, I WAS PRETTY LUCKY.
HEH.

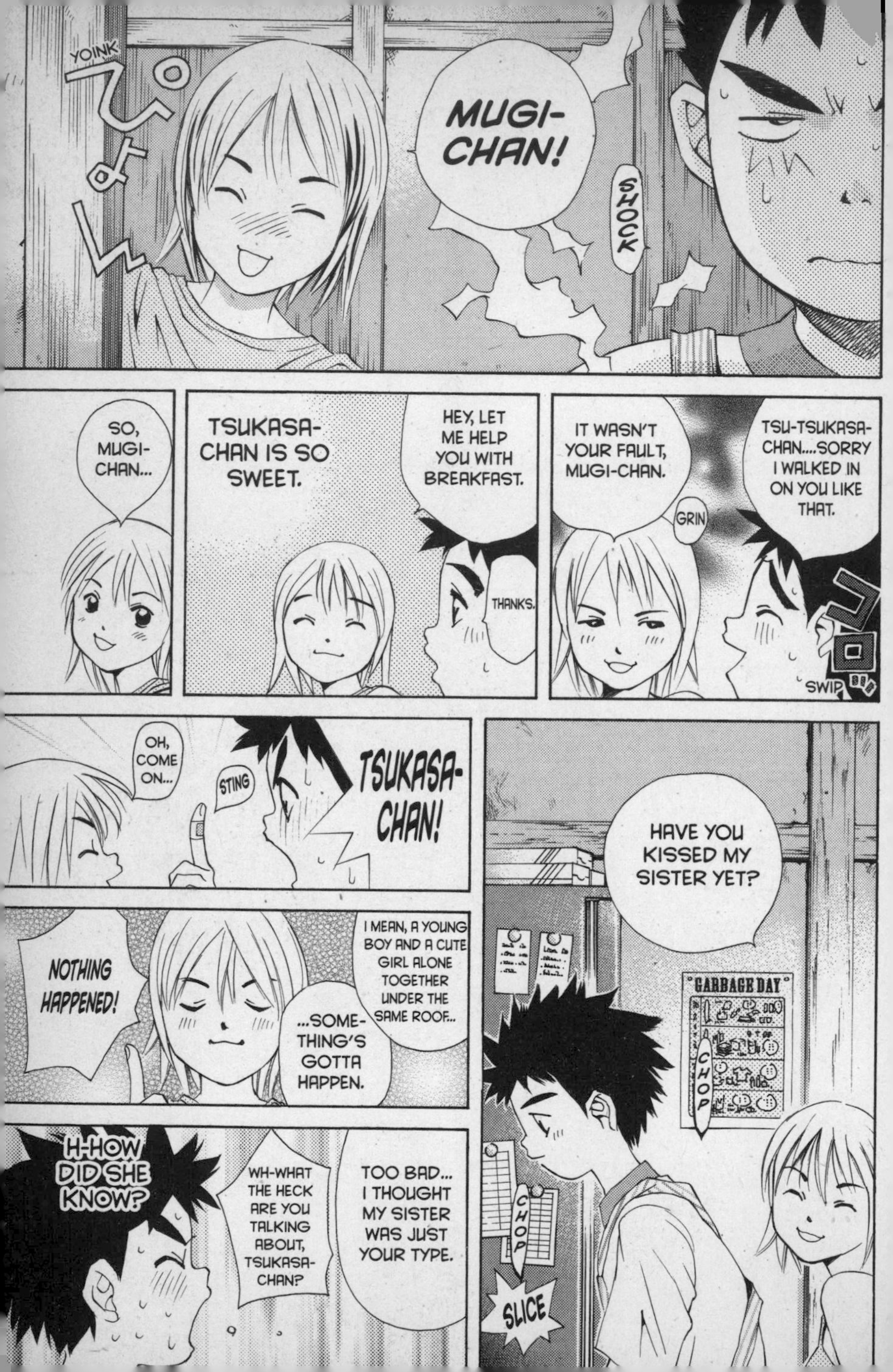
SHOCK
MUGI-CHAN!
YOINK
TSU-TSUKASA-CHAN....SORRY I WALKED IN ON YOU LIKE THAT.
IT WASN'T YOUR FAULT, MUGI-CHAN.
GRIN
SWIP
HEY, LET ME HELP YOU WITH BREAKFAST.
TSUKASA-CHAN IS SO SWEET.
THANKS.
SO, MUGI-CHAN...
HAVE YOU KISSED MY SISTER YET?
GARBAGE DAY
CHOP
CHOP
SLICE
TSUKASA-CHAN!
STING
OH, COME ON...
I MEAN, A YOUNG BOY AND A CUTE GIRL ALONE TOGETHER UNDER THE SAME ROOF...
...SOMETHING'S GOTTA HAPPEN.
NOTHING HAPPENED!
TOO BAD... I THOUGHT MY SISTER WAS JUST YOUR TYPE.
WH-WHAT THE HECK ARE YOU TALKING ABOUT, TSUKASA-CHAN?
H-HOW DID SHE KNOW?

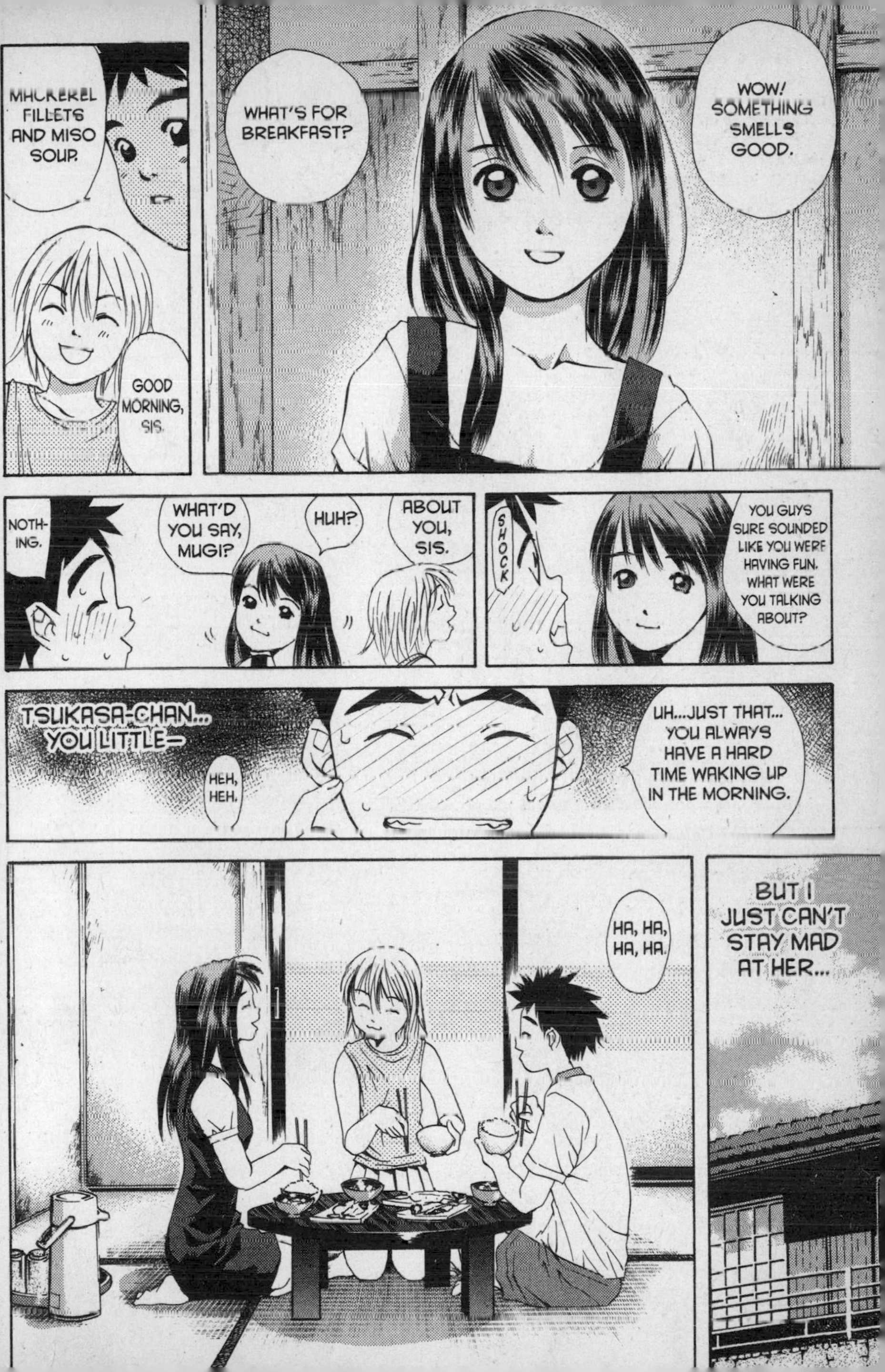
WOW! SOMETHING SMELLS GOOD.
WHAT'S FOR BREAKFAST?
MACKEREL FILLETS AND MISO SOUP.
GOOD MORNING, SIS.
YOU GUYS SURE SOUNDED LIKE YOU WERE HAVING FUN. WHAT WERE YOU TALKING ABOUT?
SHOCK
ABOUT YOU, SIS.
HUH?
WHAT'D YOU SAY, MUGI?
NOTH-ING.
UH...JUST THAT... YOU ALWAYS HAVE A HARD TIME WAKING UP IN THE MORNING.
HEH, HEH.
TSUKASA-CHAN... YOU LITTLE—
BUT I JUST CAN'T STAY MAD AT HER...
HA, HA, HA, HA.

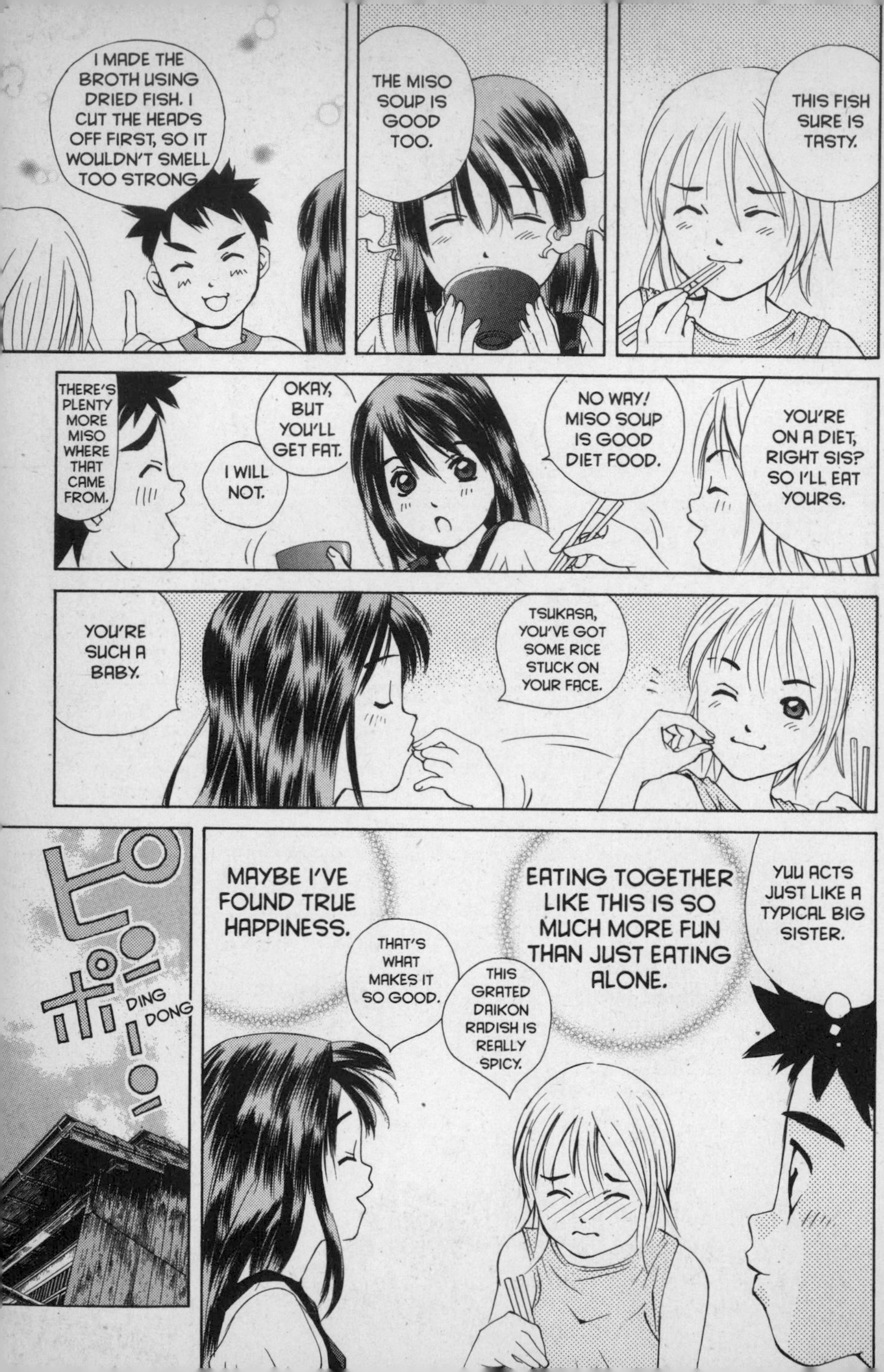
THIS FISH SURE IS TASTY.
THE MISO SOUP IS GOOD TOO.
I MADE THE BROTH USING DRIED FISH. I CUT THE HEADS OFF FIRST, SO IT WOULDN'T SMELL TOO STRONG.
YOU'RE ON A DIET, RIGHT SIS? SO I'LL EAT YOURS.
NO WAY! MISO SOUP IS GOOD DIET FOOD.
OKAY, BUT YOU'LL GET FAT.
I WILL NOT.
THERE'S PLENTY MORE MISO WHERE THAT CAME FROM.
TSUKASA, YOU'VE GOT SOME RICE STUCK ON YOUR FACE.
YOU'RE SUCH A BABY.
YUU ACTS JUST LIKE A TYPICAL BIG SISTER.
EATING TOGETHER LIKE THIS IS SO MUCH MORE FUN THAN JUST EATING ALONE.
THIS GRATED DAIKON RADISH IS REALLY SPICY.
MAYBE I'VE FOUND TRUE HAPPINESS.
THAT'S WHAT MAKES IT SO GOOD.
DING DONG

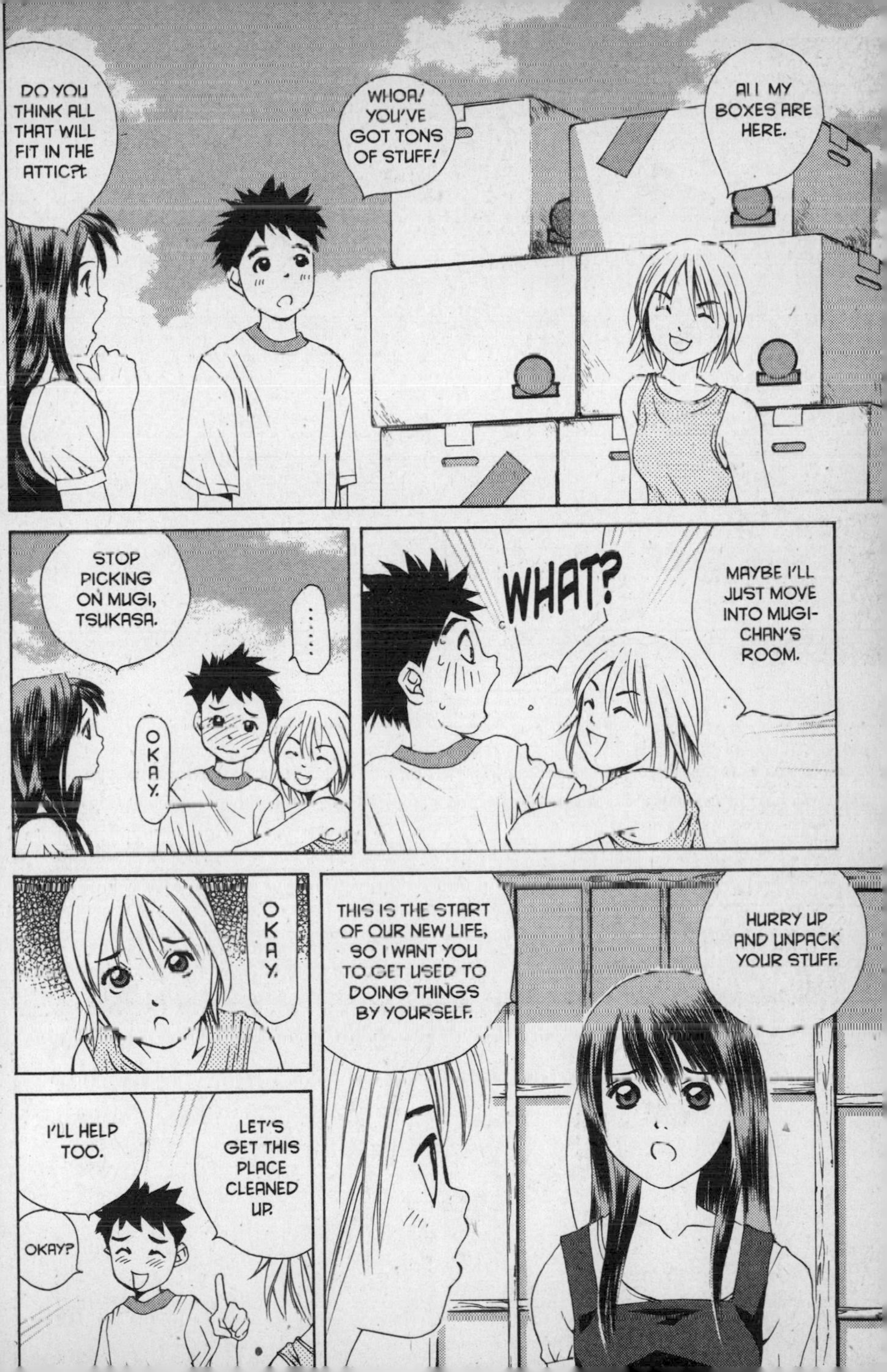
ALL MY BOXES ARE HERE.
WHOA! YOU'VE GOT TONS OF STUFF!
DO YOU THINK ALL THAT WILL FIT IN THE ATTIC?!
MAYBE I'LL JUST MOVE INTO MUGI-CHAN'S ROOM.
WHAT?
STOP PICKING ON MUGI, TSUKASA.
......
OKAY.
HURRY UP AND UNPACK YOUR STUFF.
THIS IS THE START OF OUR NEW LIFE, SO I WANT YOU TO GET USED TO DOING THINGS BY YOURSELF.
OKAY.
LET'S GET THIS PLACE CLEANED UP.
I'LL HELP TOO.
OKAY?

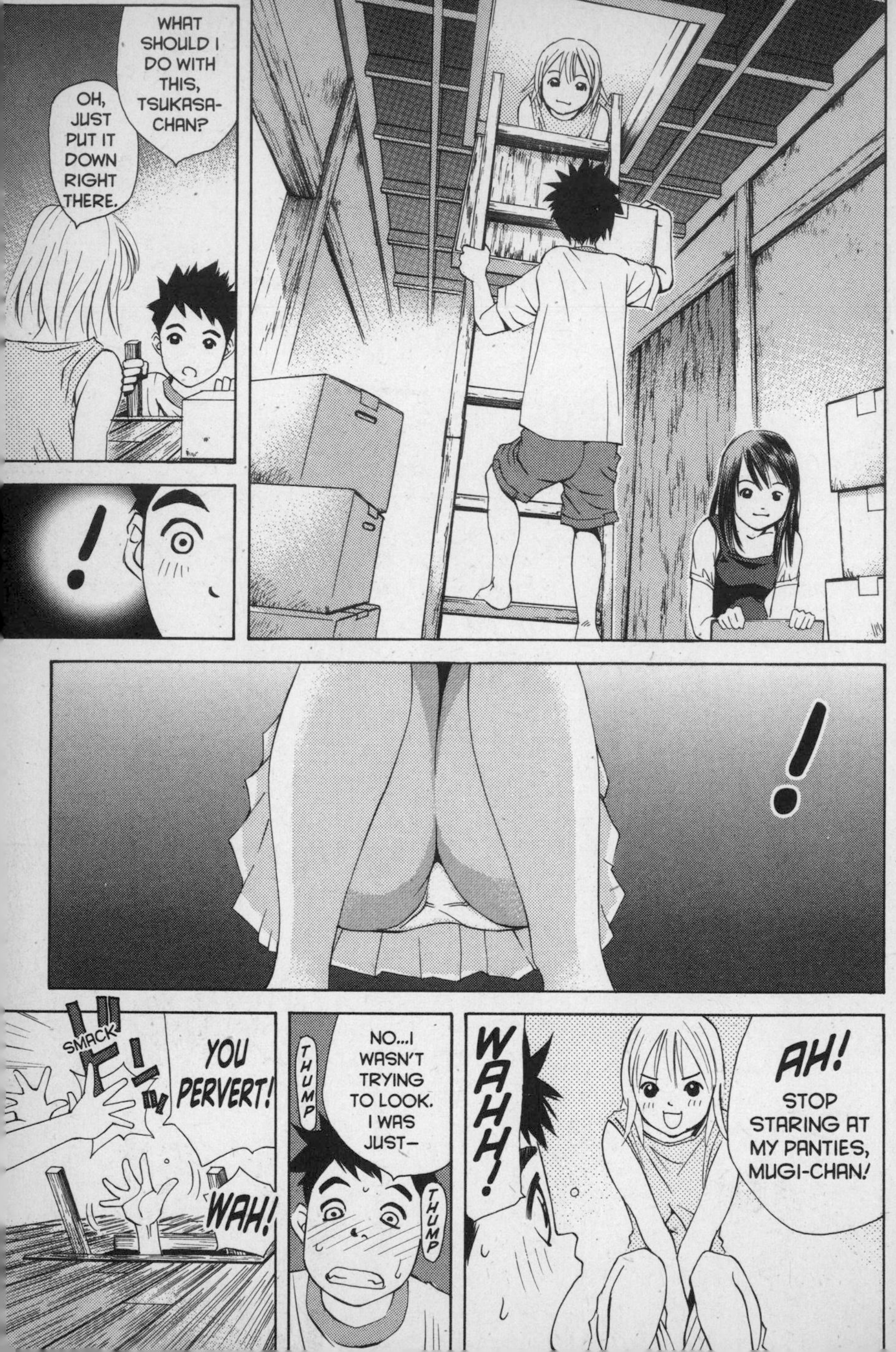
WHAT SHOULD I DO WITH THIS, TSUKASA-CHAN?
OH, JUST PUT IT DOWN RIGHT THERE.
!
!
AH! STOP STARING AT MY PANTIES, MUGI-CHAN!
WAHH!
NO...I WASN'T TRYING TO LOOK. I WAS JUST—
THUMP
THUMP
SMACK
YOU PERVERT!
WAH!

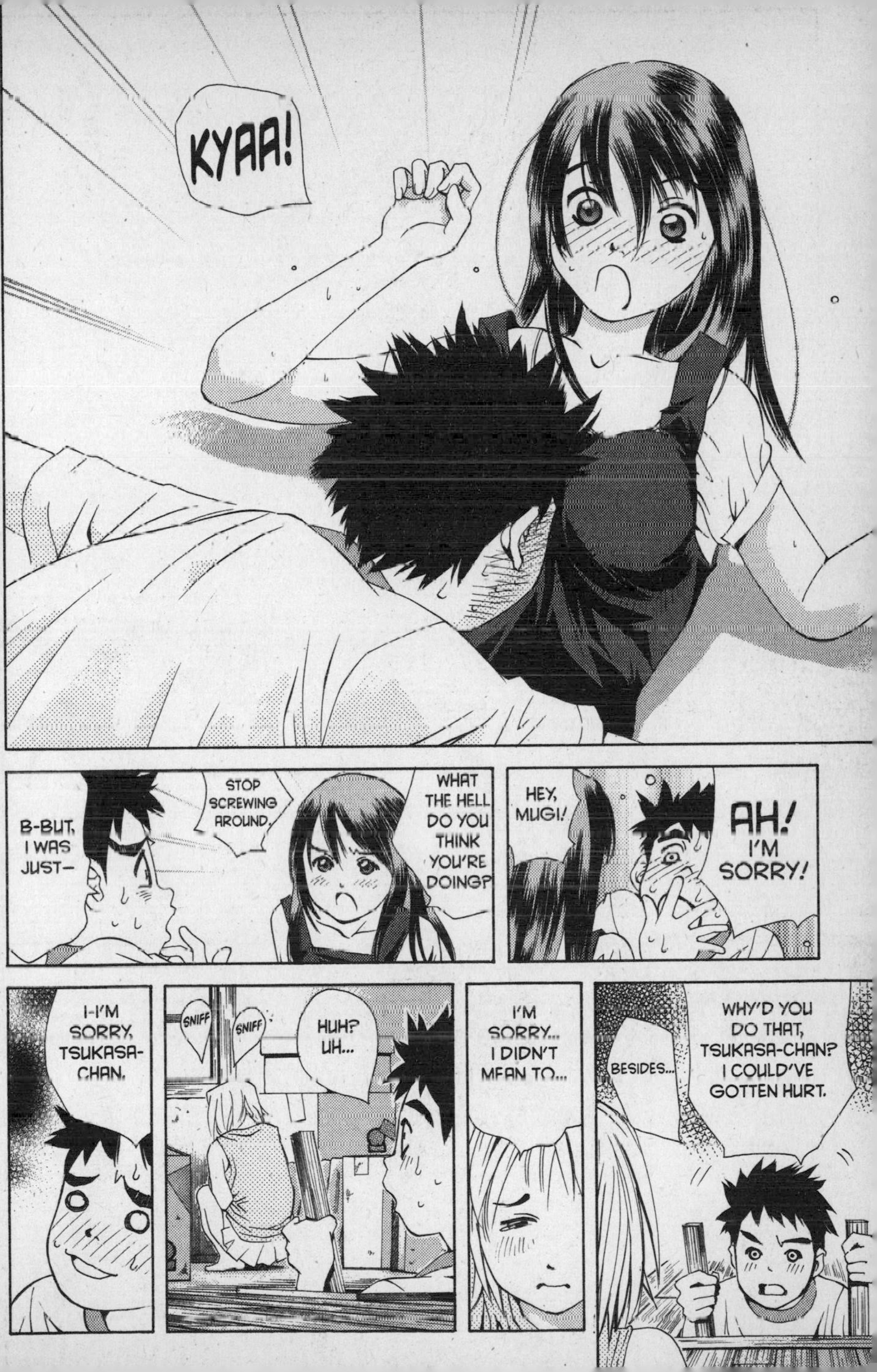
KYAA!
HEY, MUGI!
AH! I'M SORRY!
WHAT THE HELL DO YOU THINK YOU'RE DOING?
STOP SCREWING AROUND.
B-BUT, I WAS JUST—
WHY'D YOU DO THAT, TSUKASA-CHAN? I COULD'VE GOTTEN HURT.
BESIDES...
I'M SORRY... I DIDN'T MEAN TO...
HUH? UH...
SNIFF
SNIFF
I-I'M SORRY, TSUKASA-CHAN.

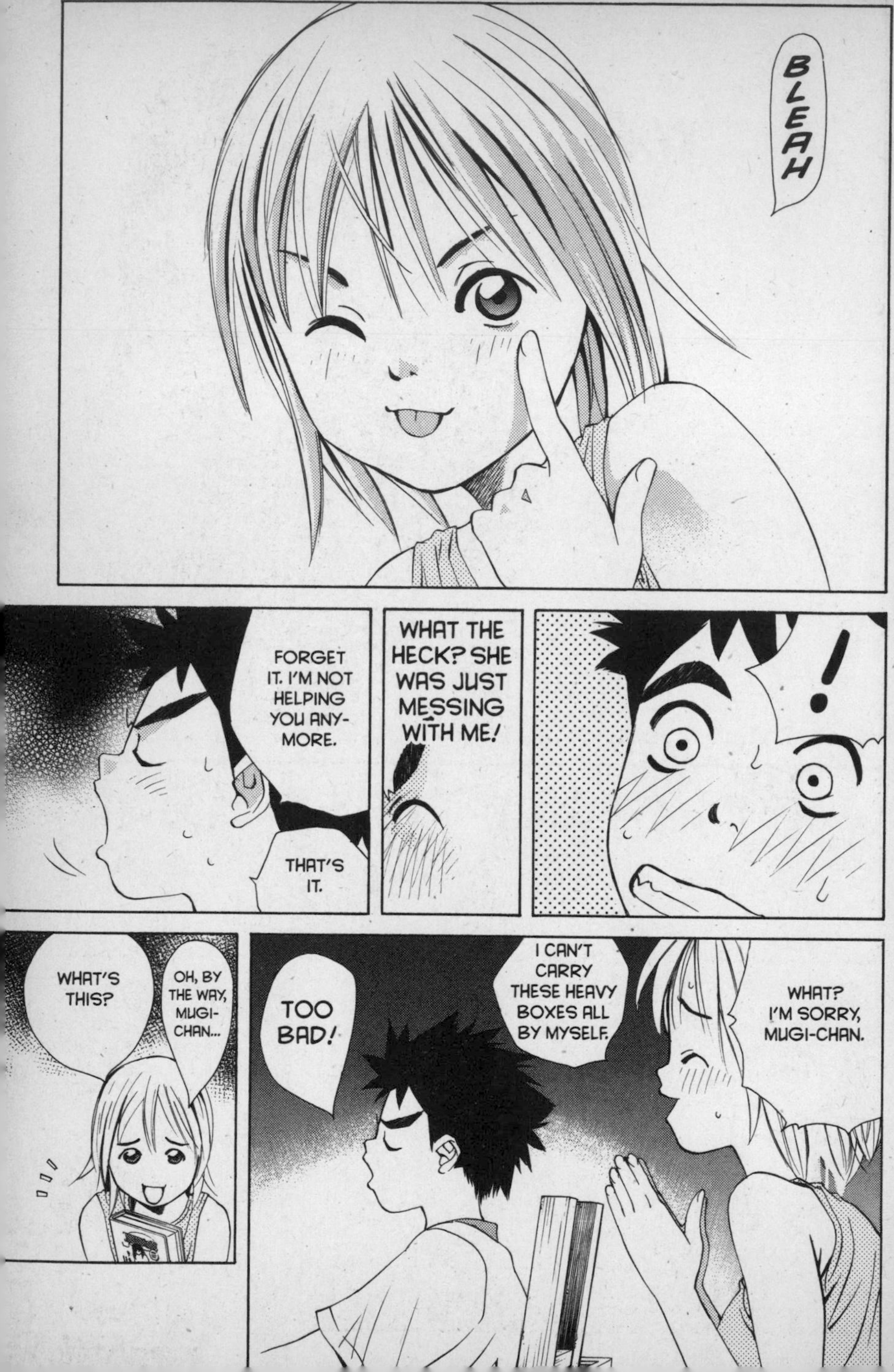
BLEAH
!
WHAT THE HECK? SHE WAS JUST MESSING WITH ME!
FORGET IT. I'M NOT HELPING YOU ANY-MORE.
THAT'S IT.
WHAT? I'M SORRY, MUGI-CHAN.
I CAN'T CARRY THESE HEAVY BOXES ALL BY MYSELF.
TOO BAD!
OH, BY THE WAY, MUGI-CHAN...
WHAT'S THIS?

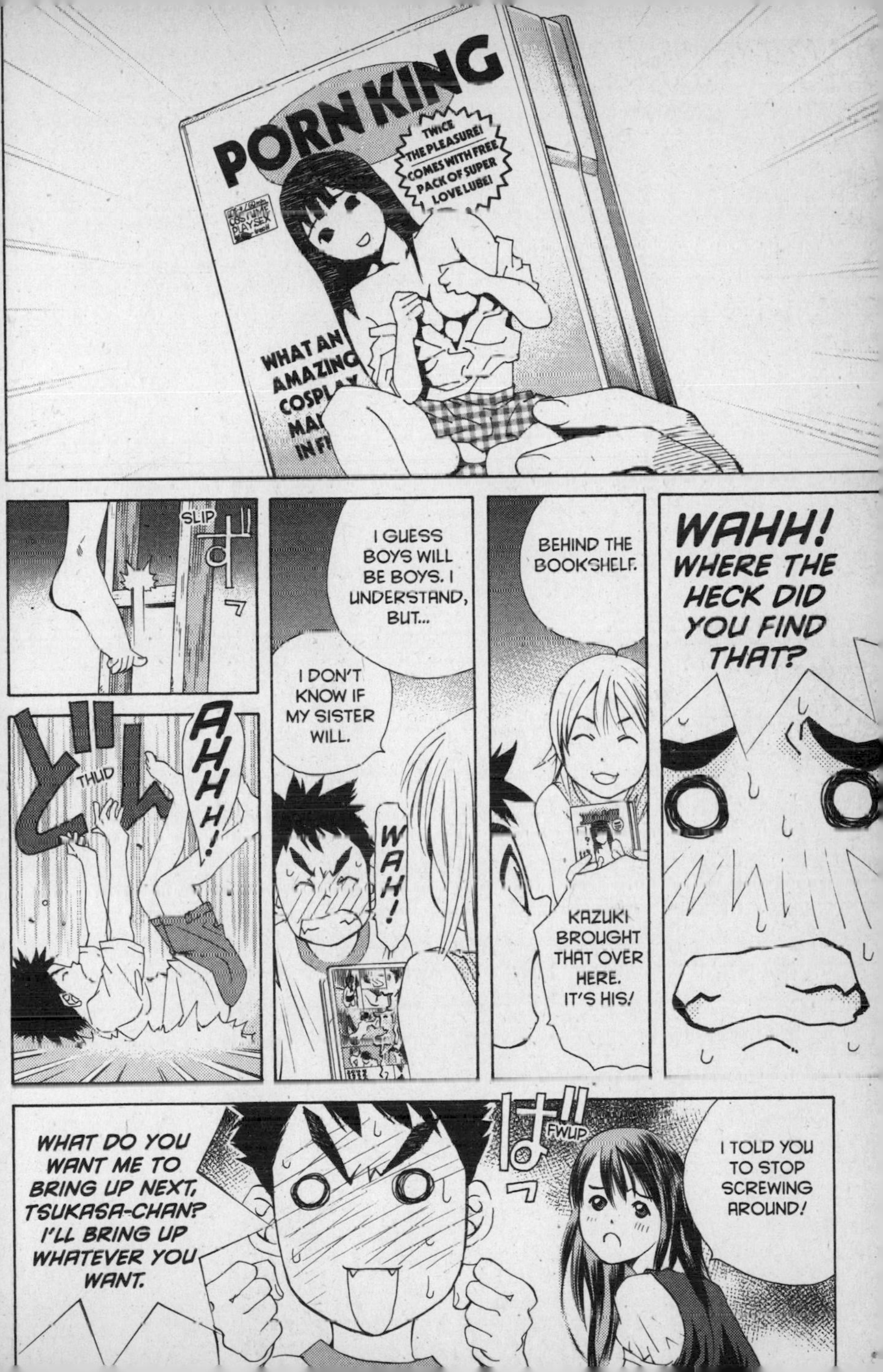
PORN KING
TWICE THE PLEASURE! COMES WITH FREE PACK OF SUPER LOVE LUBE!
WHAT AN AMAZING COSPLAY
WAHH! WHERE THE HECK DID YOU FIND THAT?
BEHIND THE BOOKSHELF.
KAZUKI BROUGHT THAT OVER HERE. IT'S HIS!
I GUESS BOYS WILL BE BOYS. I UNDERSTAND, BUT...
I DON'T KNOW IF MY SISTER WILL.
WAH!
SLIP
THUD
AHHH!
I TOLD YOU TO STOP SCREWING AROUND!
FWUP
WHAT DO YOU WANT ME TO BRING UP NEXT, TSUKASA-CHAN? I'LL BRING UP WHATEVER YOU WANT.

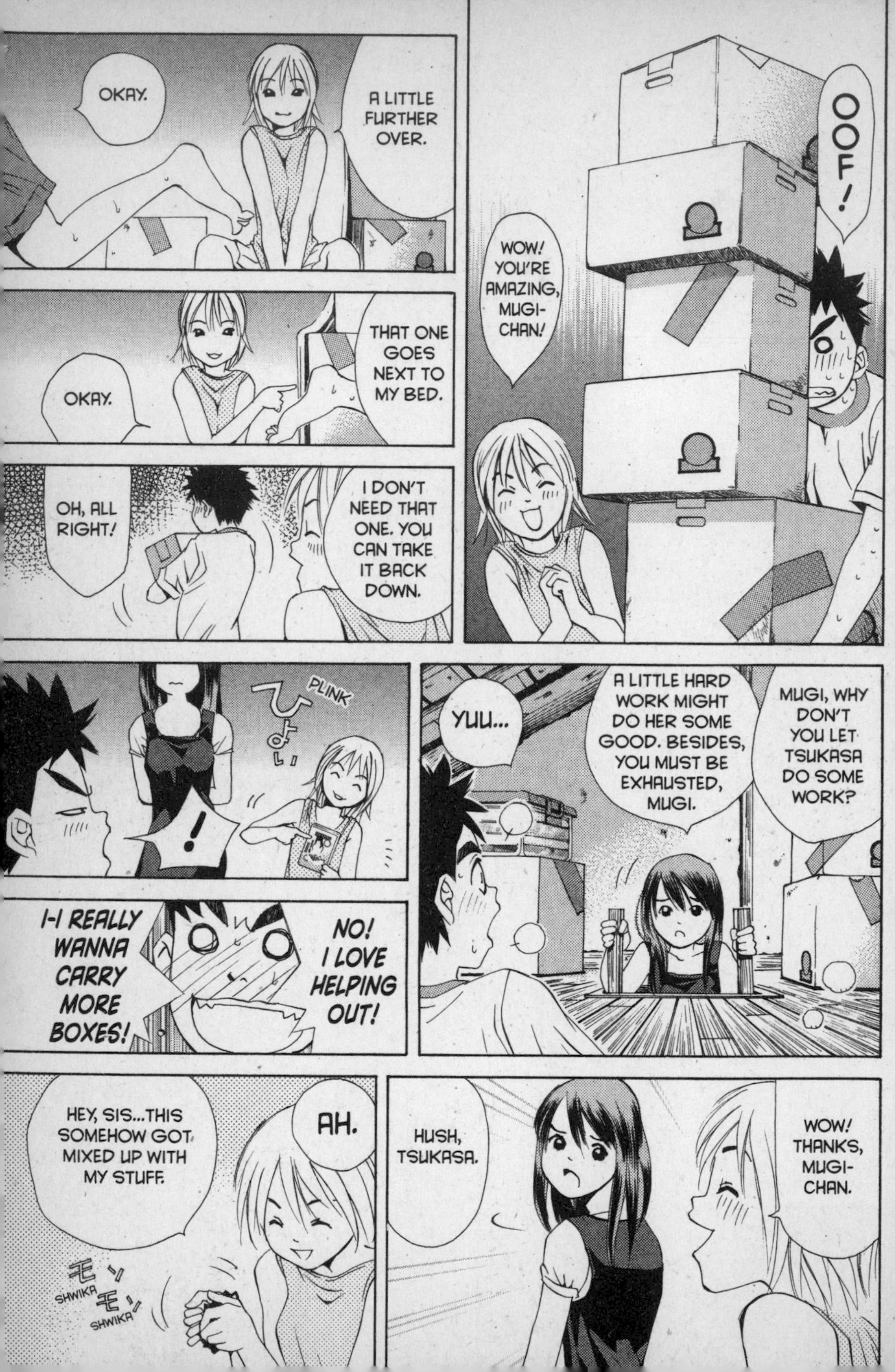

OOF!
WOW! YOU'RE AMAZING, MUGI-CHAN!
A LITTLE FURTHER OVER.
OKAY.
THAT ONE GOES NEXT TO MY BED.
OKAY.
I DON'T NEED THAT ONE. YOU CAN TAKE IT BACK DOWN.
OH, ALL RIGHT!
MUGI, WHY DON'T YOU LET TSUKASA DO SOME WORK?
A LITTLE HARD WORK MIGHT DO HER SOME GOOD. BESIDES, YOU MUST BE EXHAUSTED, MUGI.
YUU...
PLINK
!
NO! I LOVE HELPING OUT!
I-I REALLY WANNA CARRY MORE BOXES!
WOW! THANKS, MUGI-CHAN.
HUSH, TSUKASA.
AH.
HEY, SIS...THIS SOMEHOW GOT MIXED UP WITH MY STUFF.
SHWIKA
SHWIKA

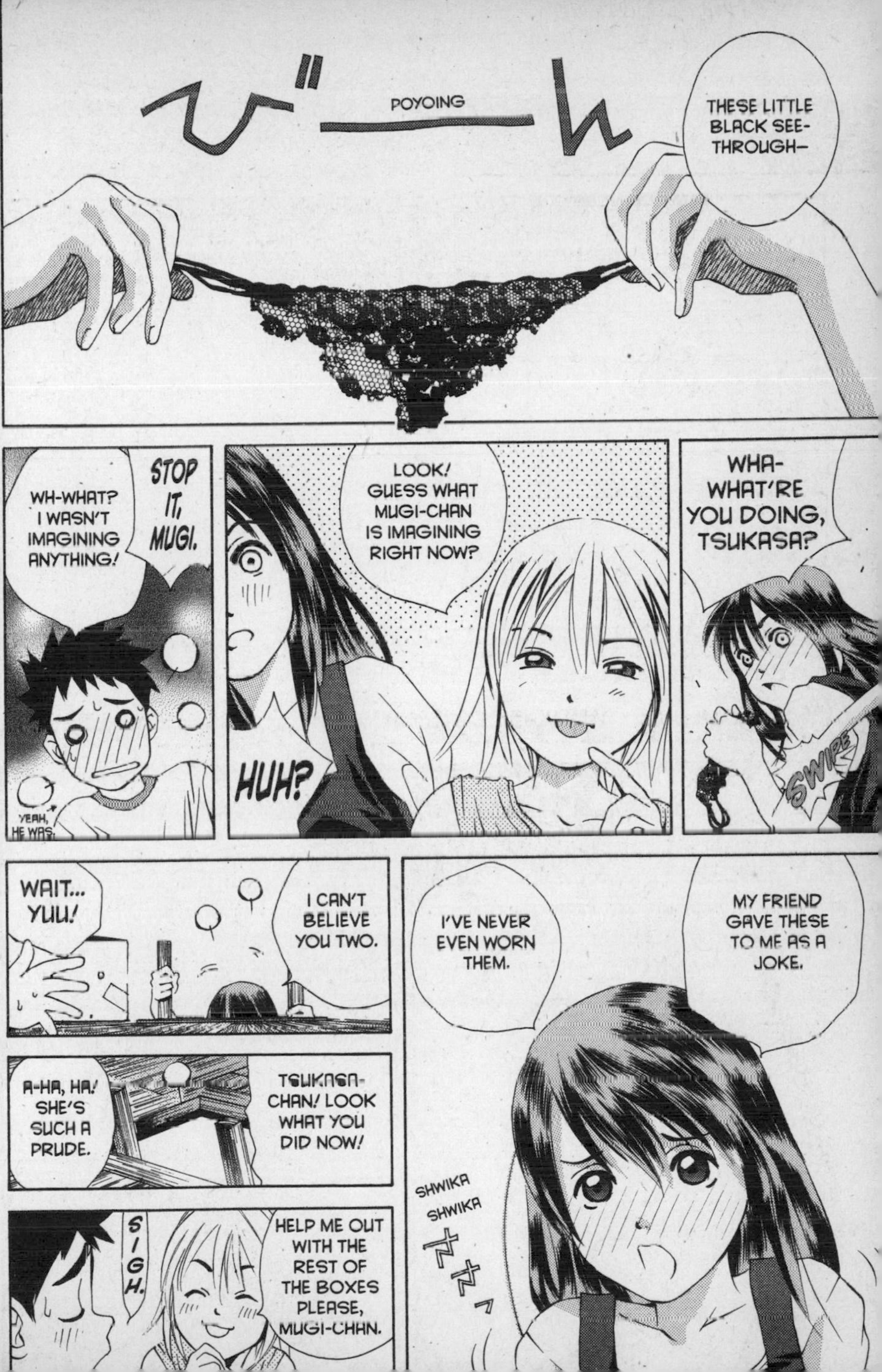
THESE LITTLE BLACK SEE-THROUGH–
POYOING
WHA- WHAT'RE YOU DOING, TSUKASA?
SWIPE
LOOK! GUESS WHAT MUGI-CHAN IS IMAGINING RIGHT NOW?
HUH?
STOP IT, MUGI.
WH-WHAT? I WASN'T IMAGINING ANYTHING!
YEAH, HE WAS.
MY FRIEND GAVE THESE TO ME AS A JOKE.
I'VE NEVER EVEN WORN THEM.
SHWIKA SHWIKA
I CAN'T BELIEVE YOU TWO.
WAIT... YUU!
TSUKASA-CHAN! LOOK WHAT YOU DID NOW!
A-HA, HA! SHE'S SUCH A PRUDE.
HELP ME OUT WITH THE REST OF THE BOXES PLEASE, MUGI-CHAN.
SIGH.

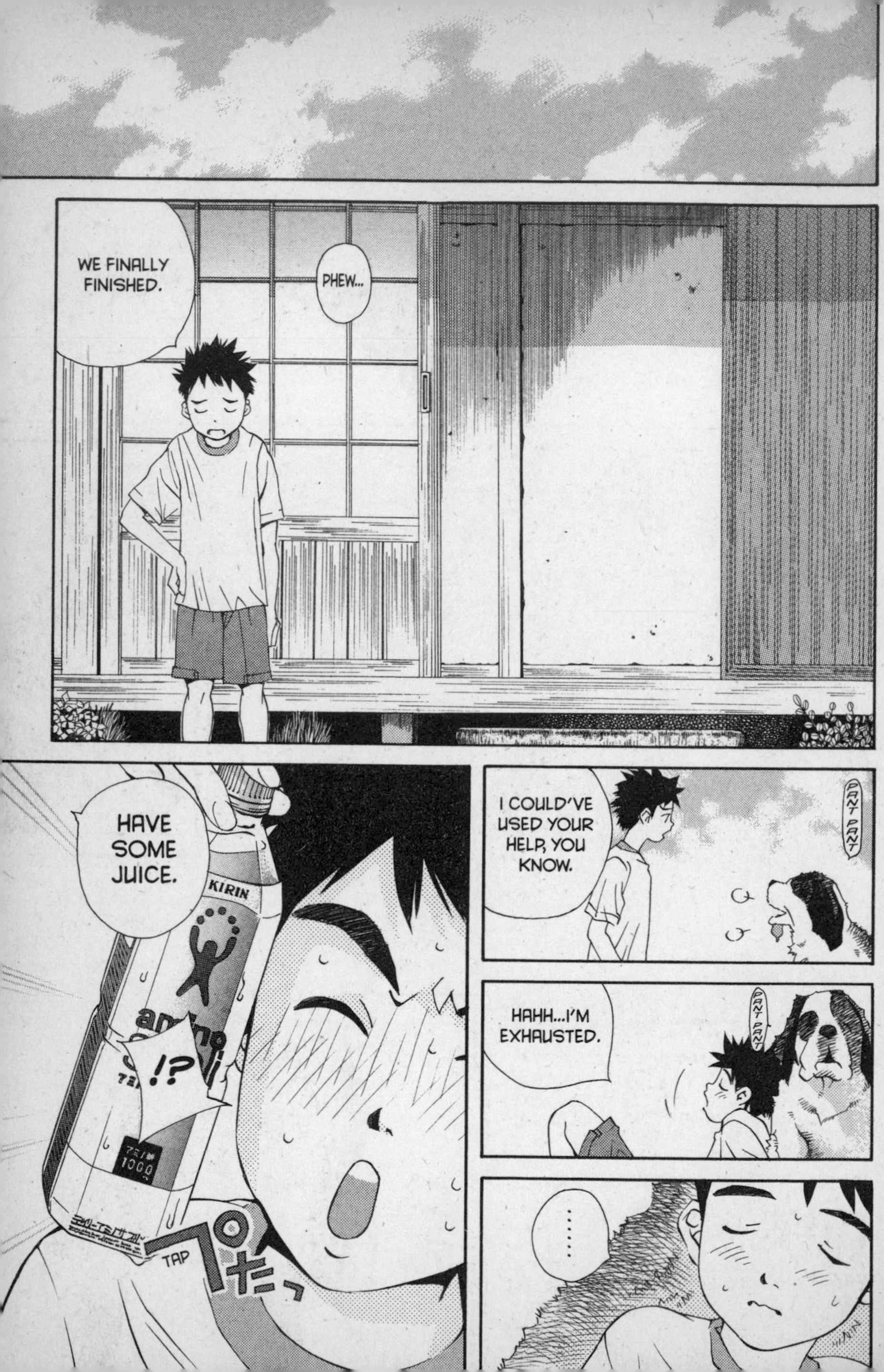
PHEW...
WE FINALLY FINISHED.
PANT PANT
I COULD'VE USED YOUR HELP, YOU KNOW.
PANT PANT
HAHH...I'M EXHAUSTED.
......
HAVE SOME JUICE.
KIRIN
!?
TAP

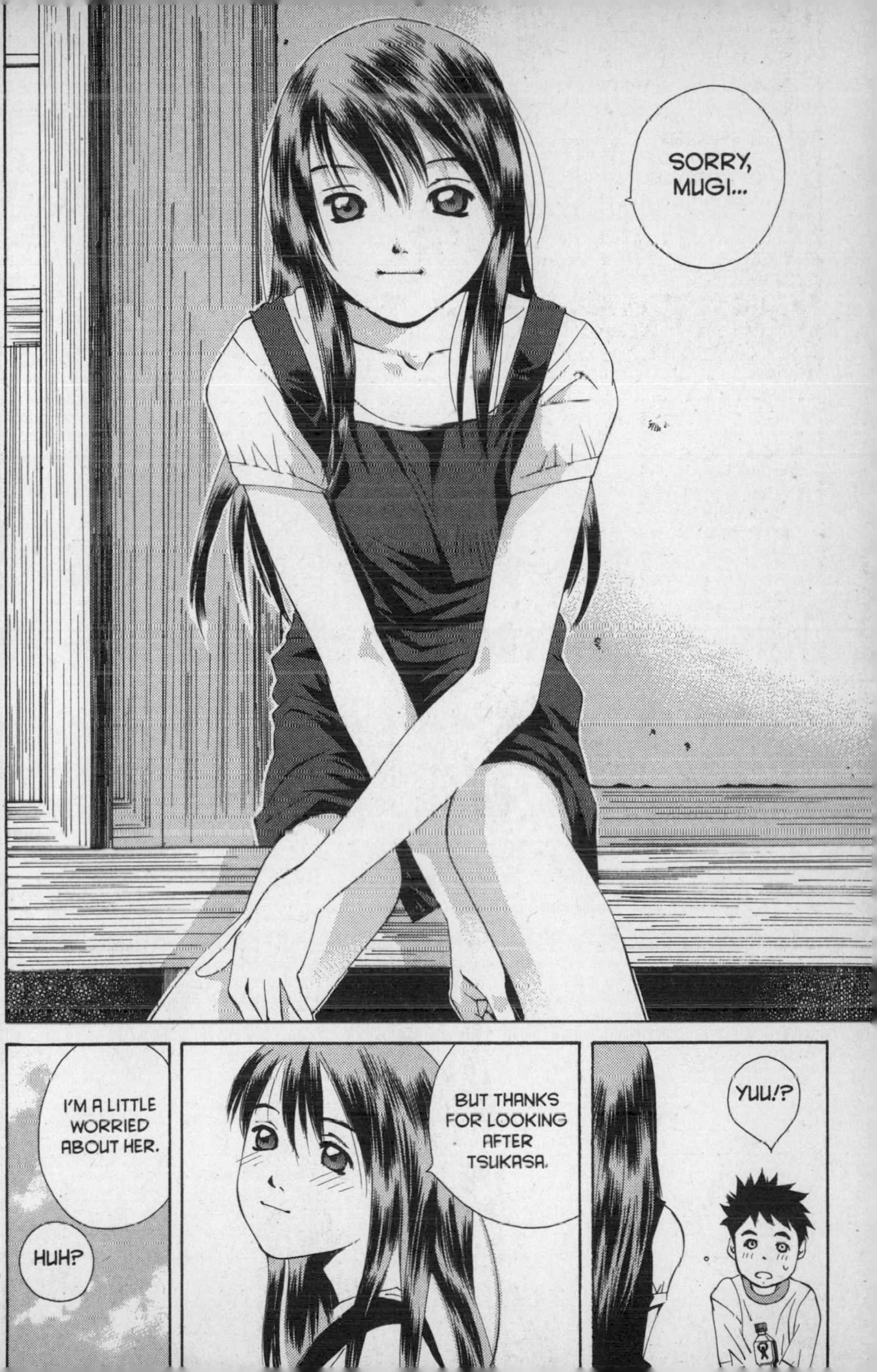
SORRY, MUGI...
YUU!?
BUT THANKS FOR LOOKING AFTER TSUKASA.
I'M A LITTLE WORRIED ABOUT HER.
HUH?

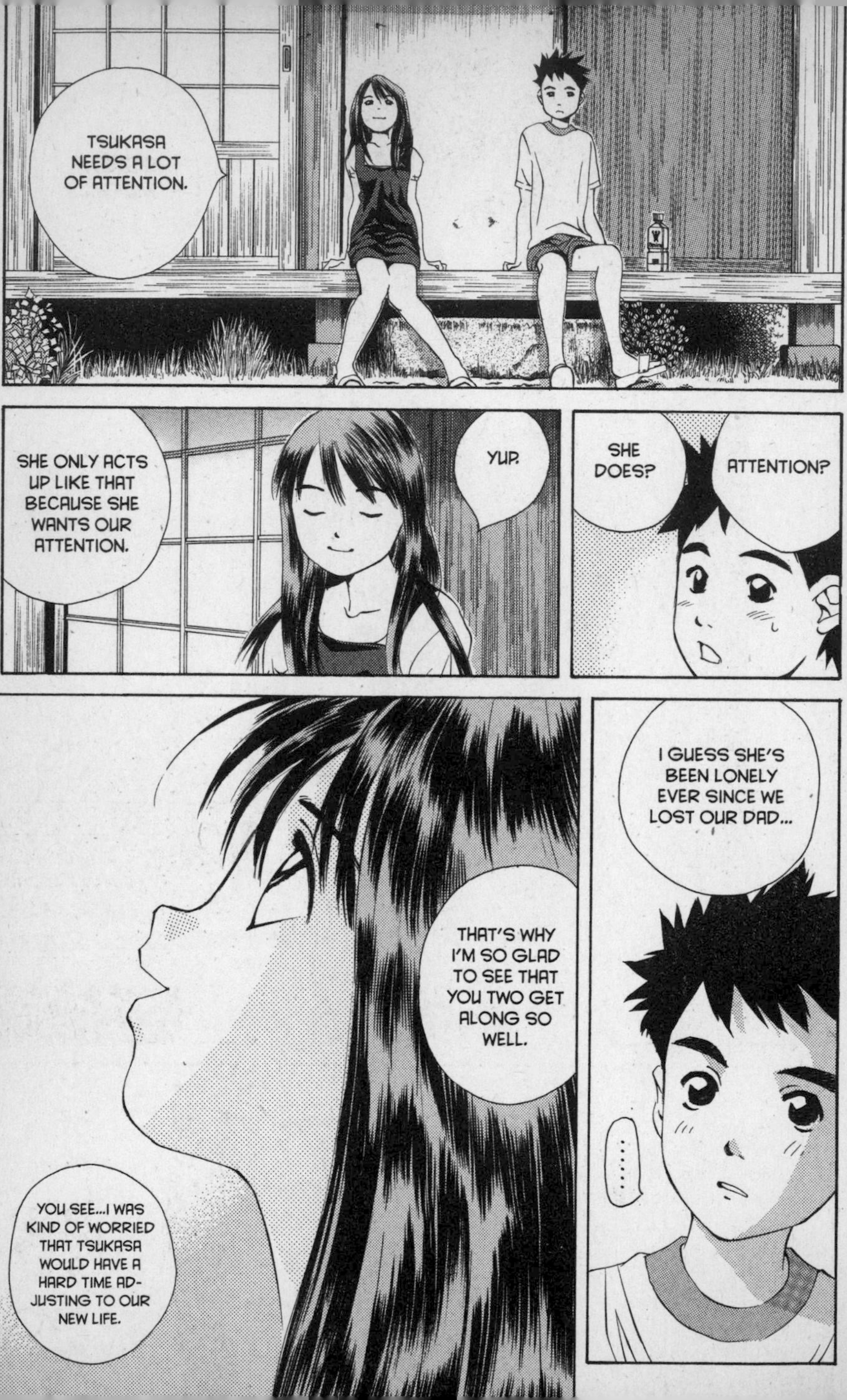
TSUKASA NEEDS A LOT OF ATTENTION.
ATTENTION?
SHE DOES?
YUP.
SHE ONLY ACTS UP LIKE THAT BECAUSE SHE WANTS OUR ATTENTION.
I GUESS SHE'S BEEN LONELY EVER SINCE WE LOST OUR DAD...
......
THAT'S WHY I'M SO GLAD TO SEE THAT YOU TWO GET ALONG SO WELL.
YOU SEE...I WAS KIND OF WORRIED THAT TSUKASA WOULD HAVE A HARD TIME AD-JUSTING TO OUR NEW LIFE.

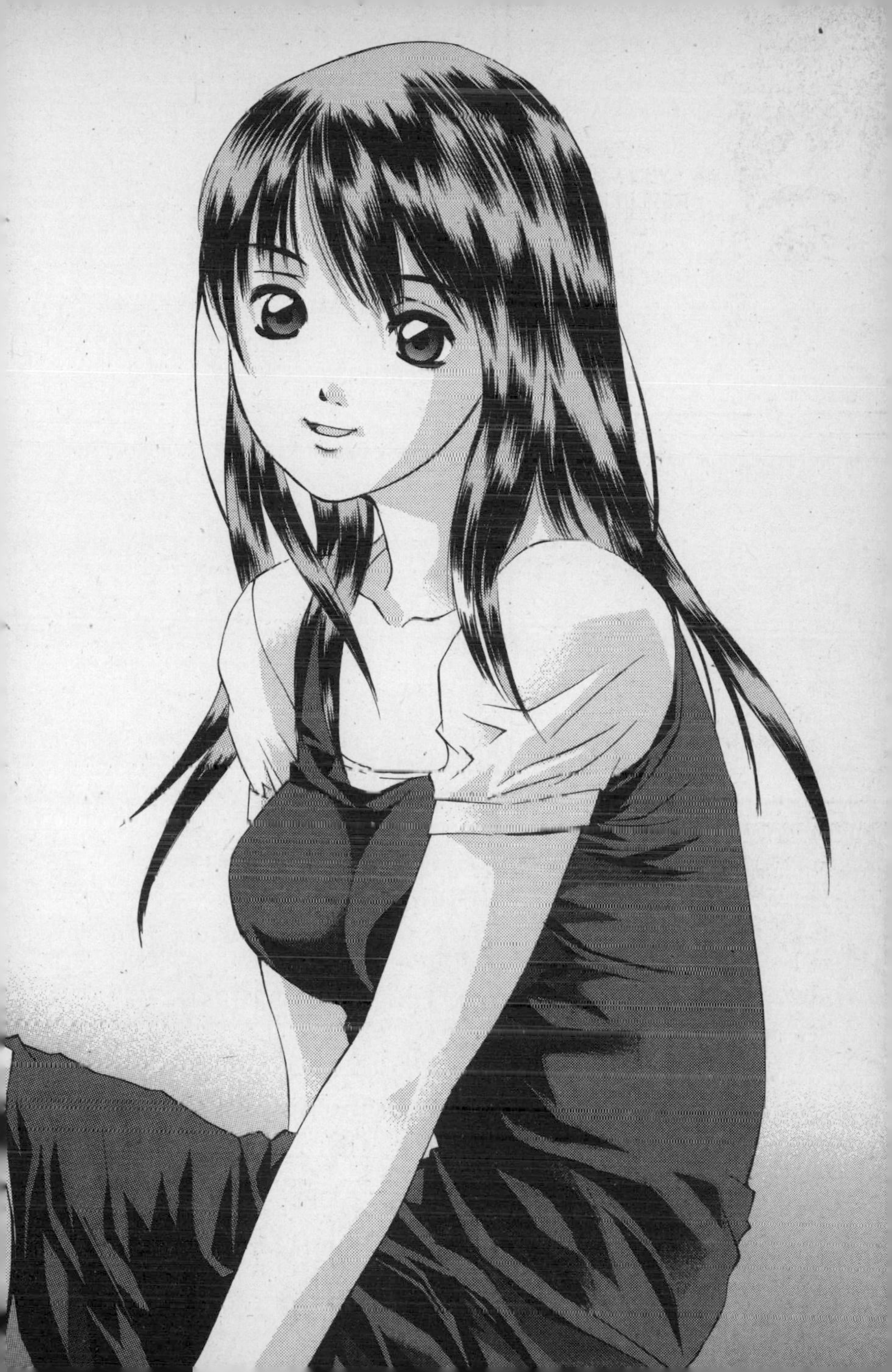

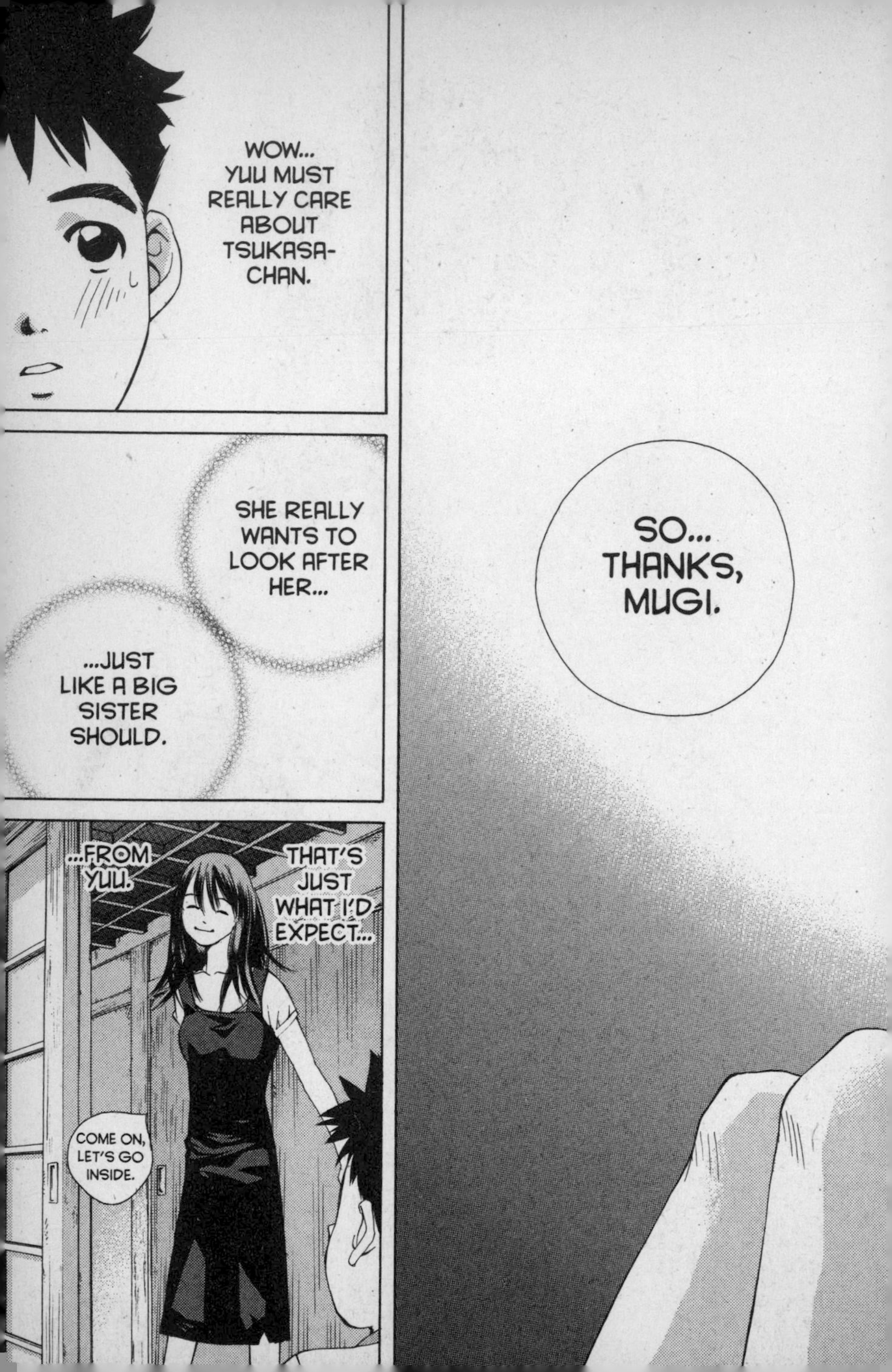
SO... THANKS, MUGI.
WOW... YUU MUST REALLY CARE ABOUT TSUKASA-CHAN.
SHE REALLY WANTS TO LOOK AFTER HER...
...JUST LIKE A BIG SISTER SHOULD.
THAT'S JUST WHAT I'D EXPECT...
...FROM YUU.
COME ON, LET'S GO INSIDE.

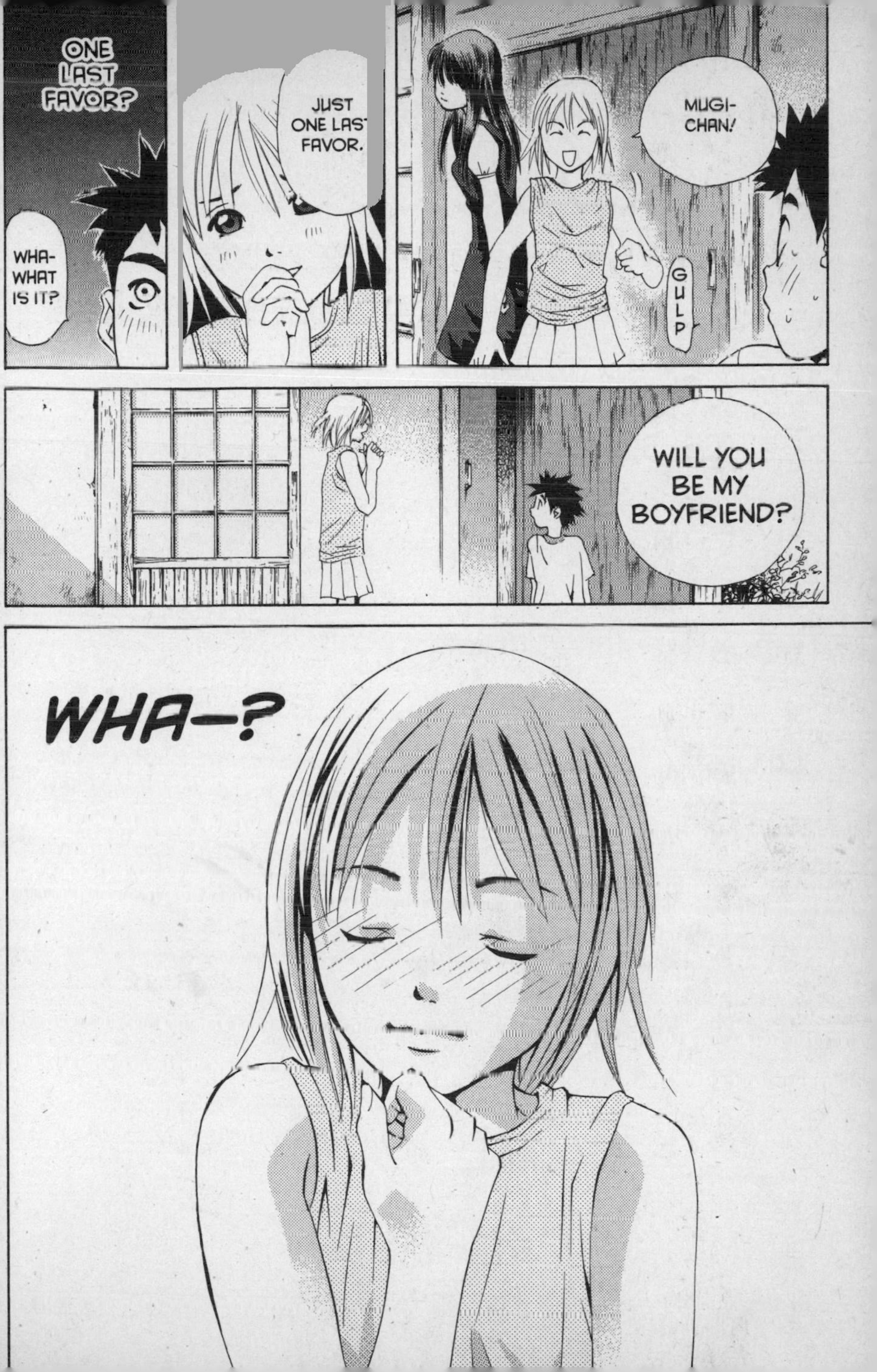
MUGI-CHAN!
GULP
JUST ONE LAST FAVOR.
ONE LAST FAVOR?
WHA-WHAT IS IT?
WILL YOU BE MY BOYFRIEND?
WHA-?

Pastel

MIRACLE 8: GOOD LUCK TO AN HONEST MAN!

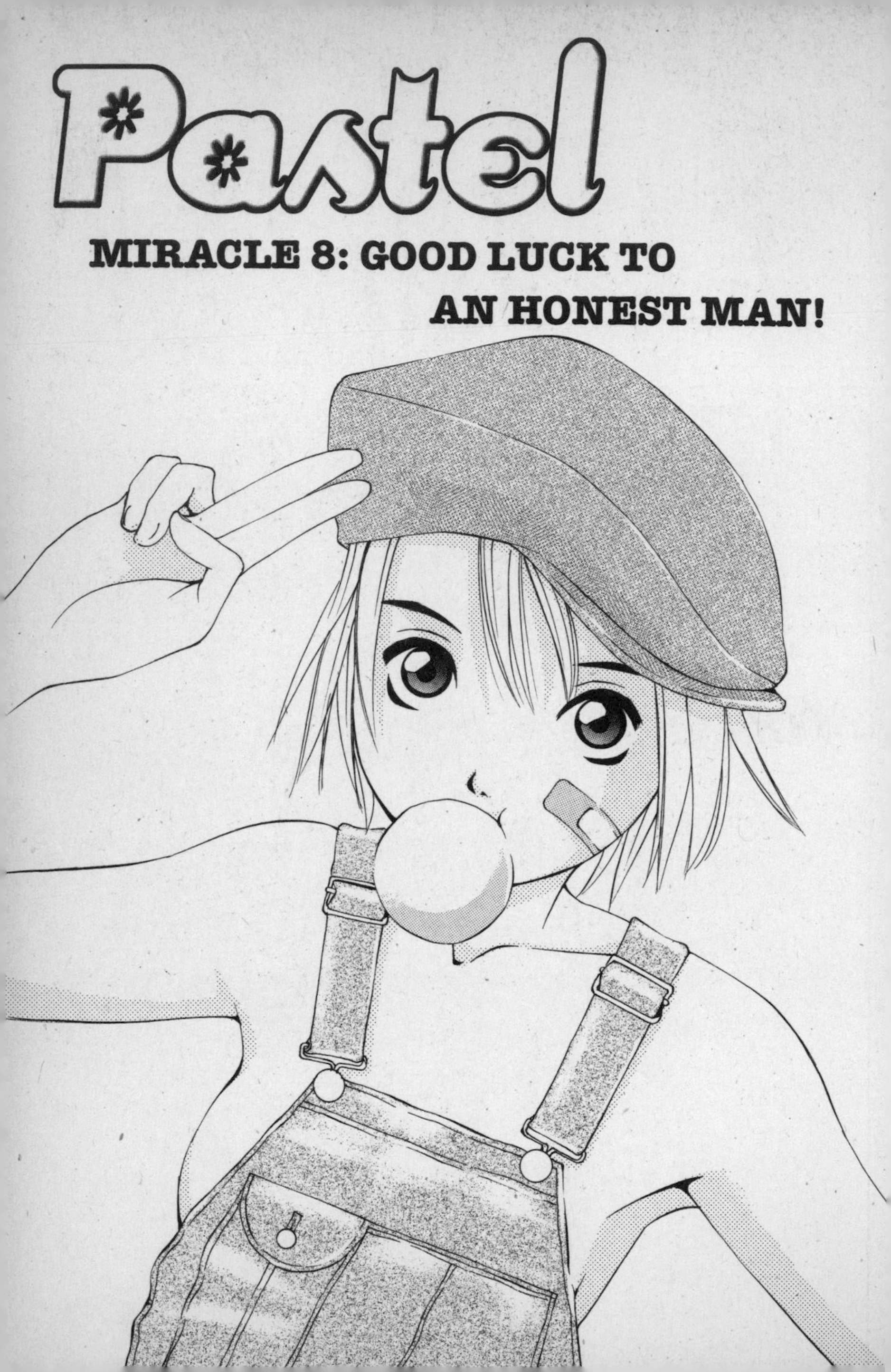

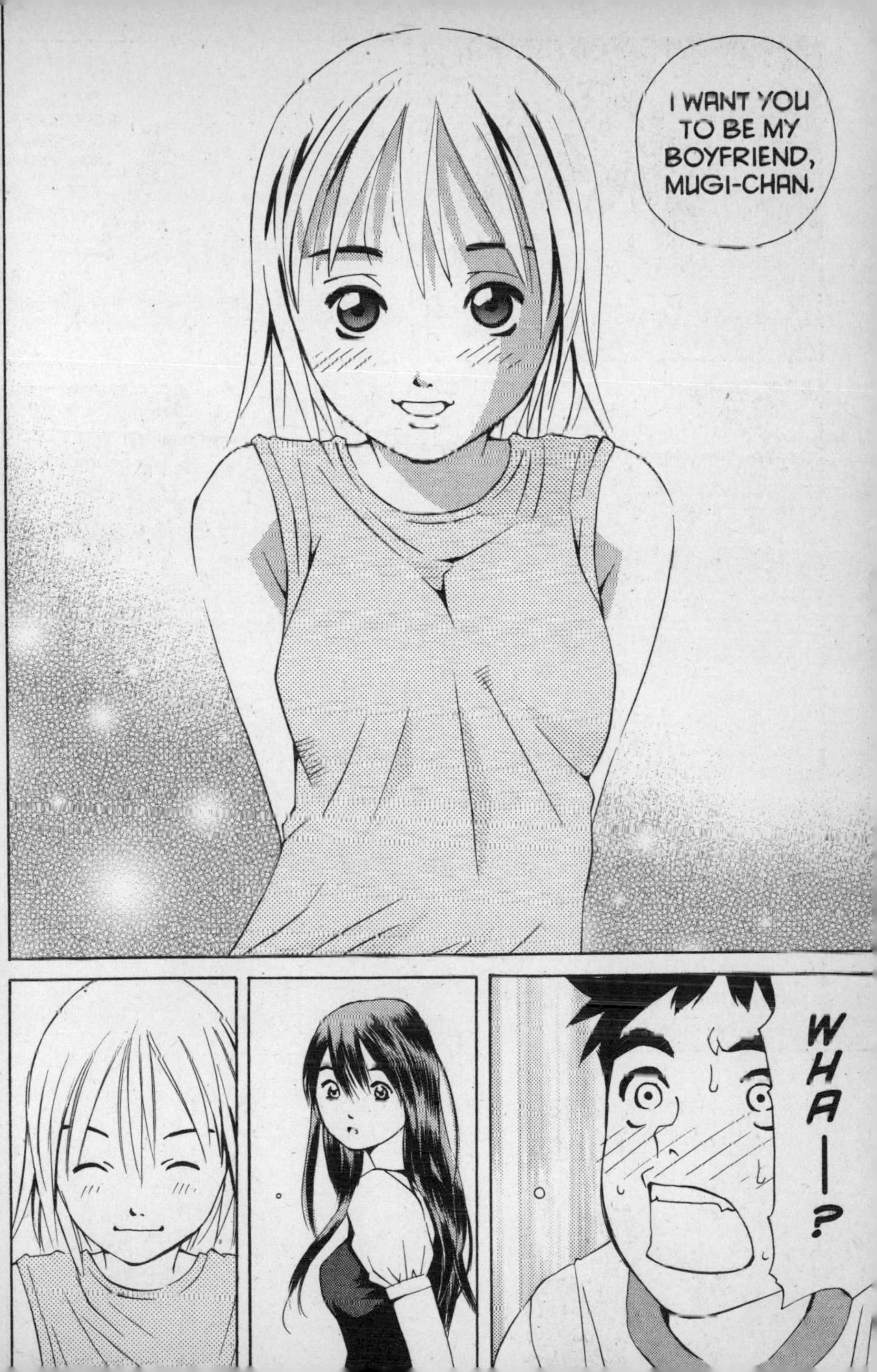
I WANT YOU TO BE MY BOYFRIEND, MUGI-CHAN.
WHA--?

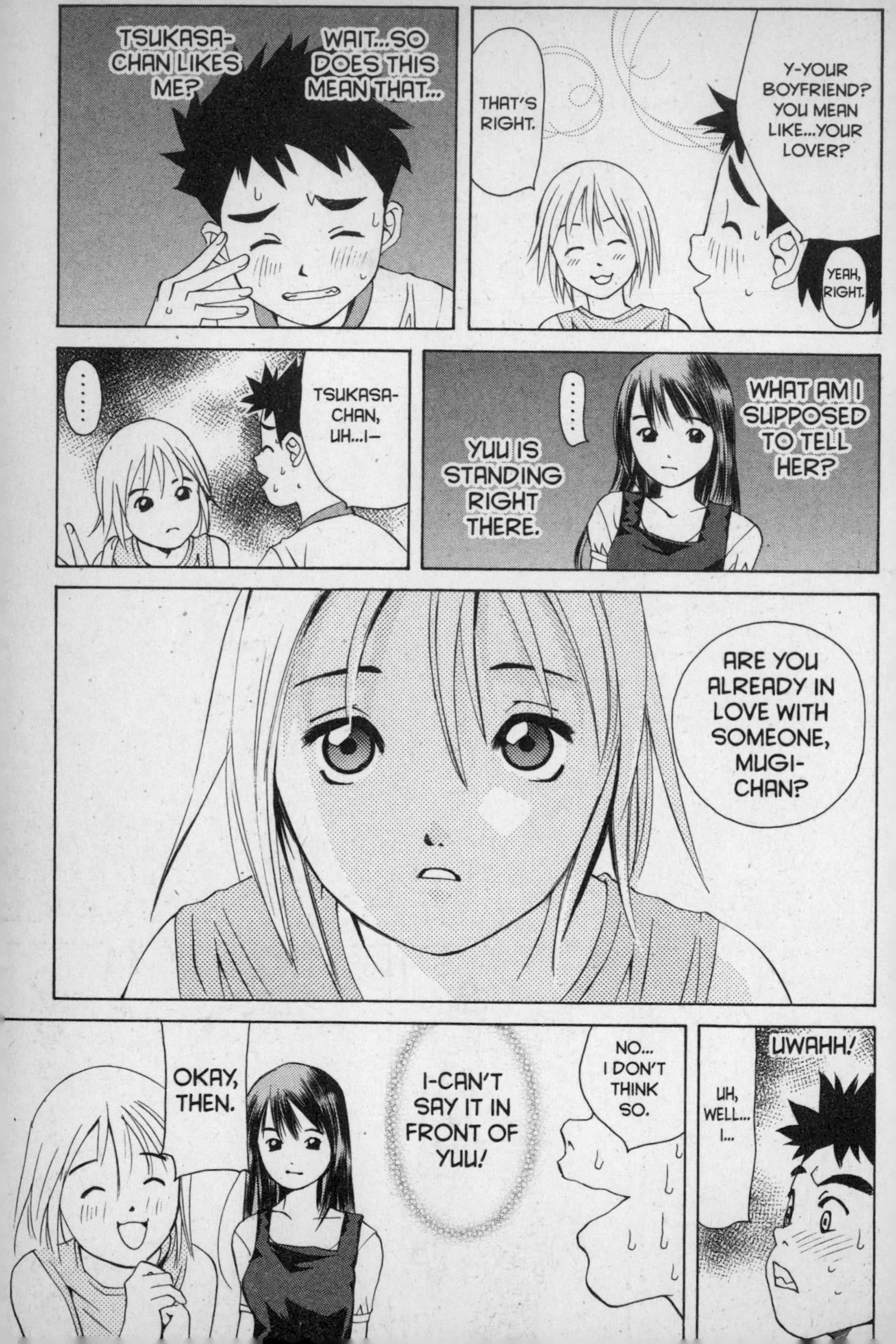
Y-YOUR BOYFRIEND? YOU MEAN LIKE...YOUR LOVER?
THAT'S RIGHT.
YEAH, RIGHT.
WAIT...SO DOES THIS MEAN THAT...
TSUKASA-CHAN LIKES ME?
WHAT AM I SUPPOSED TO TELL HER?
......
YUU IS STANDING RIGHT THERE.
TSUKASA-CHAN, UH...I–
......
ARE YOU ALREADY IN LOVE WITH SOMEONE, MUGI-CHAN?
UWAHH!
UH, WELL... I...
NO... I DON'T THINK SO.
I-CAN'T SAY IT IN FRONT OF YUU!
OKAY, THEN.

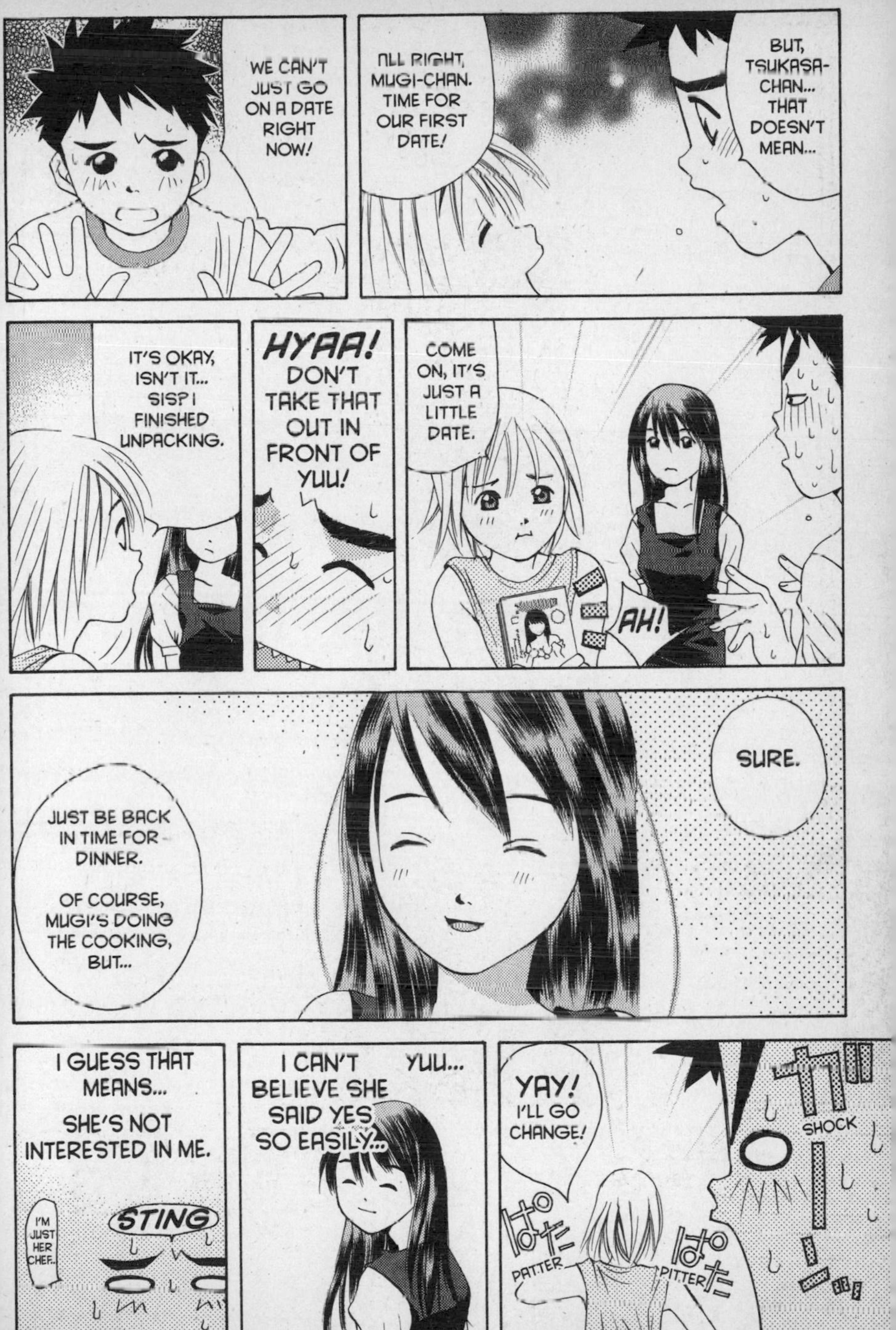
BUT, TSUKASA-CHAN... THAT DOESN'T MEAN...
ALL RIGHT, MUGI-CHAN. TIME FOR OUR FIRST DATE!
WE CAN'T JUST GO ON A DATE RIGHT NOW!
COME ON, IT'S JUST A LITTLE DATE.
AH!
HYAA! DON'T TAKE THAT OUT IN FRONT OF YUU!
IT'S OKAY, ISN'T IT... SIS? I FINISHED UNPACKING.
SURE.
JUST BE BACK IN TIME FOR DINNER.
OF COURSE, MUGI'S DOING THE COOKING, BUT...
SHOCK
YAY! I'LL GO CHANGE!
ぱた
PITTER
ぱた
PATTER
YUU...
I CAN'T BELIEVE SHE SAID YES SO EASILY...
I GUESS THAT MEANS...
SHE'S NOT INTERESTED IN ME.
STING
I'M JUST HER CHEF...

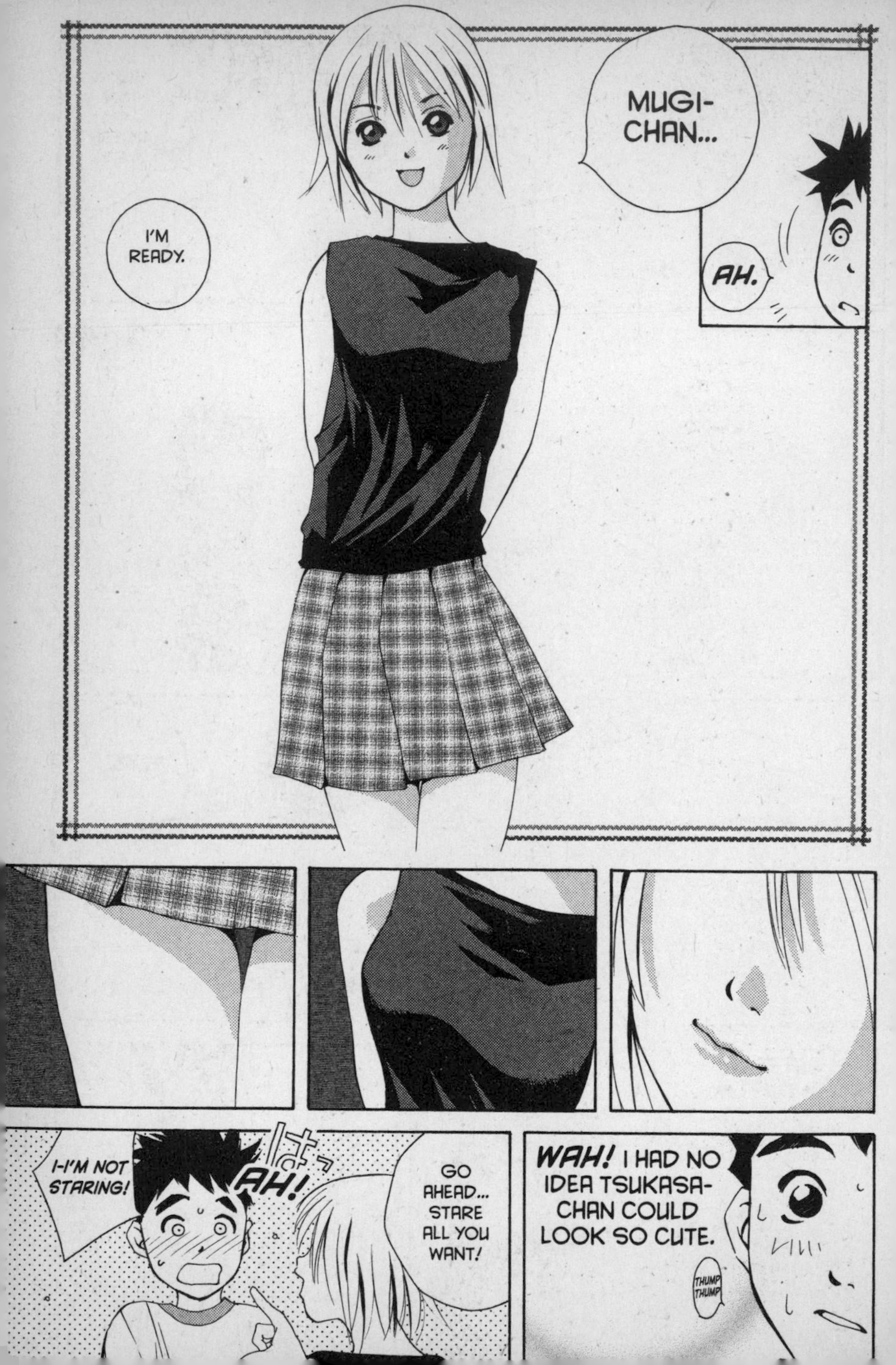
MUGI-CHAN...
AH.
I'M READY.
WAH! I HAD NO IDEA TSUKASA-CHAN COULD LOOK SO CUTE.
THUMP THUMP
GO AHEAD... STARE ALL YOU WANT!
はっ
AH!
I-I'M NOT STARING!

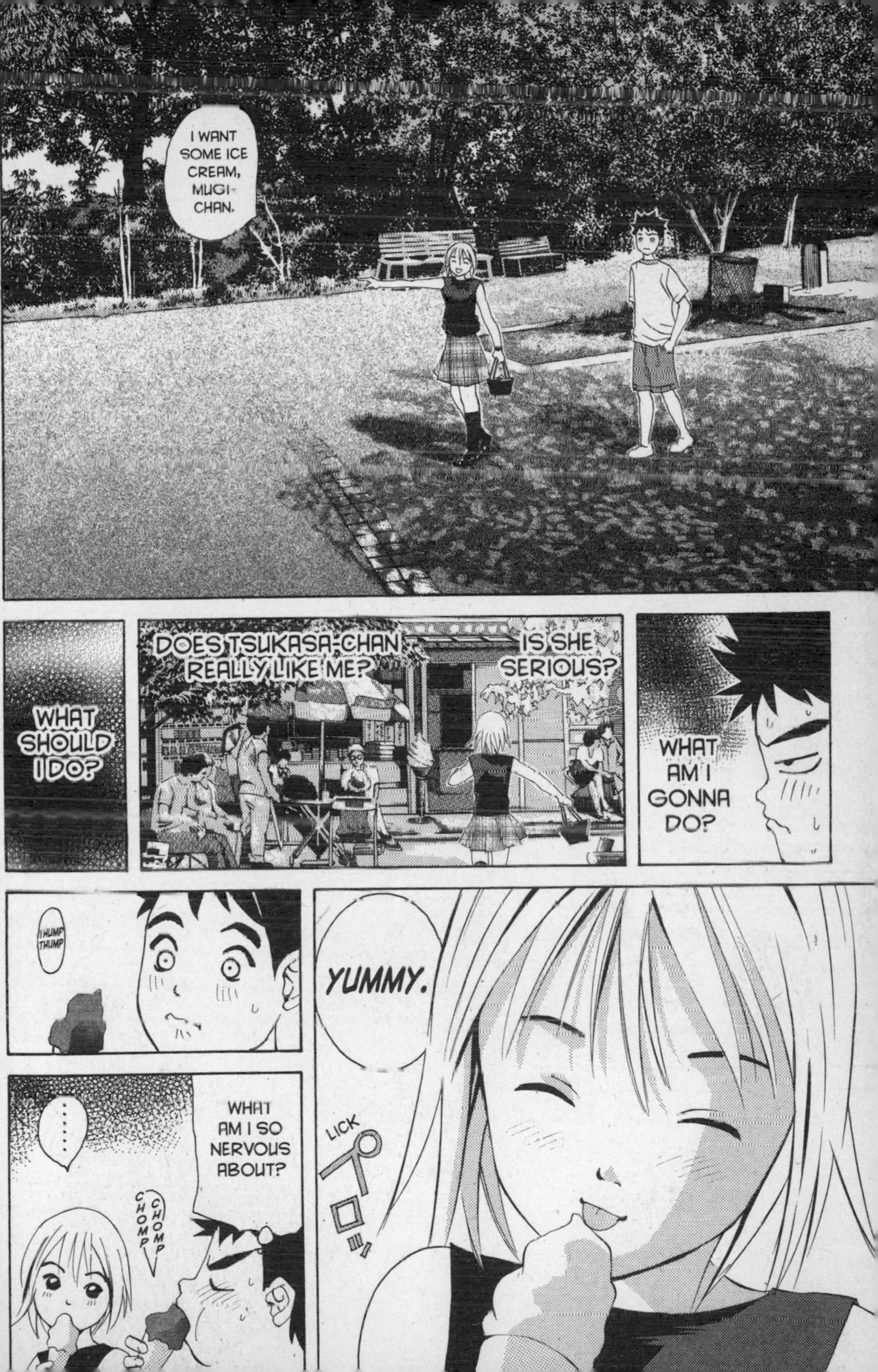
I WANT SOME ICE CREAM, MUGI-CHAN.
WHAT AM I GONNA DO?
IS SHE SERIOUS?
DOES TSUKASA-CHAN REALLY LIKE ME?
WHAT SHOULD I DO?
YUMMY.
LICK
THUMP THUMP
. . . . .
WHAT AM I SO NERVOUS ABOUT?
CHOMP CHOMP

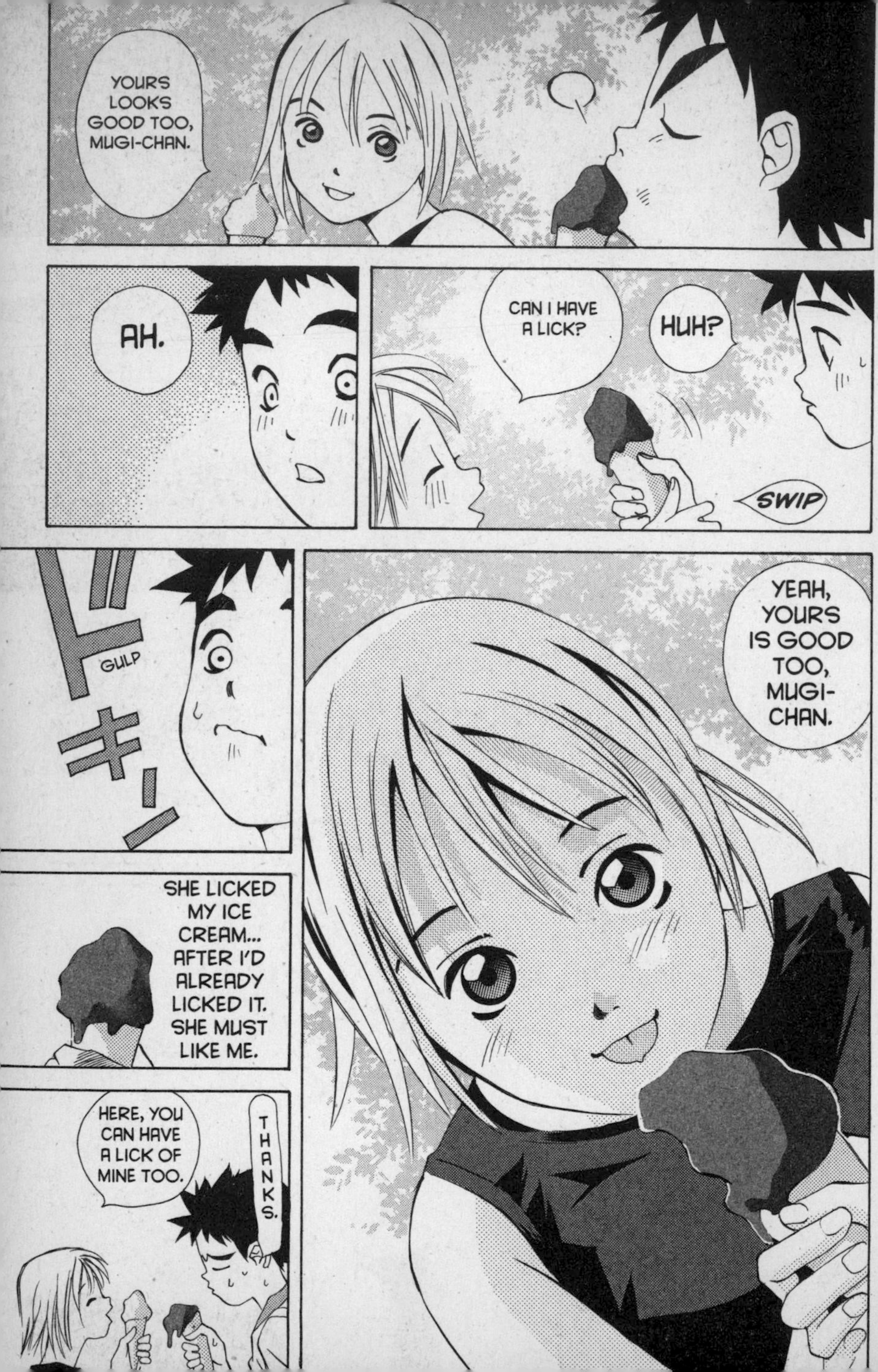
YOURS LOOKS GOOD TOO, MUGI-CHAN.
CAN I HAVE A LICK?
HUH?
SWIP
AH.
YEAH, YOURS IS GOOD TOO, MUGI-CHAN.
GULP
SHE LICKED MY ICE CREAM... AFTER I'D ALREADY LICKED IT. SHE MUST LIKE ME.
THANKS.
HERE, YOU CAN HAVE A LICK OF MINE TOO.

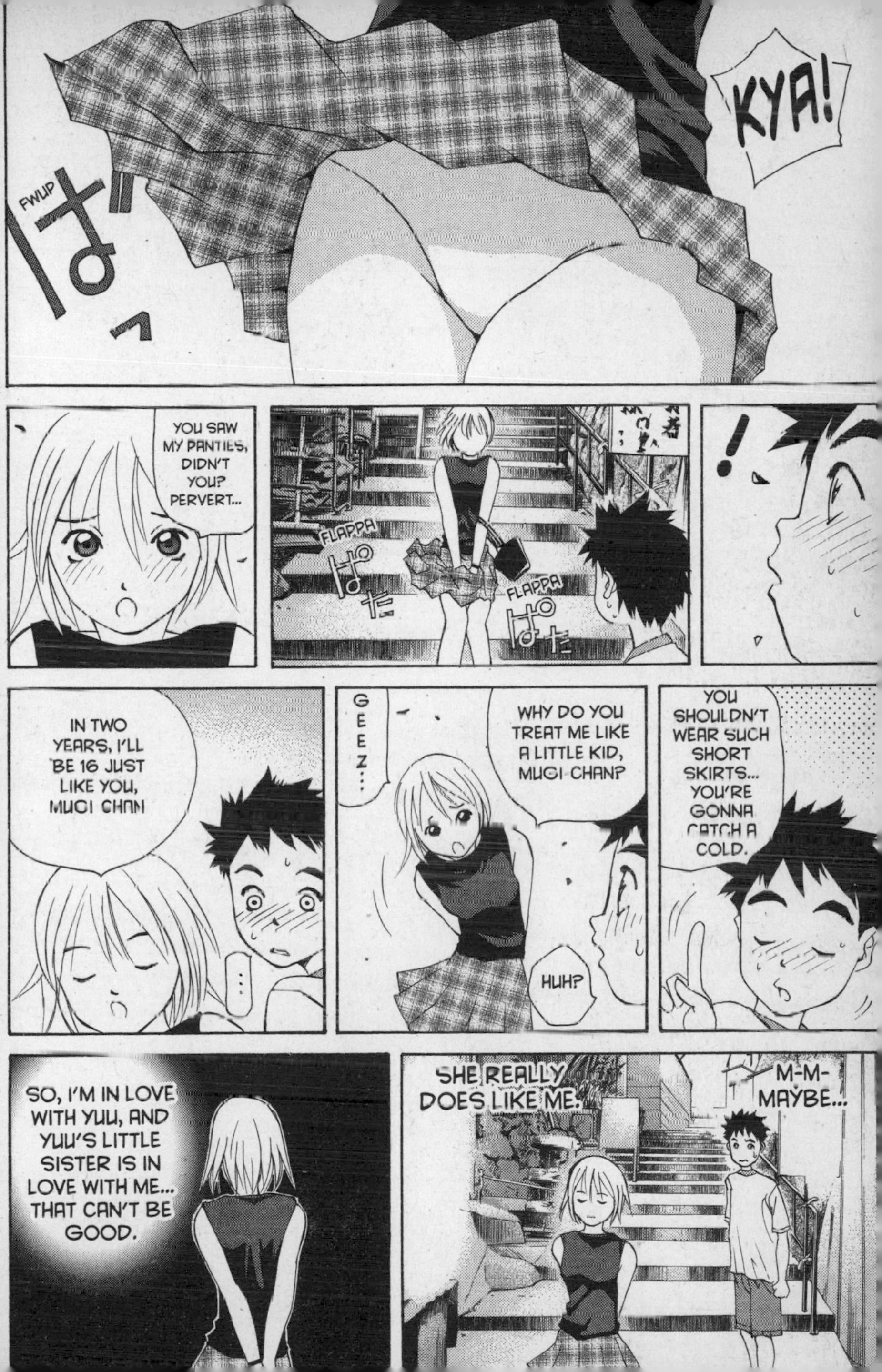
KYA!
FWUP
!
FLAPPA
FLAPPA
YOU SAW MY PANTIES, DIDN'T YOU? PERVERT...
YOU SHOULDN'T WEAR SUCH SHORT SKIRTS... YOU'RE GONNA CATCH A COLD.
WHY DO YOU TREAT ME LIKE A LITTLE KID, MUGI CHAN?
GEEZ...
HUH?
IN TWO YEARS, I'LL BE 16 JUST LIKE YOU, MUGI CHAN
...
M-M-MAYBE...
SHE REALLY DOES LIKE ME.
SO, I'M IN LOVE WITH YUU, AND YUU'S LITTLE SISTER IS IN LOVE WITH ME... THAT CAN'T BE GOOD.

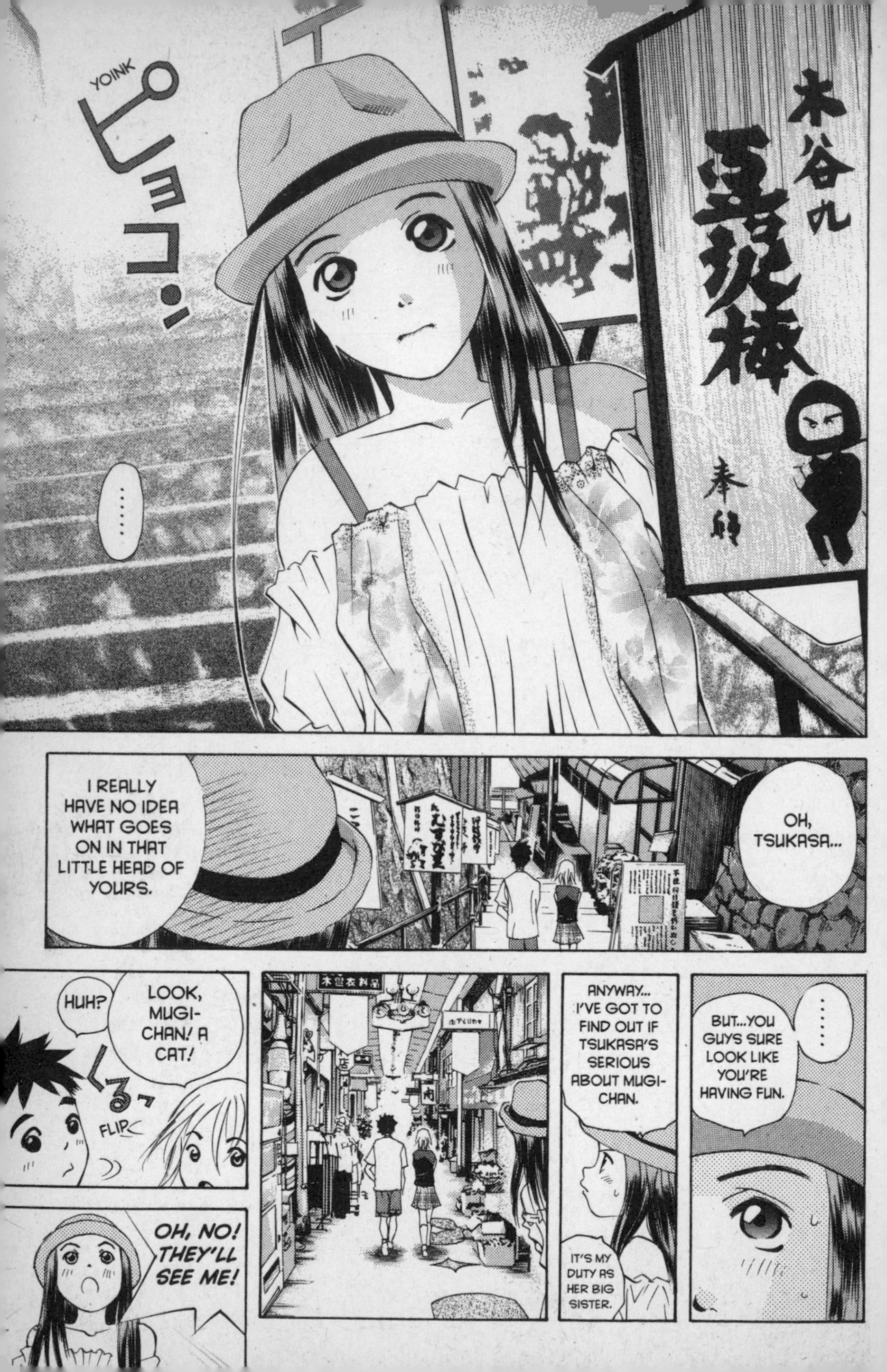
ピョコン
YOINK
......
OH, TSUKASA...
I REALLY HAVE NO IDEA WHAT GOES ON IN THAT LITTLE HEAD OF YOURS.
......
BUT...YOU GUYS SURE LOOK LIKE YOU'RE HAVING FUN.
ANYWAY... I'VE GOT TO FIND OUT IF TSUKASA'S SERIOUS ABOUT MUGI-CHAN.
IT'S MY DUTY AS HER BIG SISTER.
LOOK, MUGI-CHAN! A CAT!
HUH?
くるっ
FLIP
OH, NO! THEY'LL SEE ME!

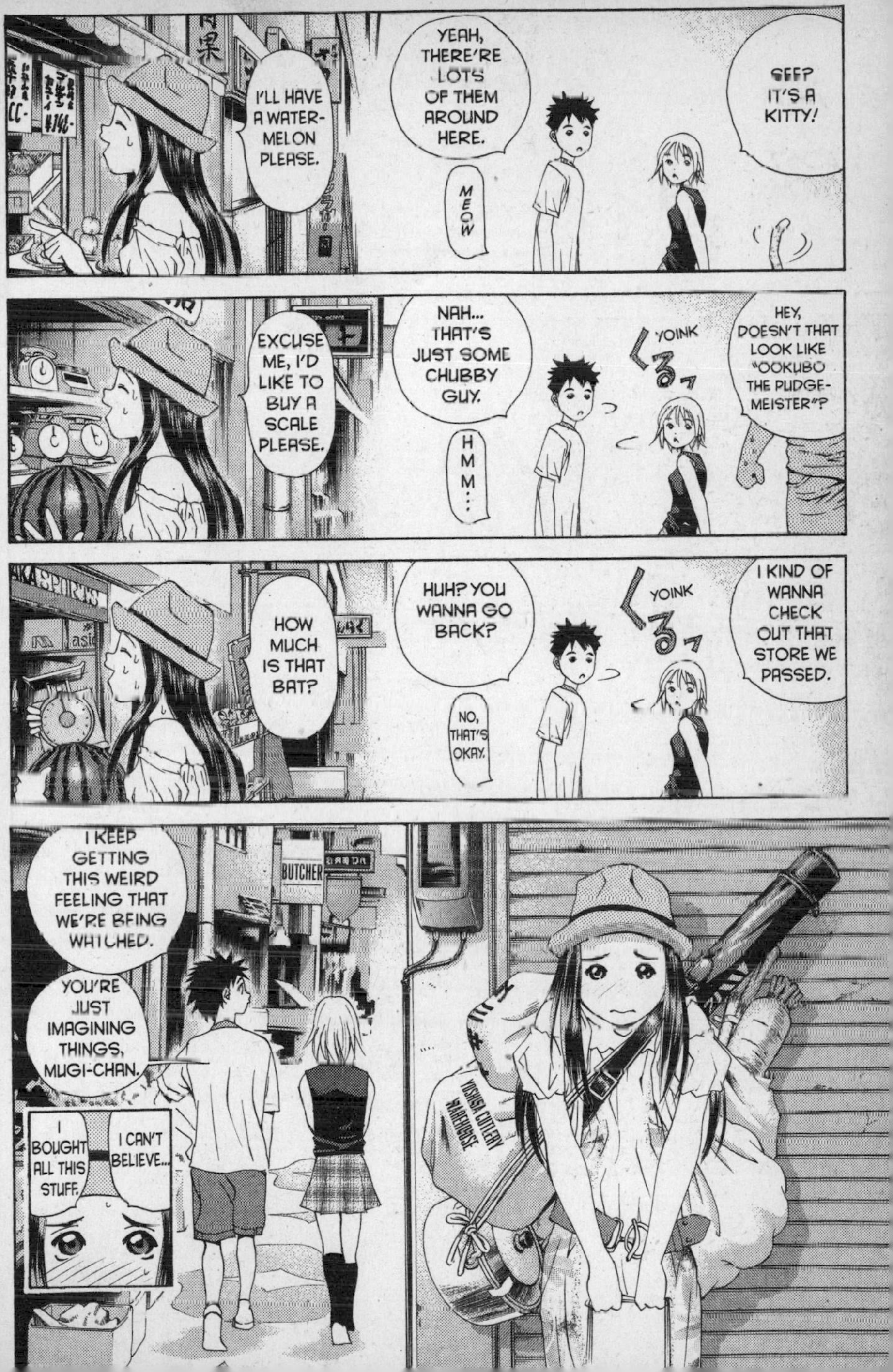
SEE? IT'S A KITTY!
YEAH, THERE'RE LOTS OF THEM AROUND HERE.
MEOW
I'LL HAVE A WATER-MELON PLEASE.
HEY, DOESN'T THAT LOOK LIKE "OOKUBO THE PUDGE-MEISTER"?
くる YOINK
NAH... THAT'S JUST SOME CHUBBY GUY.
HMM...
EXCUSE ME, I'D LIKE TO BUY A SCALE PLEASE.
I KIND OF WANNA CHECK OUT THAT STORE WE PASSED.
くる YOINK
HUH? YOU WANNA GO BACK?
NO, THAT'S OKAY.
HOW MUCH IS THAT BAT?
I KEEP GETTING THIS WEIRD FEELING THAT WE'RE BEING WATCHED.
YOU'RE JUST IMAGINING THINGS, MUGI-CHAN.
BUTCHER
I CAN'T BELIEVE...
I BOUGHT ALL THIS STUFF.

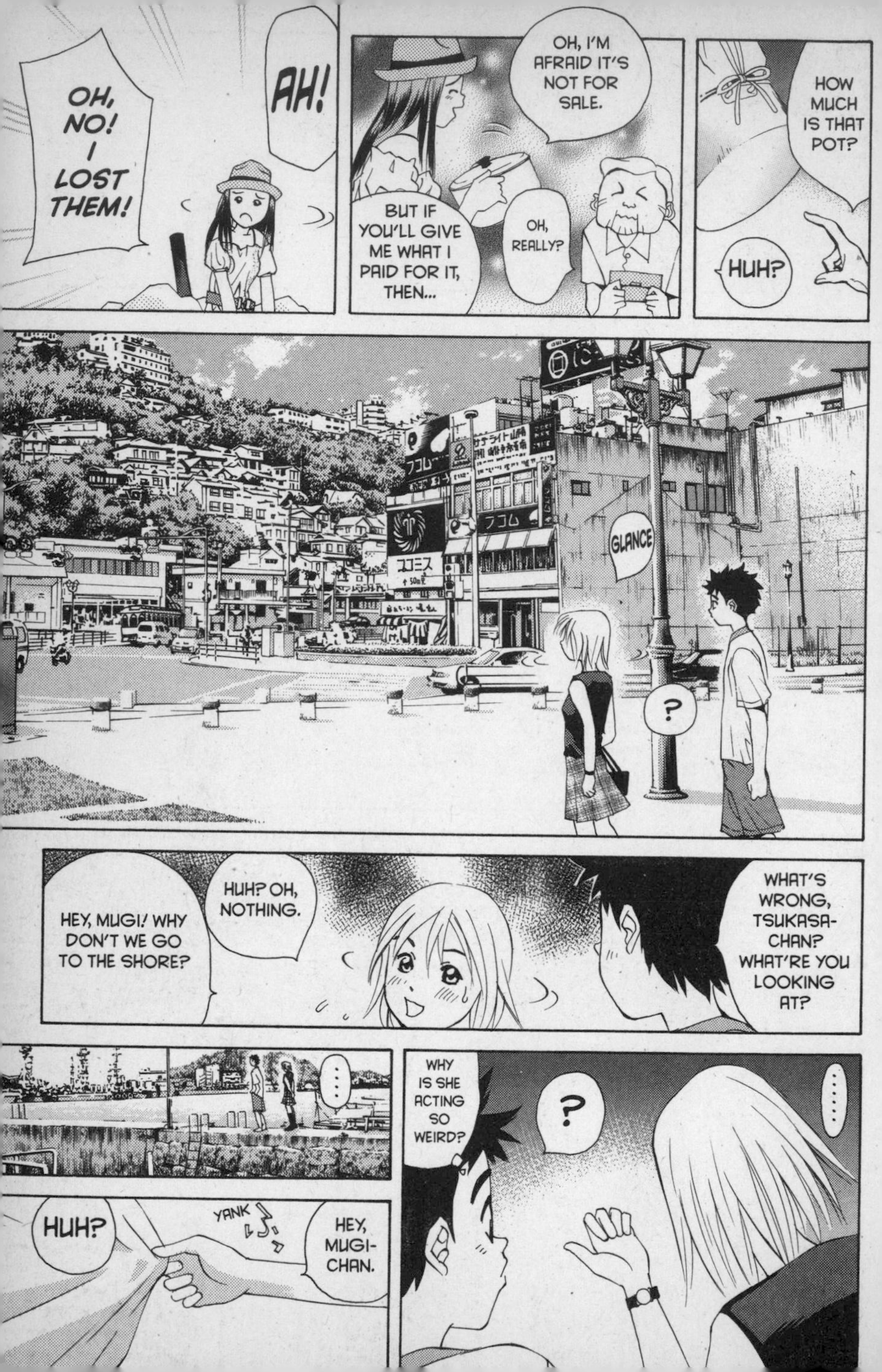
HOW MUCH IS THAT POT?
HUH?
OH, I'M AFRAID IT'S NOT FOR SALE.
OH, REALLY?
BUT IF YOU'LL GIVE ME WHAT I PAID FOR IT, THEN...
AH!
OH, NO! I LOST THEM!
GLANCE
?
WHAT'S WRONG, TSUKASA-CHAN? WHAT'RE YOU LOOKING AT?
HUH? OH, NOTHING.
HEY, MUGI! WHY DON'T WE GO TO THE SHORE?
......
?
WHY IS SHE ACTING SO WEIRD?
....
HEY, MUGI-CHAN.
YANK
HUH?

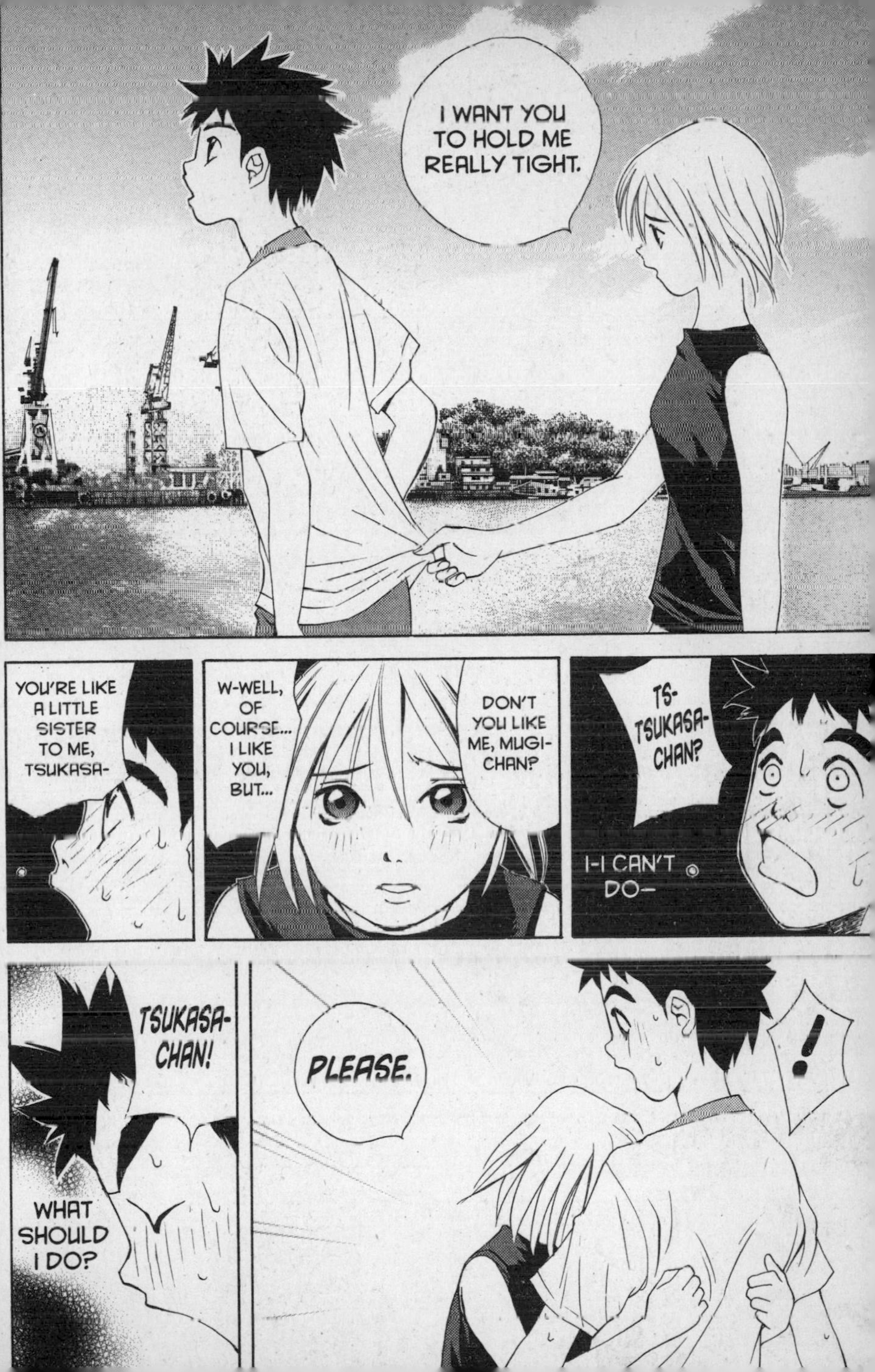
I WANT YOU TO HOLD ME REALLY TIGHT.
TS-TSUKASA-CHAN?
I-I CAN'T DO–
DON'T YOU LIKE ME, MUGI-CHAN?
W-WELL, OF COURSE... I LIKE YOU, BUT...
YOU'RE LIKE A LITTLE SISTER TO ME, TSUKASA-
!
PLEASE.
TSUKASA-CHAN!
WHAT SHOULD I DO?

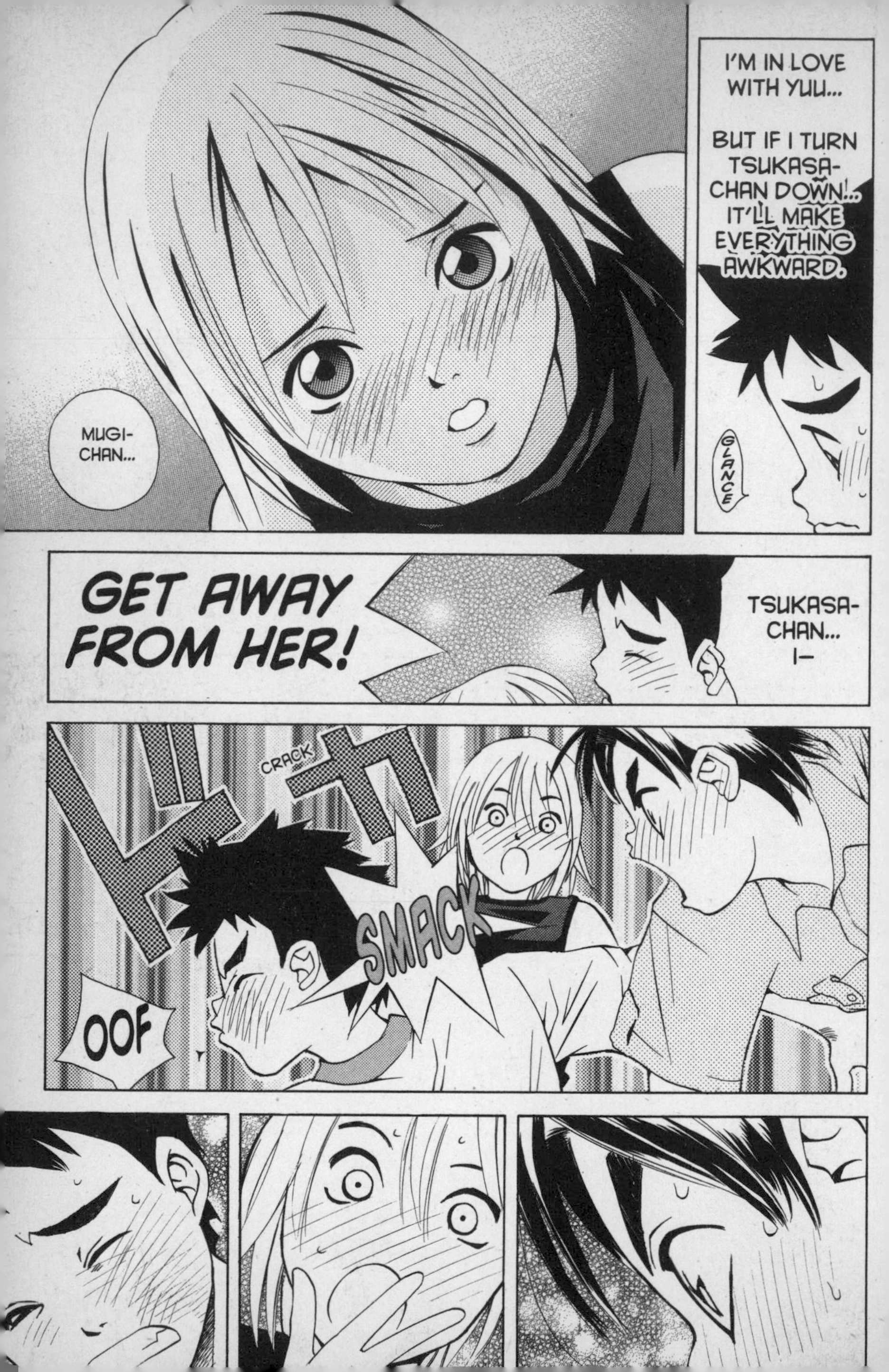
I'M IN LOVE WITH YUU...
BUT IF I TURN TSUKASA-CHAN DOWN... IT'LL MAKE EVERYTHING AWKWARD.
GLANCE
MUGI-CHAN...
TSUKASA-CHAN... I—
GET AWAY FROM HER!
CRACK
SMACK
OOF

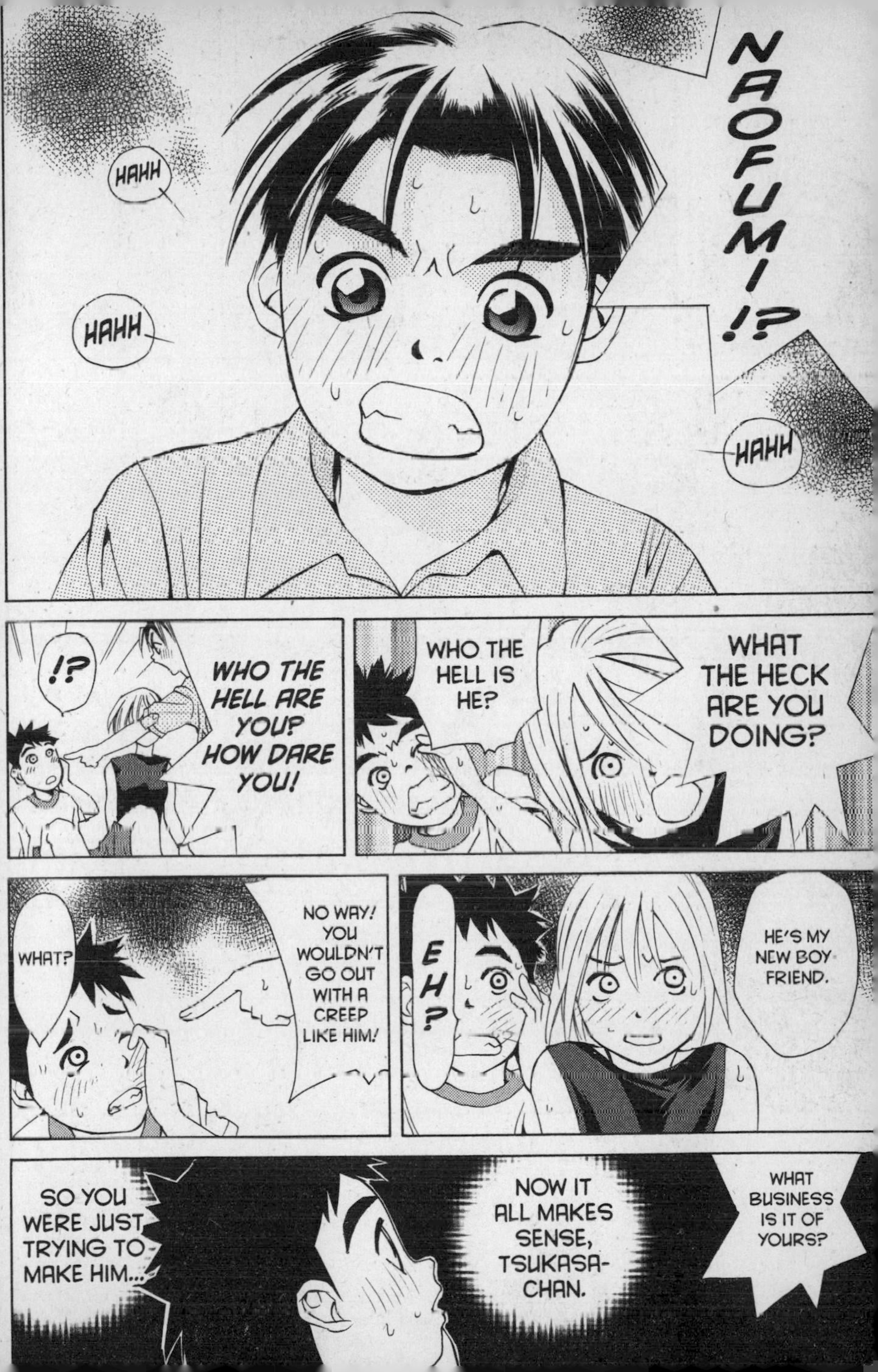
NAOFUMI!?
HAHH
HAHH
HAHH
WHAT THE HECK ARE YOU DOING?
WHO THE HELL IS HE?
WHO THE HELL ARE YOU? HOW DARE YOU!
!?
HE'S MY NEW BOY FRIEND.
EH?
NO WAY! YOU WOULDN'T GO OUT WITH A CREEP LIKE HIM!
WHAT?
WHAT BUSINESS IS IT OF YOURS?
NOW IT ALL MAKES SENSE, TSUKASA-CHAN.
SO YOU WERE JUST TRYING TO MAKE HIM...

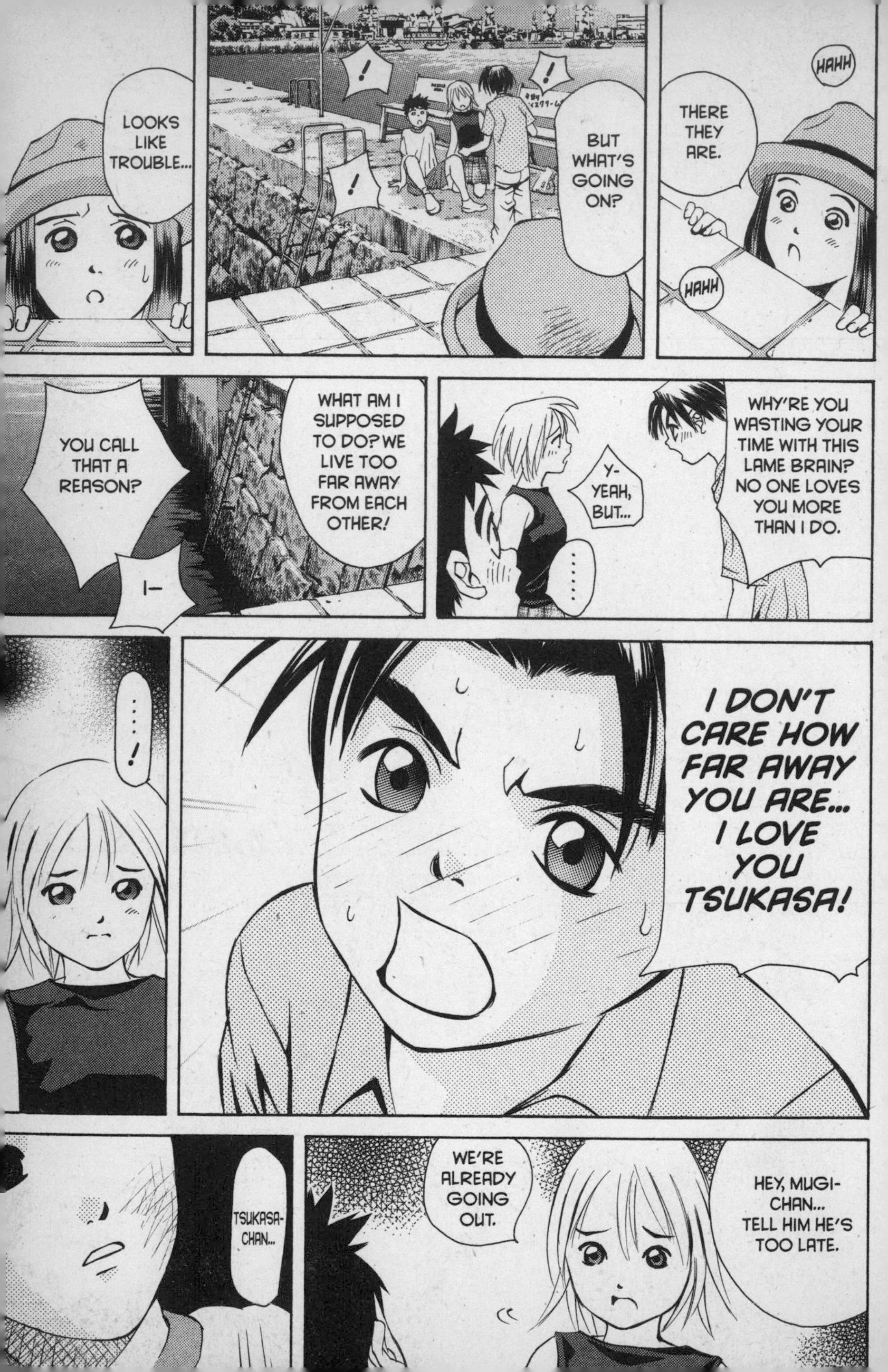
HAHH
THERE THEY ARE.
HAHH
!
!
BUT WHAT'S GOING ON?
!
LOOKS LIKE TROUBLE...
WHY'RE YOU WASTING YOUR TIME WITH THIS LAME BRAIN? NO ONE LOVES YOU MORE THAN I DO.
Y-YEAH, BUT...
......
WHAT AM I SUPPOSED TO DO? WE LIVE TOO FAR AWAY FROM EACH OTHER!
YOU CALL THAT A REASON?
I—
I DON'T CARE HOW FAR AWAY YOU ARE... I LOVE YOU TSUKASA!
....!
HEY, MUGI-CHAN... TELL HIM HE'S TOO LATE.
WE'RE ALREADY GOING OUT.
TSUKASA-CHAN...

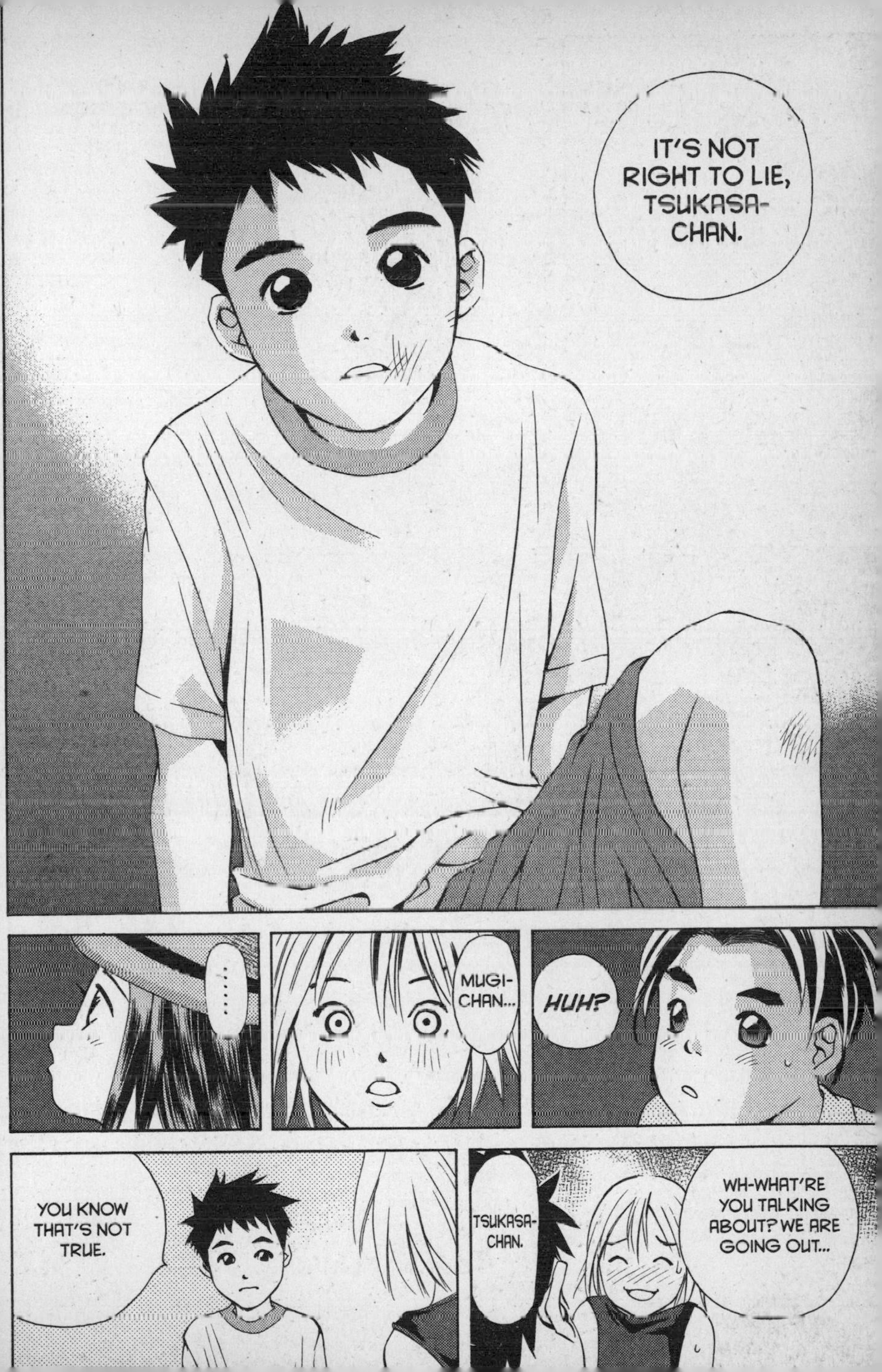
IT'S NOT RIGHT TO LIE, TSUKASA-CHAN.
HUH?
MUGI-CHAN...
......
WH-WHAT'RE YOU TALKING ABOUT? WE ARE GOING OUT...
TSUKASA-CHAN.
YOU KNOW THAT'S NOT TRUE.

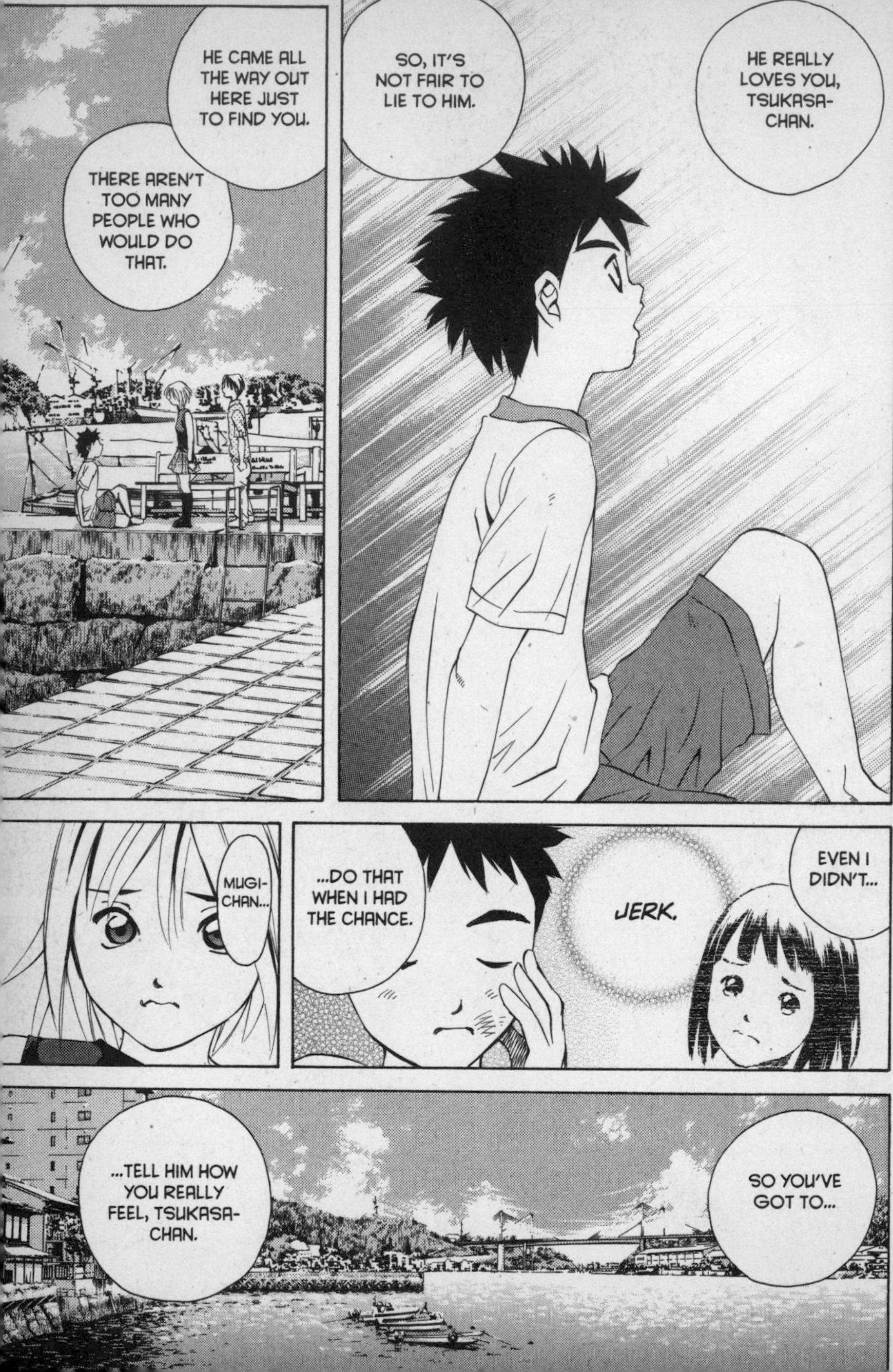
HE REALLY LOVES YOU, TSUKASA-CHAN.
SO, IT'S NOT FAIR TO LIE TO HIM.
HE CAME ALL THE WAY OUT HERE JUST TO FIND YOU.
THERE AREN'T TOO MANY PEOPLE WHO WOULD DO THAT.
EVEN I DIDN'T...
JERK.
...DO THAT WHEN I HAD THE CHANCE.
MUGI-CHAN...
SO YOU'VE GOT TO...
...TELL HIM HOW YOU REALLY FEEL, TSUKASA-CHAN.

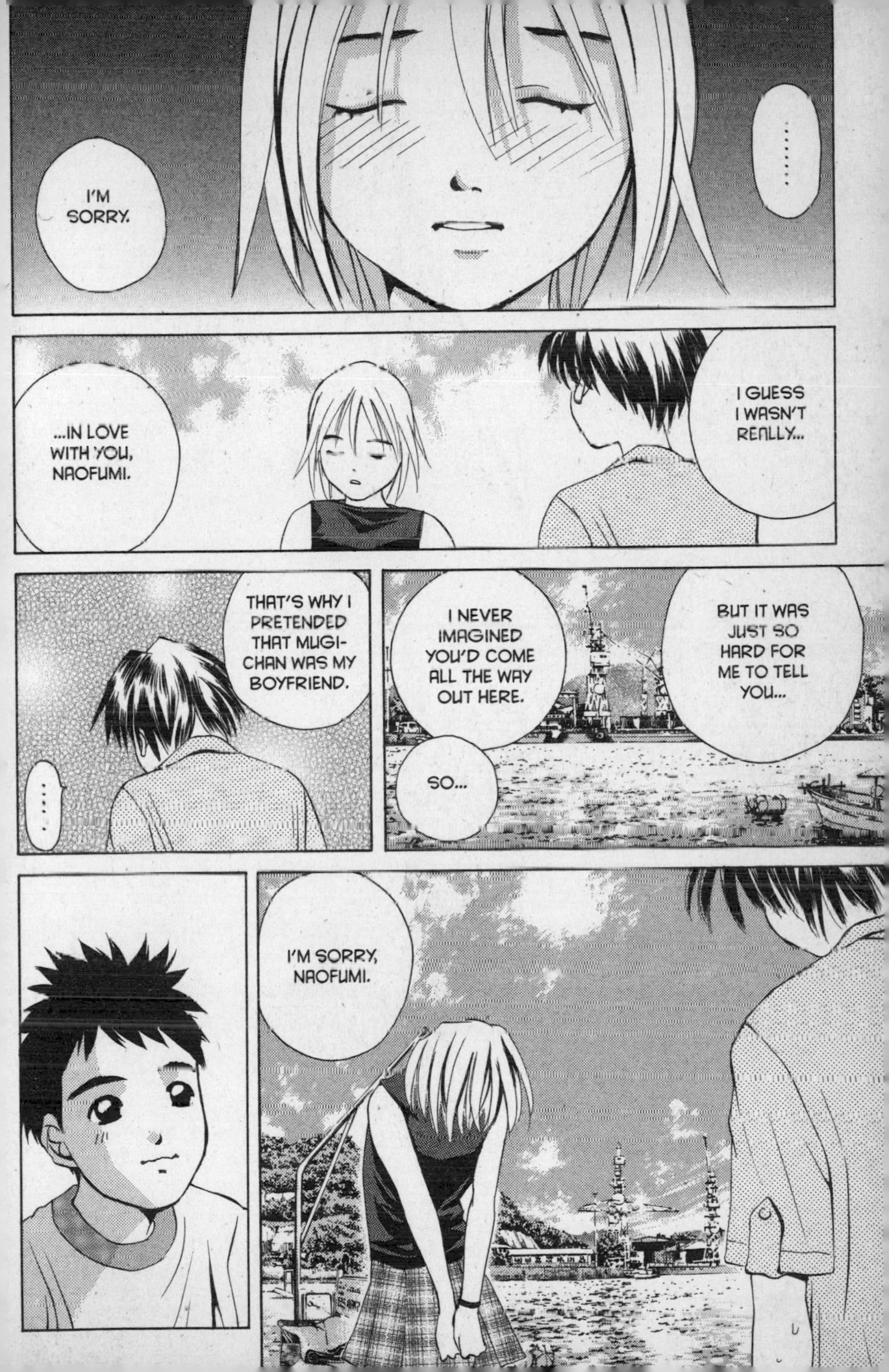
......
I'M SORRY.
I GUESS I WASN'T REALLY...
...IN LOVE WITH YOU, NAOFUMI.
BUT IT WAS JUST SO HARD FOR ME TO TELL YOU...
I NEVER IMAGINED YOU'D COME ALL THE WAY OUT HERE.
SO...
THAT'S WHY I PRETENDED THAT MUGI-CHAN WAS MY BOYFRIEND.
......
I'M SORRY, NAOFUMI.

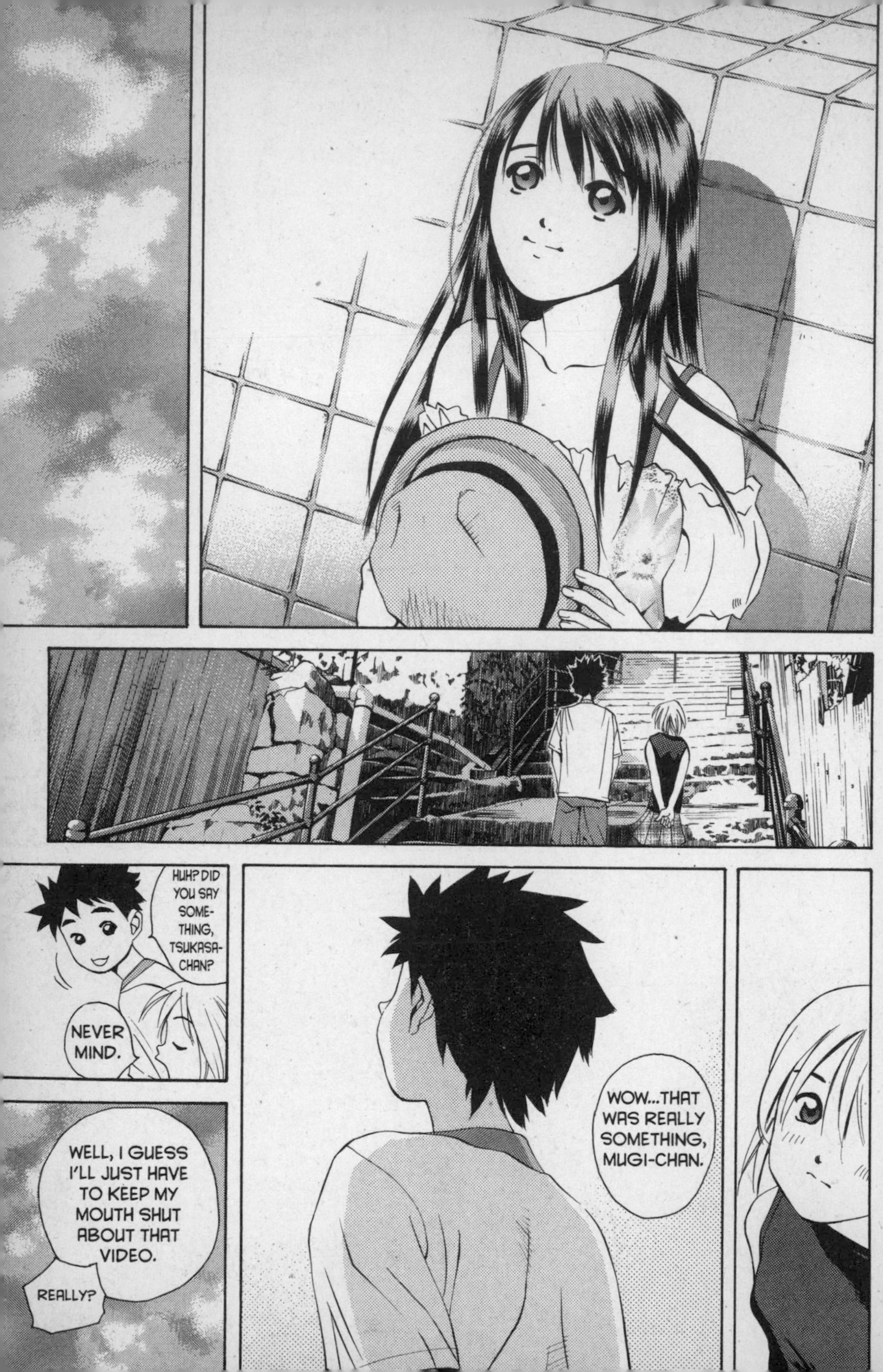
WOW...THAT WAS REALLY SOMETHING, MUGI-CHAN.
HUH? DID YOU SAY SOME-THING, TSUKASA-CHAN?
NEVER MIND.
WELL, I GUESS I'LL JUST HAVE TO KEEP MY MOUTH SHUT ABOUT THAT VIDEO.
REALLY?

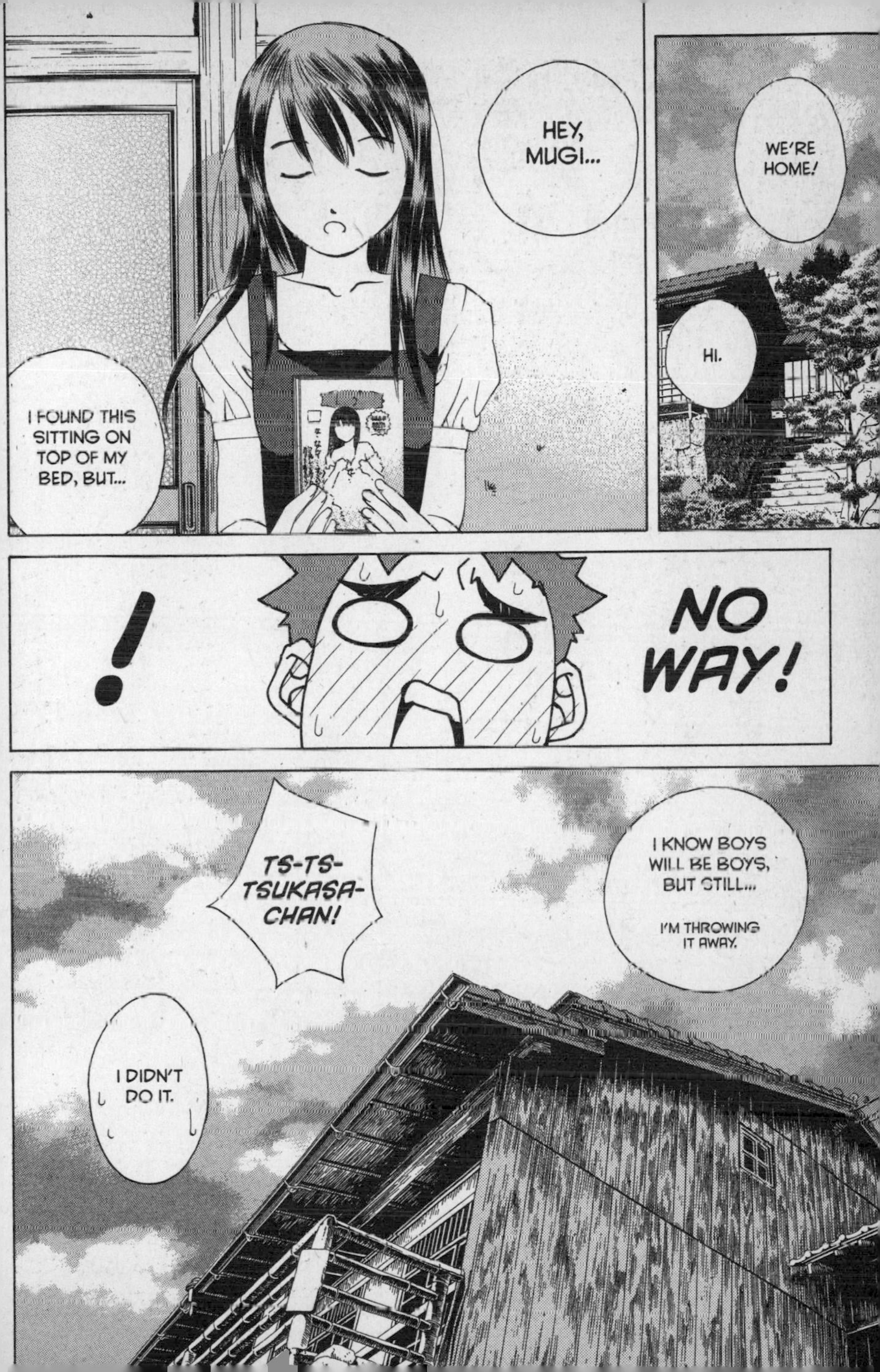
WE'RE HOME!
HI.
HEY, MUGI...
I FOUND THIS SITTING ON TOP OF MY BED, BUT...
NO WAY!
!
I KNOW BOYS WILL BE BOYS, BUT STILL...
I'M THROWING IT AWAY.
TS-TS-TSUKASA-CHAN!
I DIDN'T DO IT.

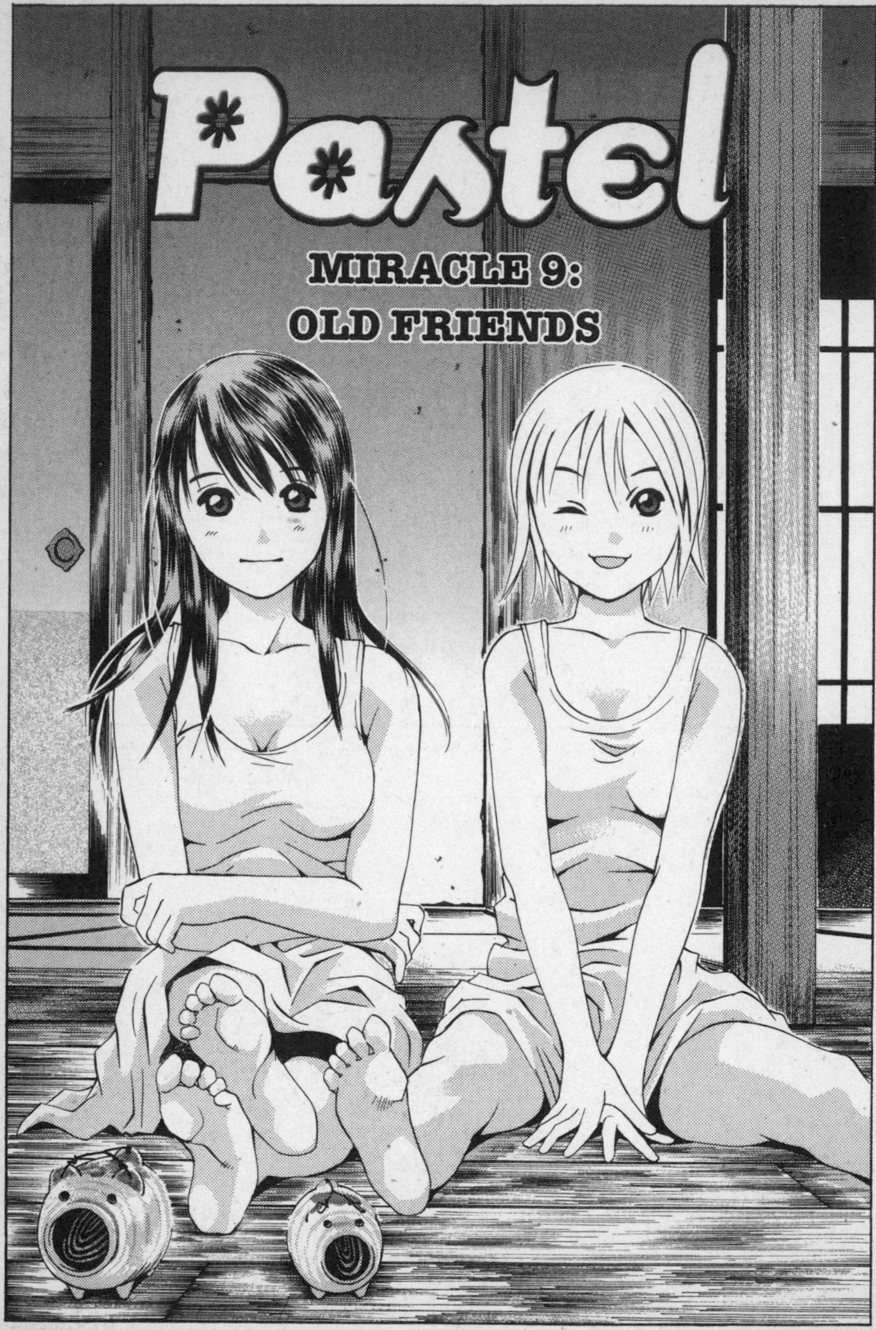
Pastel
MIRACLE 9:
OLD FRIENDS

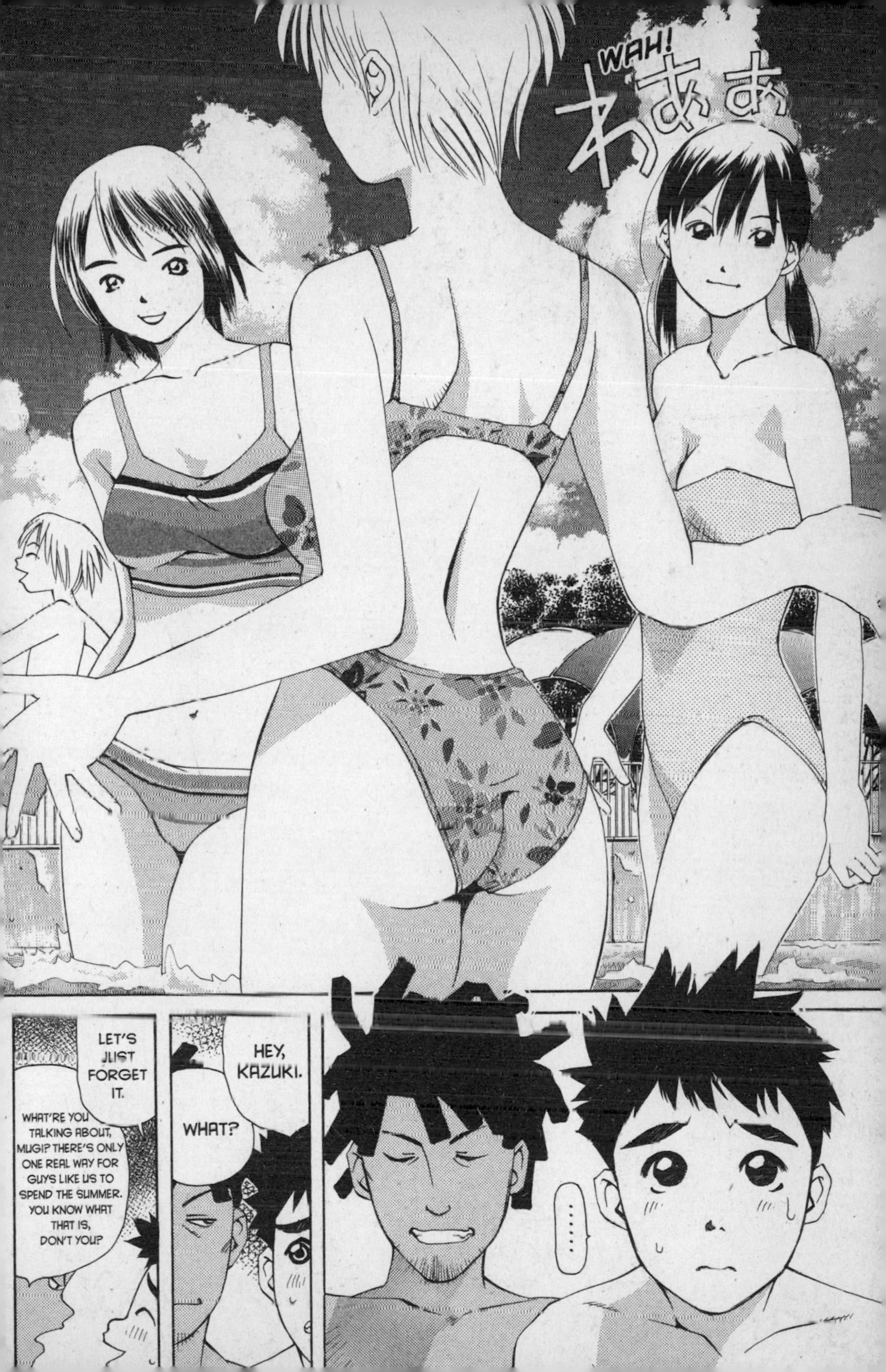
WAH!
わあぁ
......
HEY, KAZUKI.
WHAT?
LET'S JUST FORGET IT.
WHAT'RE YOU TALKING ABOUT, MUGI? THERE'S ONLY ONE REAL WAY FOR GUYS LIKE US TO SPEND THE SUMMER. YOU KNOW WHAT THAT IS, DON'T YOU?

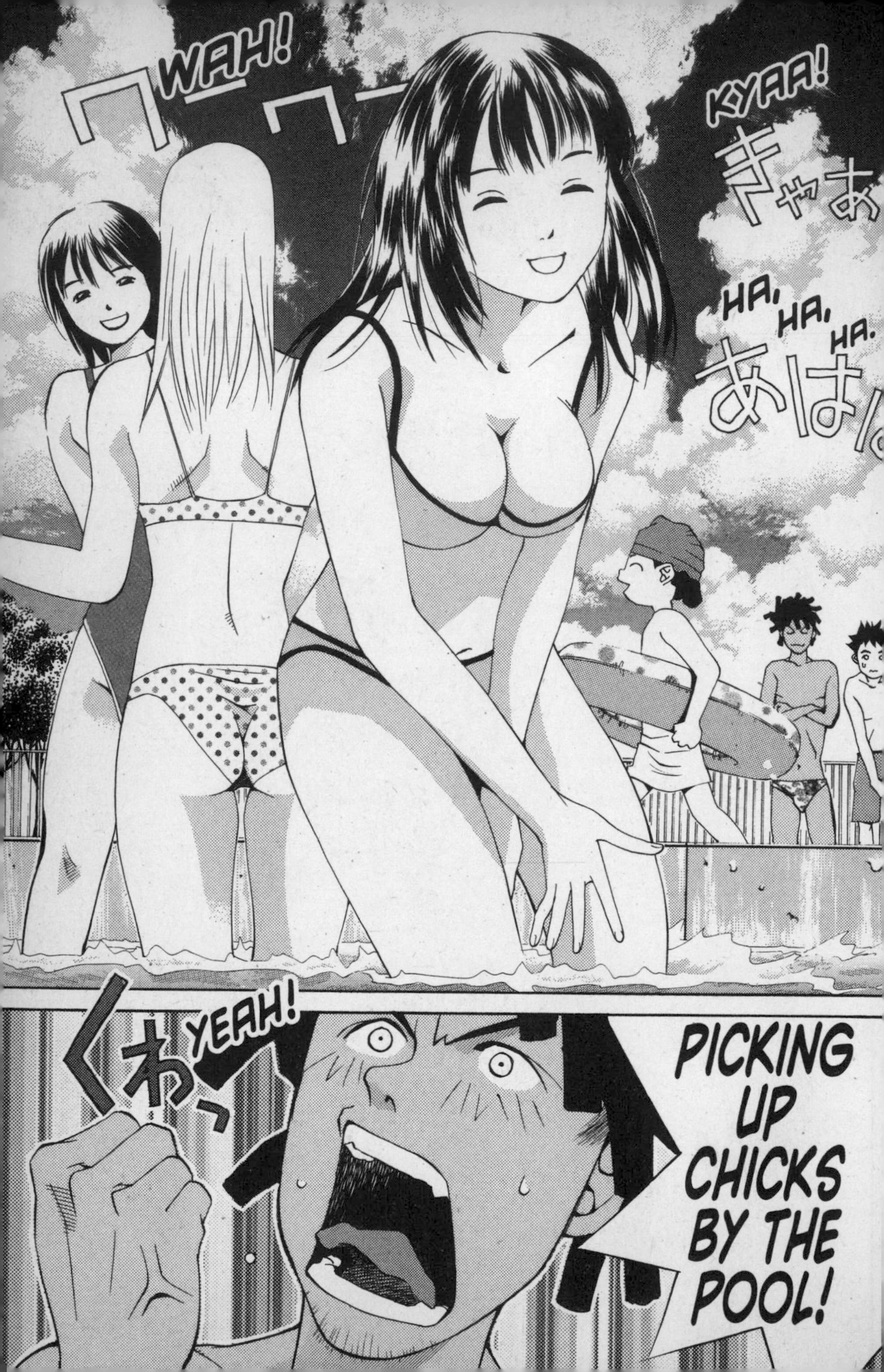
KYAA!
きゃあ
HA, HA, HA.
あは
WAH!
ワー ワー
PICKING UP CHICKS BY THE POOL!
YEAH!
くわっ

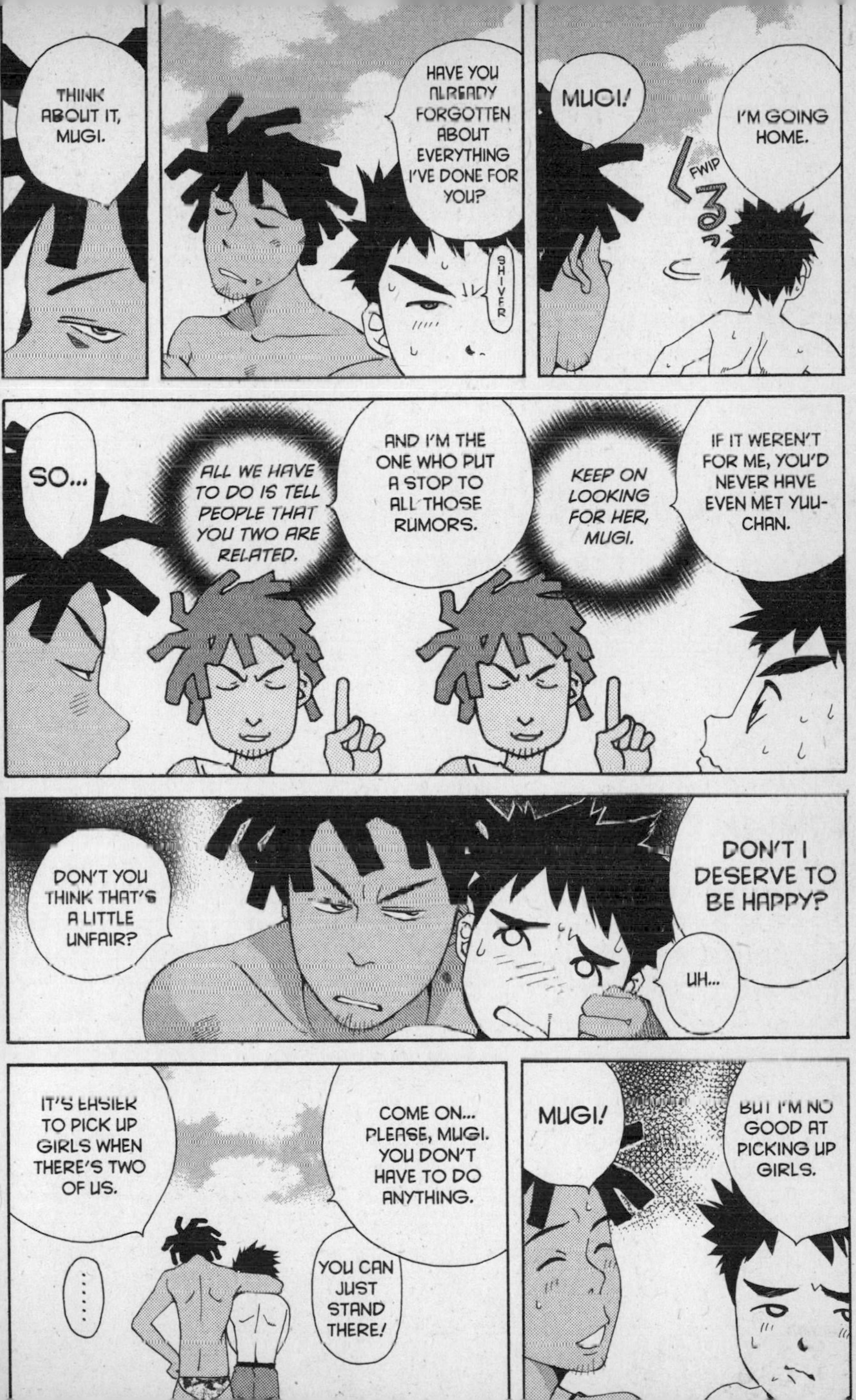
I'M GOING HOME.
FWIP
MUGI!
HAVE YOU ALREADY FORGOTTEN ABOUT EVERYTHING I'VE DONE FOR YOU?
SHIVER
THINK ABOUT IT, MUGI.
IF IT WEREN'T FOR ME, YOU'D NEVER HAVE EVEN MET YUU-CHAN.
KEEP ON LOOKING FOR HER, MUGI.
AND I'M THE ONE WHO PUT A STOP TO ALL THOSE RUMORS.
ALL WE HAVE TO DO IS TELL PEOPLE THAT YOU TWO ARE RELATED.
SO...
DON'T I DESERVE TO BE HAPPY?
UH...
DON'T YOU THINK THAT'S A LITTLE UNFAIR?
BUT I'M NO GOOD AT PICKING UP GIRLS.
MUGI!
COME ON... PLEASE, MUGI. YOU DON'T HAVE TO DO ANYTHING.
IT'S EASIER TO PICK UP GIRLS WHEN THERE'S TWO OF US.
YOU CAN JUST STAND THERE!
......

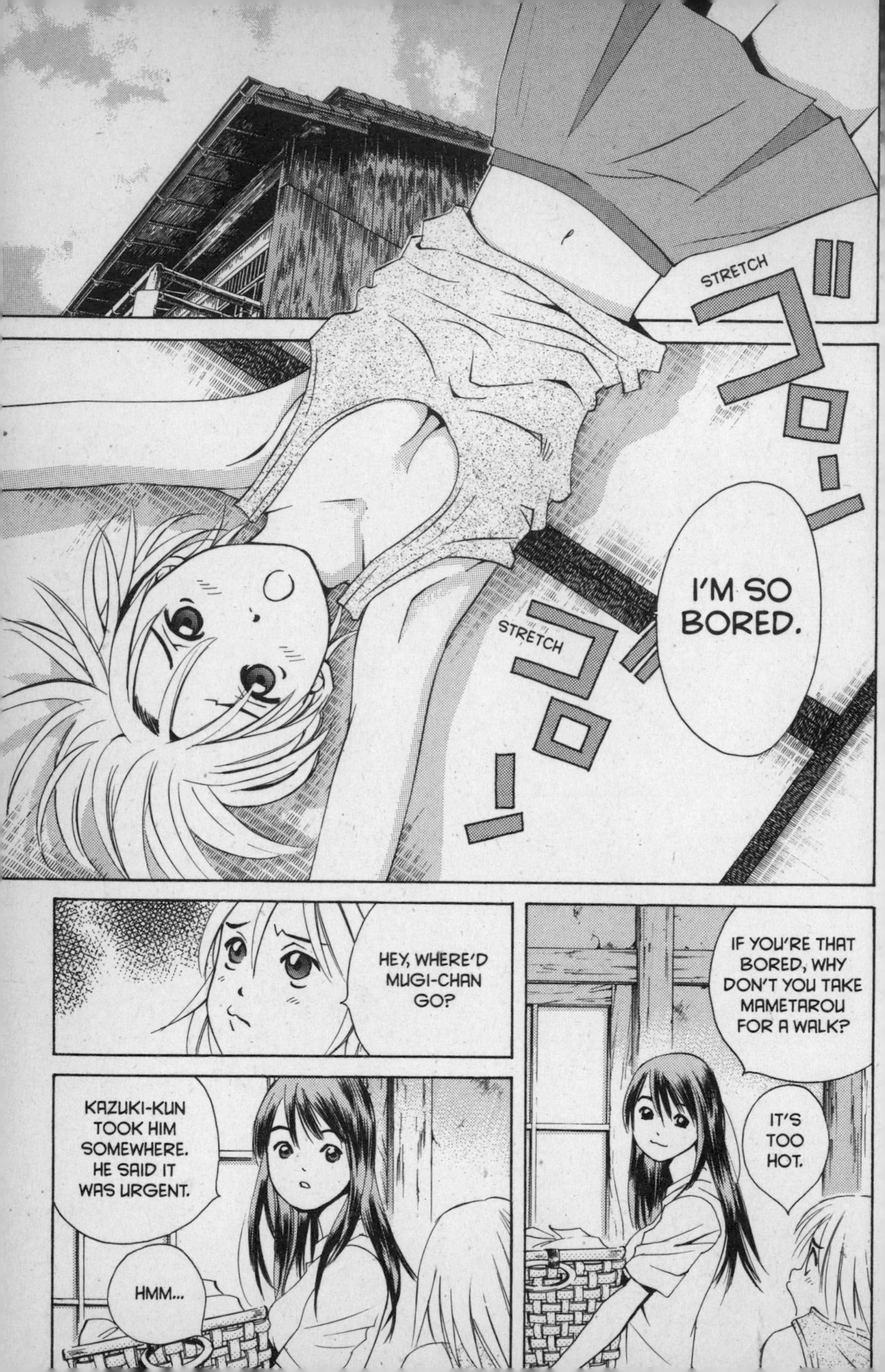
STRETCH
I'M SO BORED.
STRETCH
IF YOU'RE THAT BORED, WHY DON'T YOU TAKE MAMETAROU FOR A WALK?
IT'S TOO HOT.
HEY, WHERE'D MUGI-CHAN GO?
KAZUKI-KUN TOOK HIM SOMEWHERE. HE SAID IT WAS URGENT.
HMM...

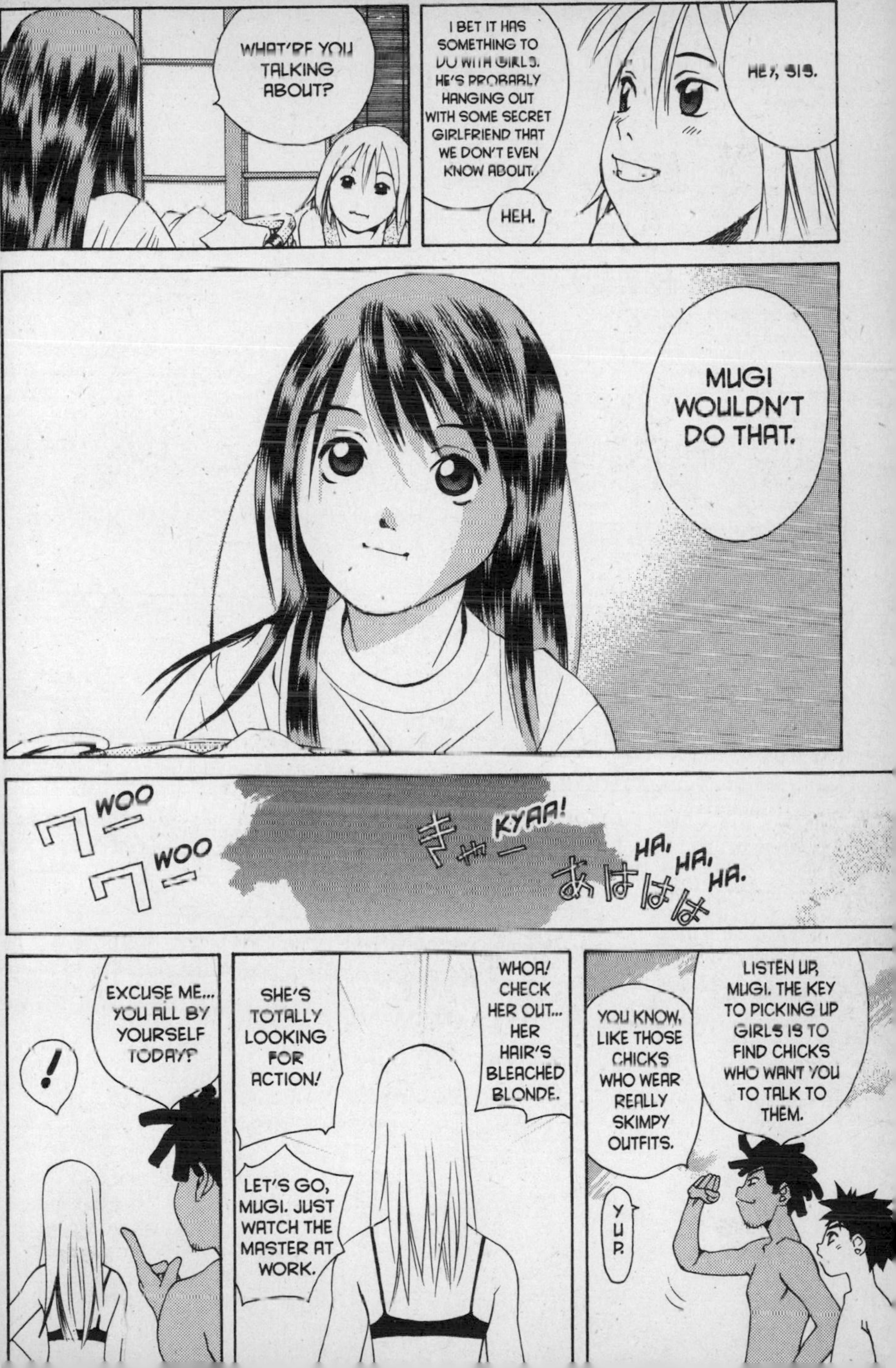
HEY, SIS.
I BET IT HAS SOMETHING TO DO WITH GIRLS. HE'S PROBABLY HANGING OUT WITH SOME SECRET GIRLFRIEND THAT WE DON'T EVEN KNOW ABOUT.
HEH.
WHAT'RE YOU TALKING ABOUT?
MUGI WOULDN'T DO THAT.
あははは HA, HA, HA.
きゃー KYAA!
ワー WOO
ワー WOO
LISTEN UP, MUGI. THE KEY TO PICKING UP GIRLS IS TO FIND CHICKS WHO WANT YOU TO TALK TO THEM.
YOU KNOW, LIKE THOSE CHICKS WHO WEAR REALLY SKIMPY OUTFITS.
YUP.
WHOA! CHECK HER OUT... HER HAIR'S BLEACHED BLONDE.
SHE'S TOTALLY LOOKING FOR ACTION!
LET'S GO, MUGI. JUST WATCH THE MASTER AT WORK.
EXCUSE ME... YOU ALL BY YOURSELF TODAY?
!

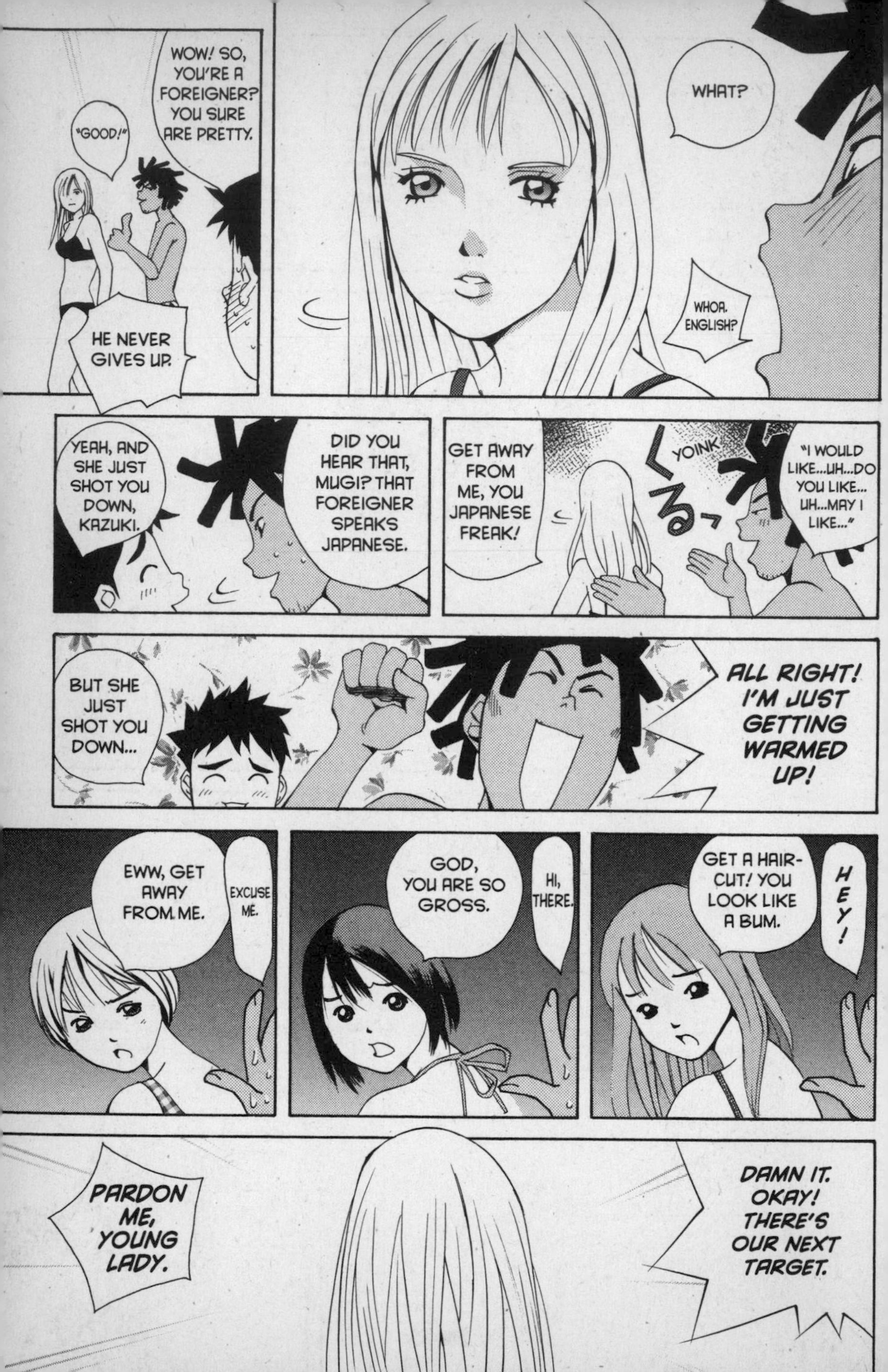
WHAT?
WHOA. ENGLISH?
WOW! SO, YOU'RE A FOREIGNER? YOU SURE ARE PRETTY.
"GOOD!"
HE NEVER GIVES UP.
"I WOULD LIKE...UH...DO YOU LIKE... UH...MAY I LIKE..."
YOINK
GET AWAY FROM ME, YOU JAPANESE FREAK!
DID YOU HEAR THAT, MUGI? THAT FOREIGNER SPEAKS JAPANESE.
YEAH, AND SHE JUST SHOT YOU DOWN, KAZUKI.
ALL RIGHT! I'M JUST GETTING WARMED UP!
BUT SHE JUST SHOT YOU DOWN...
HEY!
GET A HAIR-CUT! YOU LOOK LIKE A BUM.
HI, THERE.
GOD, YOU ARE SO GROSS.
EXCUSE ME.
EWW, GET AWAY FROM ME.
DAMN IT. OKAY! THERE'S OUR NEXT TARGET.
PARDON ME, YOUNG LADY.

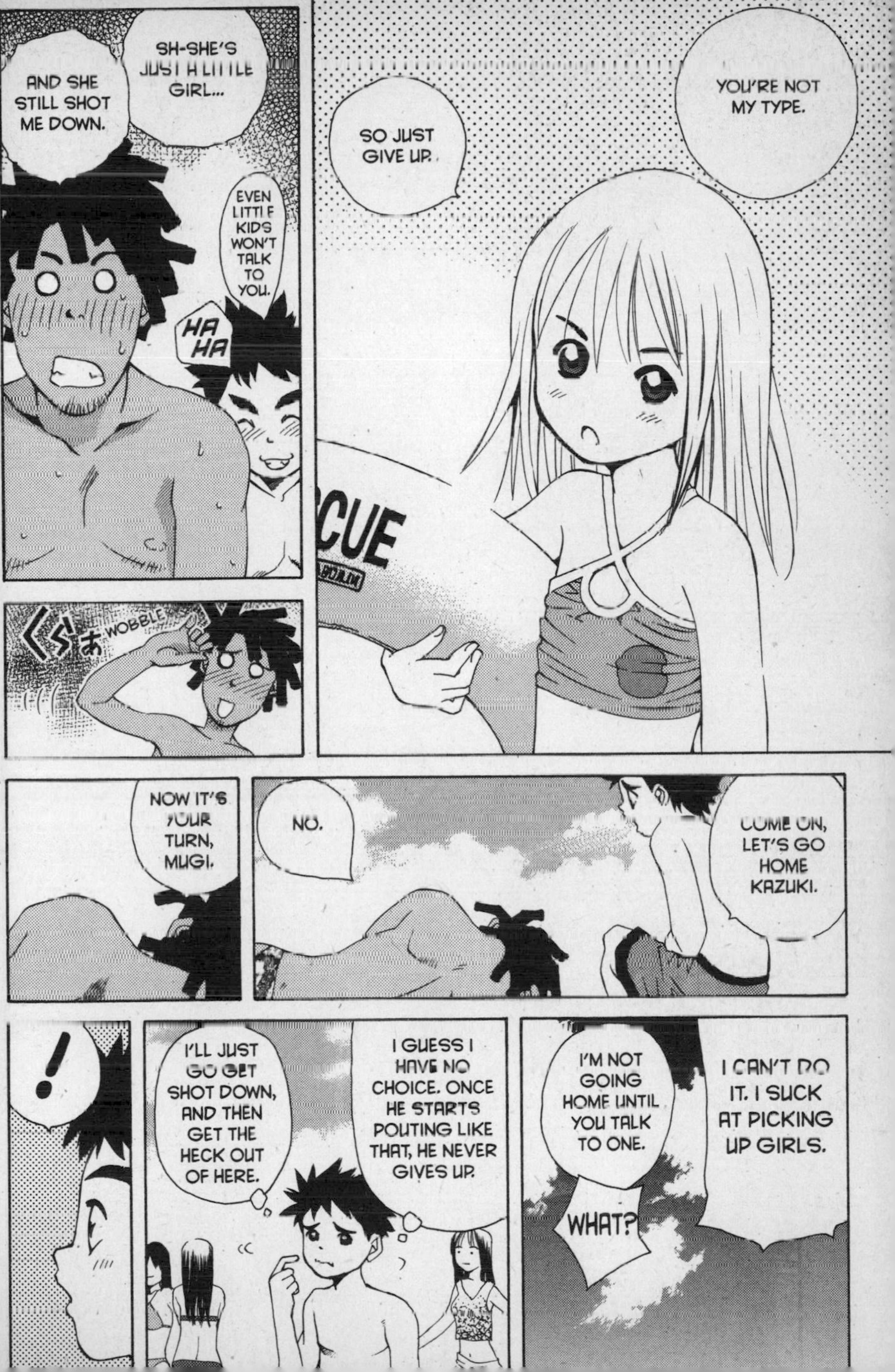
YOU'RE NOT MY TYPE.
SO JUST GIVE UP.
SH-SHE'S JUST A LITTLE GIRL...
AND SHE STILL SHOT ME DOWN.
EVEN LITTLE KIDS WON'T TALK TO YOU.
HA HA
WOBBLE
COME ON, LET'S GO HOME KAZUKI.
NO.
NOW IT'S YOUR TURN, MUGI.
I CAN'T DO IT. I SUCK AT PICKING UP GIRLS.
I'M NOT GOING HOME UNTIL YOU TALK TO ONE.
WHAT?
I GUESS I HAVE NO CHOICE. ONCE HE STARTS POUTING LIKE THAT, HE NEVER GIVES UP.
I'LL JUST GO GET SHOT DOWN, AND THEN GET THE HECK OUT OF HERE.
!

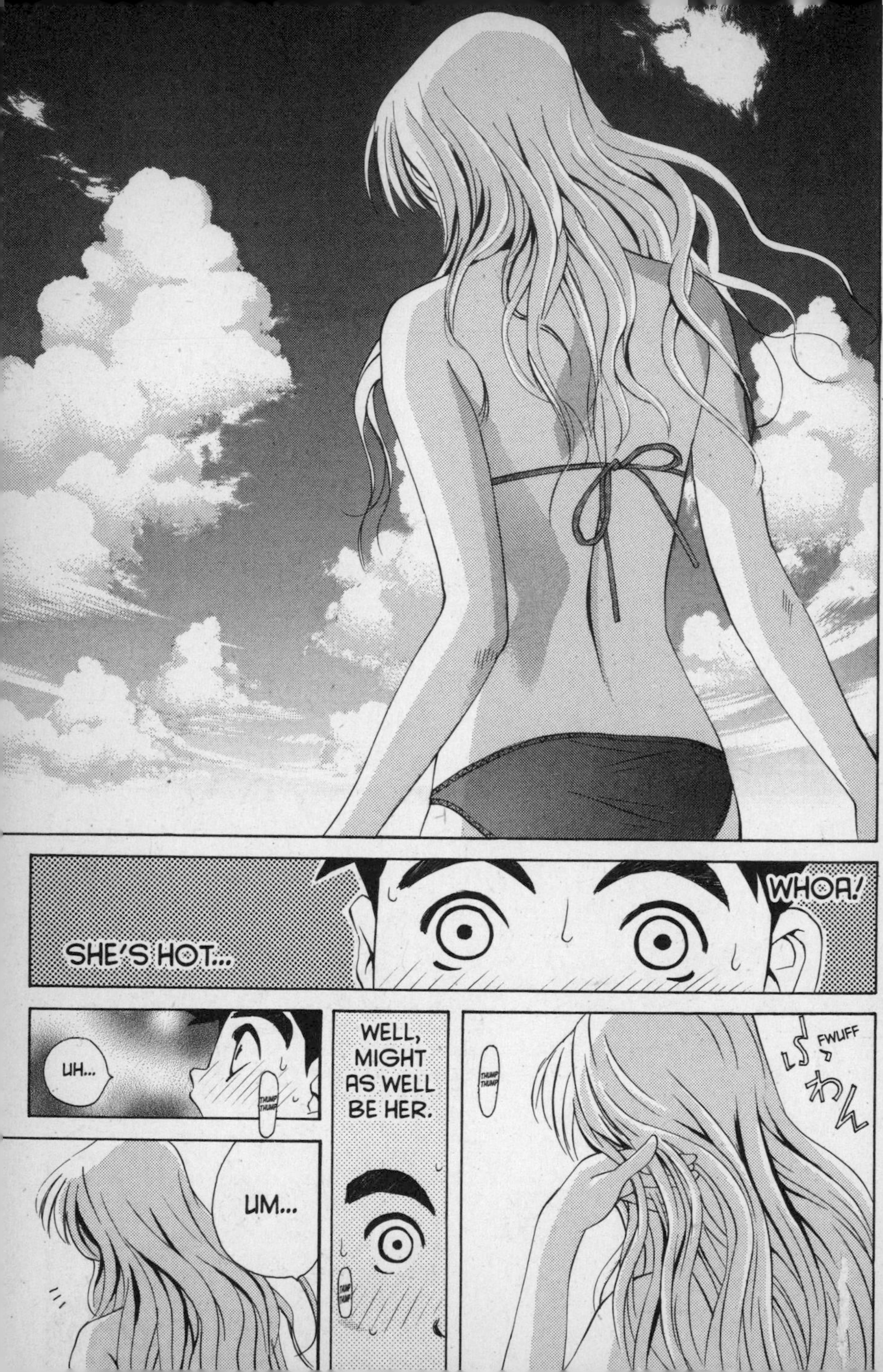

WHOA!
SHE'S HOT...
ふわん
FWUFF
THUMP THUMP
WELL, MIGHT AS WELL BE HER.
UH...
THUMP THUMP
UM...

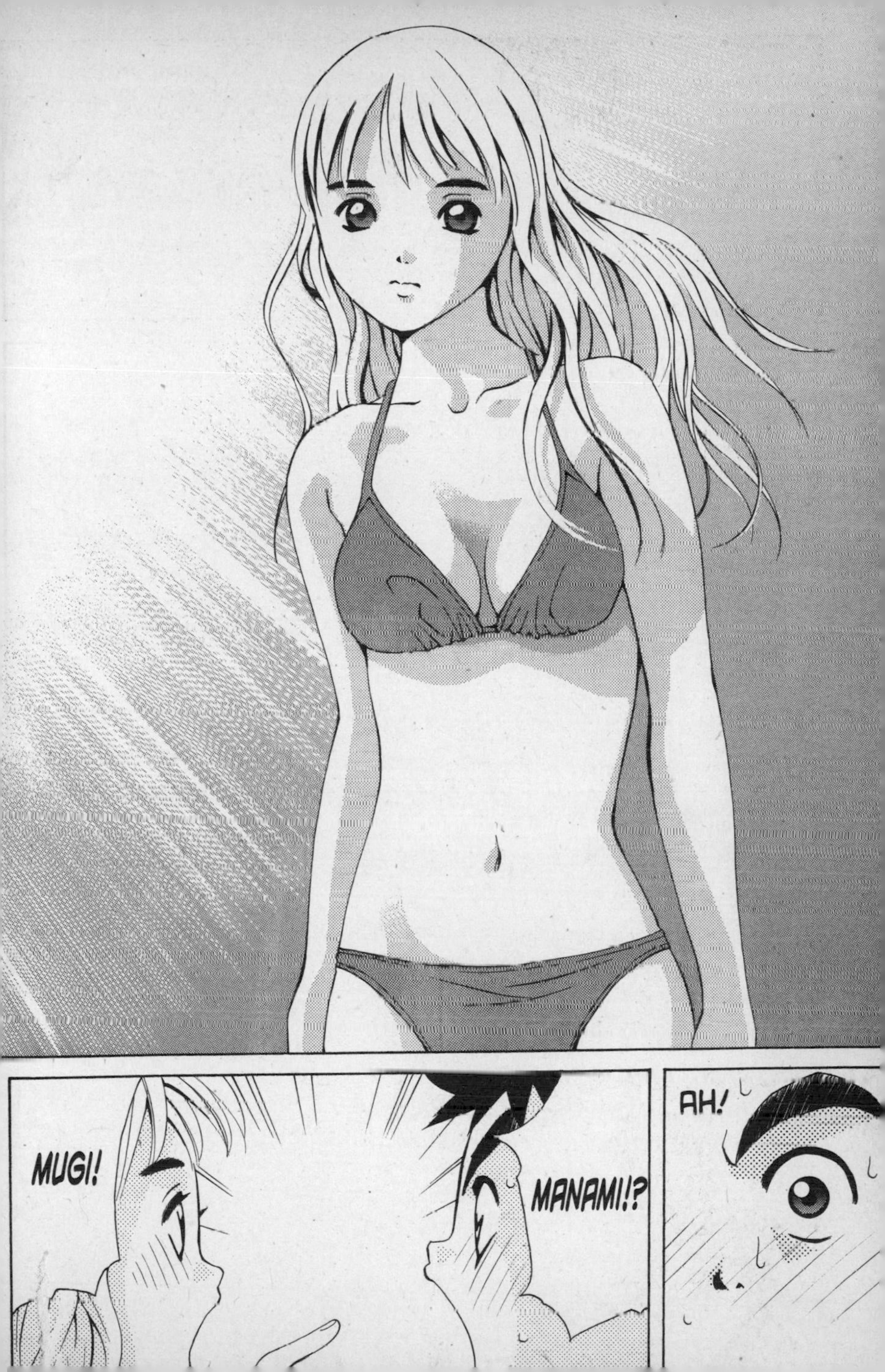
AH!
MANAMI!?
MUGI!

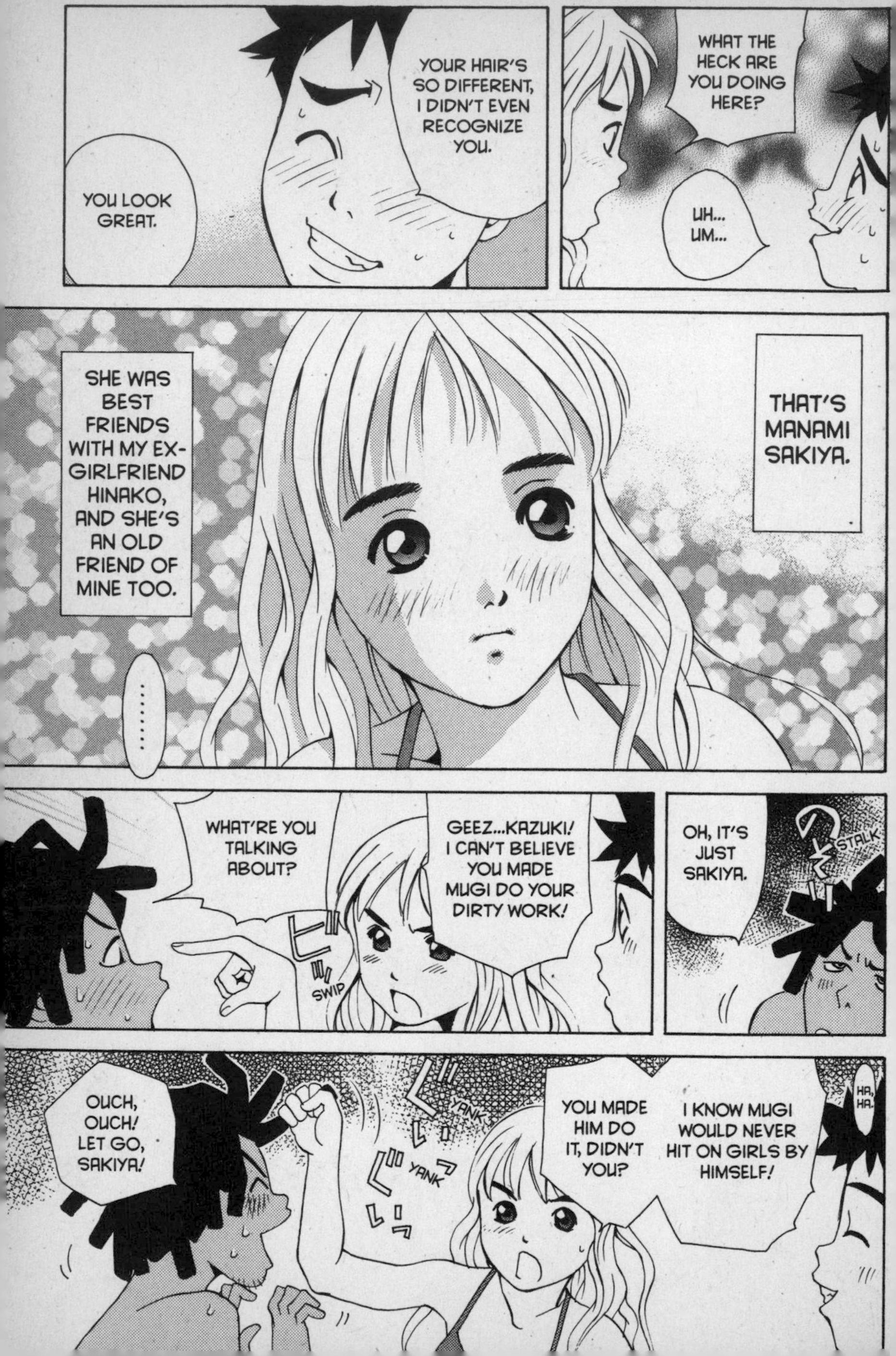
WHAT THE HECK ARE YOU DOING HERE?
UH... UM...
YOUR HAIR'S SO DIFFERENT, I DIDN'T EVEN RECOGNIZE YOU.
YOU LOOK GREAT.
THAT'S MANAMI SAKIYA.
SHE WAS BEST FRIENDS WITH MY EX-GIRLFRIEND HINAKO, AND SHE'S AN OLD FRIEND OF MINE TOO.
....
OH, IT'S JUST SAKIYA.
STALK
GEEZ...KAZUKI! I CAN'T BELIEVE YOU MADE MUGI DO YOUR DIRTY WORK!
WHAT'RE YOU TALKING ABOUT?
SWIP
HA, HA.
I KNOW MUGI WOULD NEVER HIT ON GIRLS BY HIMSELF!
YOU MADE HIM DO IT, DIDN'T YOU?
YANK
YANK
OUCH, OUCH! LET GO, SAKIYA!

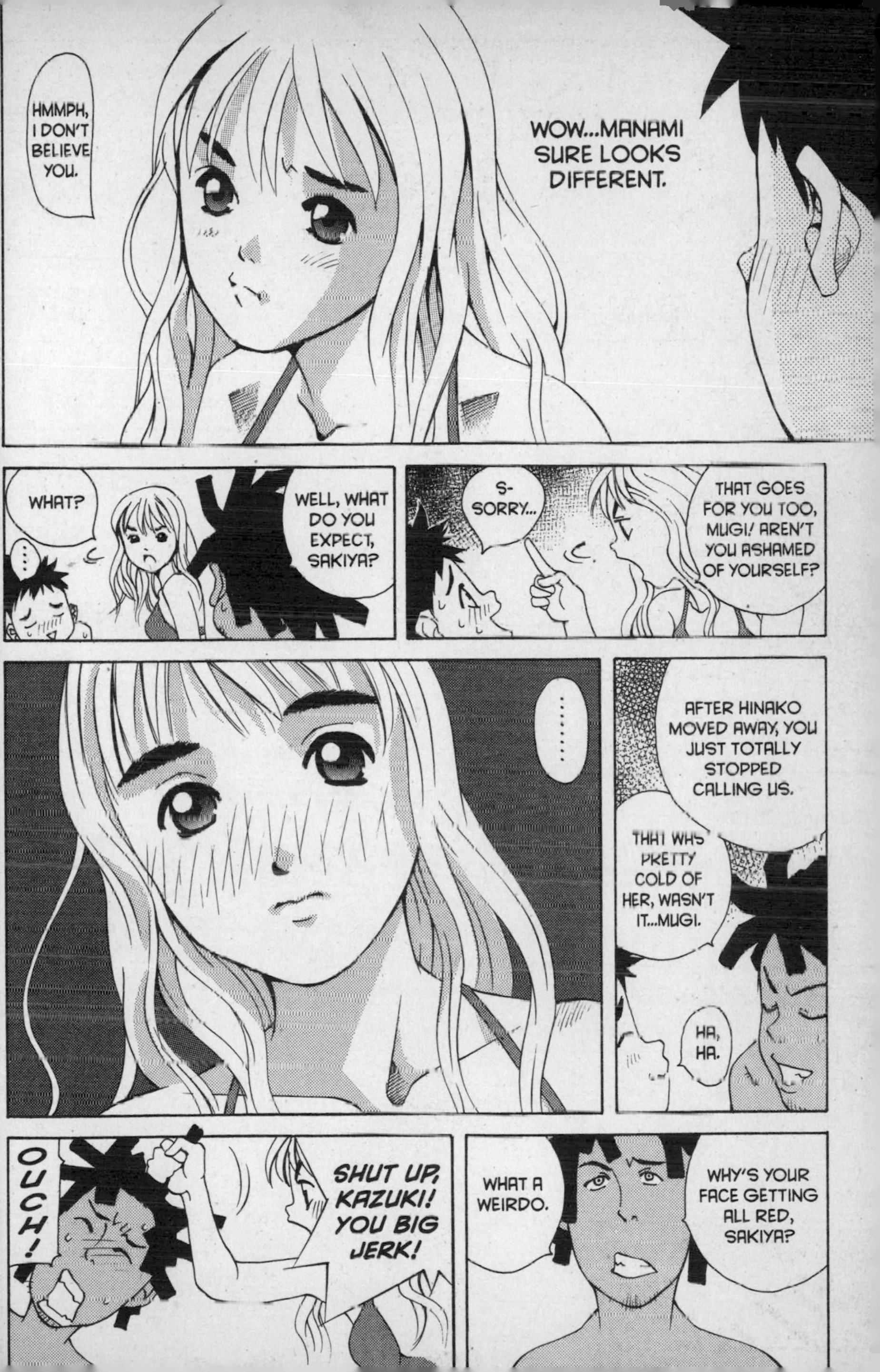
WOW...MANAMI SURE LOOKS DIFFERENT.
HMMPH, I DON'T BELIEVE YOU.
THAT GOES FOR YOU TOO, MUGI! AREN'T YOU ASHAMED OF YOURSELF?
S-SORRY...
WELL, WHAT DO YOU EXPECT, SAKIYA?
WHAT?
...
AFTER HINAKO MOVED AWAY, YOU JUST TOTALLY STOPPED CALLING US.
THAT WAS PRETTY COLD OF HER, WASN'T IT...MUGI.
HA, HA.
....
WHY'S YOUR FACE GETTING ALL RED, SAKIYA?
WHAT A WEIRDO.
SHUT UP, KAZUKI! YOU BIG JERK!
OUCH!

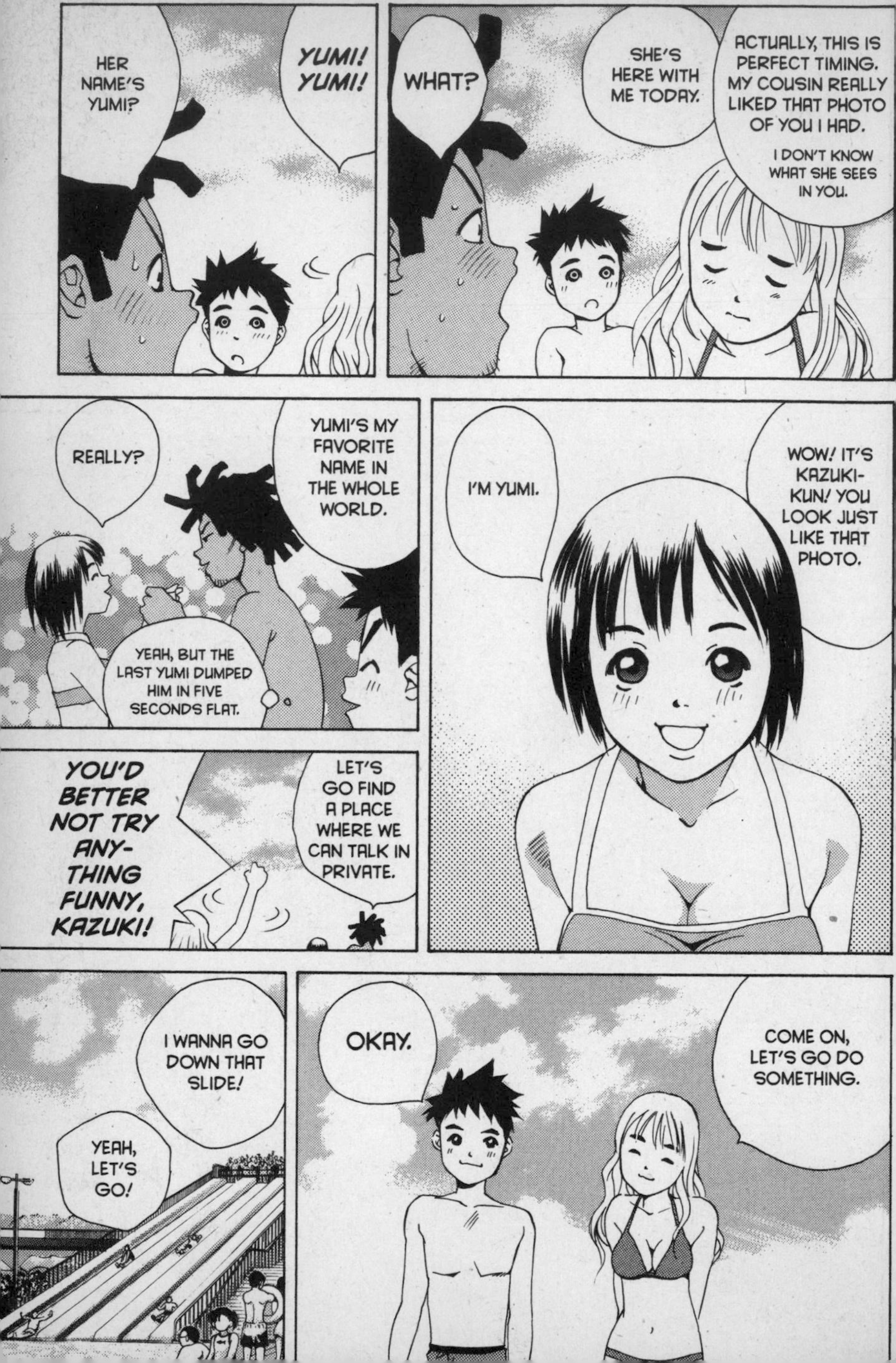
ACTUALLY, THIS IS PERFECT TIMING. MY COUSIN REALLY LIKED THAT PHOTO OF YOU I HAD.
I DON'T KNOW WHAT SHE SEES IN YOU.
SHE'S HERE WITH ME TODAY.
WHAT?
YUMI! YUMI!
HER NAME'S YUMI?
WOW! IT'S KAZUKI-KUN! YOU LOOK JUST LIKE THAT PHOTO.
I'M YUMI.
YUMI'S MY FAVORITE NAME IN THE WHOLE WORLD.
REALLY?
YEAH, BUT THE LAST YUMI DUMPED HIM IN FIVE SECONDS FLAT.
LET'S GO FIND A PLACE WHERE WE CAN TALK IN PRIVATE.
YOU'D BETTER NOT TRY ANY-THING FUNNY, KAZUKI!
COME ON, LET'S GO DO SOMETHING.
OKAY.
I WANNA GO DOWN THAT SLIDE!
YEAH, LET'S GO!

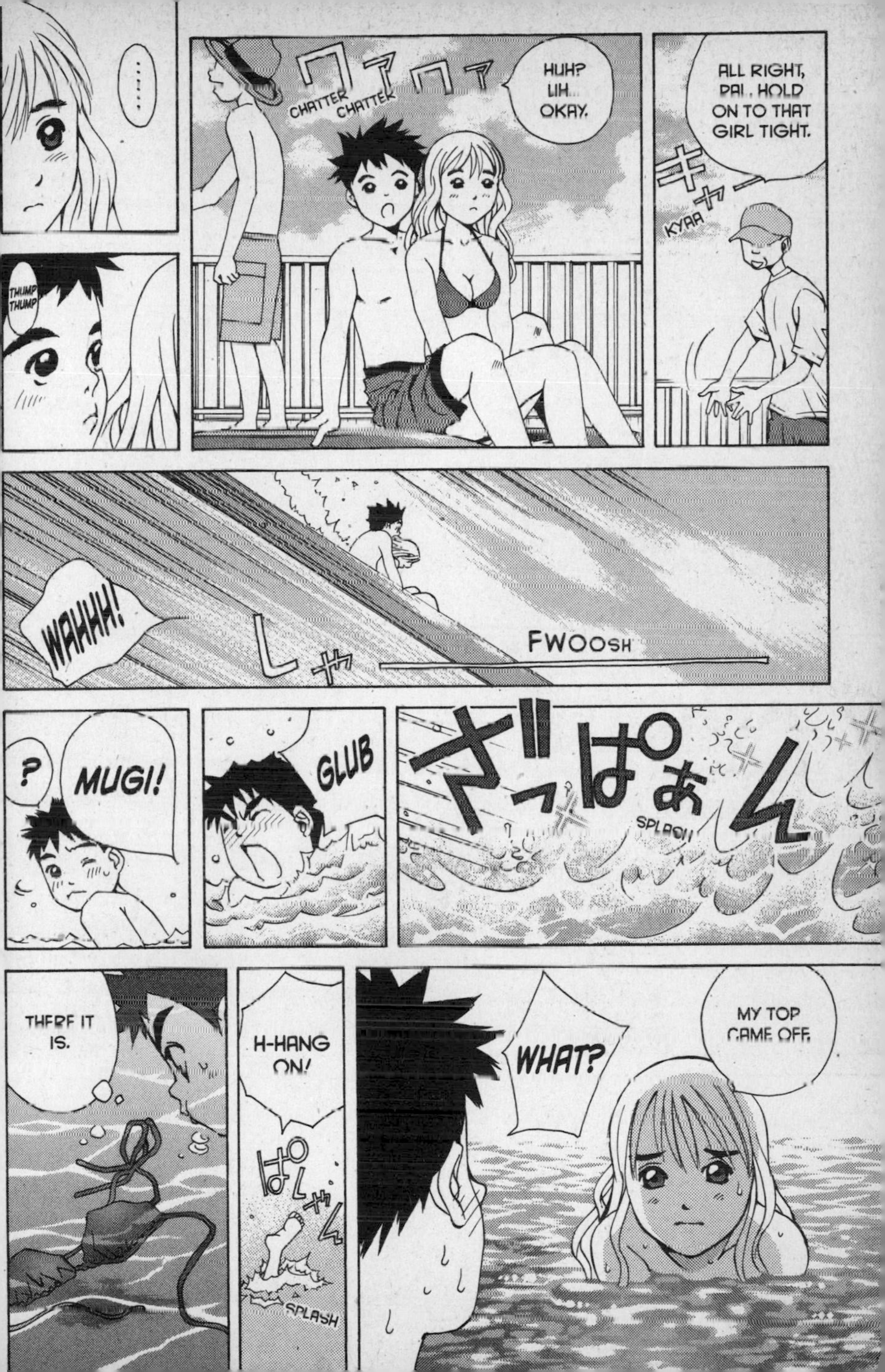
ALL RIGHT, PAL. HOLD ON TO THAT GIRL TIGHT.
キャー
KYAA
HUH? UH... OKAY.
ワァワァ
CHATTER CHATTER
......
THUMP THUMP
WAHHH!
しゃ
FWOOSH
ざっぱぁん
SPLASH!
GLUB
MUGI!
?
MY TOP CAME OFF.
WHAT?
H-HANG ON!
ぱしゃん
SPLASH
THERE IT IS.

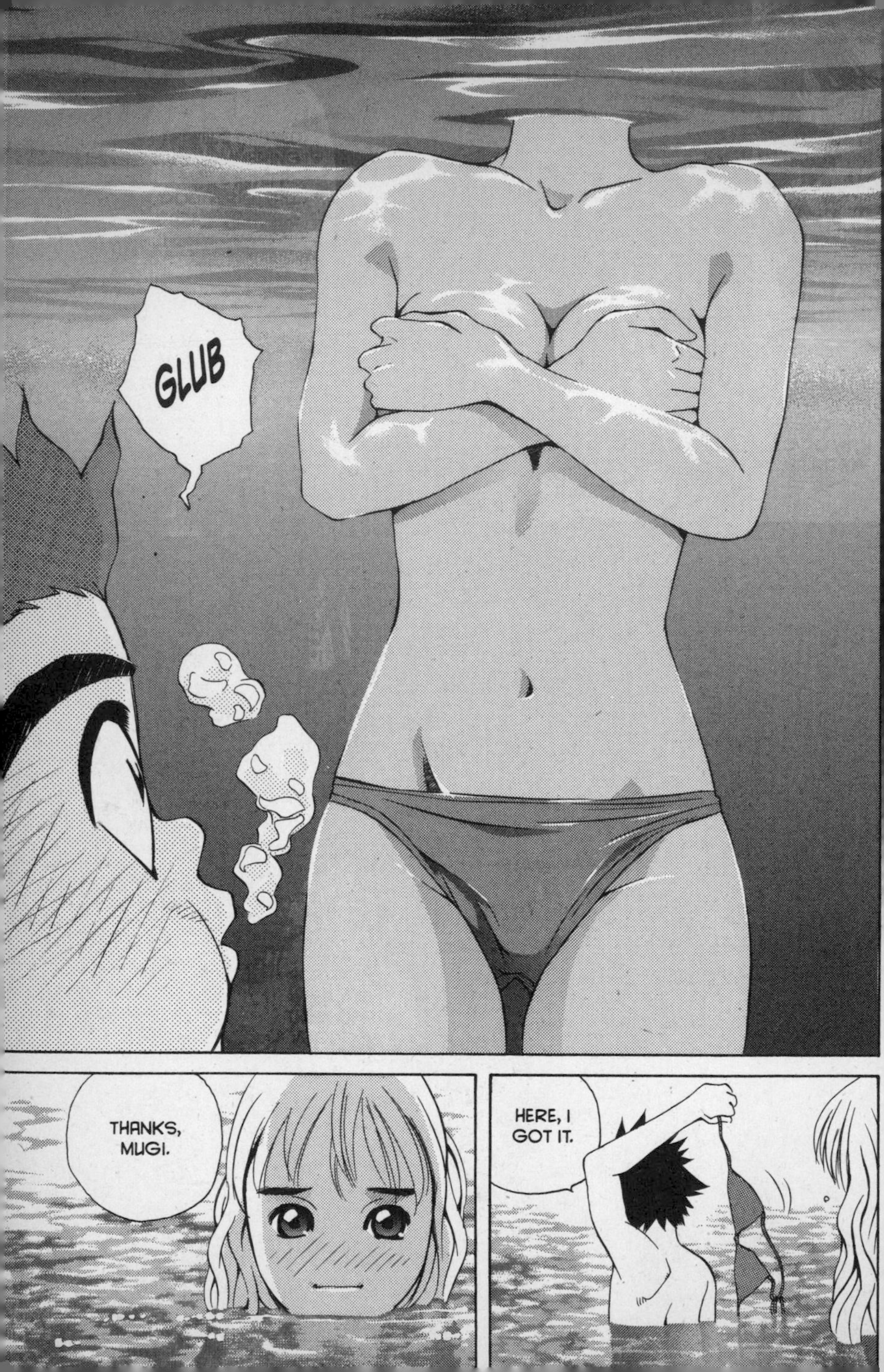
GLUB
HERE, I GOT IT.
THANKS, MUGI.

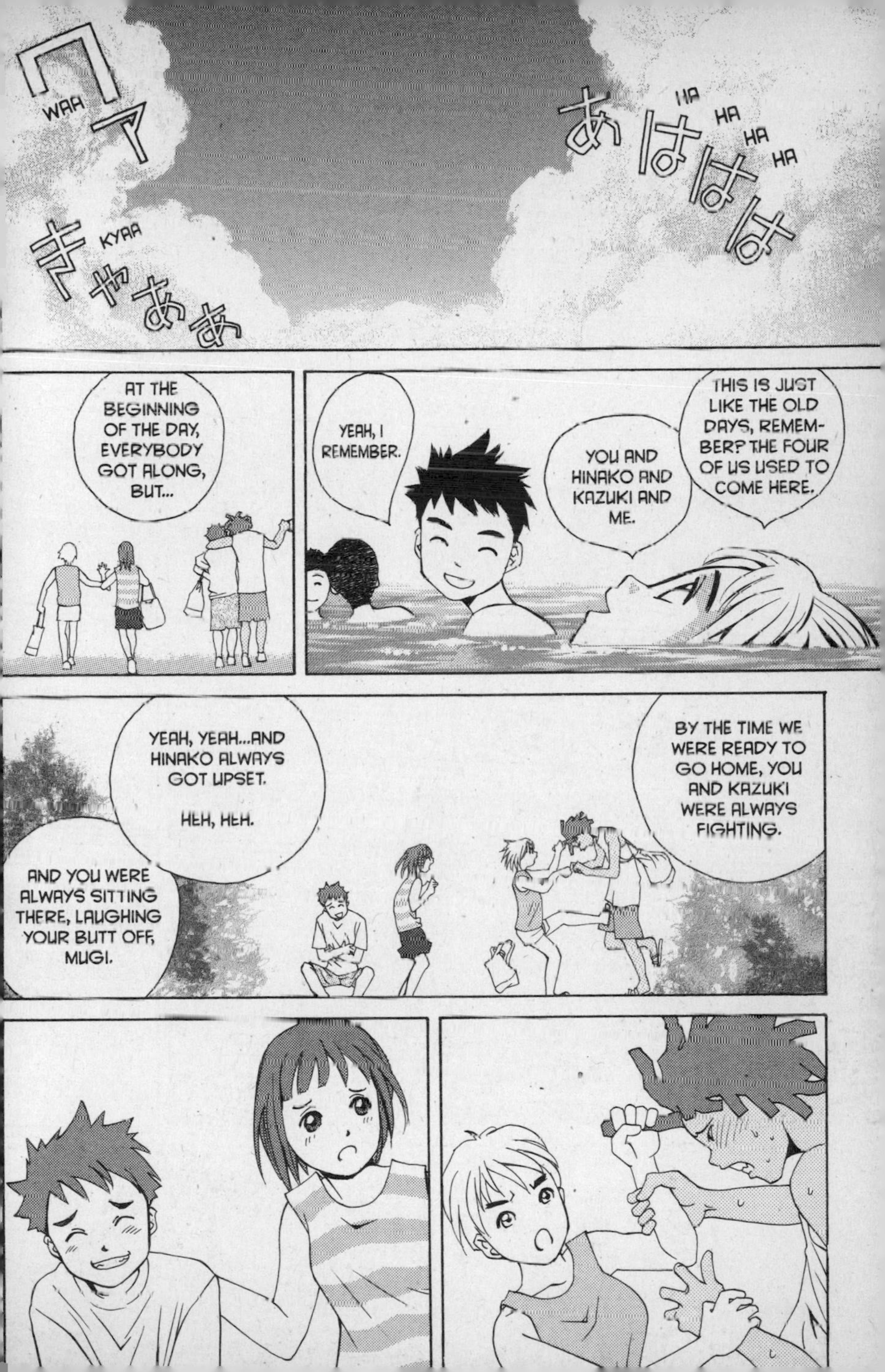
あははは
HA HA HA HA
ワァ
WAA
きゃあぁ
KYAA
THIS IS JUST LIKE THE OLD DAYS, REMEMBER? THE FOUR OF US USED TO COME HERE.
YOU AND HINAKO AND KAZUKI AND ME.
YEAH, I REMEMBER.
AT THE BEGINNING OF THE DAY, EVERYBODY GOT ALONG, BUT...
BY THE TIME WE WERE READY TO GO HOME, YOU AND KAZUKI WERE ALWAYS FIGHTING.
YEAH, YEAH...AND HINAKO ALWAYS GOT UPSET.
HEH, HEH.
AND YOU WERE ALWAYS SITTING THERE, LAUGHING YOUR BUTT OFF, MUGI.

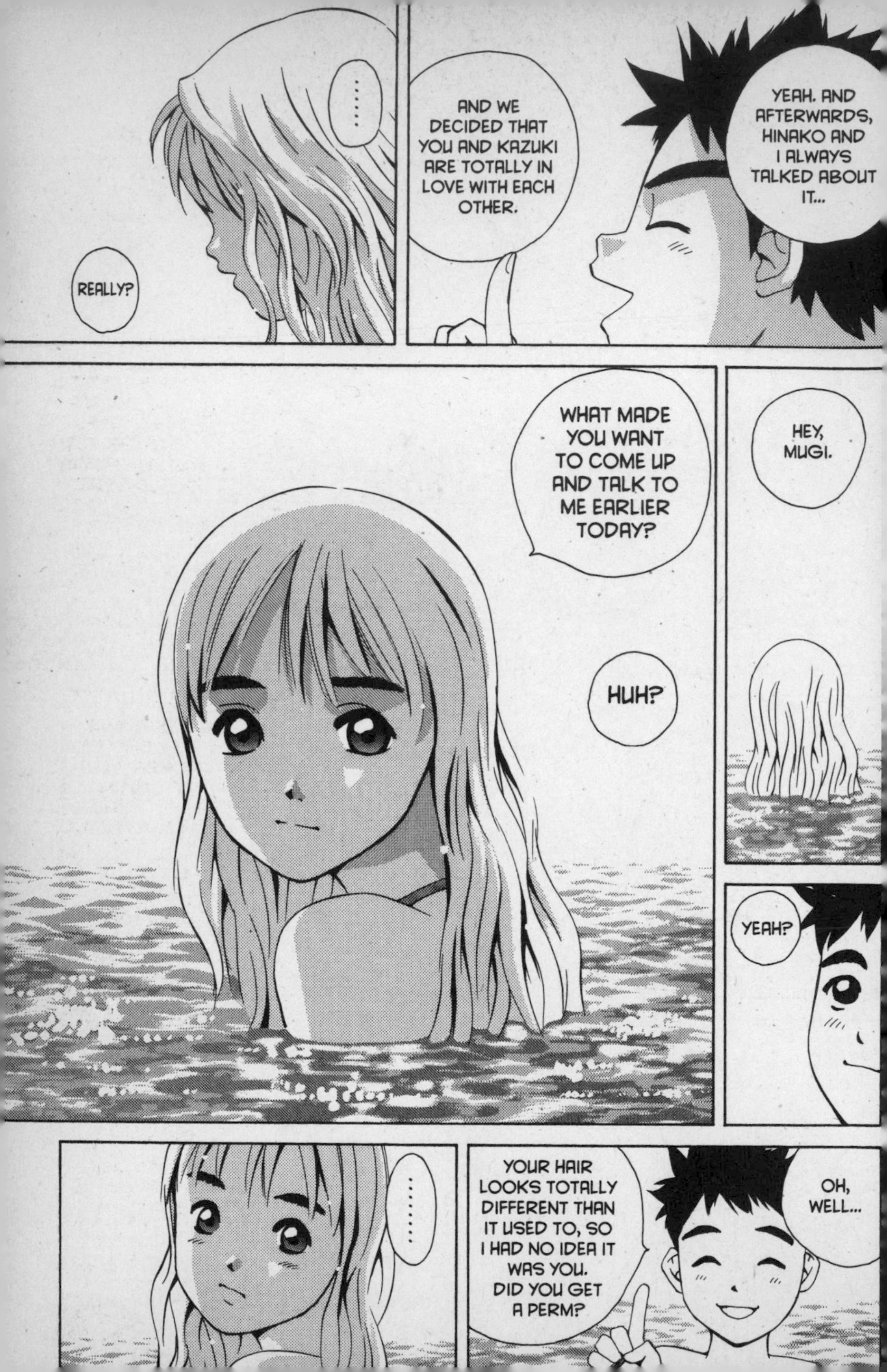
YEAH. AND AFTERWARDS, HINAKO AND I ALWAYS TALKED ABOUT IT...
AND WE DECIDED THAT YOU AND KAZUKI ARE TOTALLY IN LOVE WITH EACH OTHER.
......
REALLY?
HEY, MUGI.
YEAH?
WHAT MADE YOU WANT TO COME UP AND TALK TO ME EARLIER TODAY?
HUH?
OH, WELL...
YOUR HAIR LOOKS TOTALLY DIFFERENT THAN IT USED TO, SO I HAD NO IDEA IT WAS YOU. DID YOU GET A PERM?
......

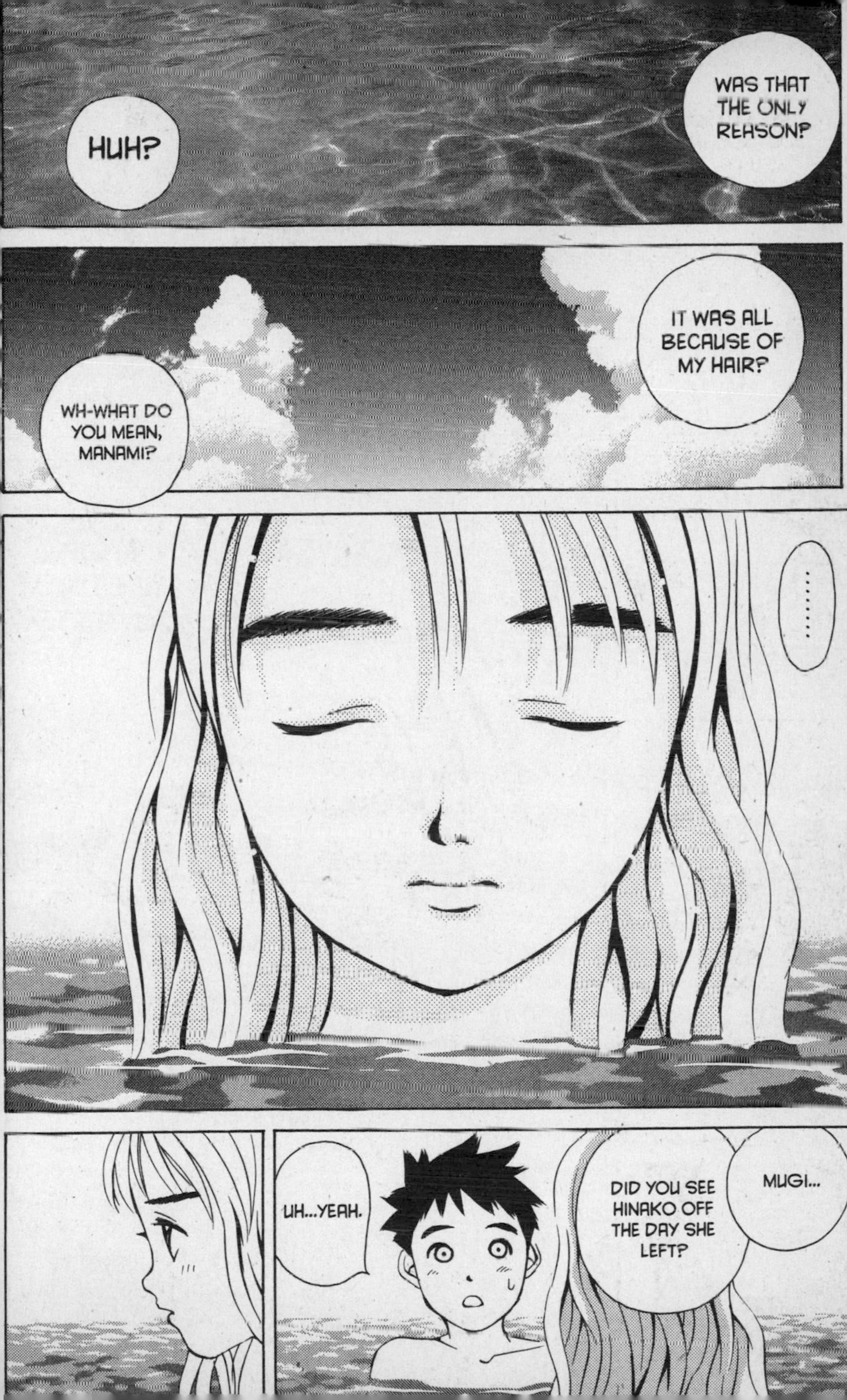
WAS THAT THE ONLY REASON?
HUH?
IT WAS ALL BECAUSE OF MY HAIR?
WH-WHAT DO YOU MEAN, MANAMI?
......
MUGI...
DID YOU SEE HINAKO OFF THE DAY SHE LEFT?
UH...YEAH.

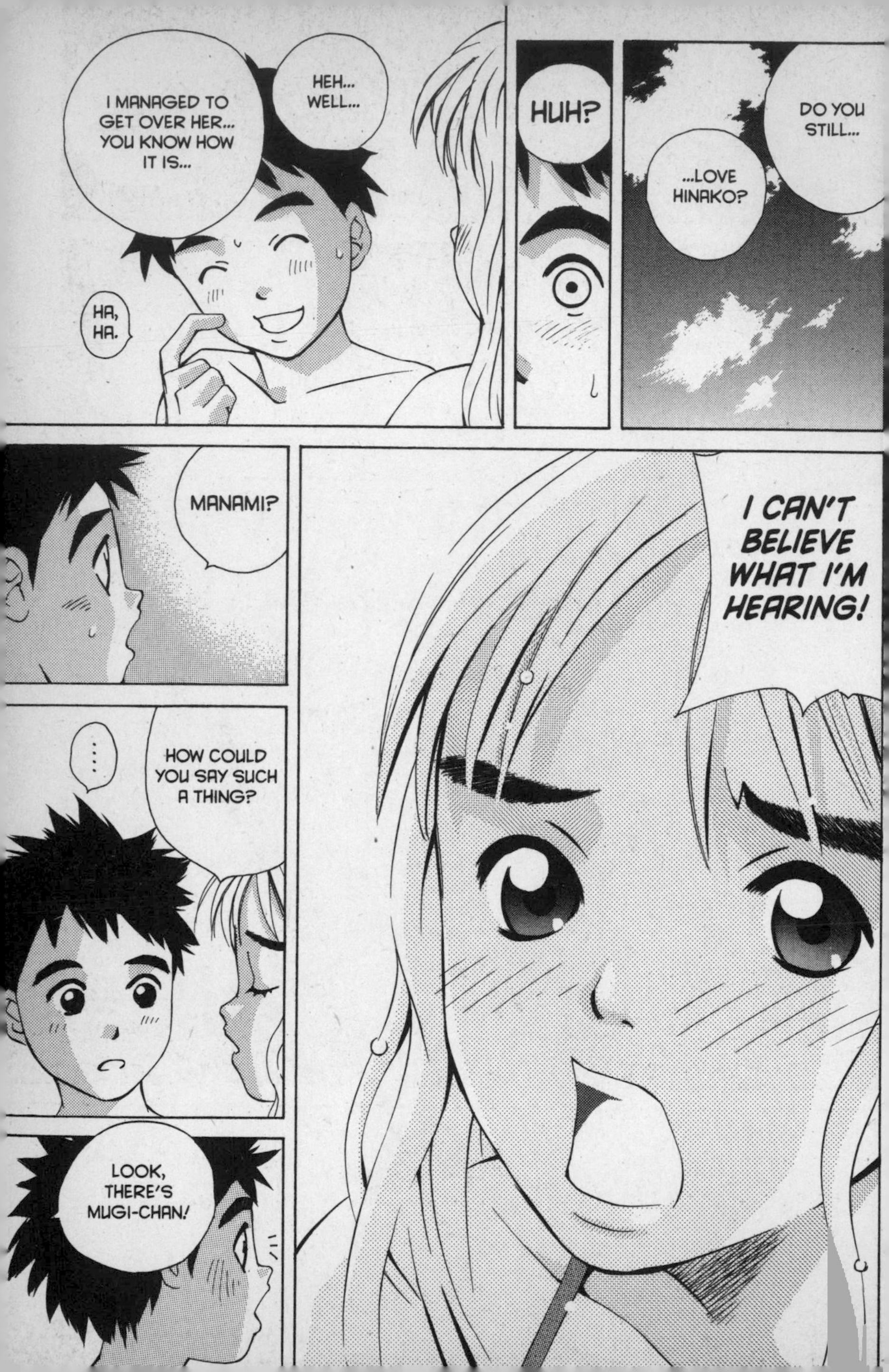
DO YOU STILL...
...LOVE HINAKO?
HUH?
HEH... WELL...
I MANAGED TO GET OVER HER... YOU KNOW HOW IT IS...
HA, HA.
I CAN'T BELIEVE WHAT I'M HEARING!
MANAMI?
HOW COULD YOU SAY SUCH A THING?
....
LOOK, THERE'S MUGI-CHAN!

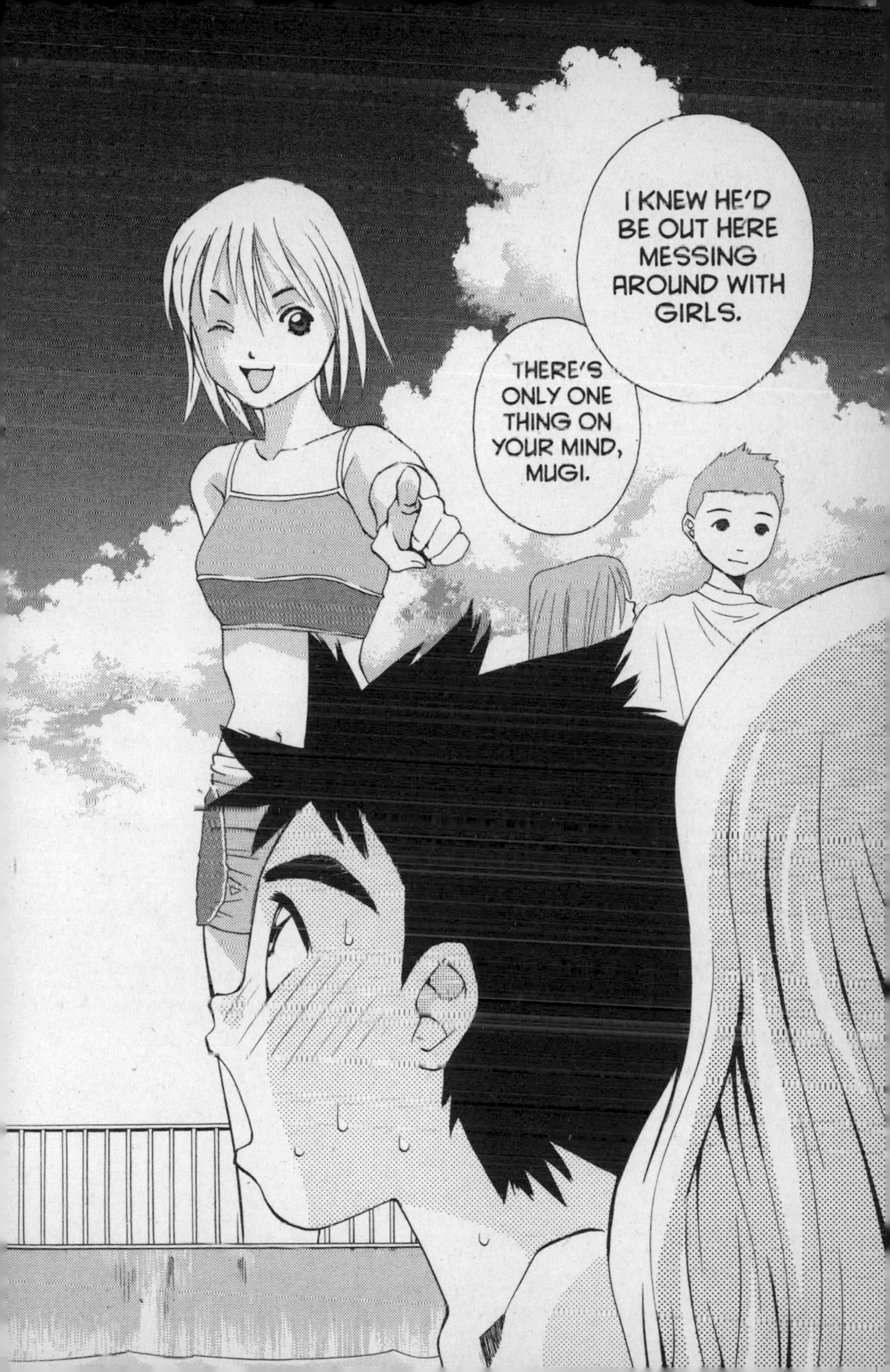
I KNEW HE'D BE OUT HERE MESSING AROUND WITH GIRLS.
THERE'S ONLY ONE THING ON YOUR MIND, MUGI.

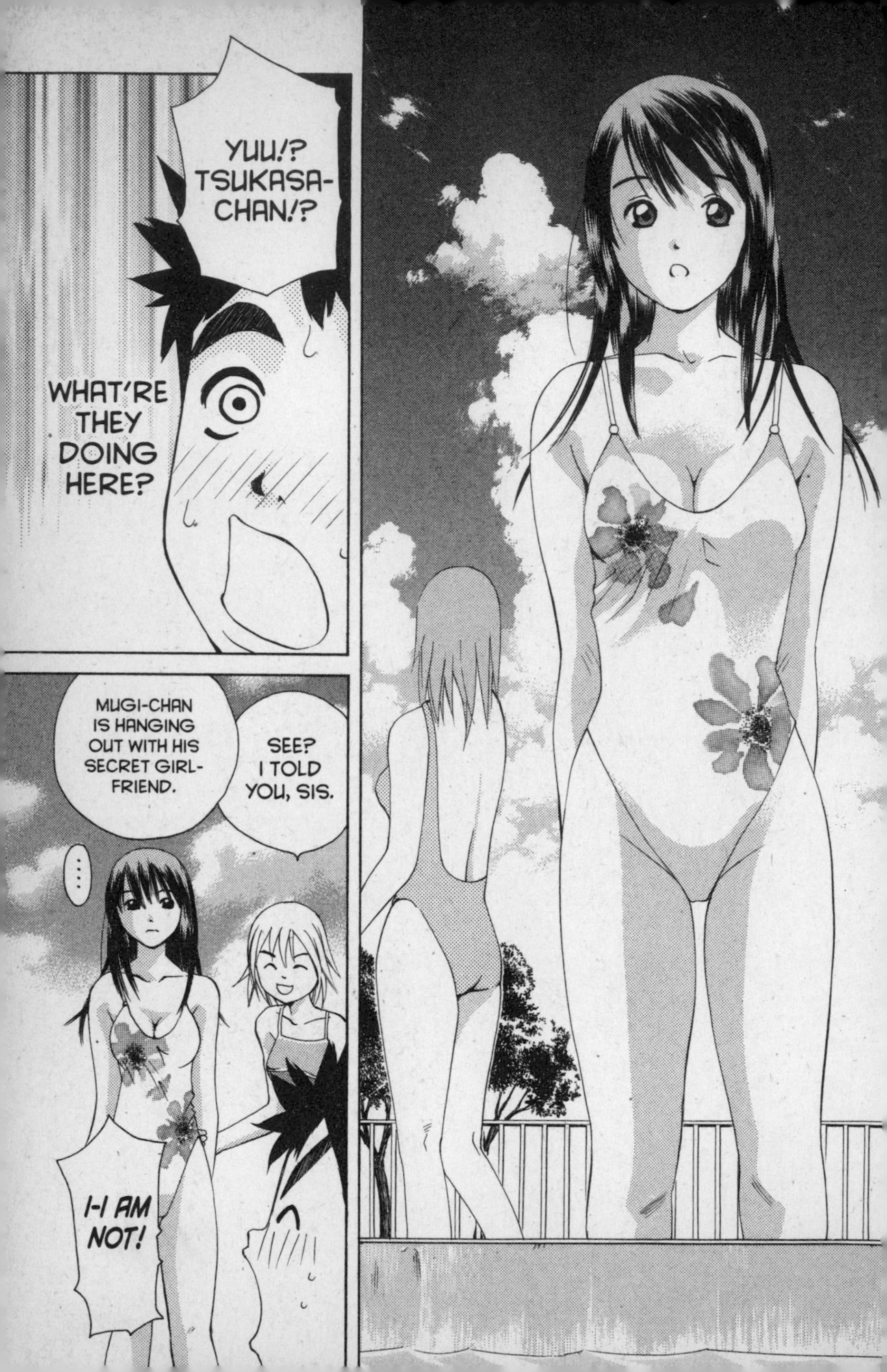
YUU!? TSUKASA-CHAN!?
WHAT'RE THEY DOING HERE?
SEE? I TOLD YOU, SIS.
MUGI-CHAN IS HANGING OUT WITH HIS SECRET GIRL-FRIEND.
....
I-I AM NOT!

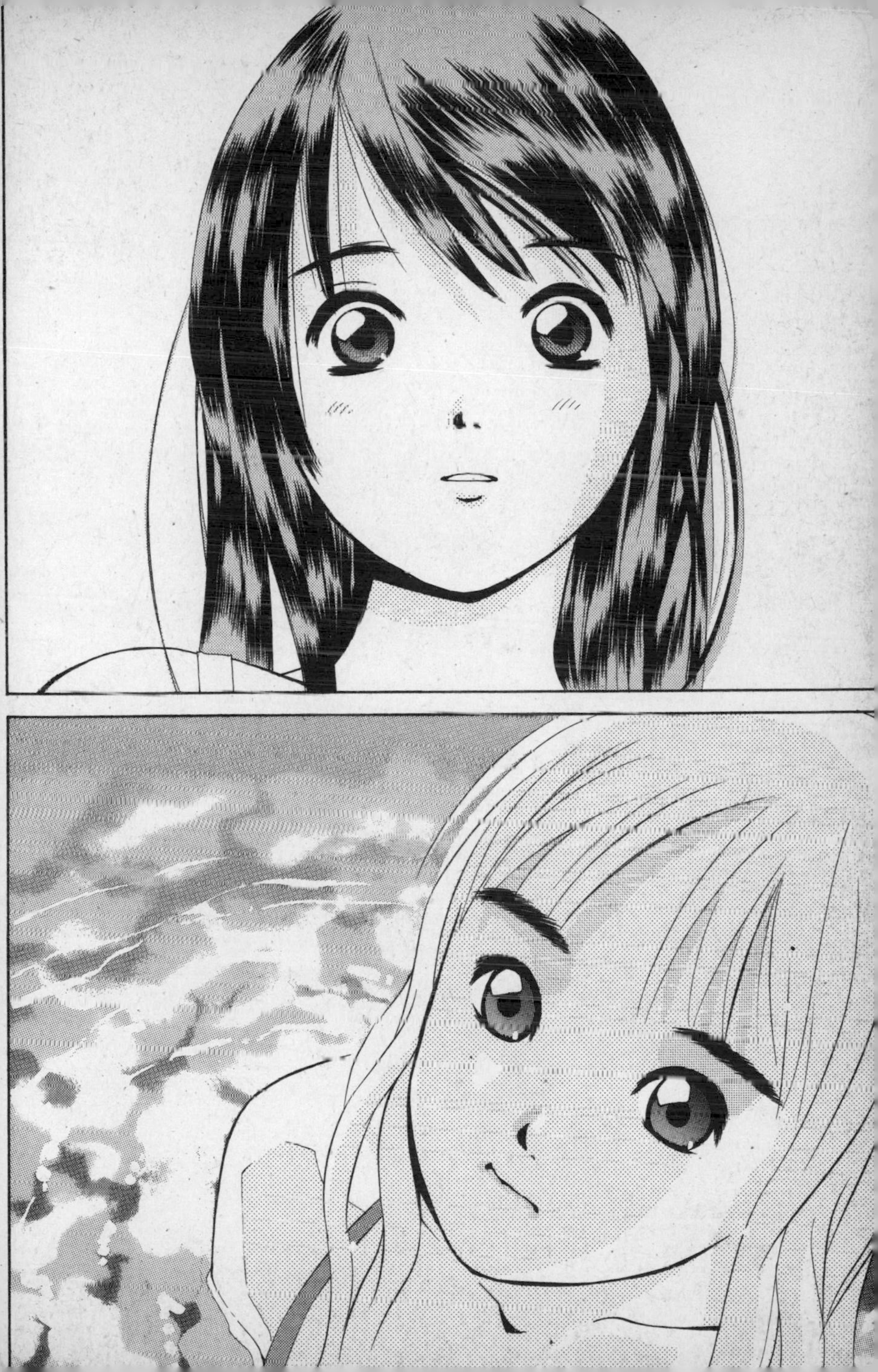

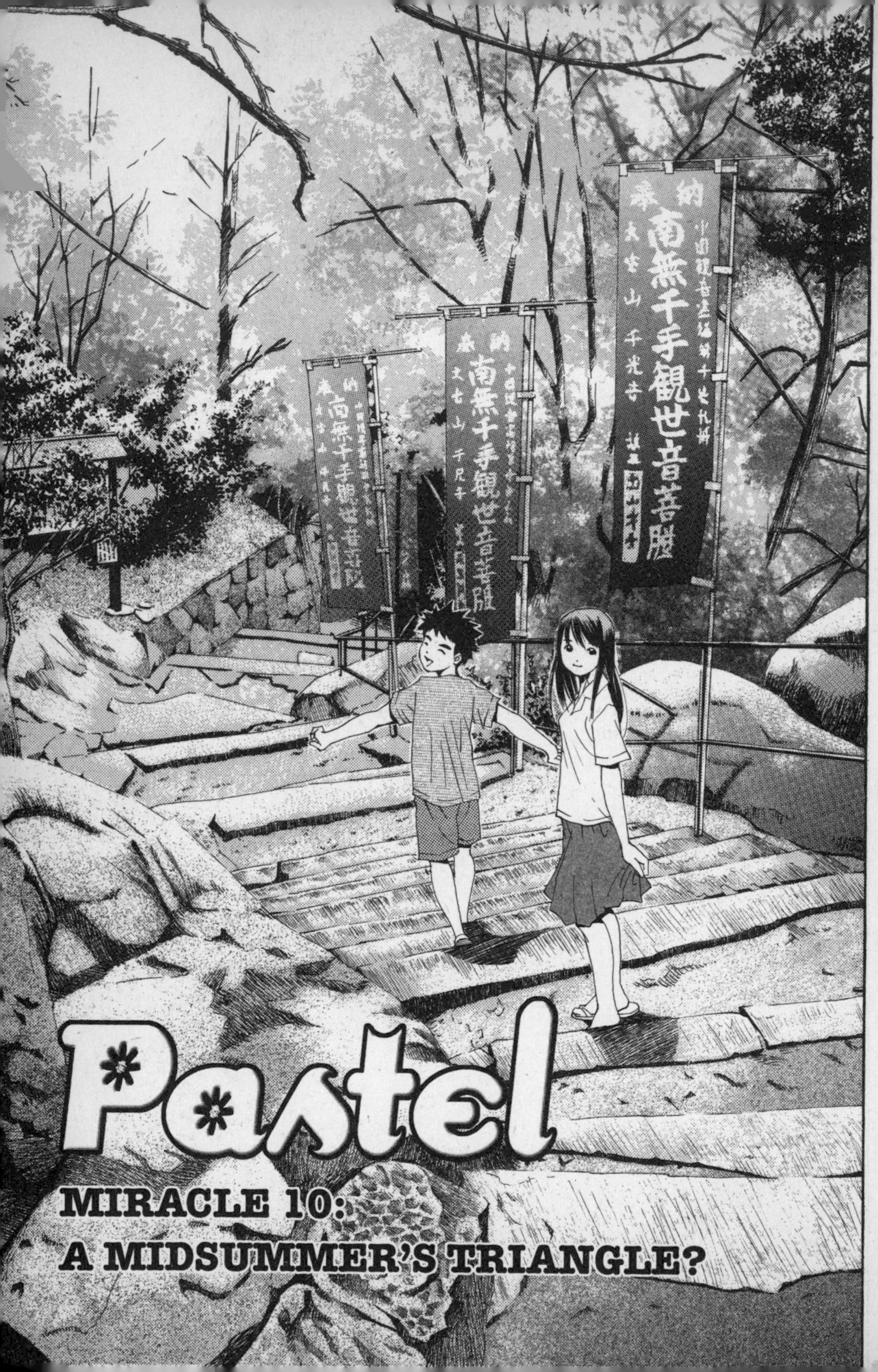
南無千手観世音菩薩
Pastel
MIRACLE 10:
A MIDSUMMER'S TRIANGLE?

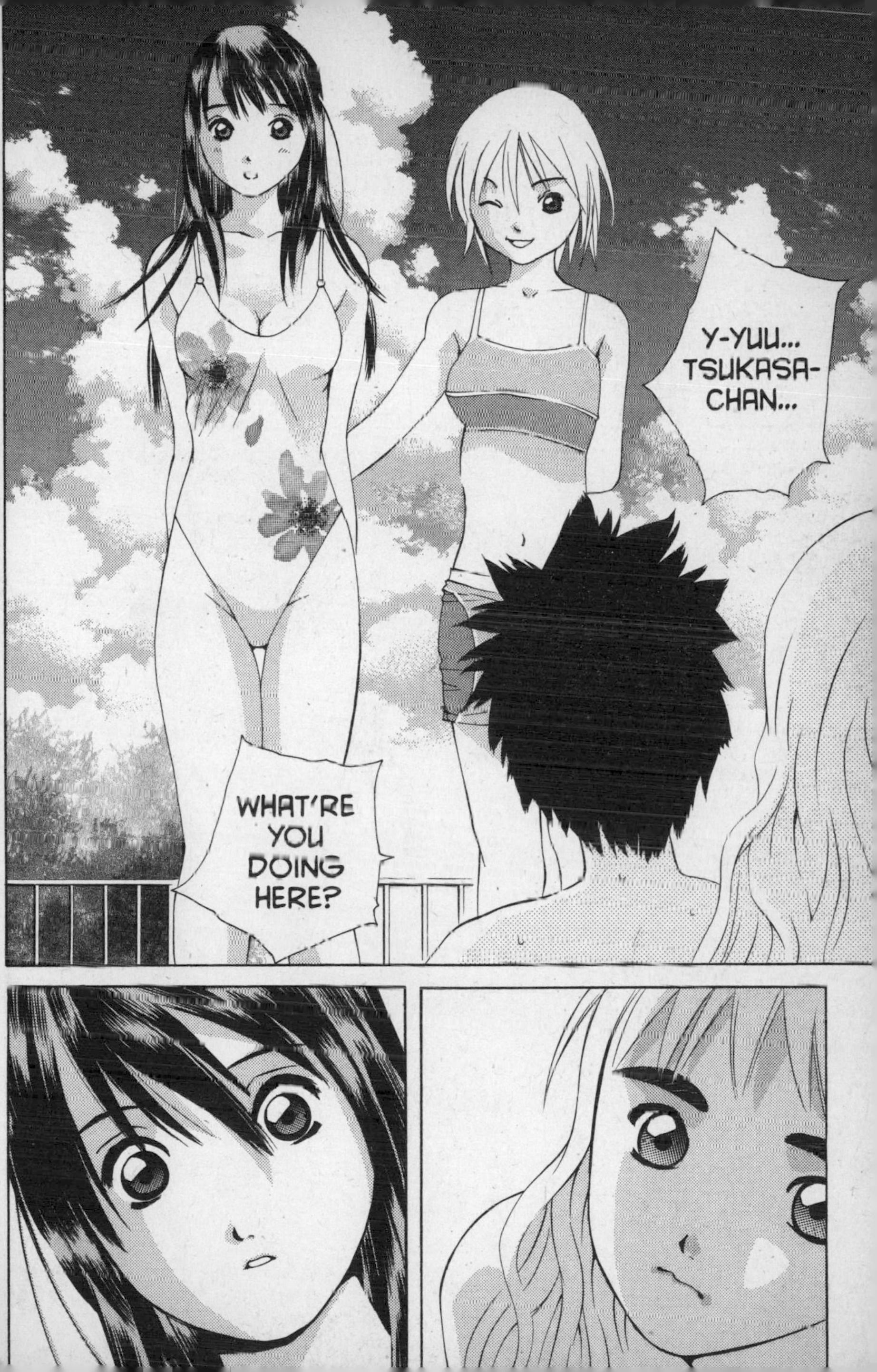
Y-YUU... TSUKASA-CHAN...
WHAT'RE YOU DOING HERE?

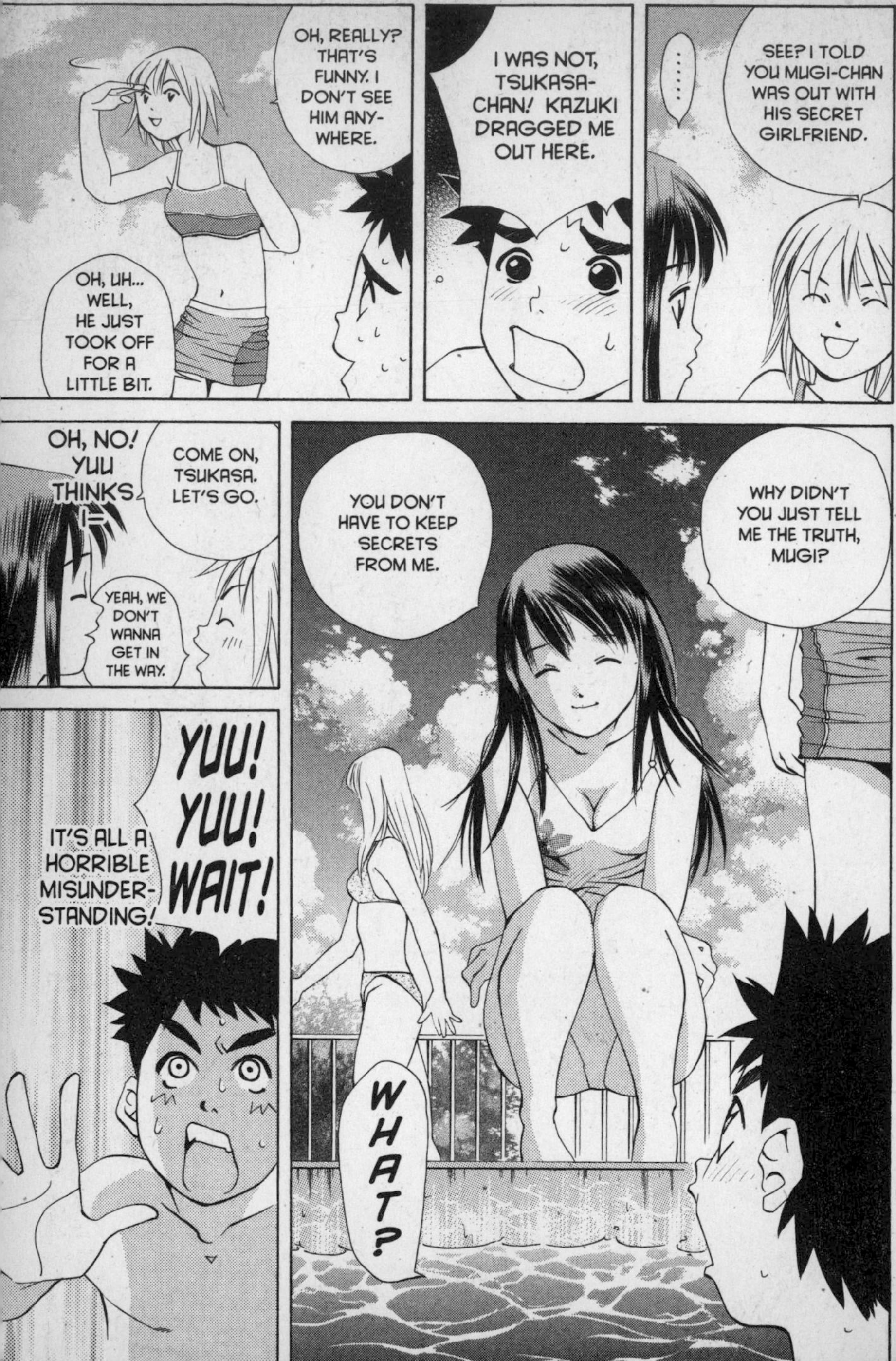
SEE? I TOLD YOU MUGI-CHAN WAS OUT WITH HIS SECRET GIRLFRIEND.
......
I WAS NOT, TSUKASA-CHAN! KAZUKI DRAGGED ME OUT HERE.
OH, REALLY? THAT'S FUNNY. I DON'T SEE HIM ANYWHERE.
OH, UH... WELL, HE JUST TOOK OFF FOR A LITTLE BIT.
WHY DIDN'T YOU JUST TELL ME THE TRUTH, MUGI?
YOU DON'T HAVE TO KEEP SECRETS FROM ME.
WHAT?
COME ON, TSUKASA. LET'S GO.
OH, NO! YUU THINKS I—
YEAH, WE DON'T WANNA GET IN THE WAY.
YUU! YUU! WAIT!
IT'S ALL A HORRIBLE MISUNDERSTANDING!

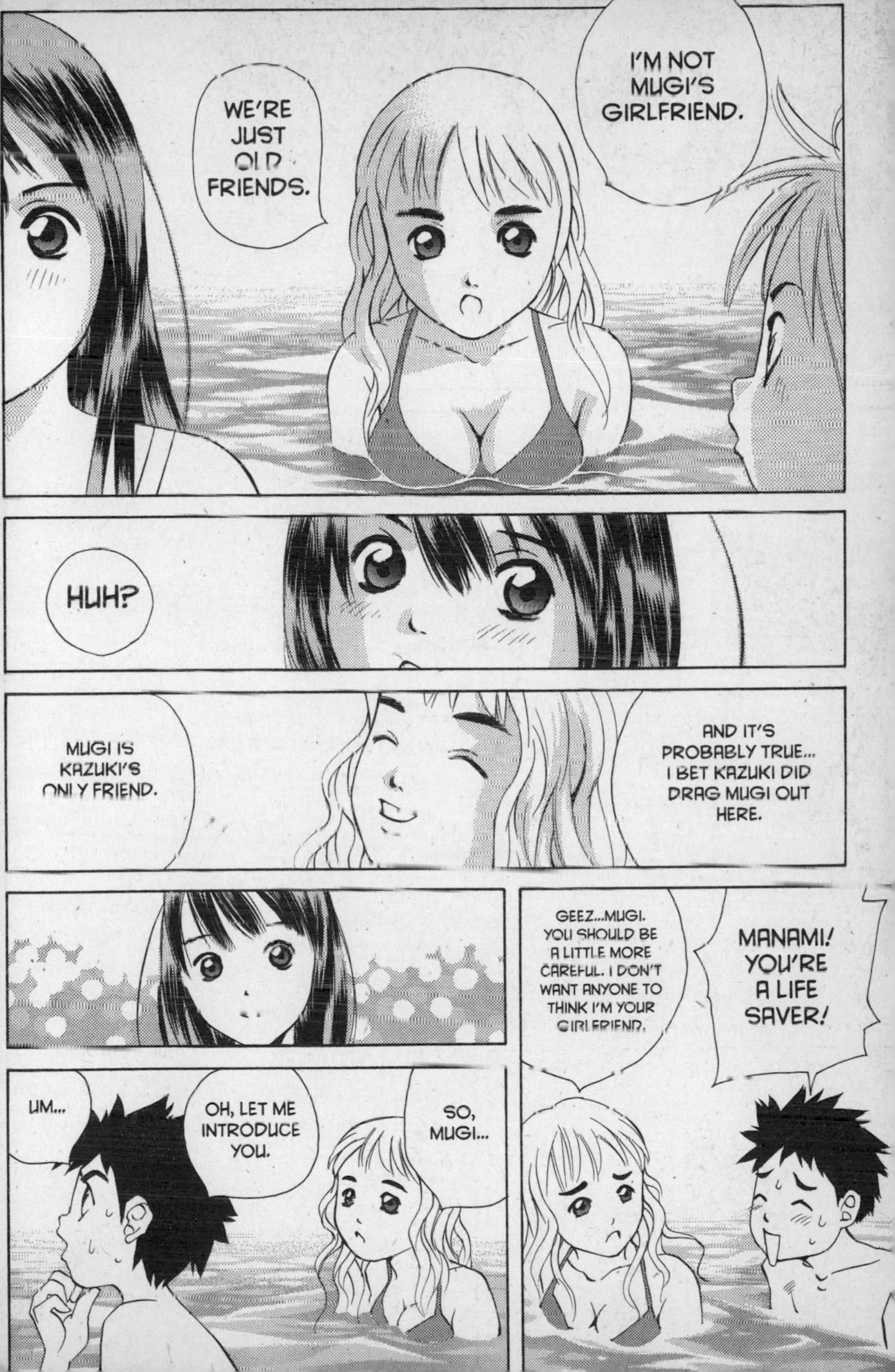
I'M NOT MUGI'S GIRLFRIEND.
WE'RE JUST OLD FRIENDS.
HUH?
AND IT'S PROBABLY TRUE... I BET KAZUKI DID DRAG MUGI OUT HERE.
MUGI IS KAZUKI'S ONLY FRIEND.
MANAMI! YOU'RE A LIFE SAVER!
GEEZ...MUGI. YOU SHOULD BE A LITTLE MORE CAREFUL. I DON'T WANT ANYONE TO THINK I'M YOUR GIRLFRIEND.
SO, MUGI...
OH, LET ME INTRODUCE YOU.
UM...

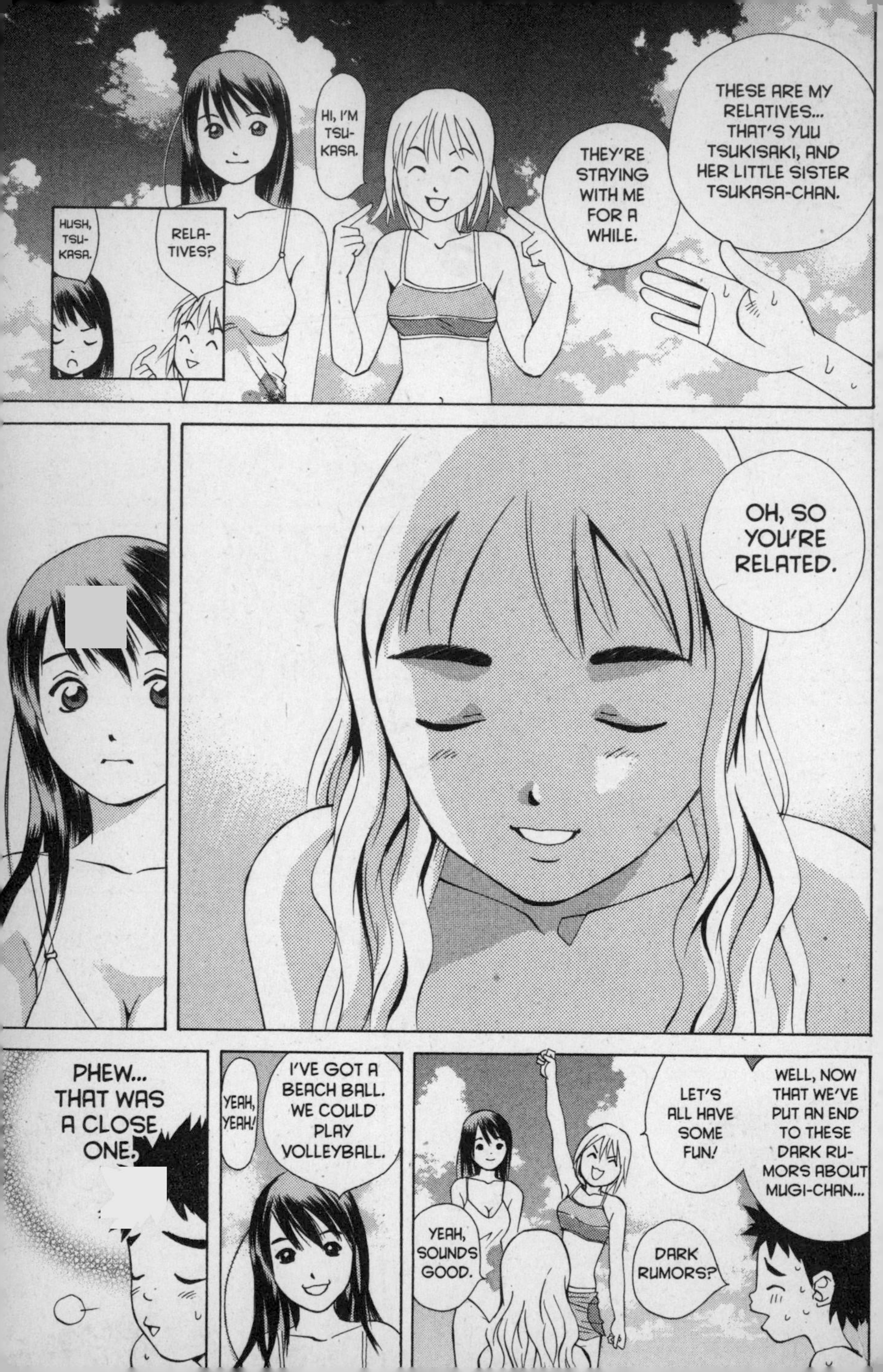
THESE ARE MY RELATIVES... THAT'S YUU TSUKISAKI, AND HER LITTLE SISTER TSUKASA-CHAN.
THEY'RE STAYING WITH ME FOR A WHILE.
HI, I'M TSU-KASA.
RELA-TIVES?
HUSH, TSU-KASA.
OH, SO YOU'RE RELATED.
WELL, NOW THAT WE'VE PUT AN END TO THESE DARK RU-MORS ABOUT MUGI-CHAN...
LET'S ALL HAVE SOME FUN!
DARK RUMORS?
YEAH, SOUNDS GOOD.
I'VE GOT A BEACH BALL. WE COULD PLAY VOLLEYBALL.
YEAH, YEAH!
PHEW... THAT WAS A CLOSE ONE.

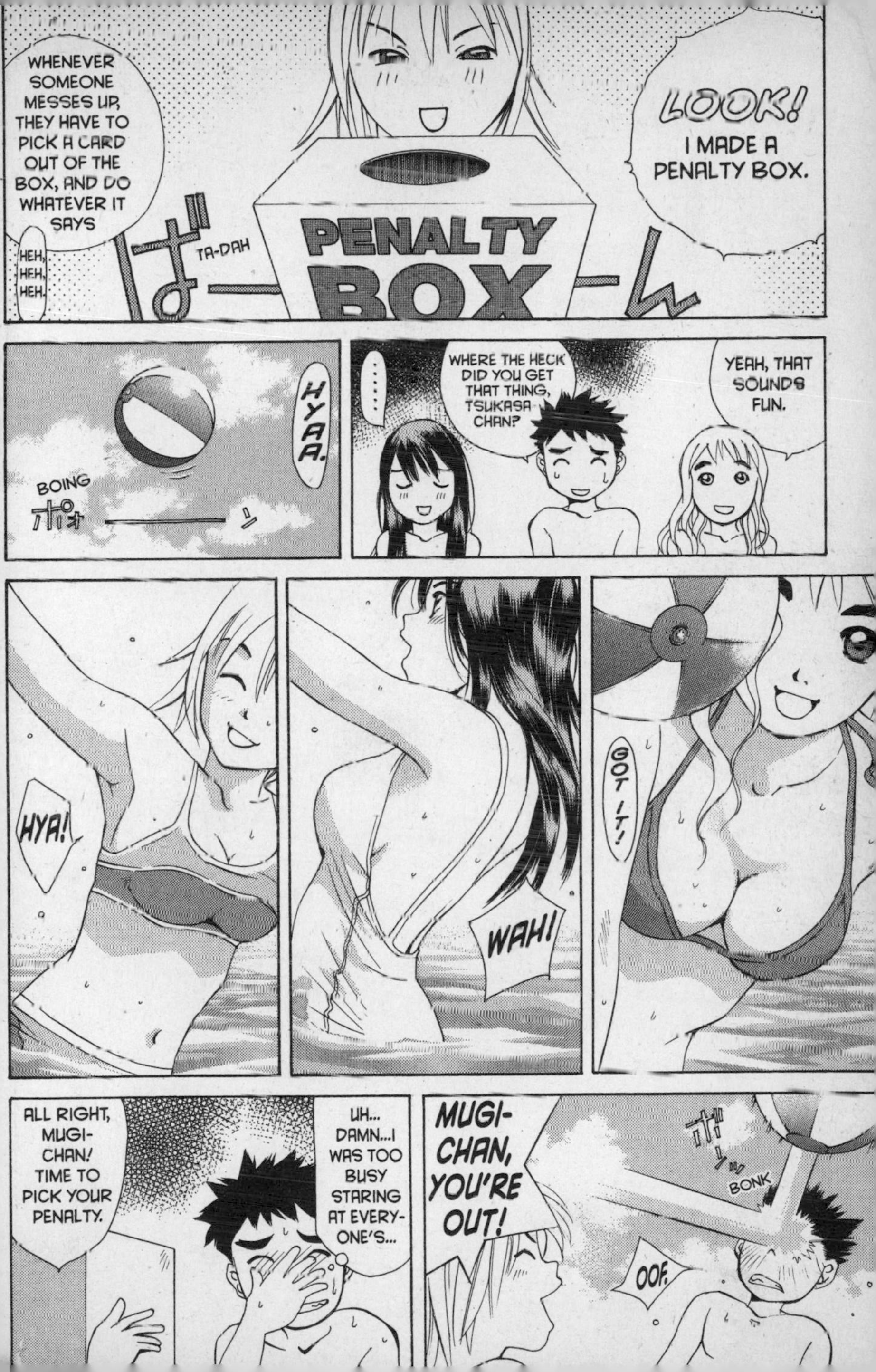
LOOK! I MADE A PENALTY BOX.
WHENEVER SOMEONE MESSES UP, THEY HAVE TO PICK A CARD OUT OF THE BOX, AND DO WHATEVER IT SAYS
PENALTY BOX
TA-DAH
HEH, HEH, HEH.
YEAH, THAT SOUNDS FUN.
WHERE THE HECK DID YOU GET THAT THING, TSUKASA-CHAN?
......
HYAA.
BOING
GOT IT!
WAH!
HYA!
MUGI-CHAN, YOU'RE OUT!
BONK
OOF.
UH... DAMN...I WAS TOO BUSY STARING AT EVERY-ONE'S...
ALL RIGHT, MUGI-CHAN! TIME TO PICK YOUR PENALTY.

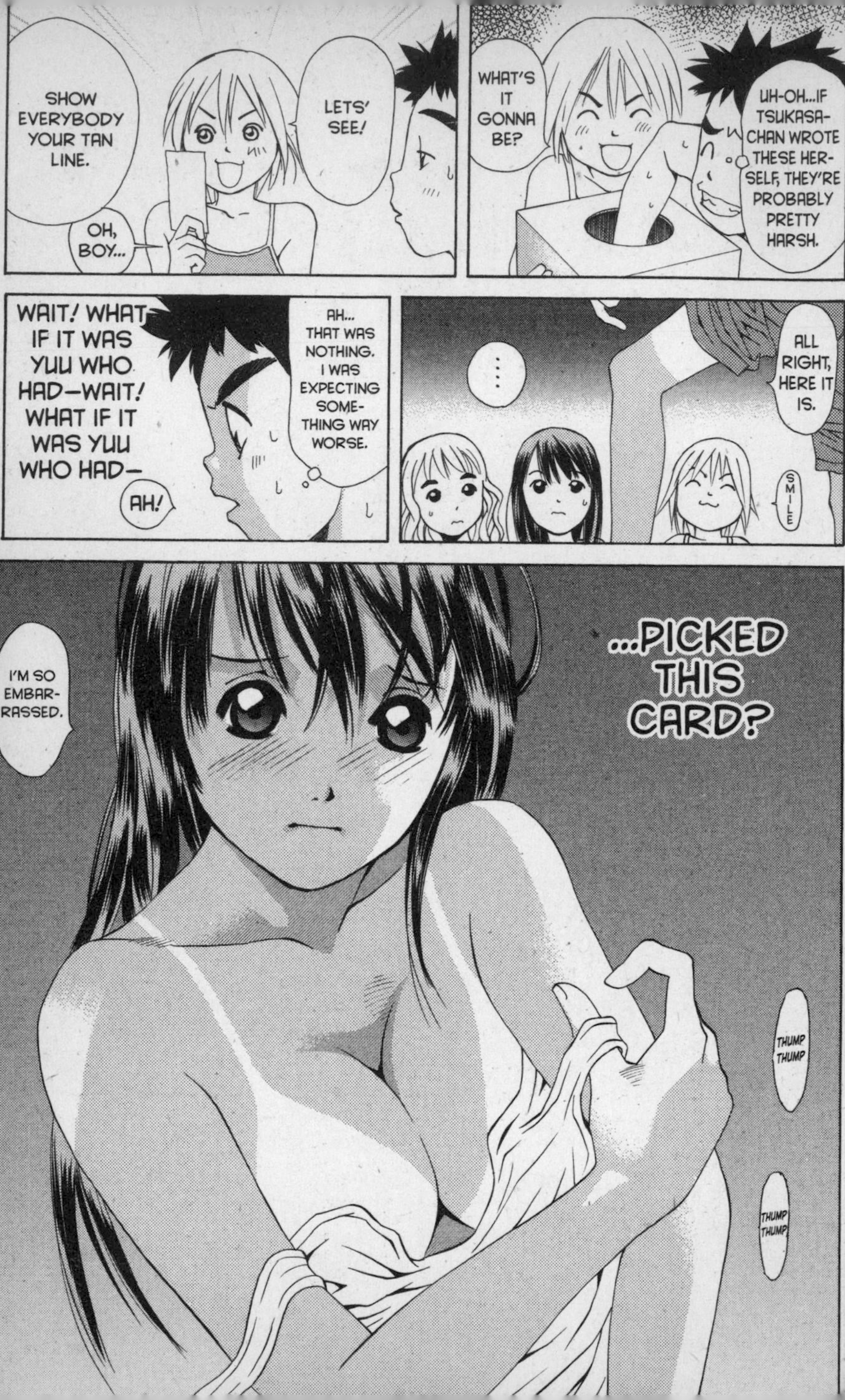
UH-OH...IF TSUKASA-CHAN WROTE THESE HERSELF, THEY'RE PROBABLY PRETTY HARSH.
WHAT'S IT GONNA BE?
LETS' SEE!
SHOW EVERYBODY YOUR TAN LINE.
OH, BOY...
ALL RIGHT, HERE IT IS.
....
SMILE
AH... THAT WAS NOTHING. I WAS EXPECTING SOMETHING WAY WORSE.
WAIT! WHAT IF IT WAS YUU WHO HAD—WAIT! WHAT IF IT WAS YUU WHO HAD—
AH!
...PICKED THIS CARD?
I'M SO EMBARRASSED.
THUMP THUMP
THUMP THUMP

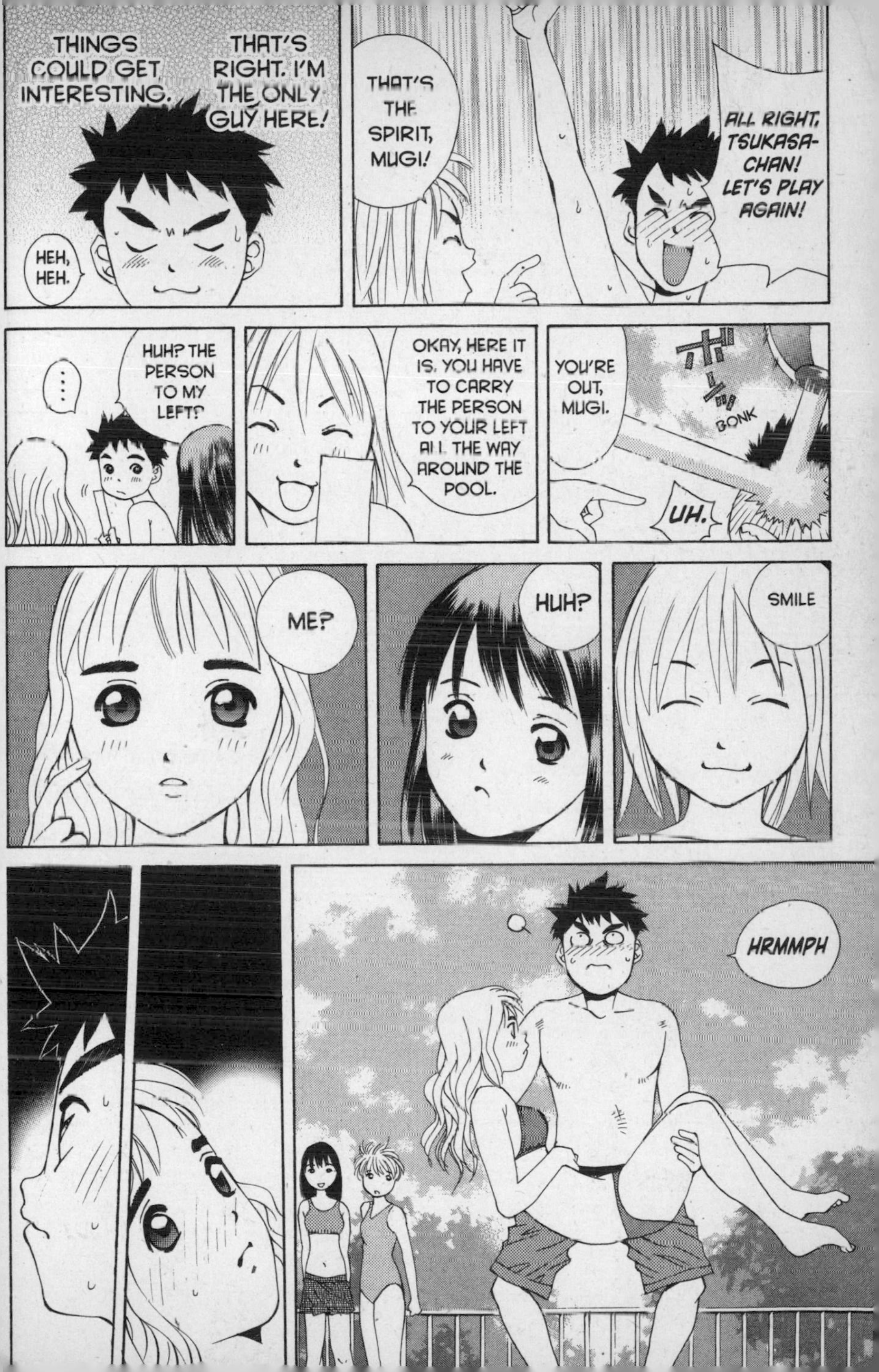
ALL RIGHT, TSUKASA-CHAN! LET'S PLAY AGAIN!
THAT'S THE SPIRIT, MUGI!
THAT'S RIGHT. I'M THE ONLY GUY HERE!
THINGS COULD GET INTERESTING.
HEH, HEH.
BONK
YOU'RE OUT, MUGI.
UH.
OKAY, HERE IT IS. YOU HAVE TO CARRY THE PERSON TO YOUR LEFT ALL THE WAY AROUND THE POOL.
HUH? THE PERSON TO MY LEFT?
....
SMILE
HUH?
ME?
HRMMPH

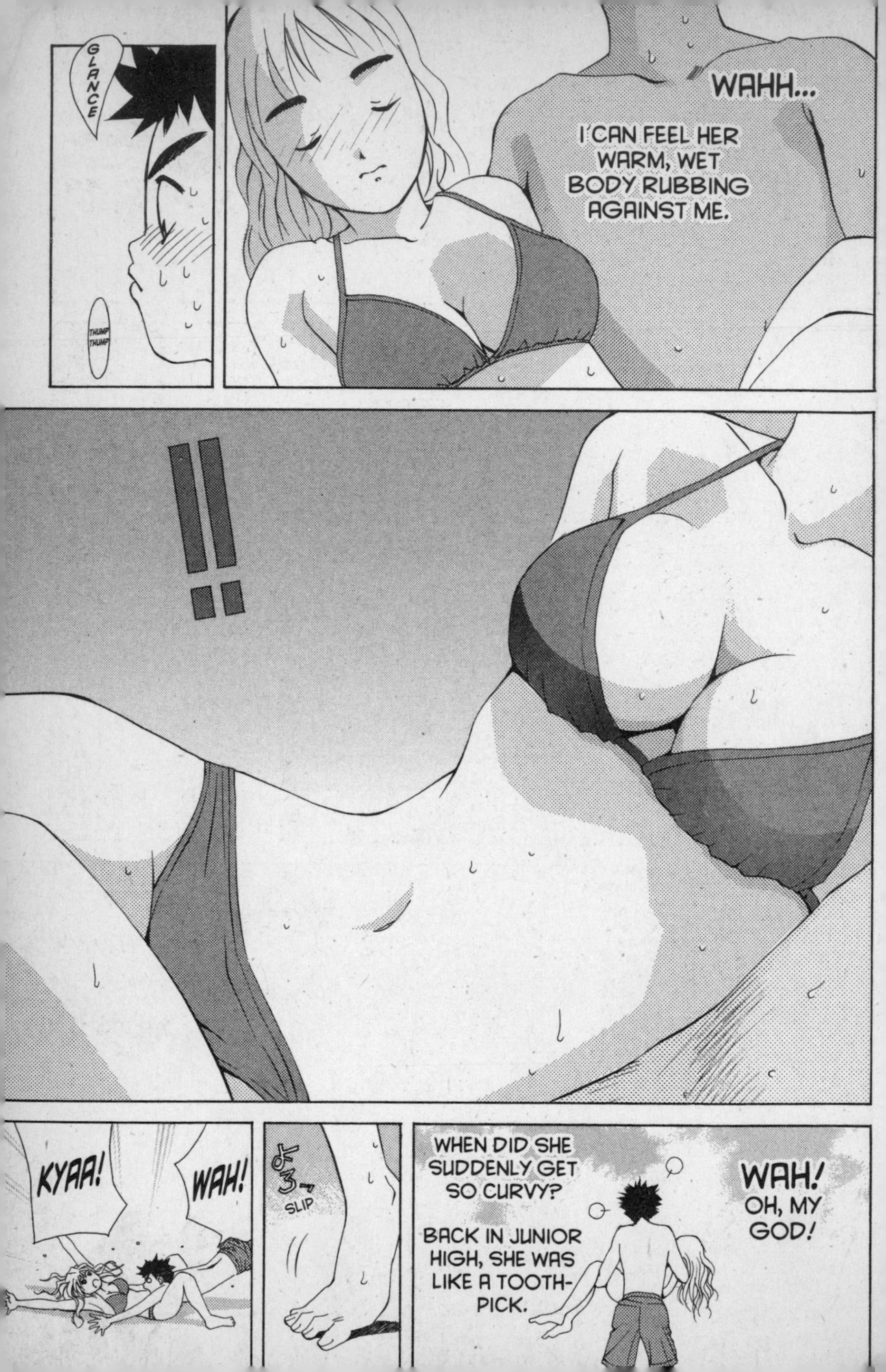
WAHH...
I CAN FEEL HER WARM, WET BODY RUBBING AGAINST ME.
GLANCE
THUMP THUMP
!!
WAH! OH, MY GOD!
WHEN DID SHE SUDDENLY GET SO CURVY?
BACK IN JUNIOR HIGH, SHE WAS LIKE A TOOTH-PICK.
SLIP
WAH!
KYAA!

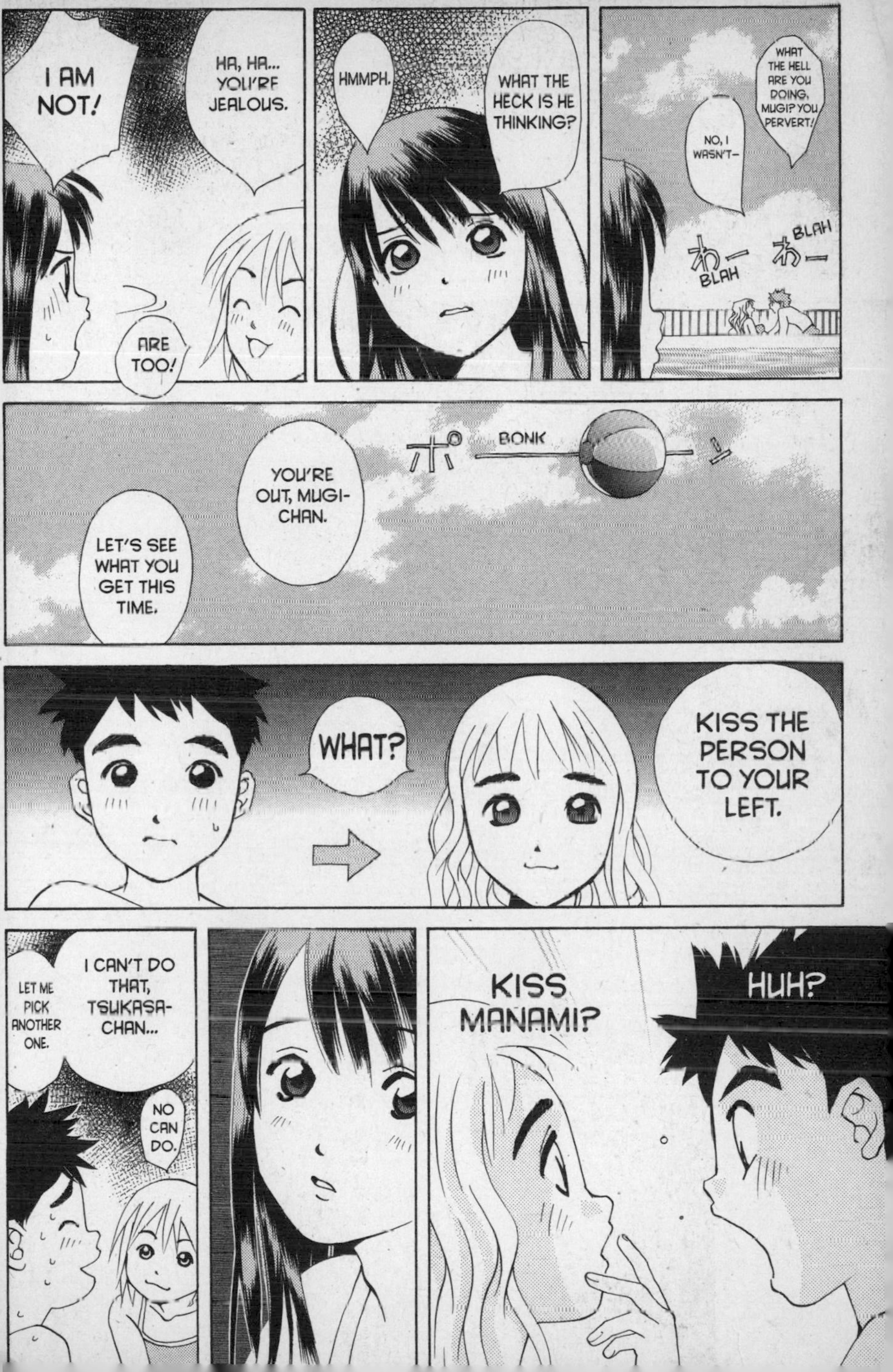
WHAT THE HELL ARE YOU DOING, MUGI? YOU PERVERT!
NO, I WASN'T—
わー BLAH
わー BLAH
WHAT THE HECK IS HE THINKING?
HMMPH.
HA, HA... YOU'RE JEALOUS.
I AM NOT!
ARE TOO!
ポ BONK
YOU'RE OUT, MUGI-CHAN.
LET'S SEE WHAT YOU GET THIS TIME.
KISS THE PERSON TO YOUR LEFT.
WHAT?
HUH?
KISS MANAMI?
I CAN'T DO THAT, TSUKASA-CHAN...
LET ME PICK ANOTHER ONE.
NO CAN DO.

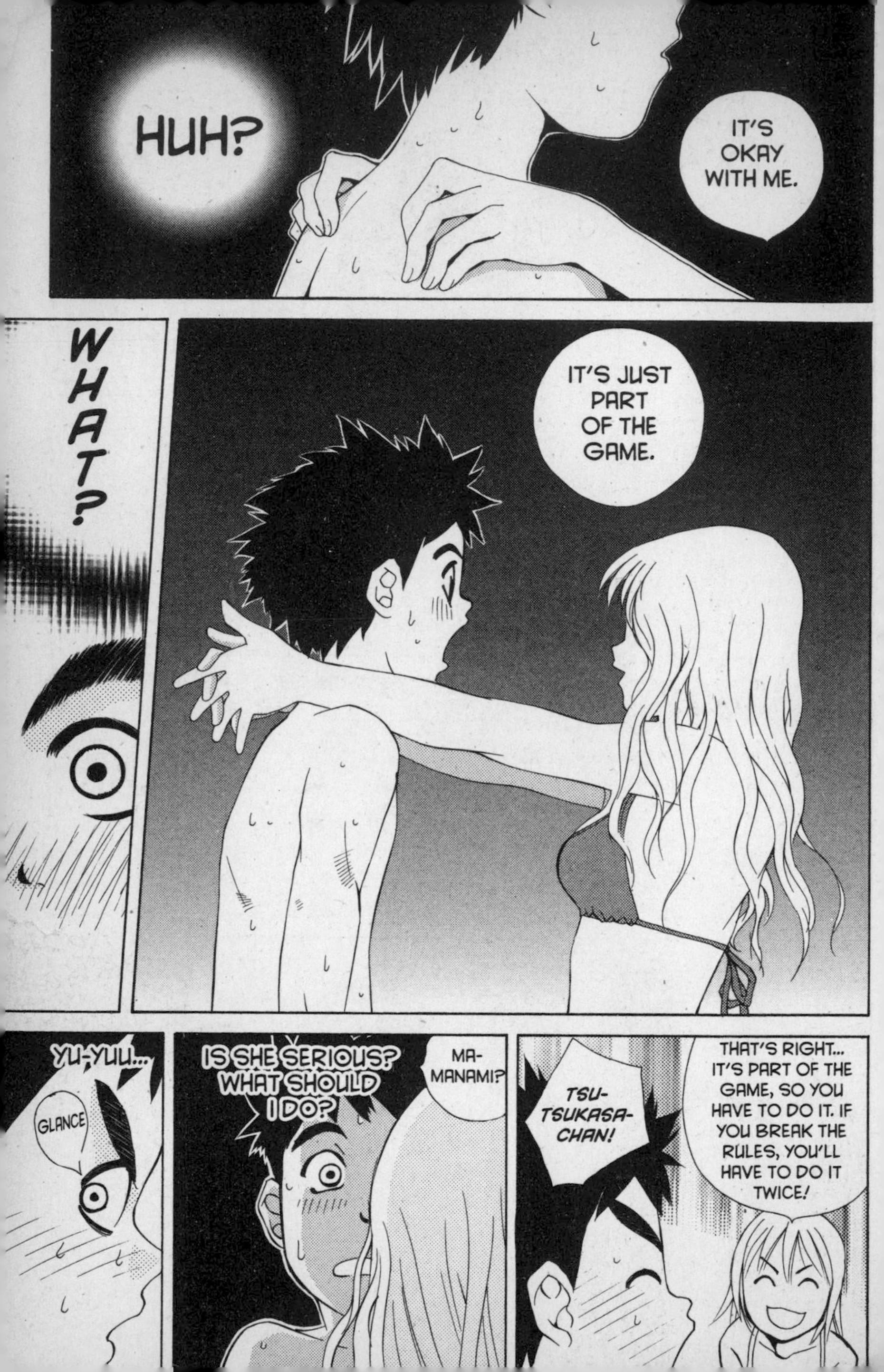
IT'S OKAY WITH ME.
HUH?
IT'S JUST PART OF THE GAME.
WHAT?
THAT'S RIGHT... IT'S PART OF THE GAME, SO YOU HAVE TO DO IT. IF YOU BREAK THE RULES, YOU'LL HAVE TO DO IT TWICE!
TSU-TSUKASA-CHAN!
MA-MANAMI?
IS SHE SERIOUS? WHAT SHOULD I DO?
YU-YUU...
GLANCE

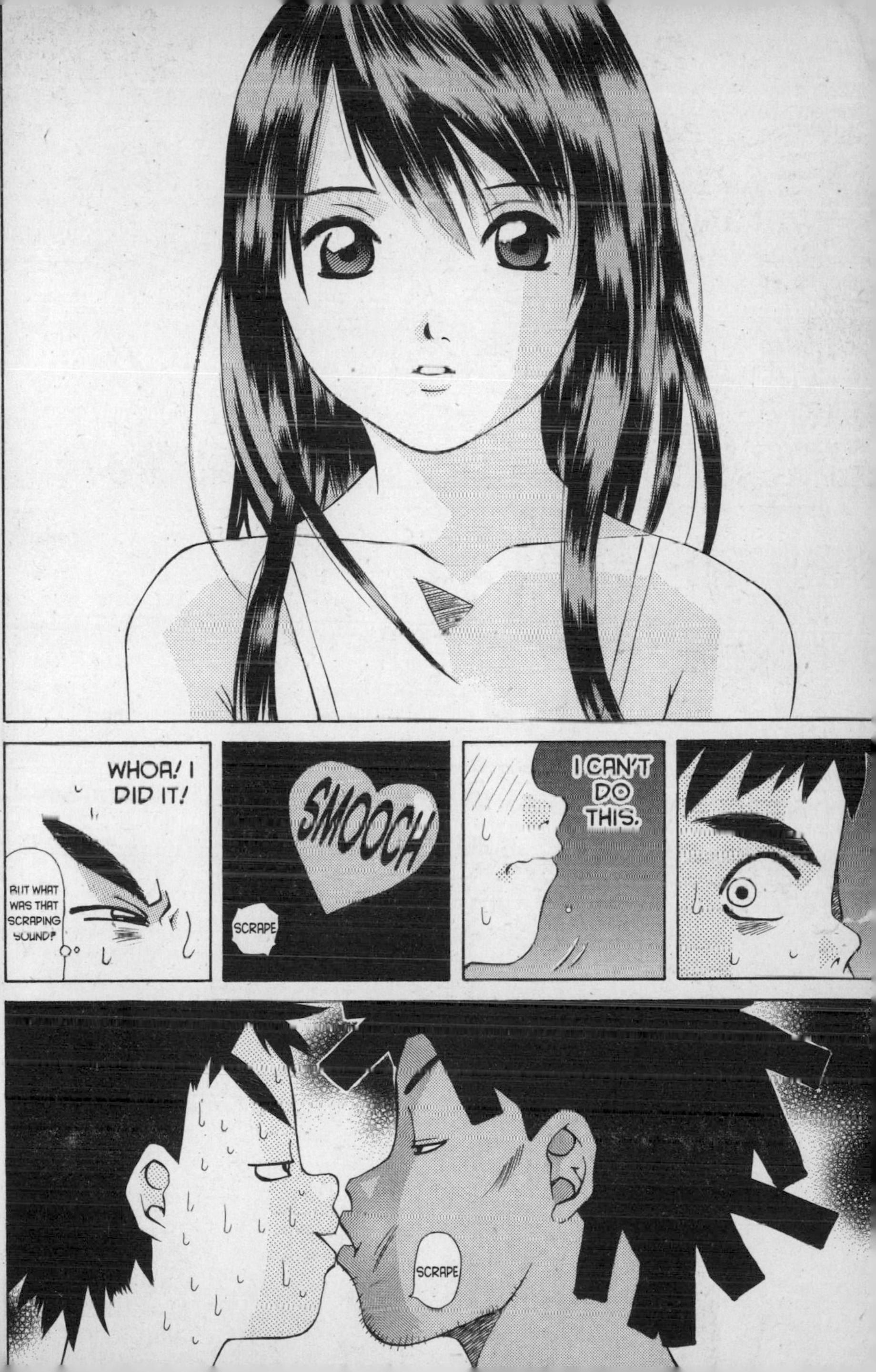
I CAN'T DO THIS.
SMOOCH
SCRAPE
WHOA! I DID IT!
BUT WHAT WAS THAT SCRAPING SOUND?
SCRAPE

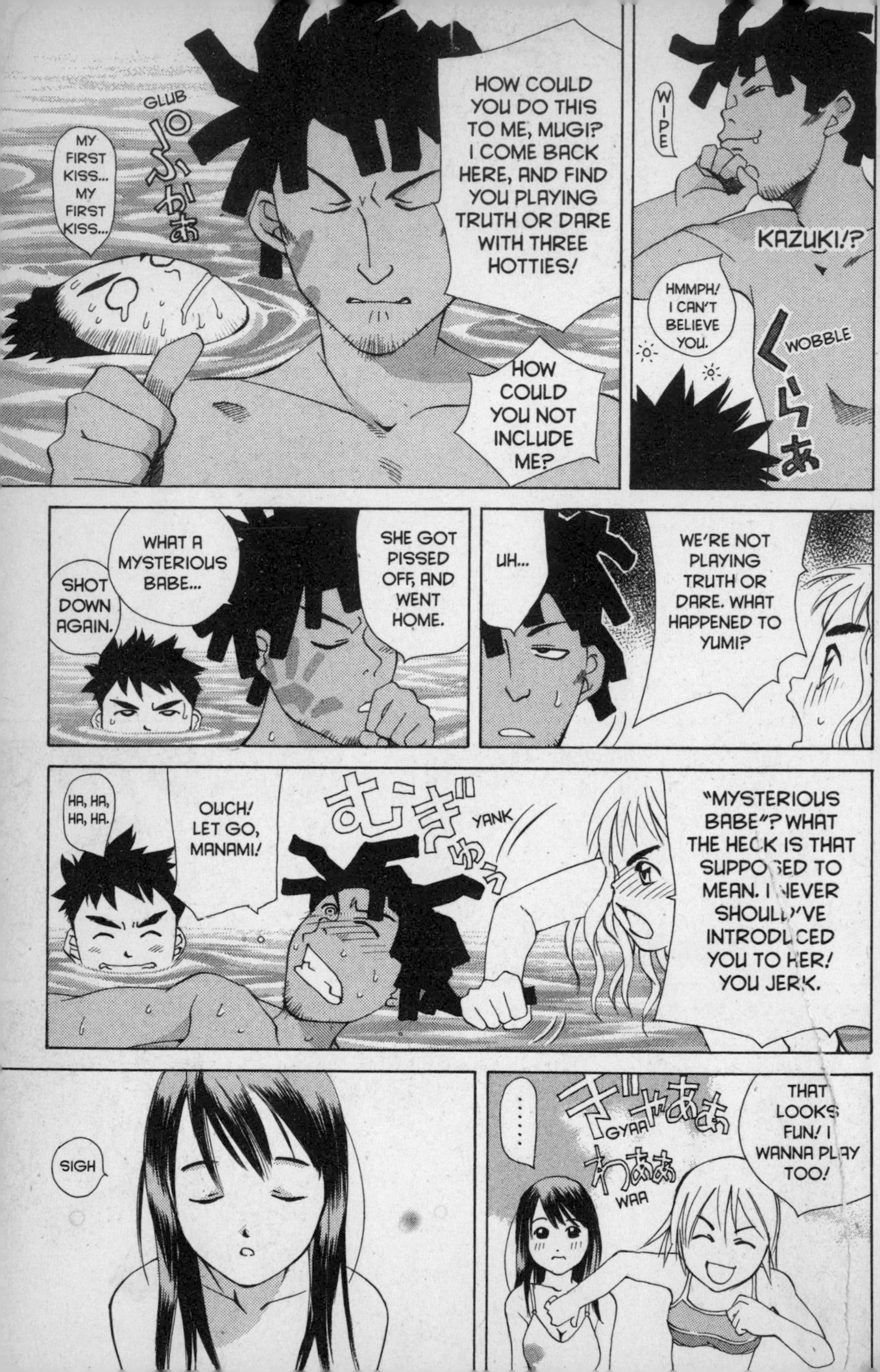
WIPE
KAZUKI!?
HMMPH! I CAN'T BELIEVE YOU.
WOBBLE
HOW COULD YOU DO THIS TO ME, MUGI? I COME BACK HERE, AND FIND YOU PLAYING TRUTH OR DARE WITH THREE HOTTIES!
HOW COULD YOU NOT INCLUDE ME?
GLUB
MY FIRST KISS... MY FIRST KISS...
WE'RE NOT PLAYING TRUTH OR DARE. WHAT HAPPENED TO YUMI?
UH...
SHE GOT PISSED OFF, AND WENT HOME.
WHAT A MYSTERIOUS BABE...
SHOT DOWN AGAIN.
"MYSTERIOUS BABE"? WHAT THE HECK IS THAT SUPPOSED TO MEAN. I NEVER SHOULD'VE INTRODUCED YOU TO HER! YOU JERK.
YANK
OUCH! LET GO, MANAMI!
HA, HA, HA, HA.
THAT LOOKS FUN! I WANNA PLAY TOO!
GYAA
WAA
......
SIGH

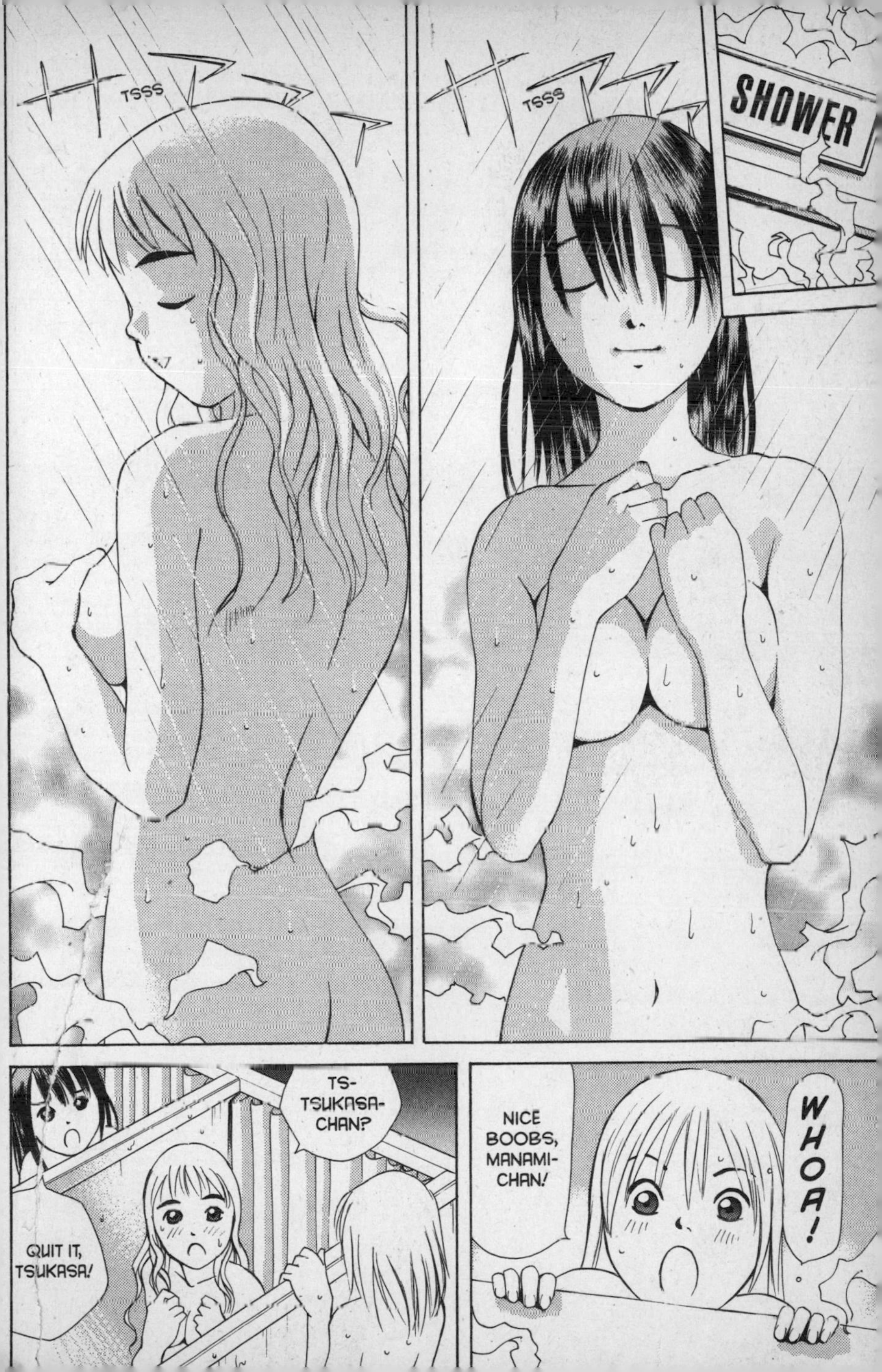
SHOWER
TSSS
TSSS
WHOA!
NICE BOOBS, MANAMI-CHAN!
TS-TSUKASA-CHAN?
QUIT IT, TSUKASA!

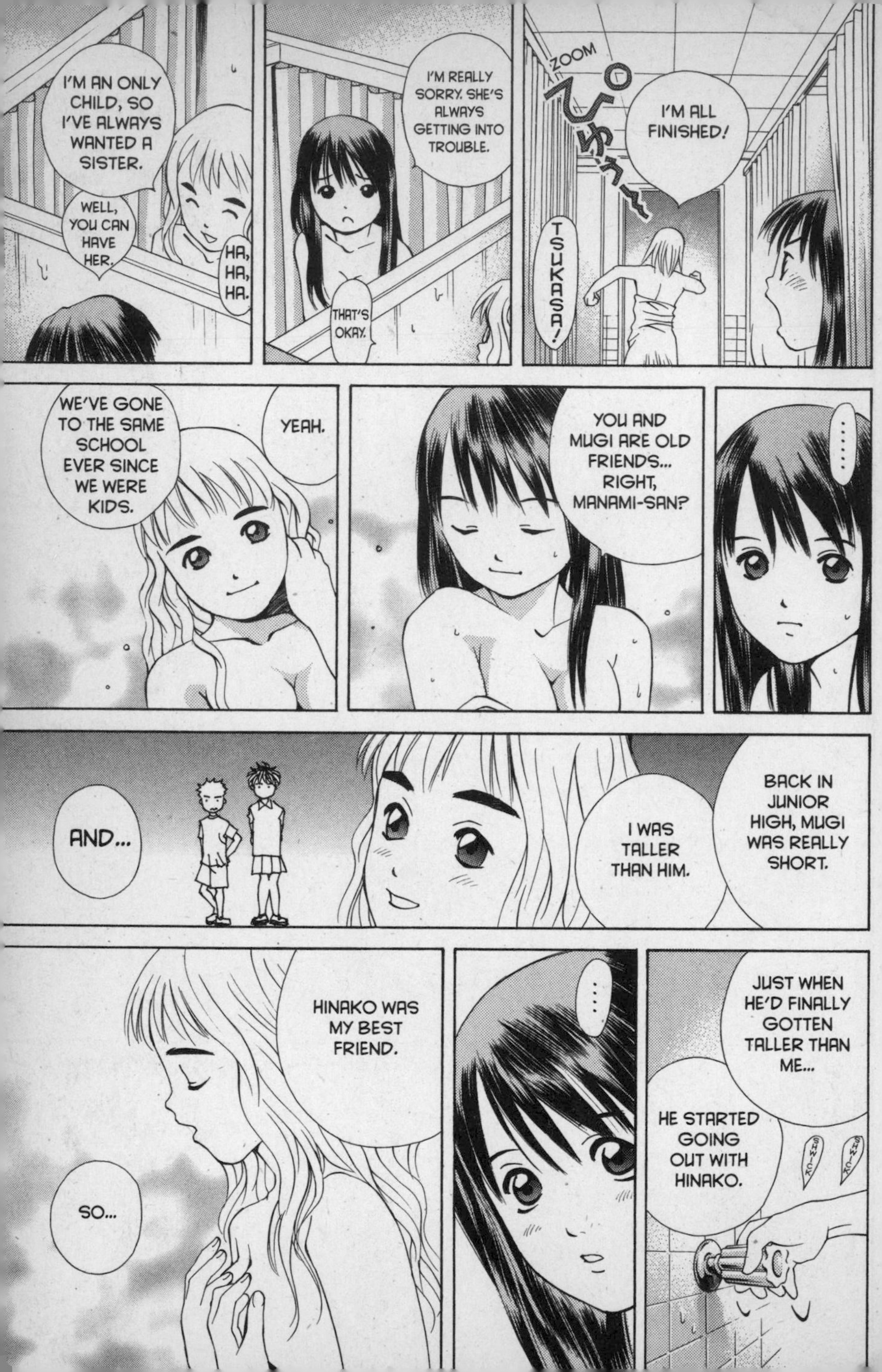
I'M ALL FINISHED!
ZOOM
TSUKASA!
I'M REALLY SORRY. SHE'S ALWAYS GETTING INTO TROUBLE.
THAT'S OKAY.
I'M AN ONLY CHILD, SO I'VE ALWAYS WANTED A SISTER.
WELL, YOU CAN HAVE HER.
HA, HA, HA.
......
YOU AND MUGI ARE OLD FRIENDS... RIGHT, MANAMI-SAN?
YEAH.
WE'VE GONE TO THE SAME SCHOOL EVER SINCE WE WERE KIDS.
BACK IN JUNIOR HIGH, MUGI WAS REALLY SHORT.
I WAS TALLER THAN HIM.
AND...
JUST WHEN HE'D FINALLY GOTTEN TALLER THAN ME...
SWICK
SWICK
HE STARTED GOING OUT WITH HINAKO.
....
HINAKO WAS MY BEST FRIEND.
SO...

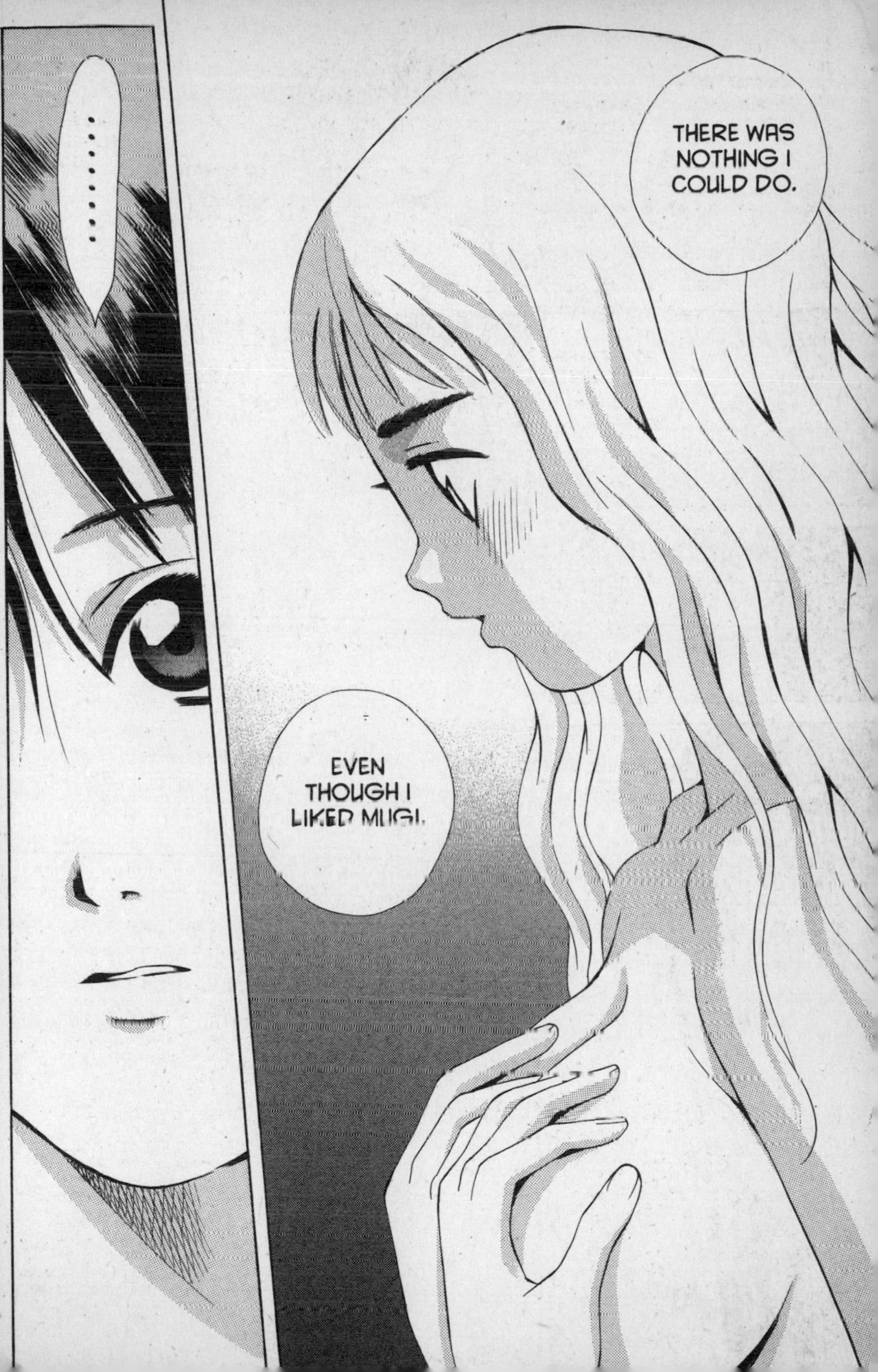
THERE WAS NOTHING I COULD DO.
EVEN THOUGH I LIKED MUGI.
......

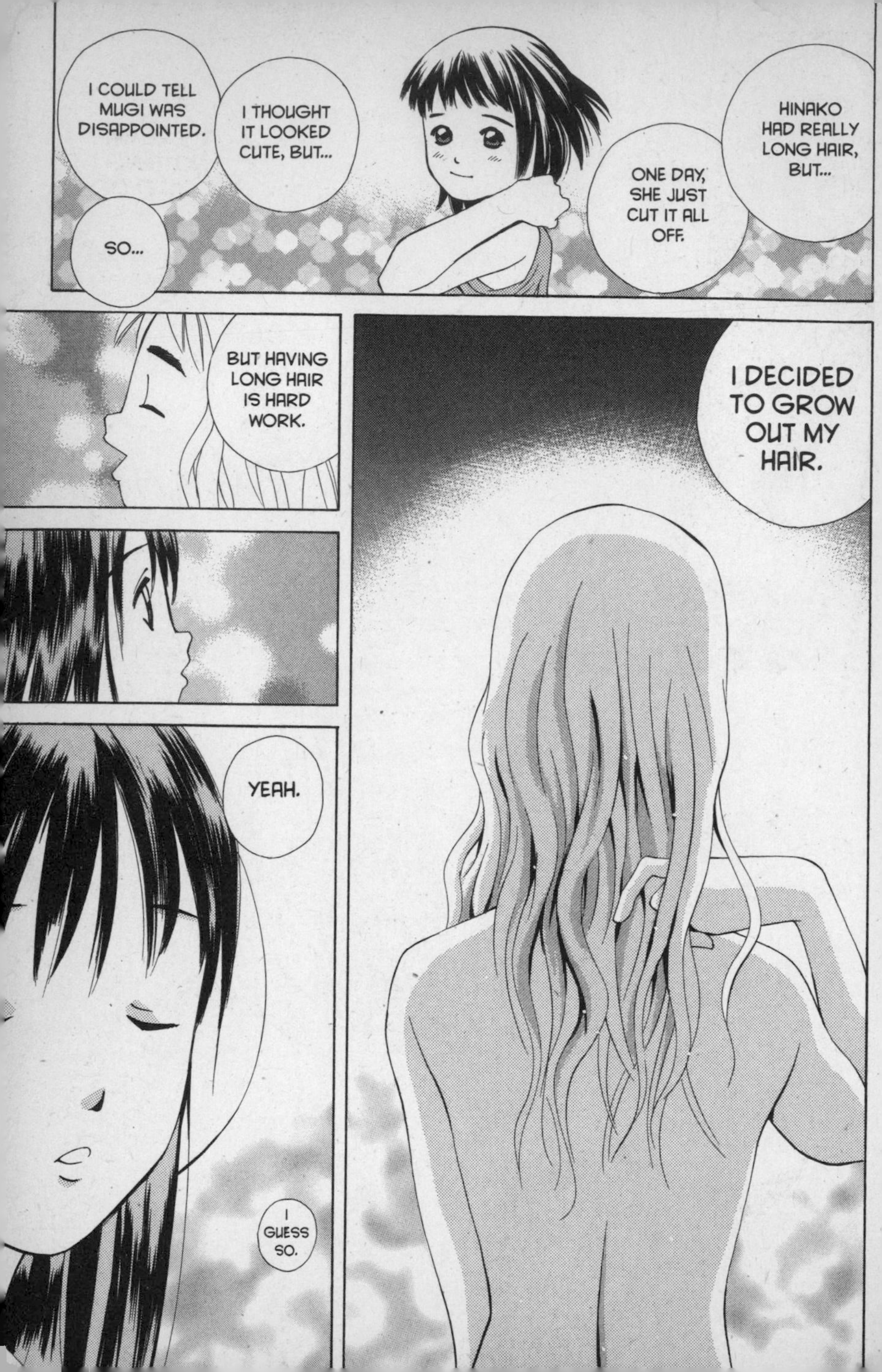
HINAKO HAD REALLY LONG HAIR, BUT...
ONE DAY, SHE JUST CUT IT ALL OFF.
I THOUGHT IT LOOKED CUTE, BUT...
I COULD TELL MUGI WAS DISAPPOINTED.
SO...
I DECIDED TO GROW OUT MY HAIR.
BUT HAVING LONG HAIR IS HARD WORK.
YEAH.
I GUESS SO.

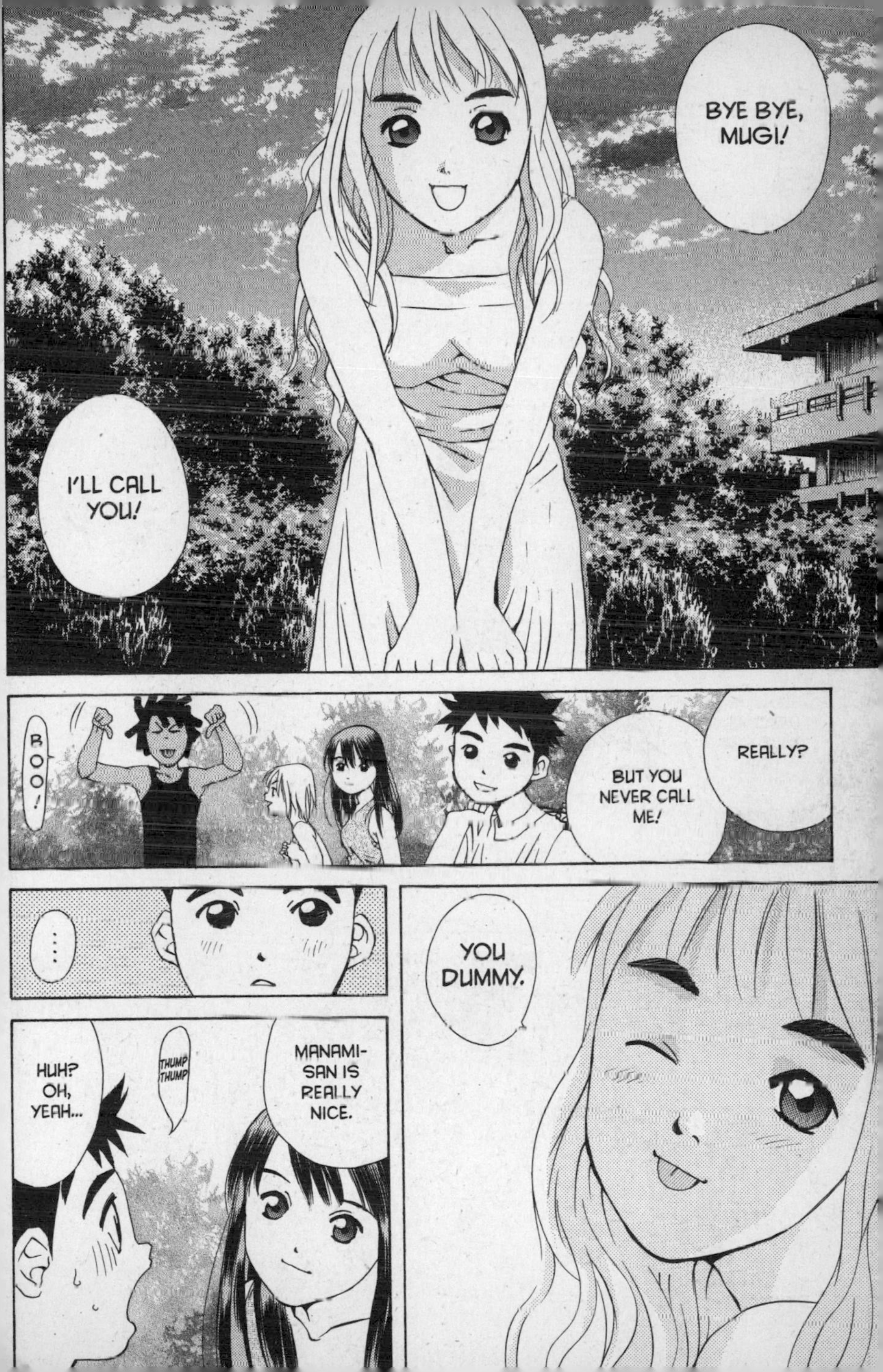
BYE BYE, MUGI!
I'LL CALL YOU!
REALLY?
BUT YOU NEVER CALL ME!
BOO!
YOU DUMMY.
....
MANAMI-SAN IS REALLY NICE.
THUMP THUMP
HUH? OH, YEAH...

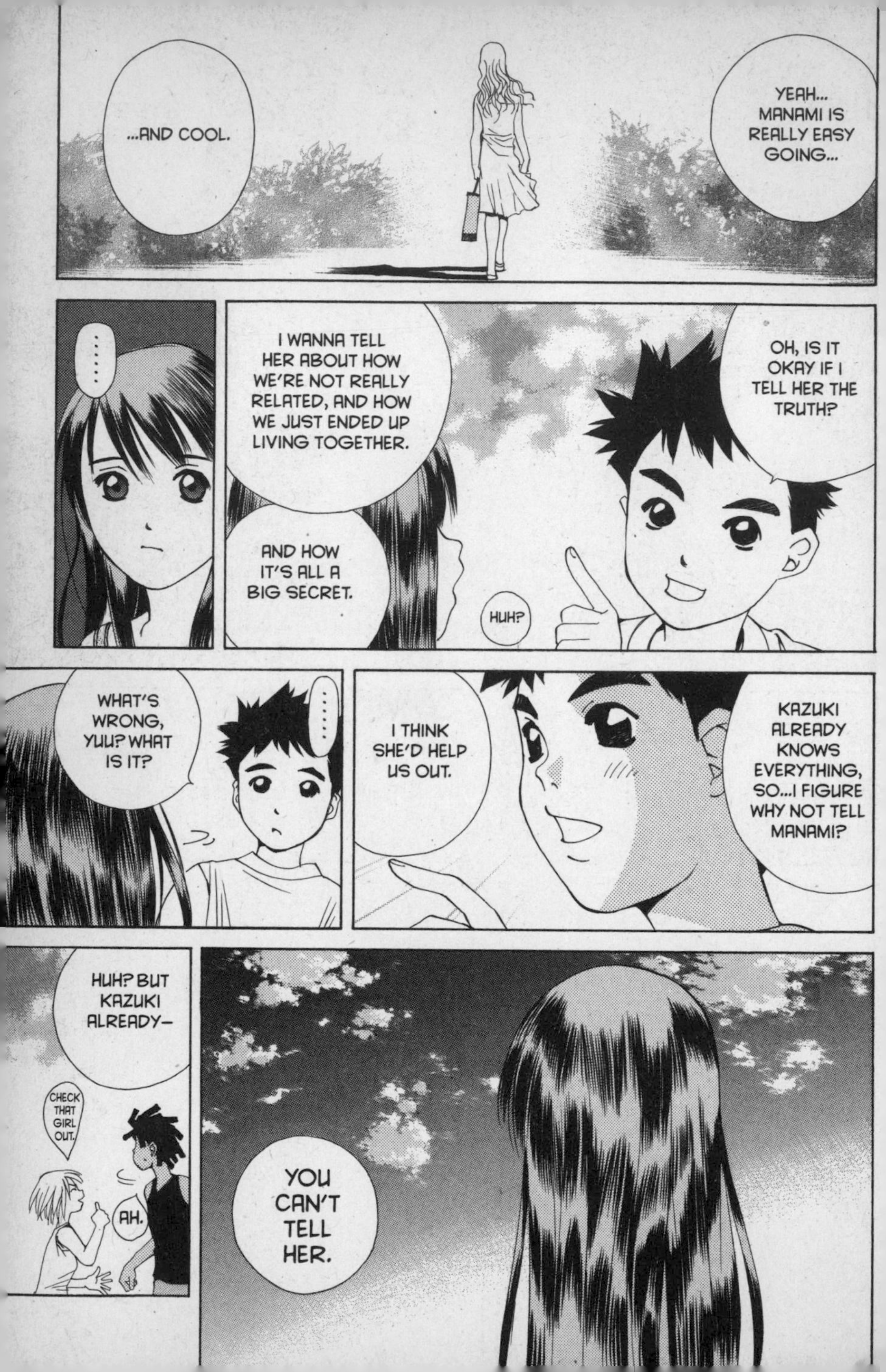
YEAH... MANAMI IS REALLY EASY GOING...
...AND COOL.
OH, IS IT OKAY IF I TELL HER THE TRUTH?
I WANNA TELL HER ABOUT HOW WE'RE NOT REALLY RELATED, AND HOW WE JUST ENDED UP LIVING TOGETHER.
HUH?
AND HOW IT'S ALL A BIG SECRET.
......
KAZUKI ALREADY KNOWS EVERYTHING, SO...I FIGURE WHY NOT TELL MANAMI?
I THINK SHE'D HELP US OUT.
......
WHAT'S WRONG, YUU? WHAT IS IT?
YOU CAN'T TELL HER.
HUH? BUT KAZUKI ALREADY—
CHECK THAT GIRL OUT.
AH.

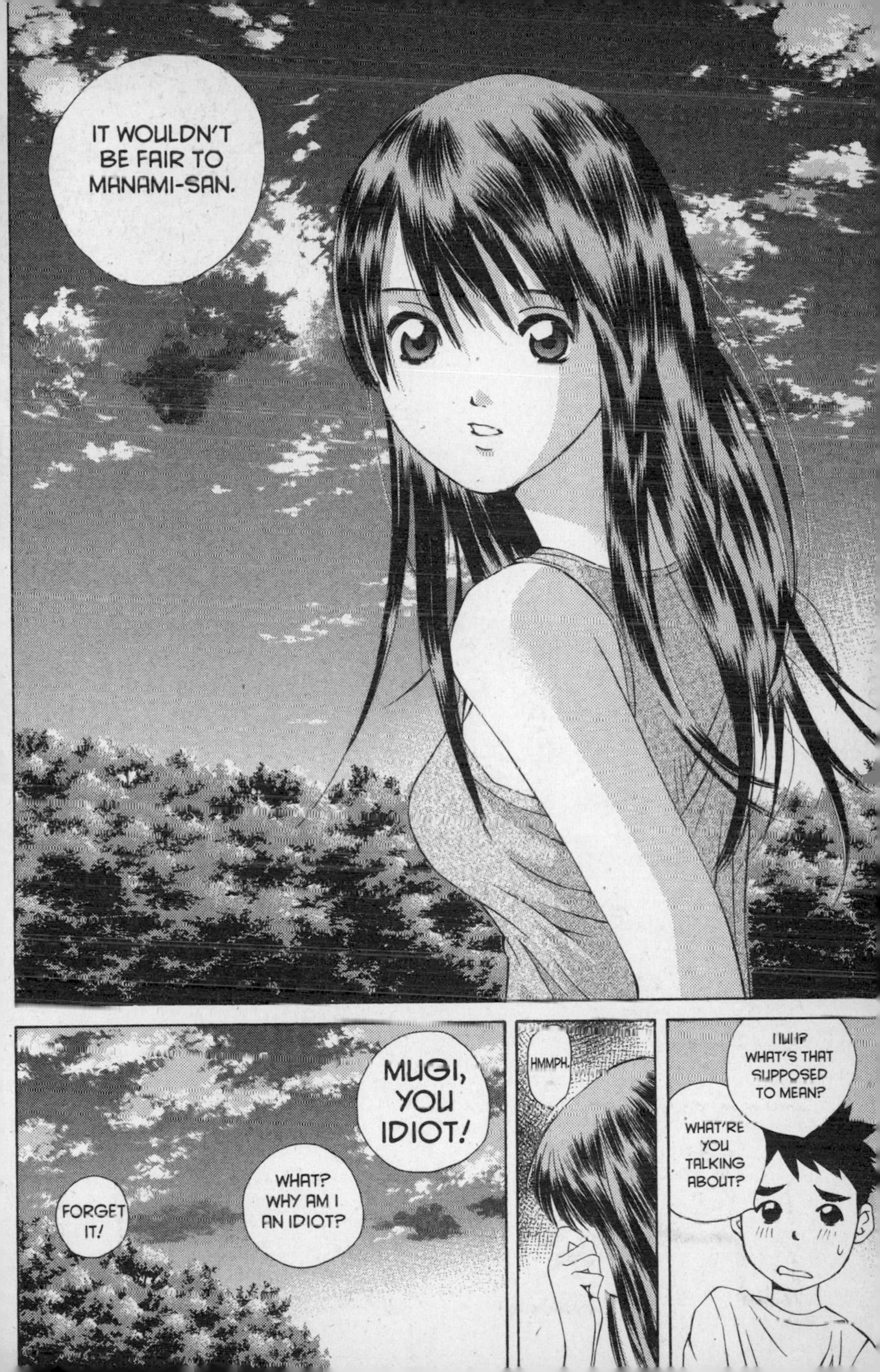
IT WOULDN'T BE FAIR TO MANAMI-SAN.
HUH? WHAT'S THAT SUPPOSED TO MEAN?
WHAT'RE YOU TALKING ABOUT?
HMMPH.
MUGI, YOU IDIOT!
WHAT? WHY AM I AN IDIOT?
FORGET IT!

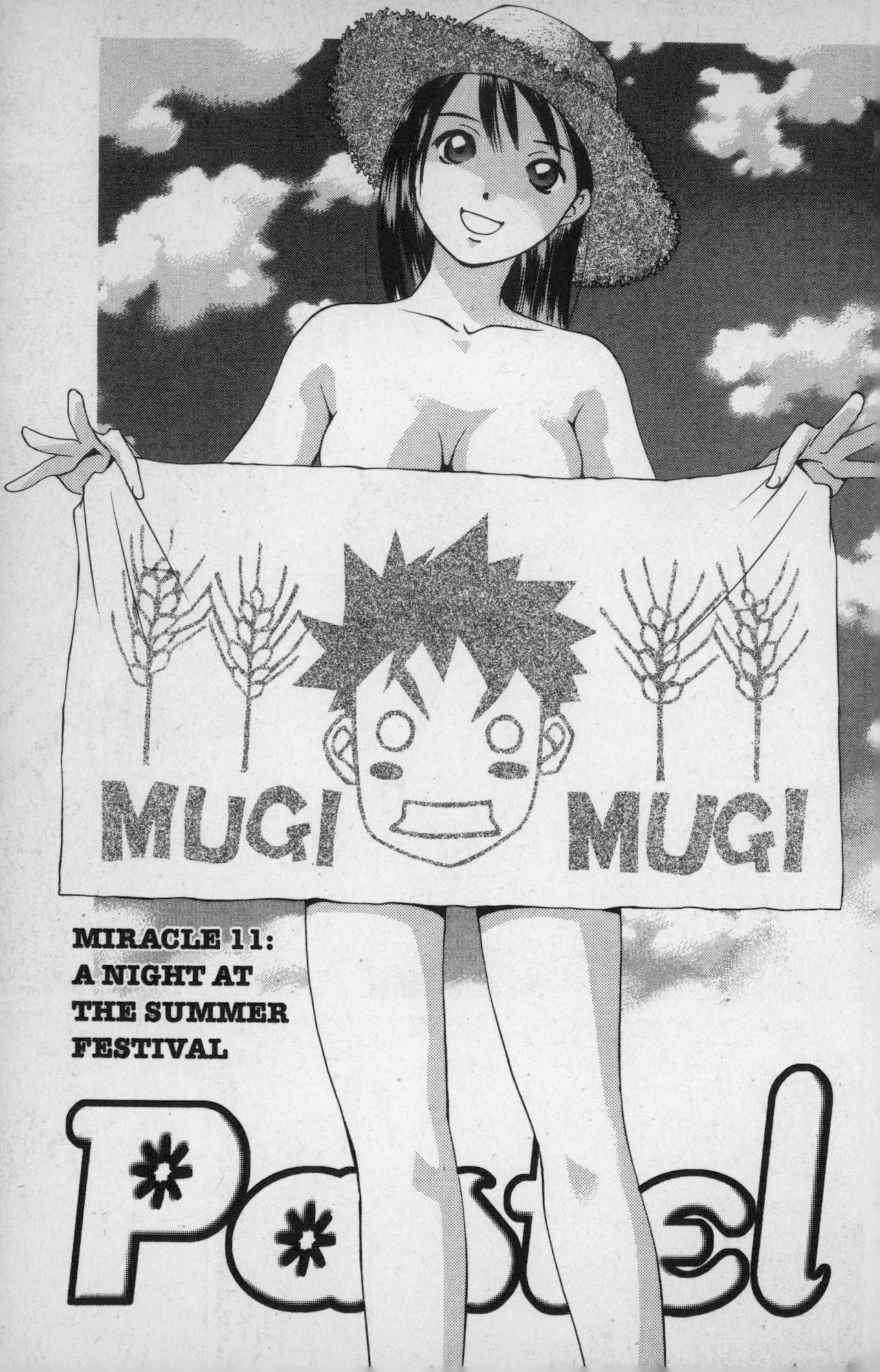
MUGI
MUGI
MIRACLE 11:
A NIGHT AT
THE SUMMER
FESTIVAL
Pastel

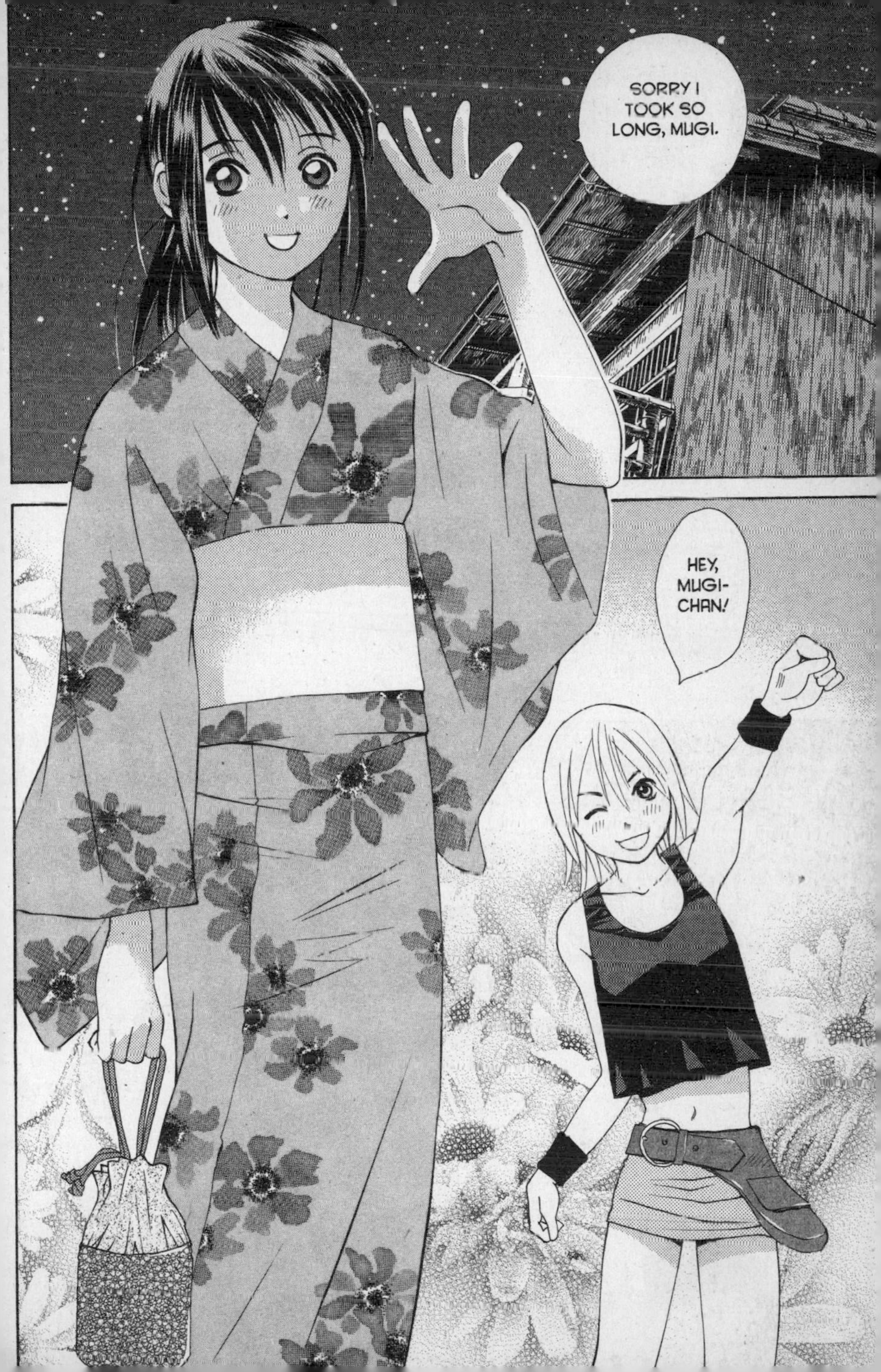
SORRY I TOOK SO LONG, MUGI.
HEY, MUGI-CHAN!

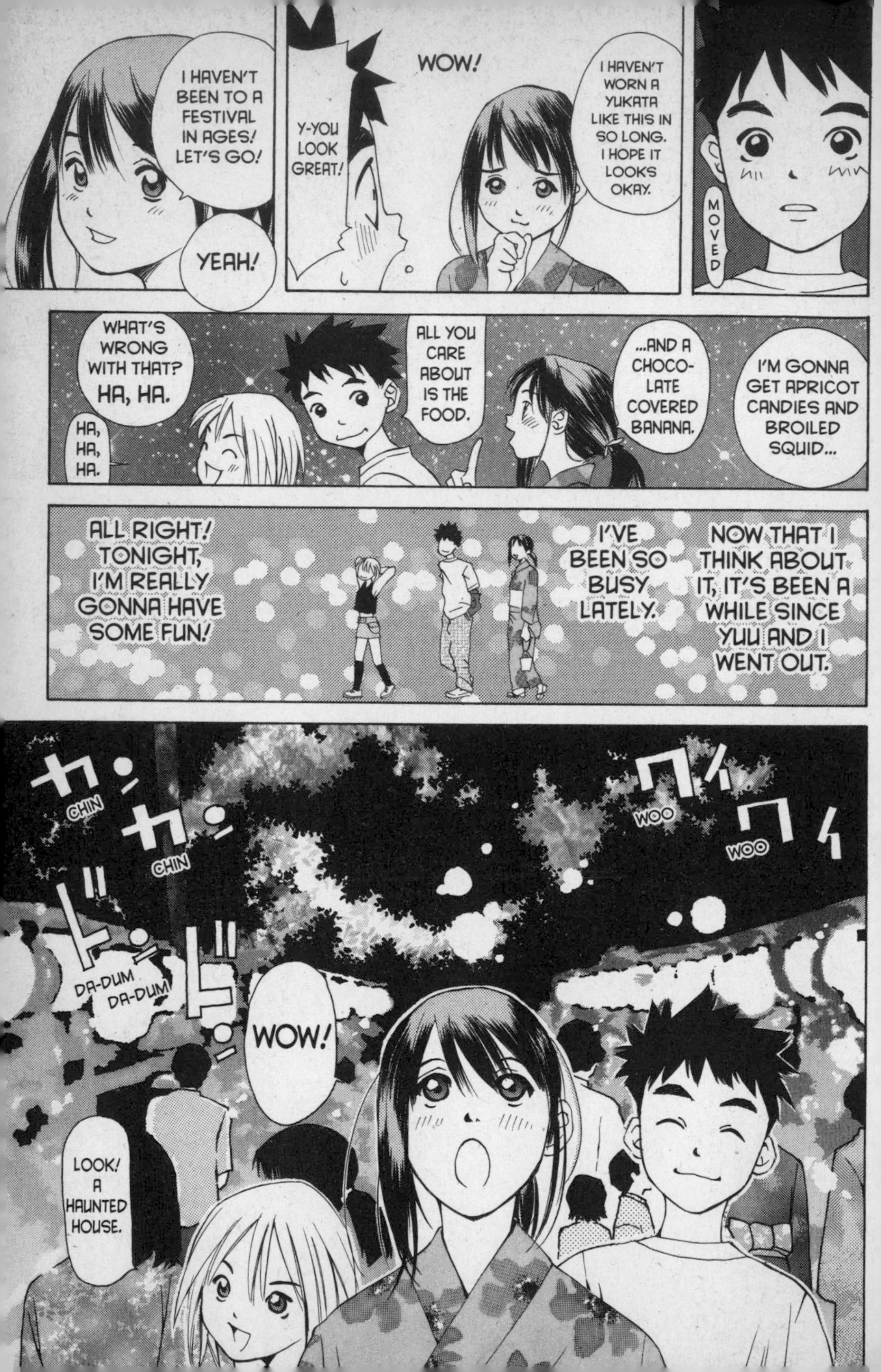
MOVED
I HAVEN'T WORN A YUKATA LIKE THIS IN SO LONG. I HOPE IT LOOKS OKAY.
WOW!
Y-YOU LOOK GREAT!
I HAVEN'T BEEN TO A FESTIVAL IN AGES! LET'S GO!
YEAH!
I'M GONNA GET APRICOT CANDIES AND BROILED SQUID...
...AND A CHOCO-LATE COVERED BANANA.
ALL YOU CARE ABOUT IS THE FOOD.
WHAT'S WRONG WITH THAT? HA, HA.
HA, HA, HA.
NOW THAT I THINK ABOUT IT, IT'S BEEN A WHILE SINCE YUU AND I WENT OUT.
I'VE BEEN SO BUSY LATELY.
ALL RIGHT! TONIGHT, I'M REALLY GONNA HAVE SOME FUN!
WOO
WOO
CHIN
CHIN
DA-DUM
DA-DUM
WOW!
LOOK! A HAUNTED HOUSE.

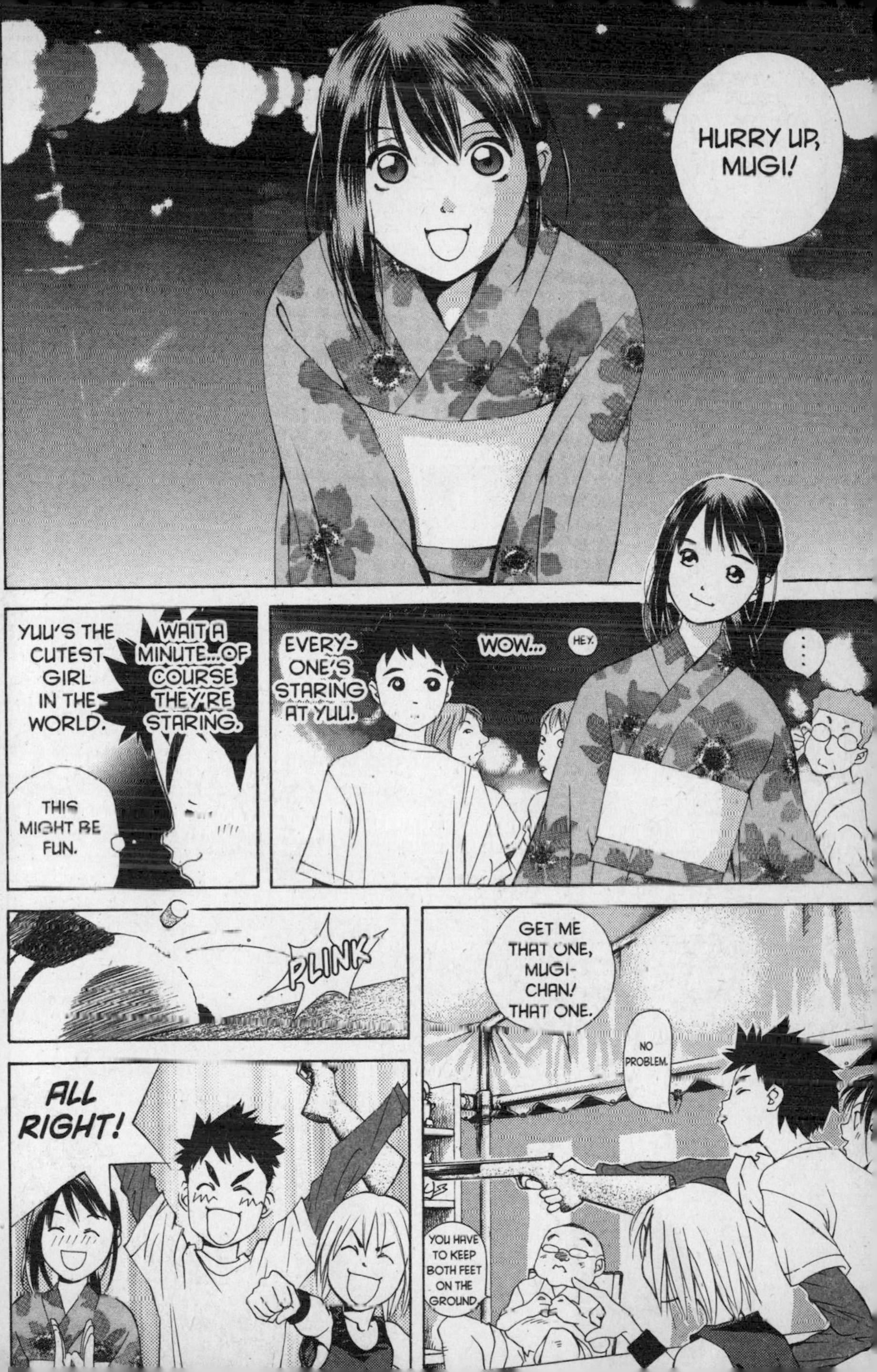
HURRY UP, MUGI!
....
HEY.
WOW...
EVERY-ONE'S STARING AT YUU.
WAIT A MINUTE...OF COURSE THEY'RE STARING.
YUU'S THE CUTEST GIRL IN THE WORLD.
THIS MIGHT BE FUN.
GET ME THAT ONE, MUGI-CHAN! THAT ONE.
NO PROBLEM.
YOU HAVE TO KEEP BOTH FEET ON THE GROUND.
PLINK
ALL RIGHT!

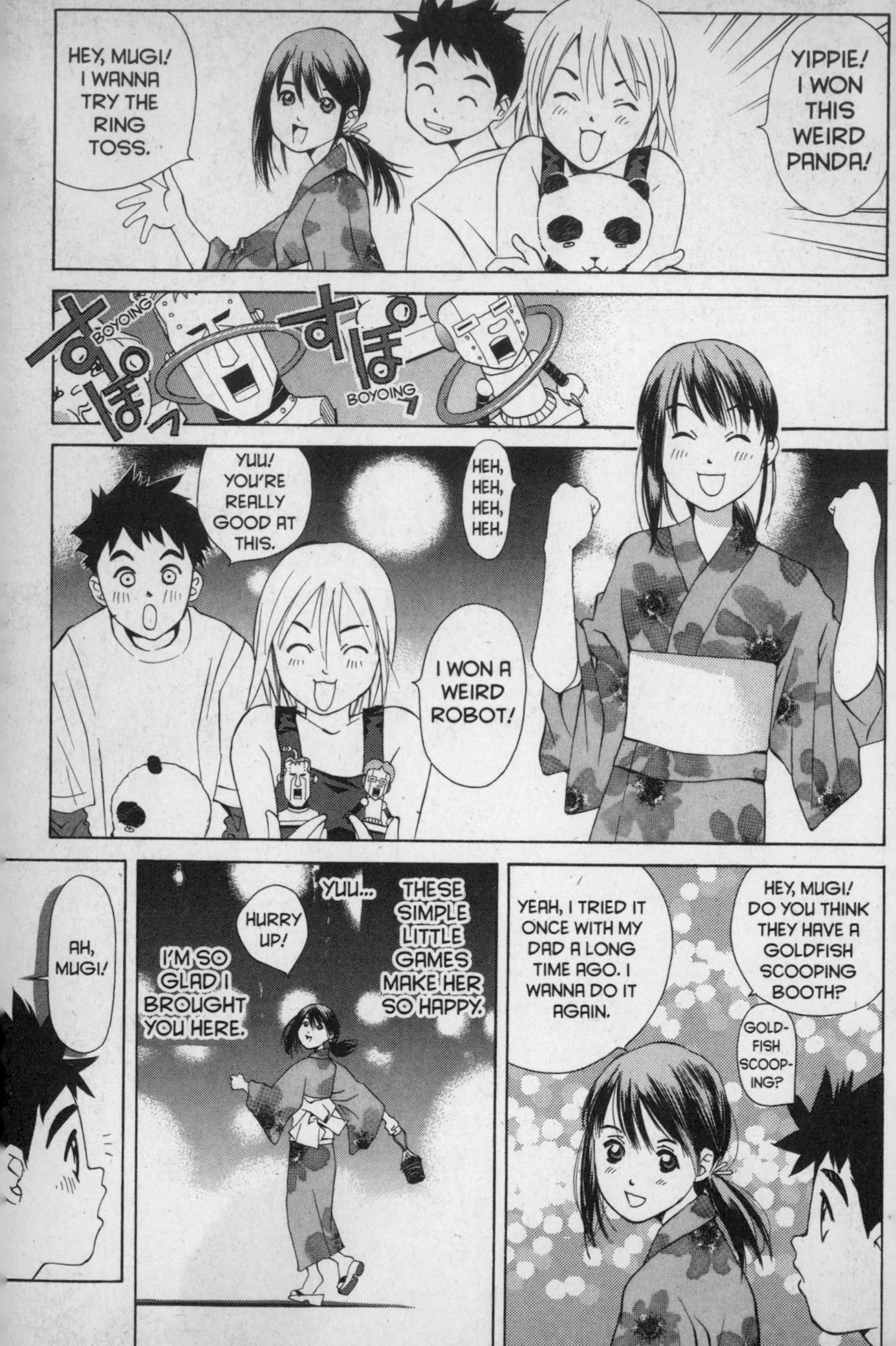
YIPPIE! I WON THIS WEIRD PANDA!
HEY, MUGI! I WANNA TRY THE RING TOSS.
すぽ
BOYOING
すぽっ
BOYOING
HEH, HEH, HEH, HEH.
YUU! YOU'RE REALLY GOOD AT THIS.
I WON A WEIRD ROBOT!
HEY, MUGI! DO YOU THINK THEY HAVE A GOLDFISH SCOOPING BOOTH?
GOLD-FISH SCOOP-ING?
YEAH, I TRIED IT ONCE WITH MY DAD A LONG TIME AGO. I WANNA DO IT AGAIN.
THESE SIMPLE LITTLE GAMES MAKE HER SO HAPPY.
YUU...
HURRY UP!
I'M SO GLAD I BROUGHT YOU HERE.
AH, MUGI!

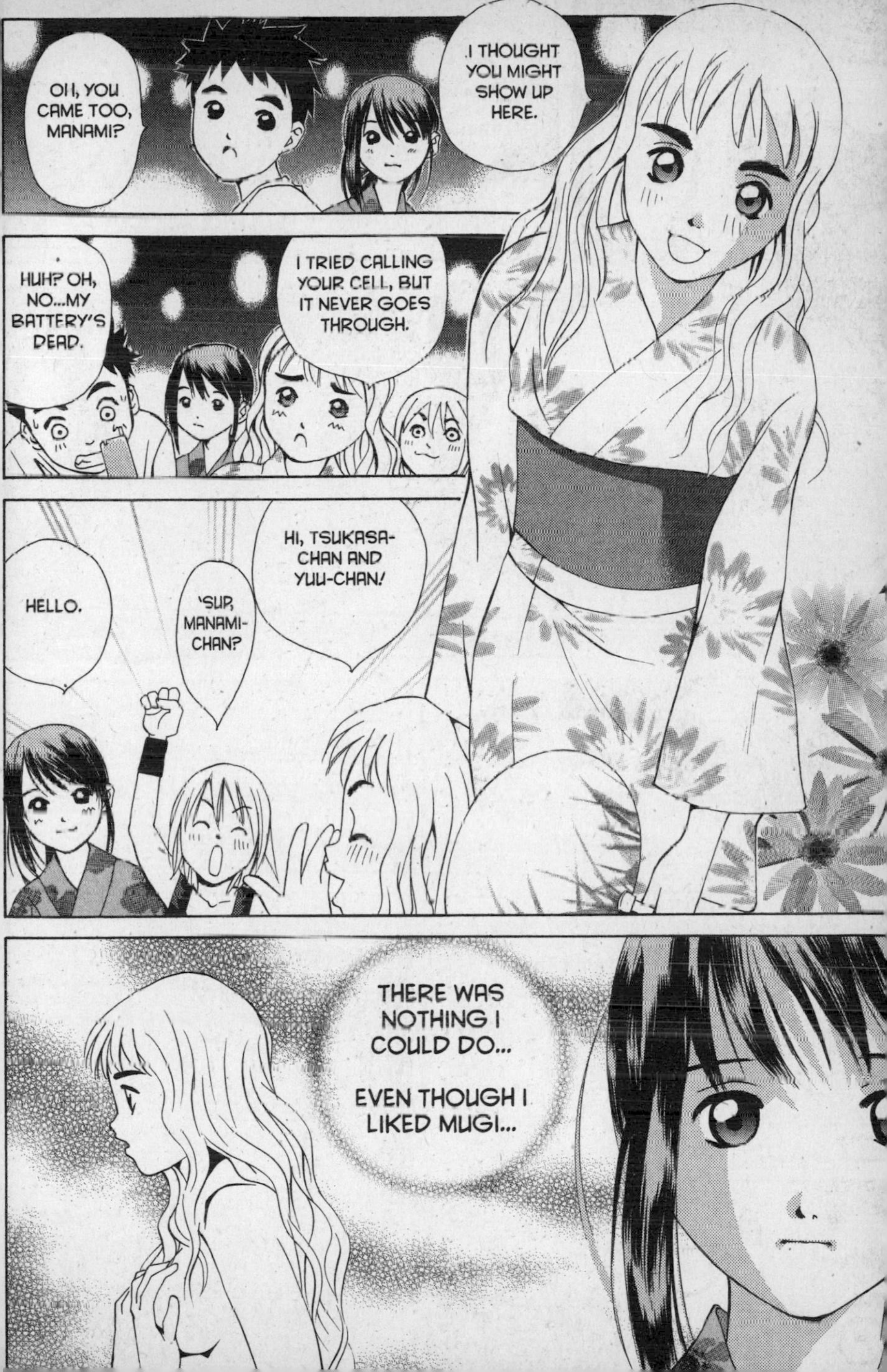
I THOUGHT YOU MIGHT SHOW UP HERE.
OH, YOU CAME TOO, MANAMI?
I TRIED CALLING YOUR CELL, BUT IT NEVER GOES THROUGH.
HUH? OH, NO...MY BATTERY'S DEAD.
HI, TSUKASA-CHAN AND YUU-CHAN!
'SUP, MANAMI-CHAN?
HELLO.
THERE WAS NOTHING I COULD DO...
EVEN THOUGH I LIKED MUGI...

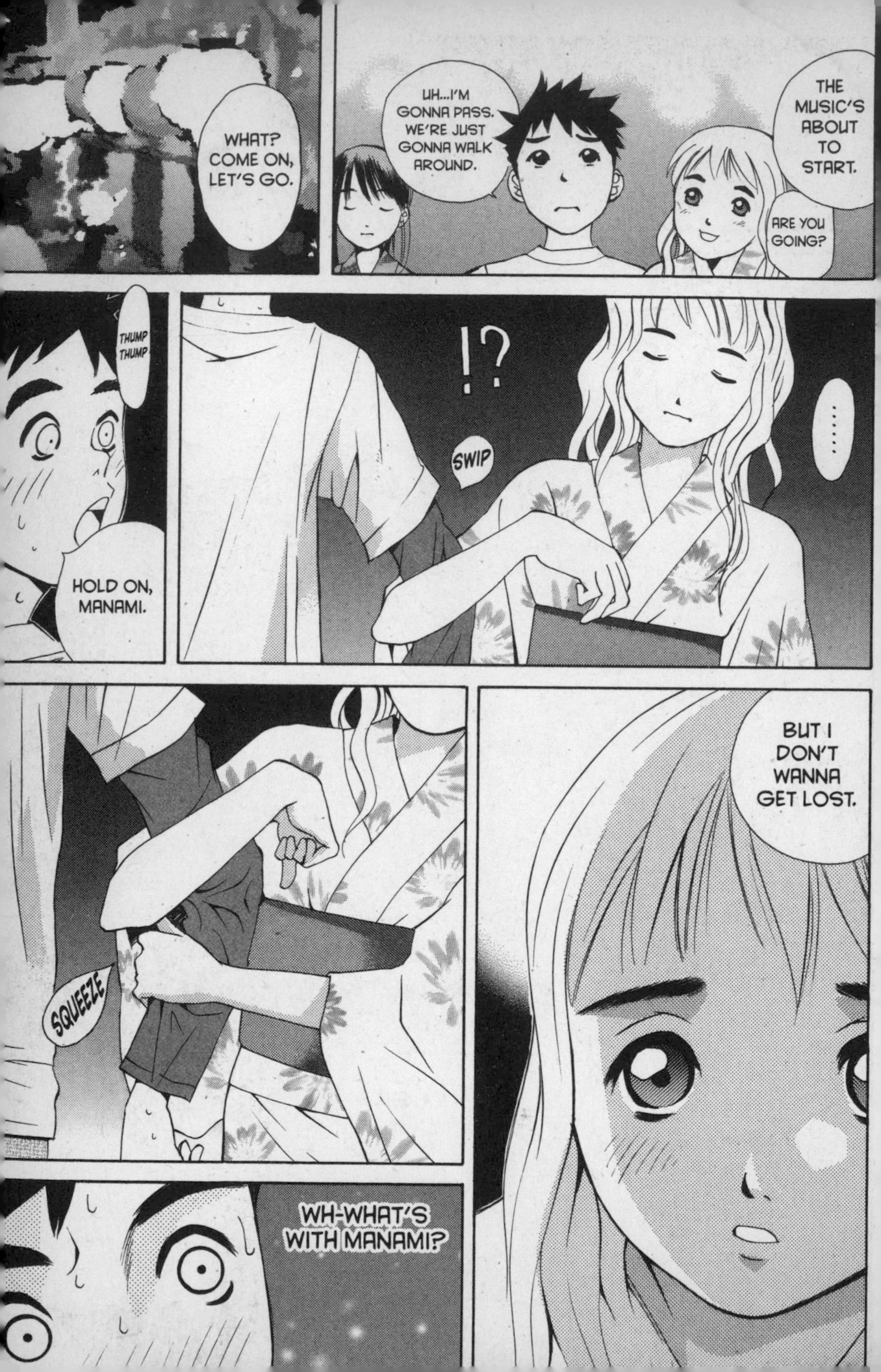
THE MUSIC'S ABOUT TO START.
ARE YOU GOING?
UH...I'M GONNA PASS. WE'RE JUST GONNA WALK AROUND.
WHAT? COME ON, LET'S GO.
......
!?
SWIP
THUMP THUMP
HOLD ON, MANAMI.
BUT I DON'T WANNA GET LOST.
SQUEEZE
WH-WHAT'S WITH MANAMI?

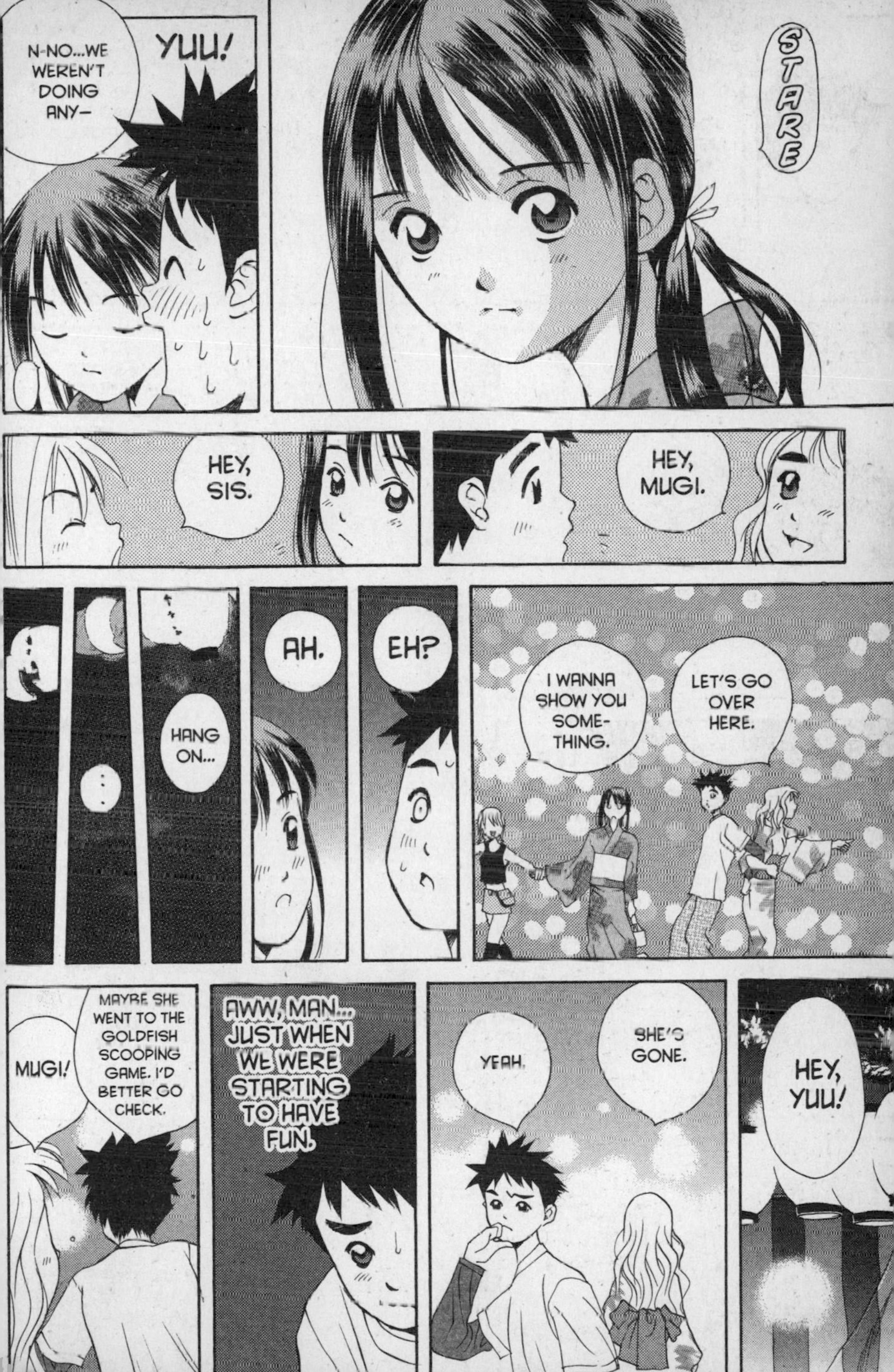
STARE
YUU!
N-NO...WE WEREN'T DOING ANY—
HEY, MUGI.
HEY, SIS.
LET'S GO OVER HERE.
I WANNA SHOW YOU SOME-THING.
EH?
AH.
HANG ON...
...
HEY, YUU!
SHE'S GONE.
YEAH.
AWW, MAN... JUST WHEN WE WERE STARTING TO HAVE FUN.
MAYBE SHE WENT TO THE GOLDFISH SCOOPING GAME. I'D BETTER GO CHECK.
MUGI!

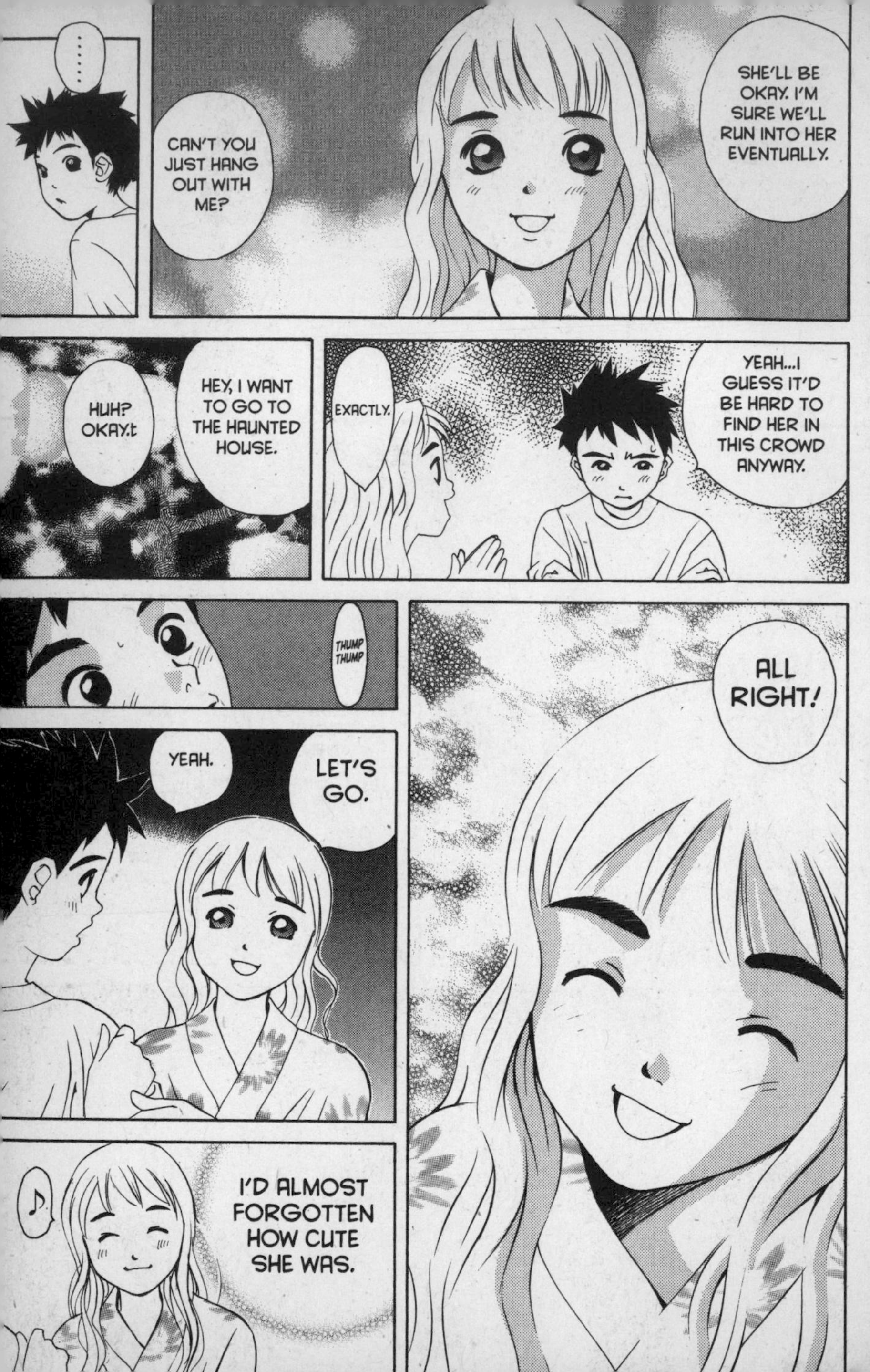
SHE'LL BE OKAY. I'M SURE WE'LL RUN INTO HER EVENTUALLY.
CAN'T YOU JUST HANG OUT WITH ME?
......
YEAH...I GUESS IT'D BE HARD TO FIND HER IN THIS CROWD ANYWAY.
EXACTLY.
HEY, I WANT TO GO TO THE HAUNTED HOUSE.
HUH? OKAY.
ALL RIGHT!
THUMP THUMP
LET'S GO.
YEAH.
♪
I'D ALMOST FORGOTTEN HOW CUTE SHE WAS.

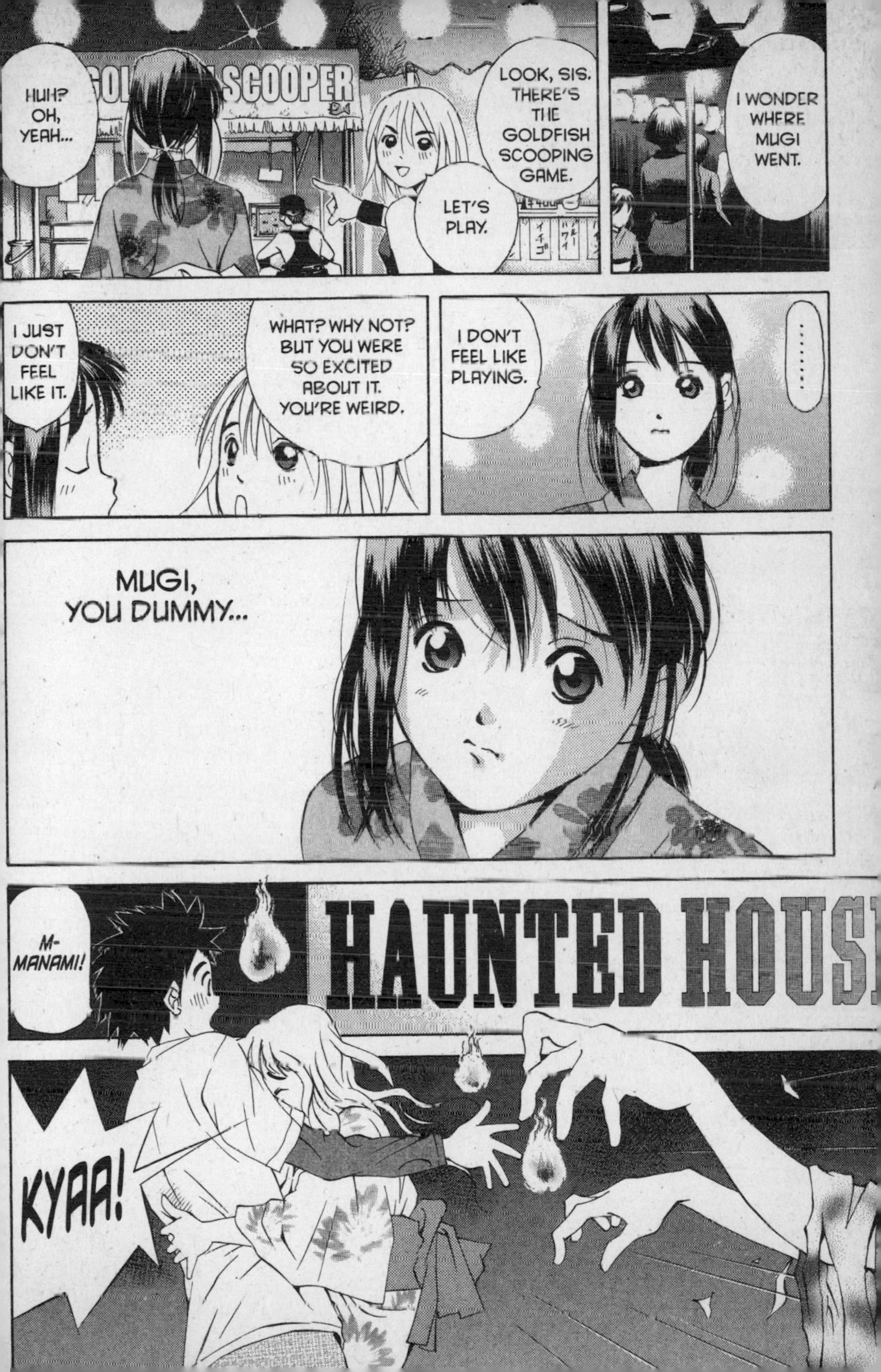
I WONDER WHERE MUGI WENT.
LOOK, SIS. THERE'S THE GOLDFISH SCOOPING GAME.
LET'S PLAY.
SCOOPER
HUH? OH, YEAH...
……
I DON'T FEEL LIKE PLAYING.
WHAT? WHY NOT? BUT YOU WERE SO EXCITED ABOUT IT. YOU'RE WEIRD.
I JUST DON'T FEEL LIKE IT.
MUGI, YOU DUMMY...
HAUNTED HOUS
M-MANAMI!
KYAA!

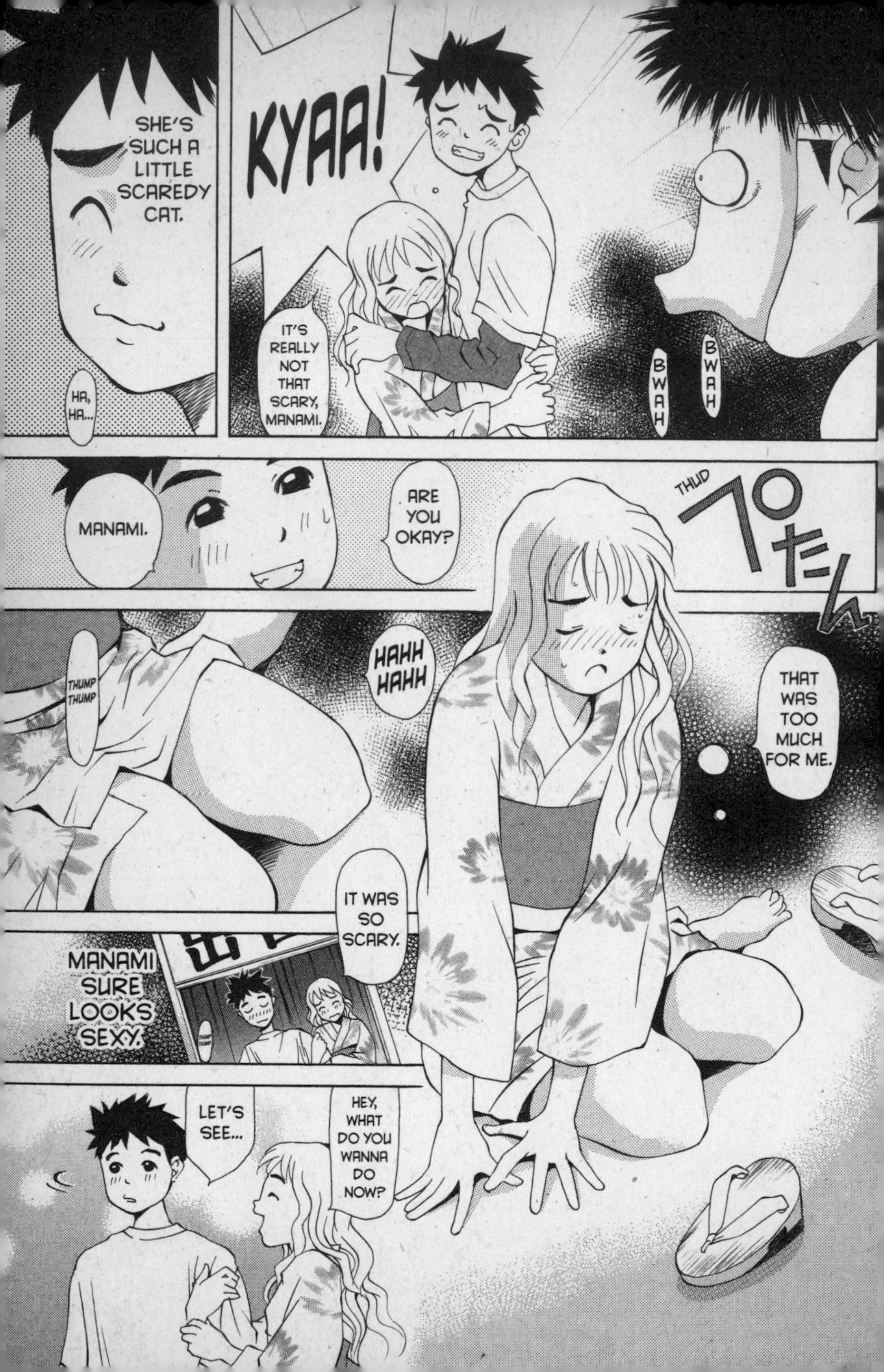
BWAH
BWAH
KYAA!
IT'S REALLY NOT THAT SCARY, MANAMI.
SHE'S SUCH A LITTLE SCAREDY CAT.
HA, HA...
THUD
ぺたん
THAT WAS TOO MUCH FOR ME.
IT WAS SO SCARY.
ARE YOU OKAY?
MANAMI.
HAHH HAHH
THUMP THUMP
MANAMI SURE LOOKS SEXY.
HEY, WHAT DO YOU WANNA DO NOW?
LET'S SEE...

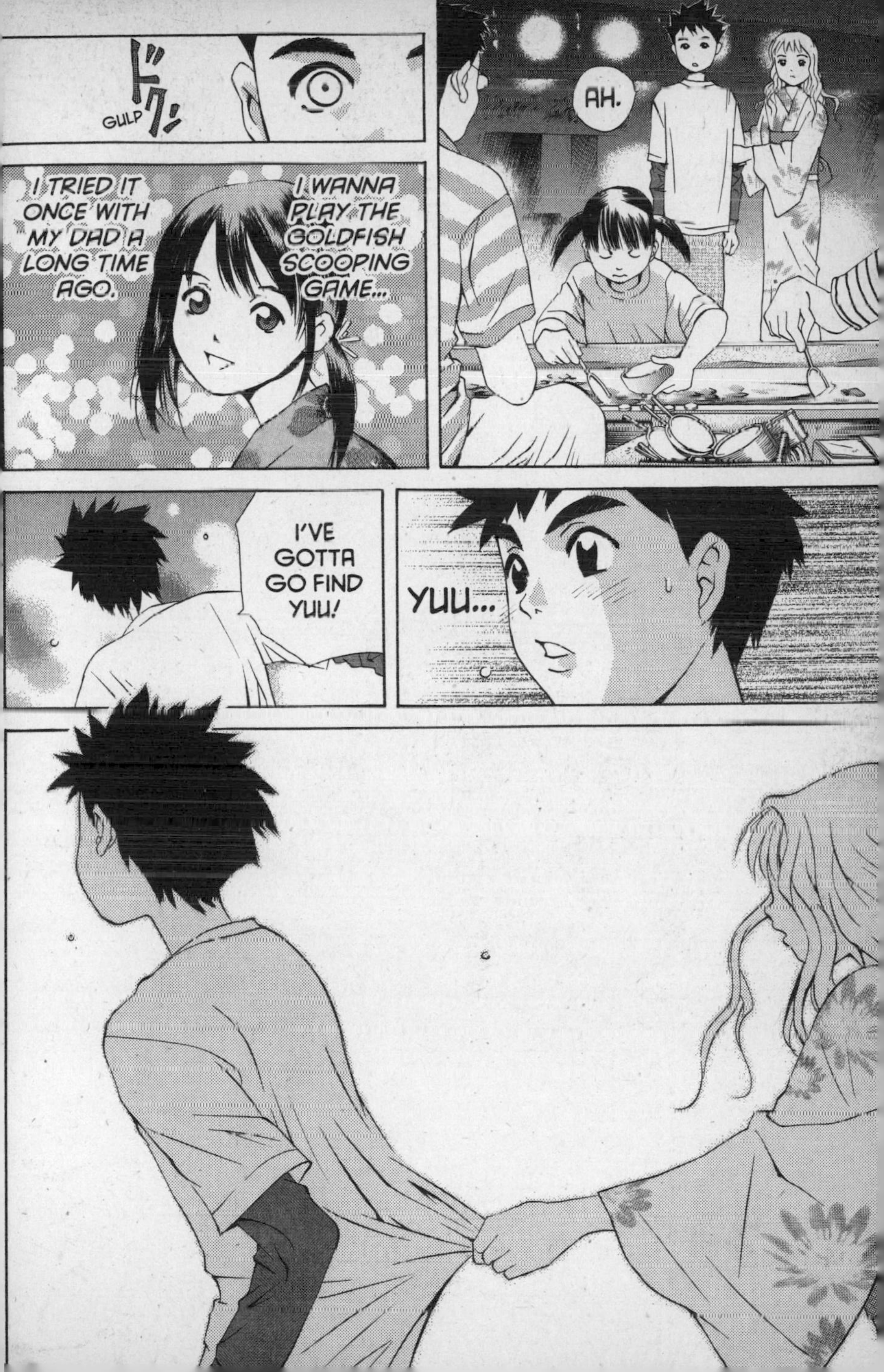
AH.
ドクン
GULP
I WANNA PLAY THE GOLDFISH SCOOPING GAME...
I TRIED IT ONCE WITH MY DAD A LONG TIME AGO.
YUU...
I'VE GOTTA GO FIND YUU!

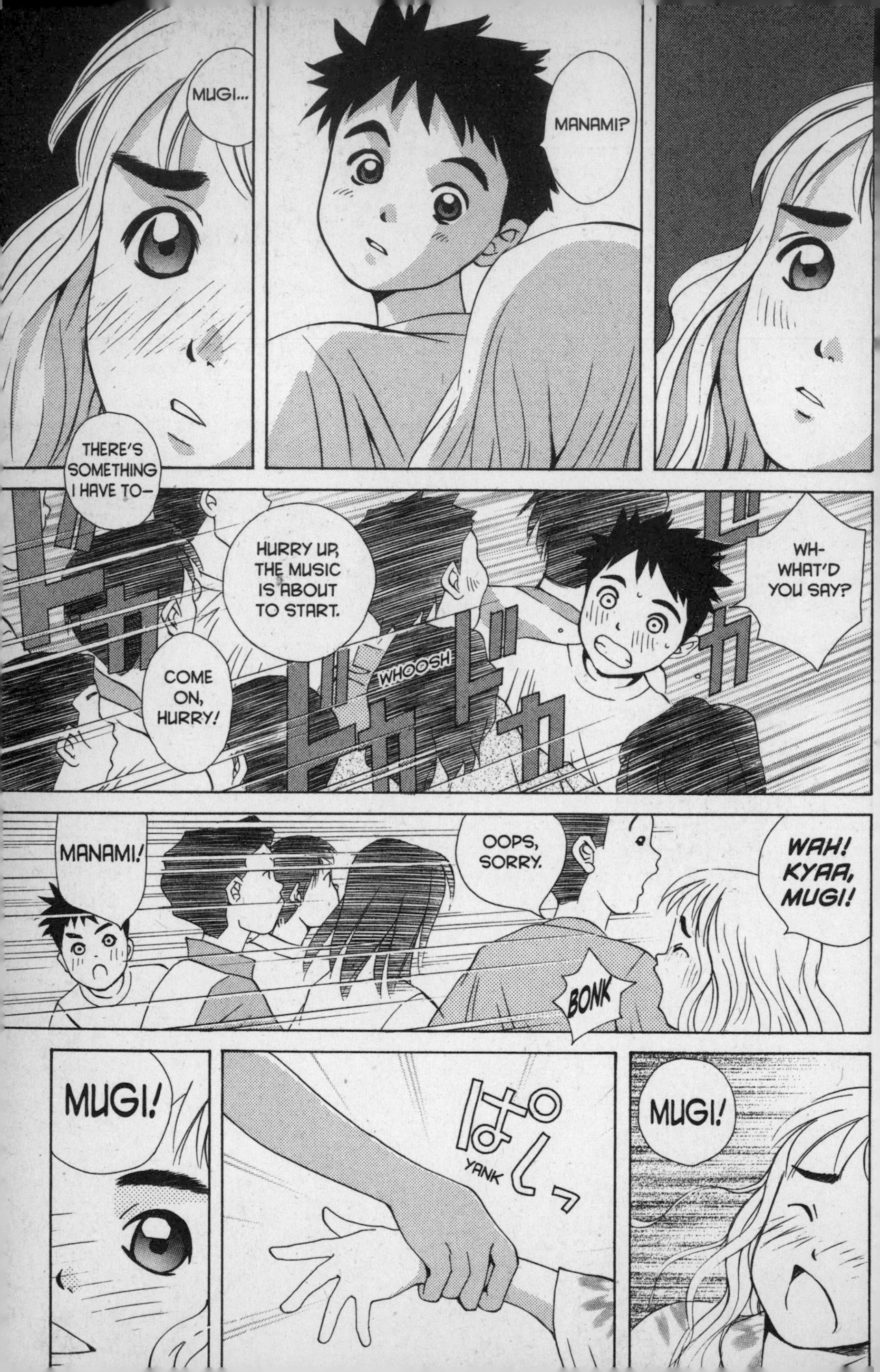
MANAMI?
MUGI...
THERE'S SOMETHING I HAVE TO—
WH- WHAT'D YOU SAY?
HURRY UP, THE MUSIC IS ABOUT TO START.
WHOOSH
COME ON, HURRY!
WAH! KYAA, MUGI!
OOPS, SORRY.
BONK
MANAMI!
MUGI!
ぱしっ
YANK
MUGI!

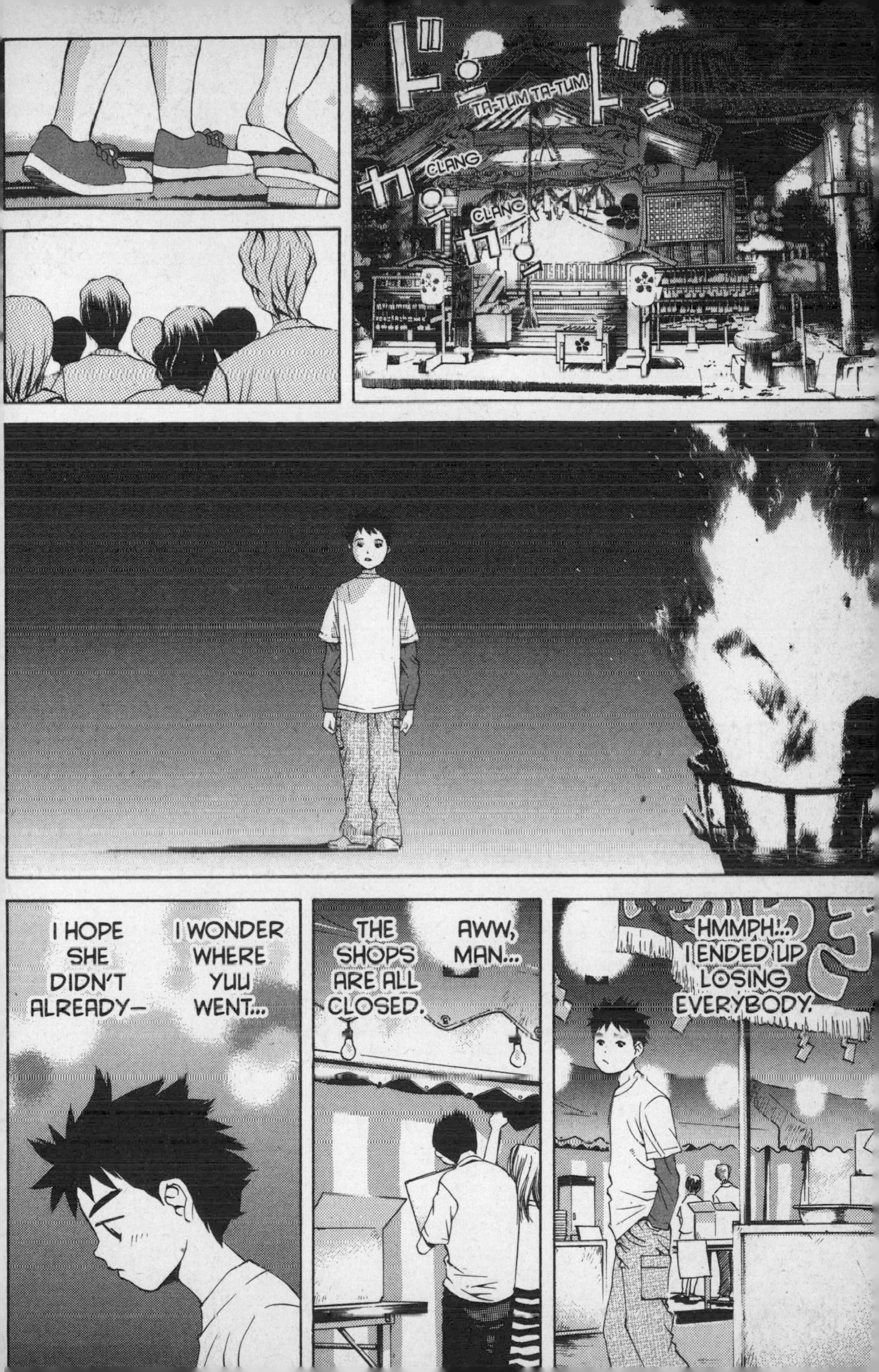
TA-TUM TA-TUM
CLANG
CLANG
HMMPH!... I ENDED UP LOSING EVERYBODY.
AWW, MAN...
THE SHOPS ARE ALL CLOSED.
I WONDER WHERE YUU WENT...
I HOPE SHE DIDN'T ALREADY—

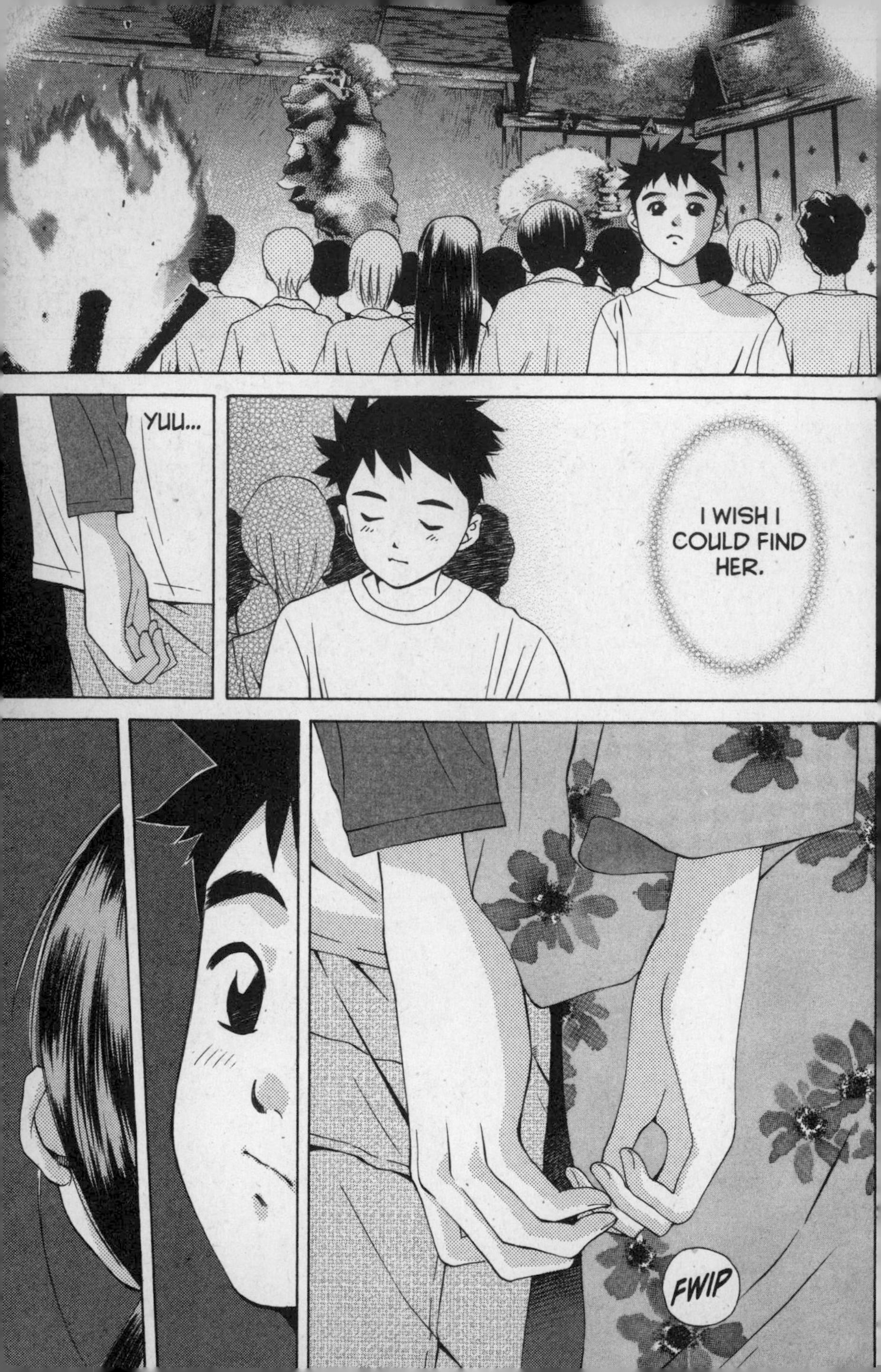
I WISH I COULD FIND HER.
YUU...
FWIP

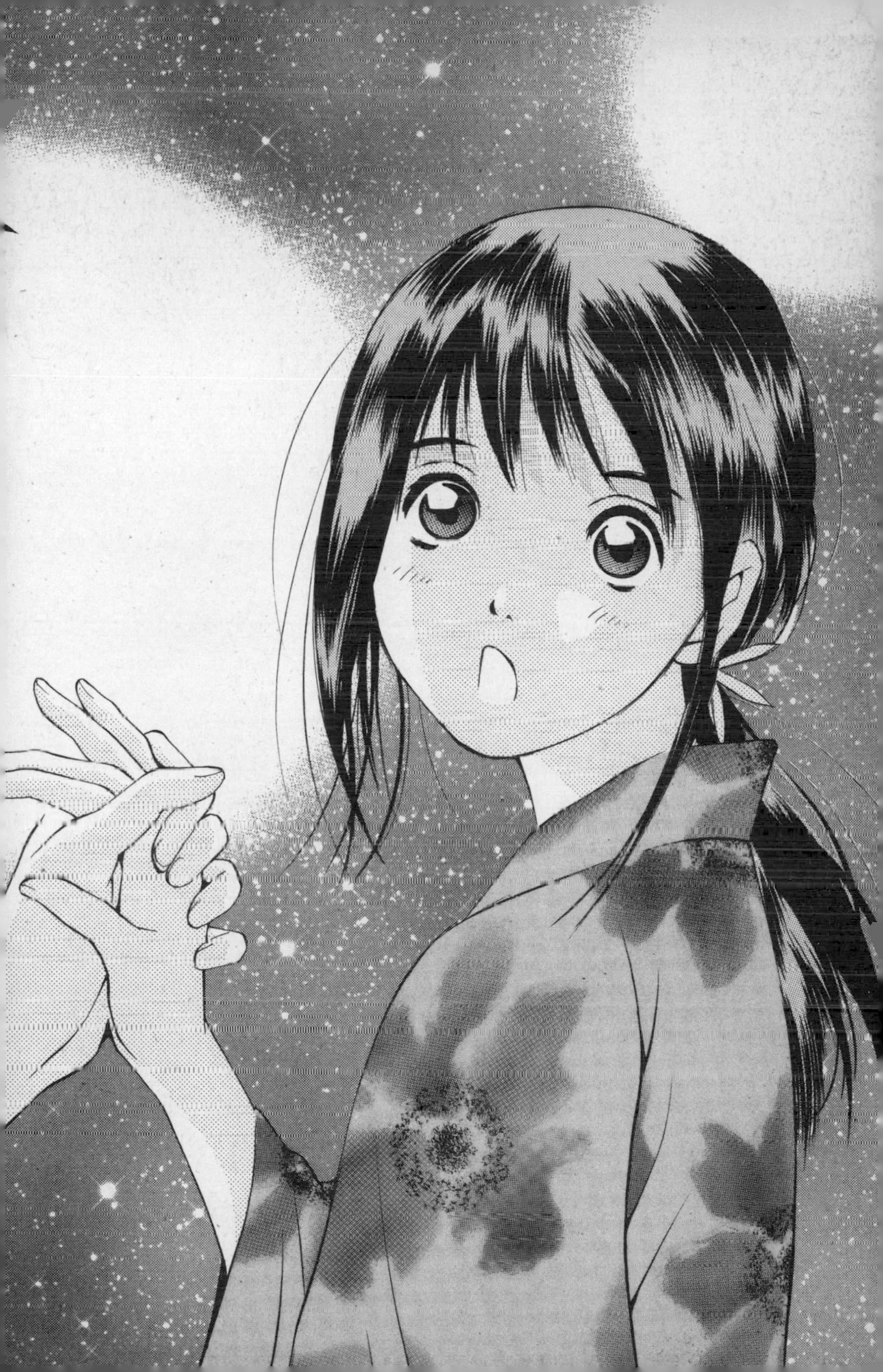

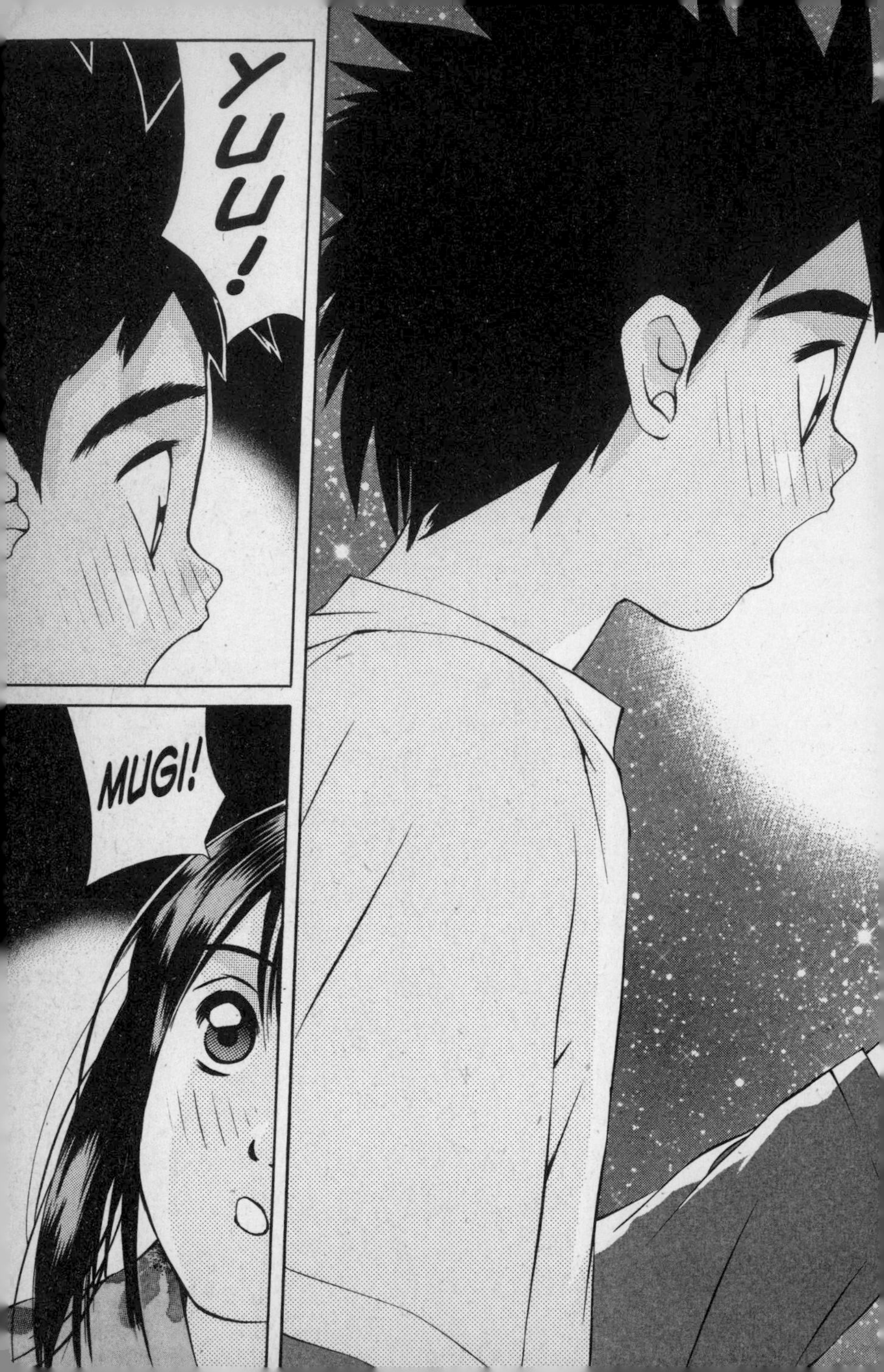
YUU!
MUGI!

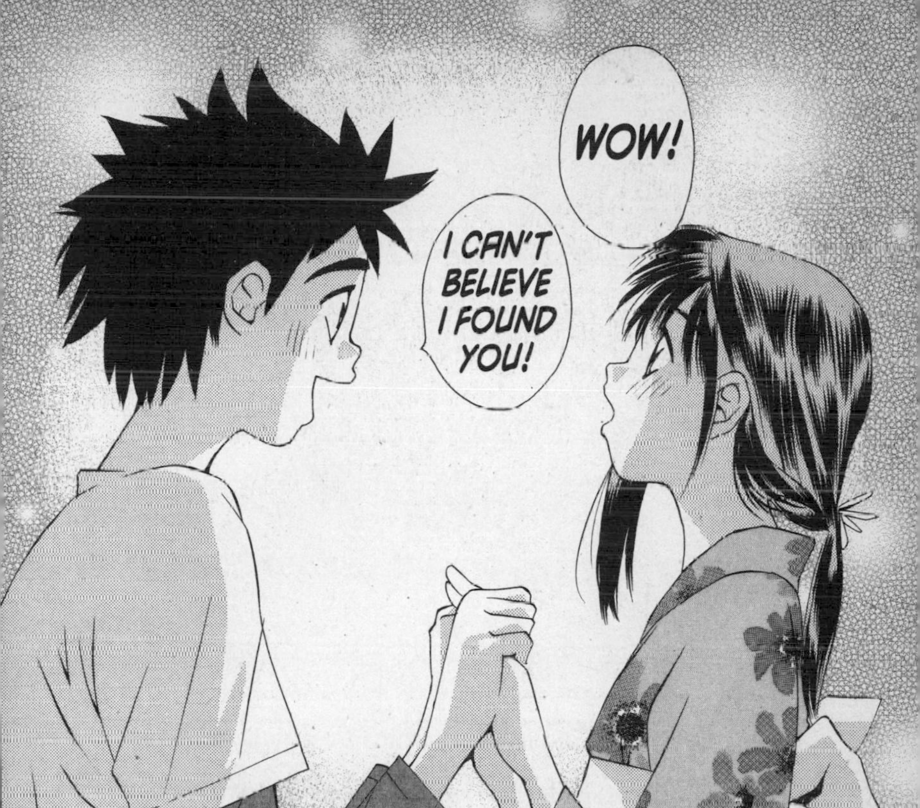
WOW!
I CAN'T BELIEVE I FOUND YOU!

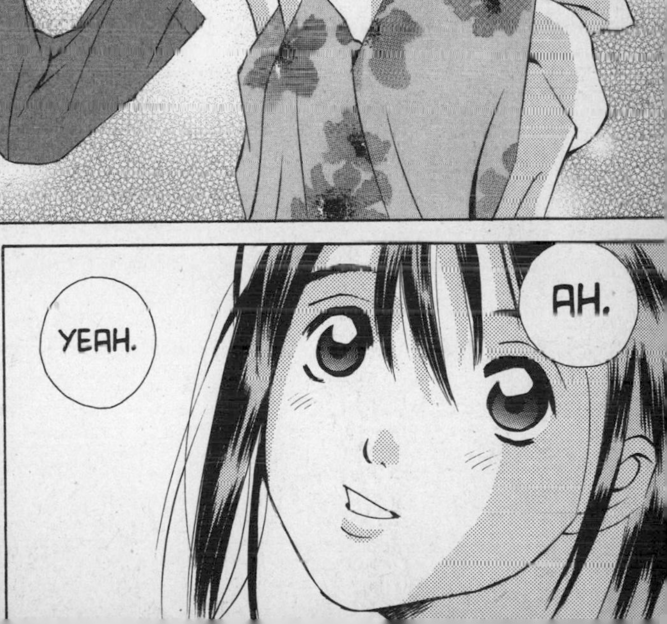
AH.
YEAH.

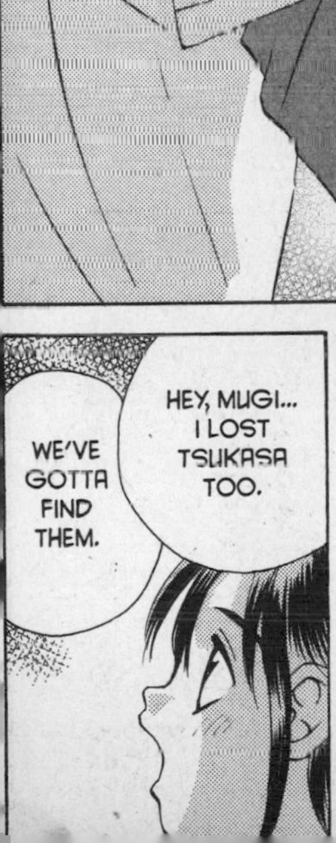
HEY, MUGI... I LOST TSUKASA TOO.
WE'VE GOTTA FIND THEM.

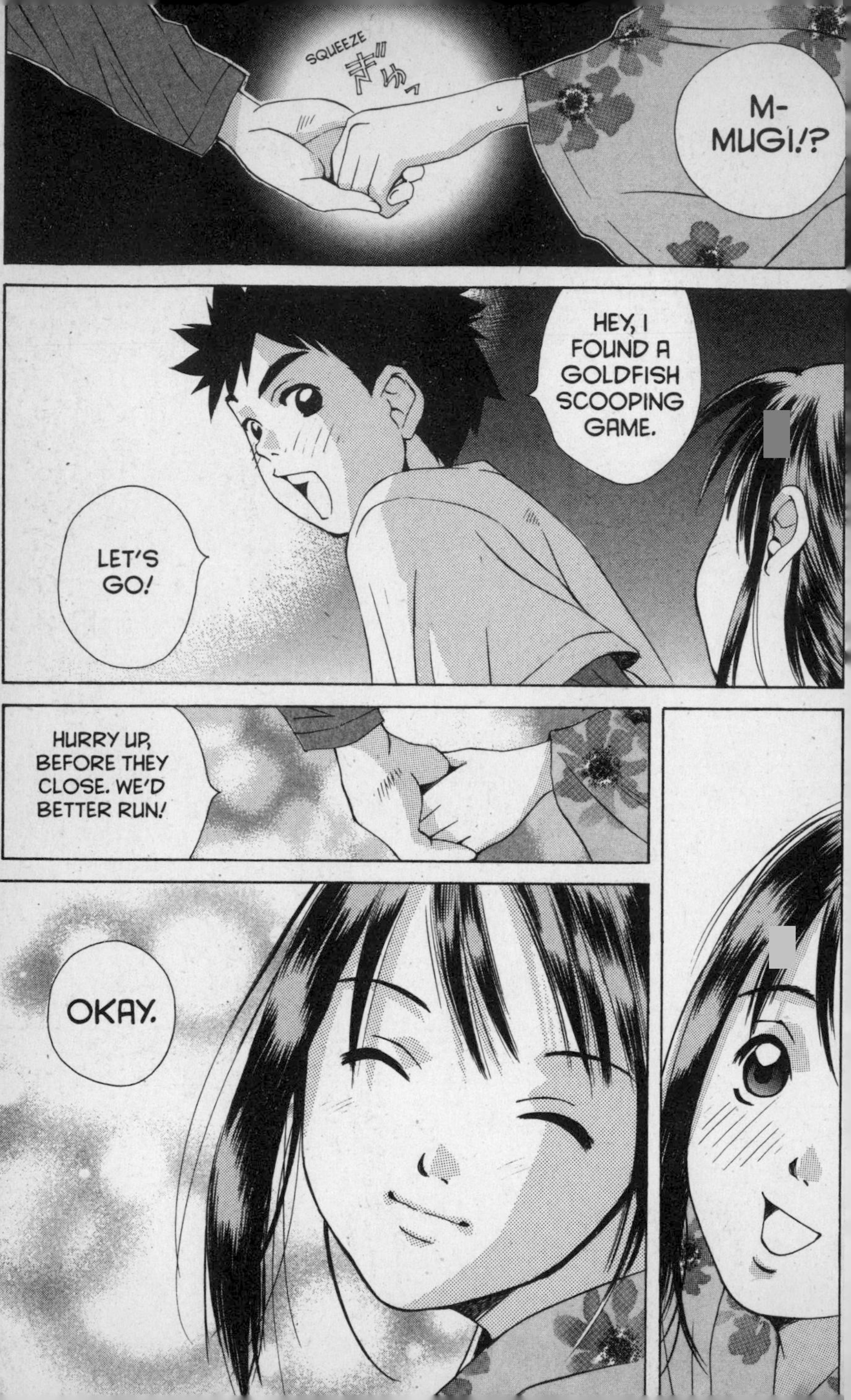
M-MUGI!?
SQUEEZE
HEY, I FOUND A GOLDFISH SCOOPING GAME.
LET'S GO!
HURRY UP, BEFORE THEY CLOSE. WE'D BETTER RUN!
OKAY.

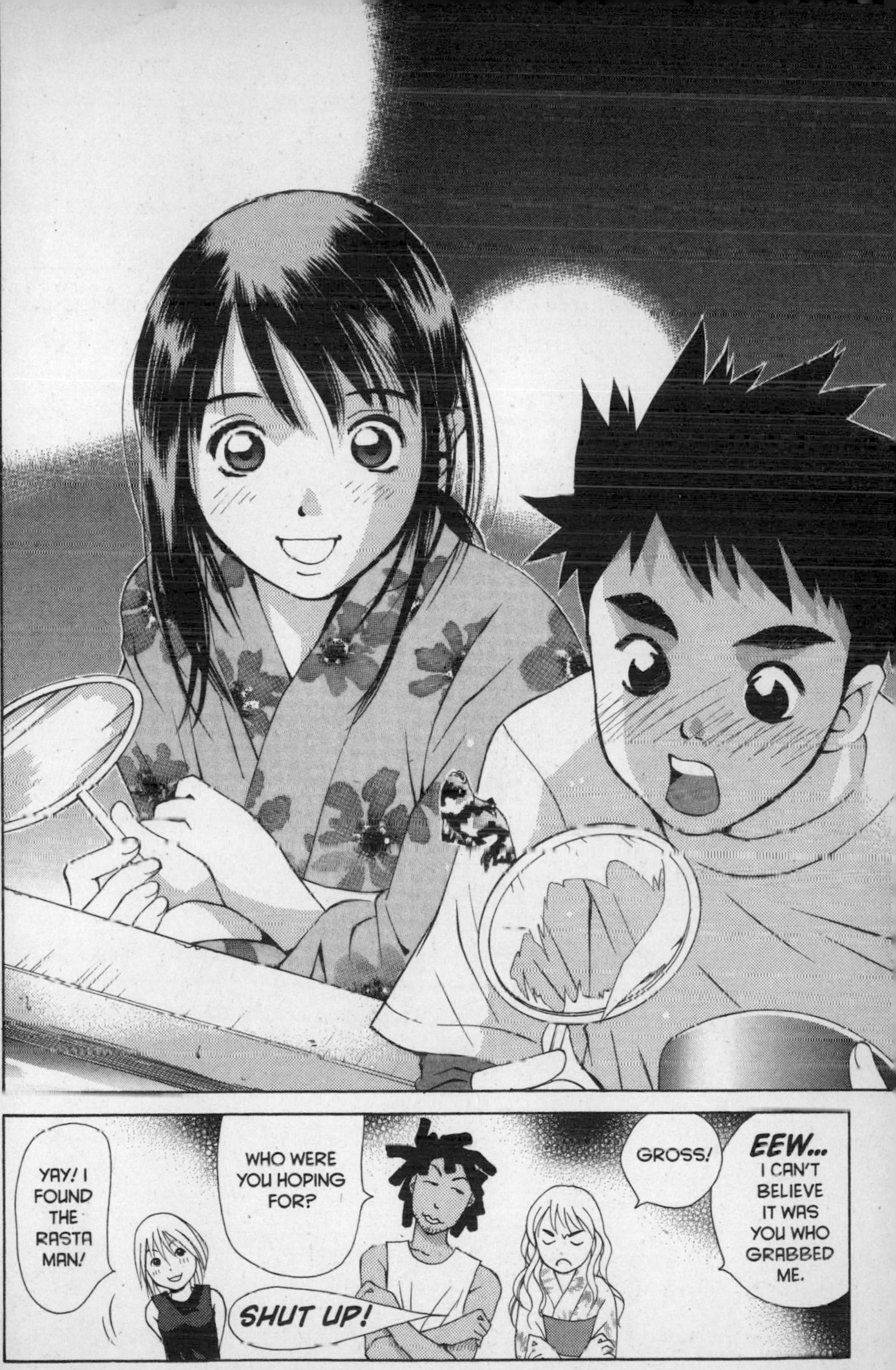
EEW... I CAN'T BELIEVE IT WAS YOU WHO GRABBED ME.
GROSS!
WHO WERE YOU HOPING FOR?
SHUT UP!
YAY! I FOUND THE RASTA MAN!

Pastel

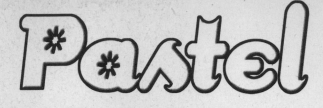

MIRACLE 12: FRAGMENTS OF LOVE

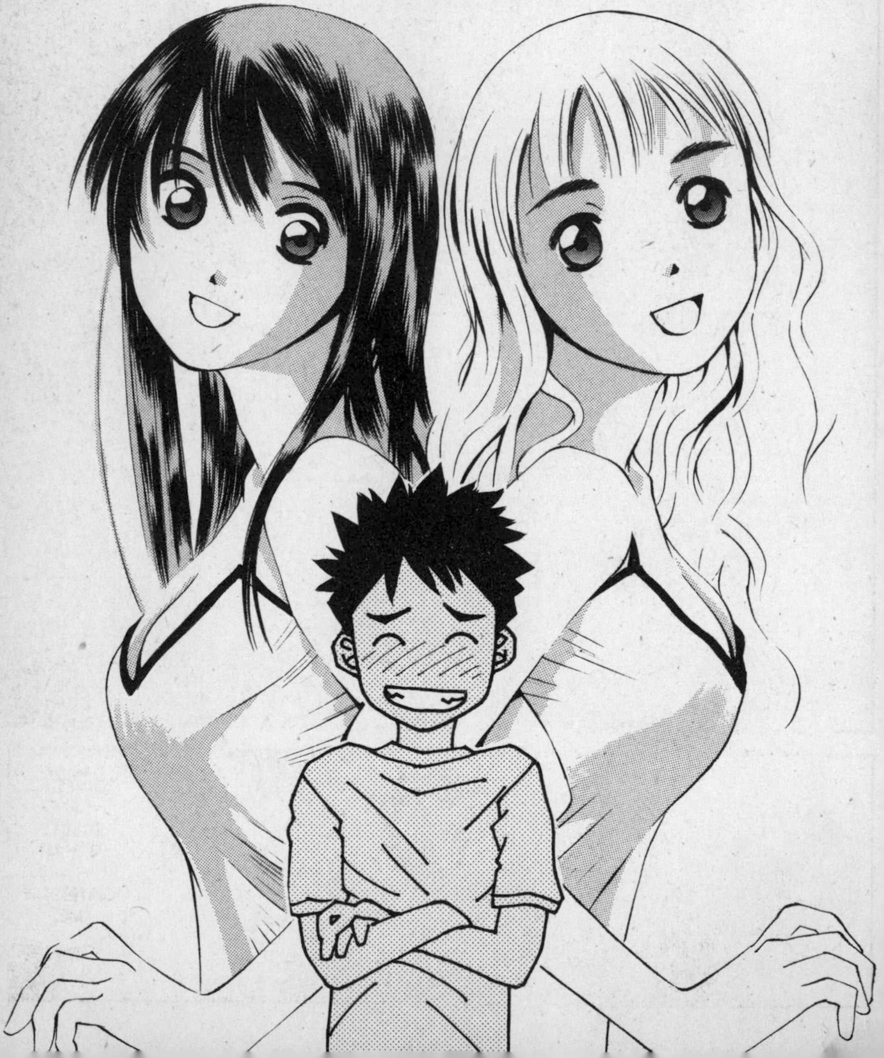

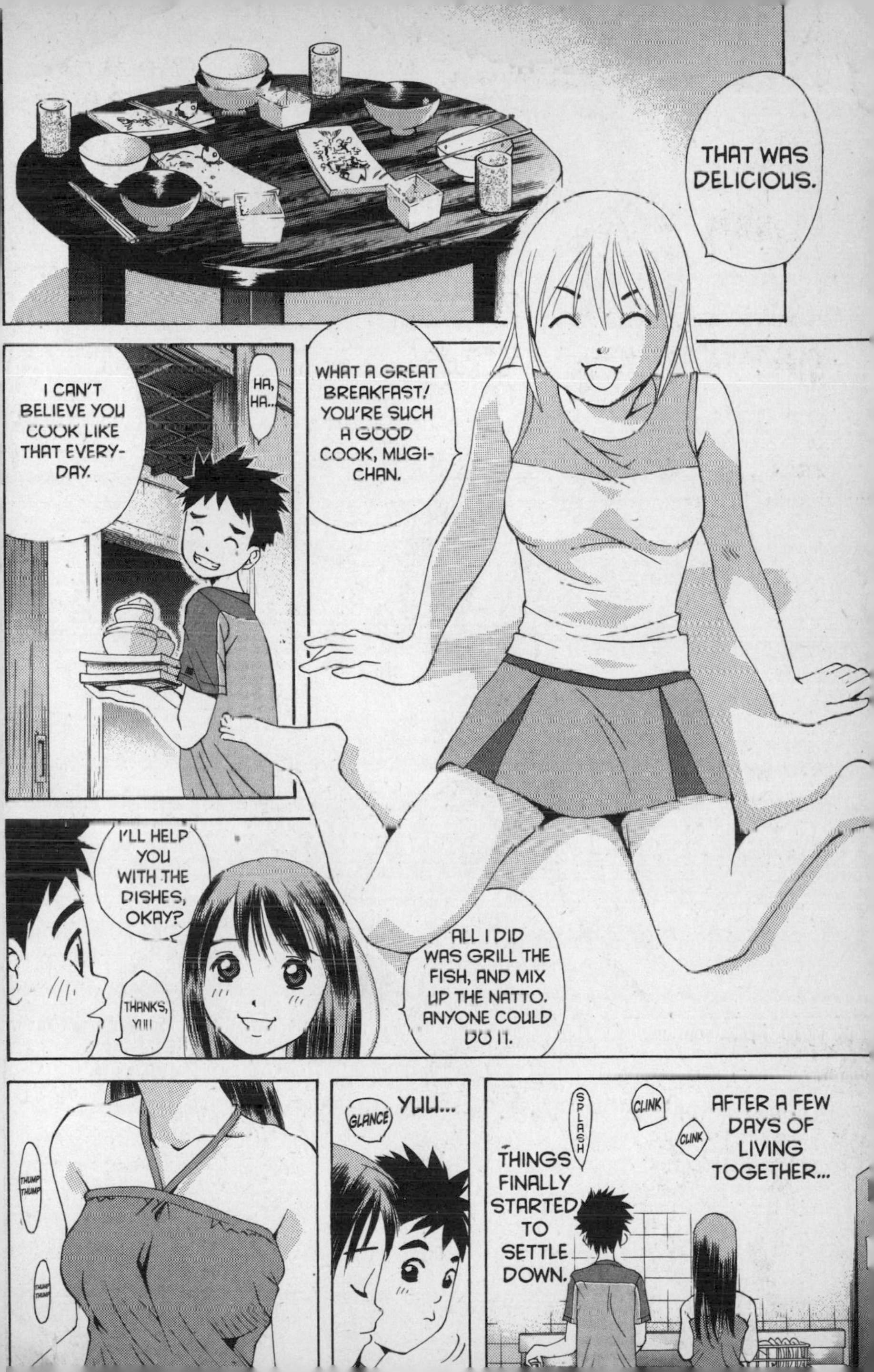
THAT WAS DELICIOUS.
WHAT A GREAT BREAKFAST! YOU'RE SUCH A GOOD COOK, MUGI-CHAN.
HA, HA...
I CAN'T BELIEVE YOU COOK LIKE THAT EVERY-DAY.
ALL I DID WAS GRILL THE FISH, AND MIX UP THE NATTO. ANYONE COULD DO IT.
I'LL HELP YOU WITH THE DISHES, OKAY?
THANKS, YUU!
AFTER A FEW DAYS OF LIVING TOGETHER...
CLINK
CLINK
SPLASH
THINGS FINALLY STARTED TO SETTLE DOWN.
YUU...
GLANCE
THUMP THUMP
THUMP THUMP

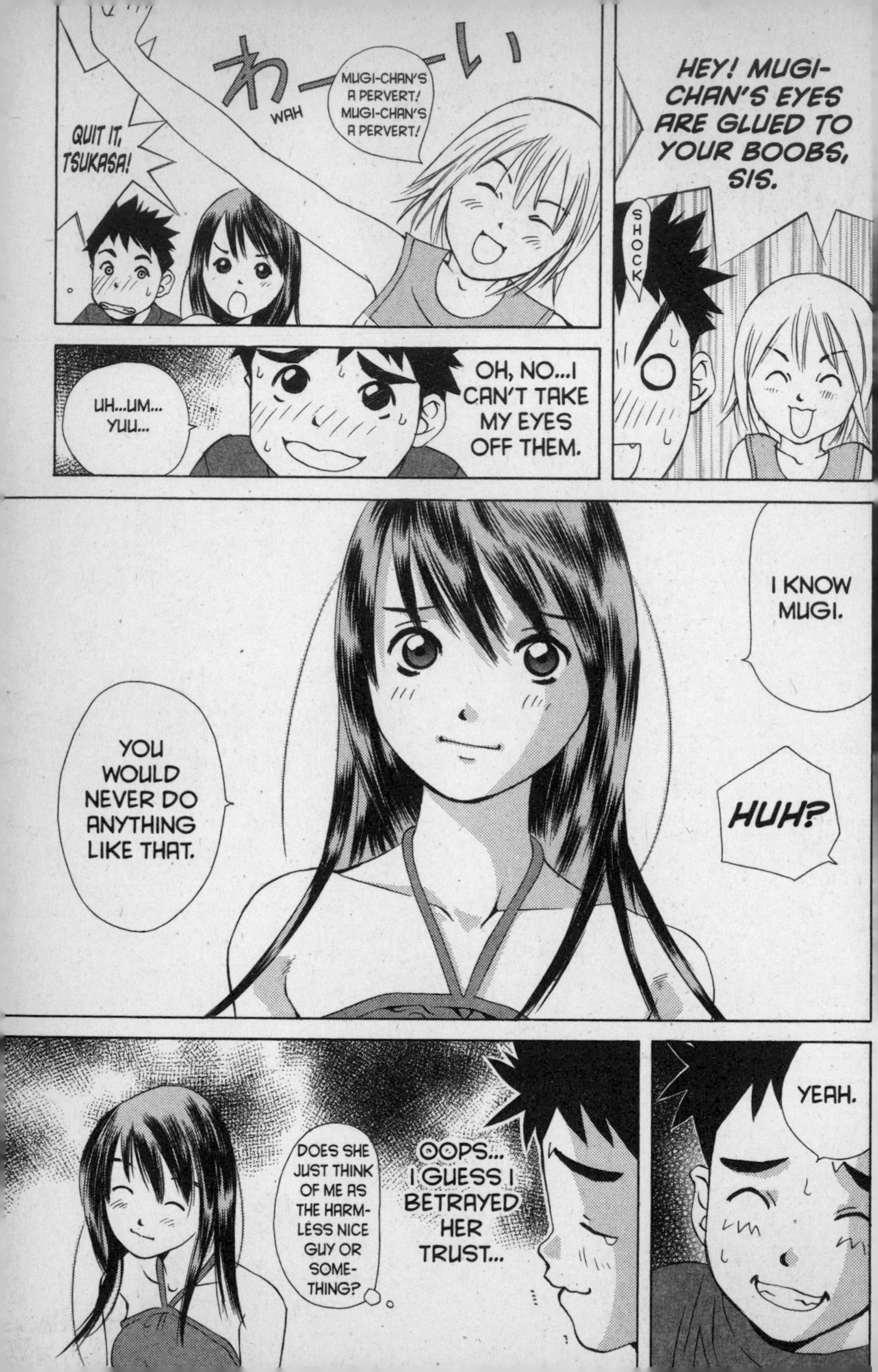
HEY! MUGI-CHAN'S EYES ARE GLUED TO YOUR BOOBS, SIS.
SHOCK
わーーい
WAH
MUGI-CHAN'S A PERVERT! MUGI-CHAN'S A PERVERT!
QUIT IT, TSUKASA!
OH, NO...I CAN'T TAKE MY EYES OFF THEM.
UH...UM... YUU...
I KNOW MUGI.
HUH?
YOU WOULD NEVER DO ANYTHING LIKE THAT.
YEAH.
OOPS... I GUESS I BETRAYED HER TRUST...
DOES SHE JUST THINK OF ME AS THE HARM-LESS NICE GUY OR SOME-THING?

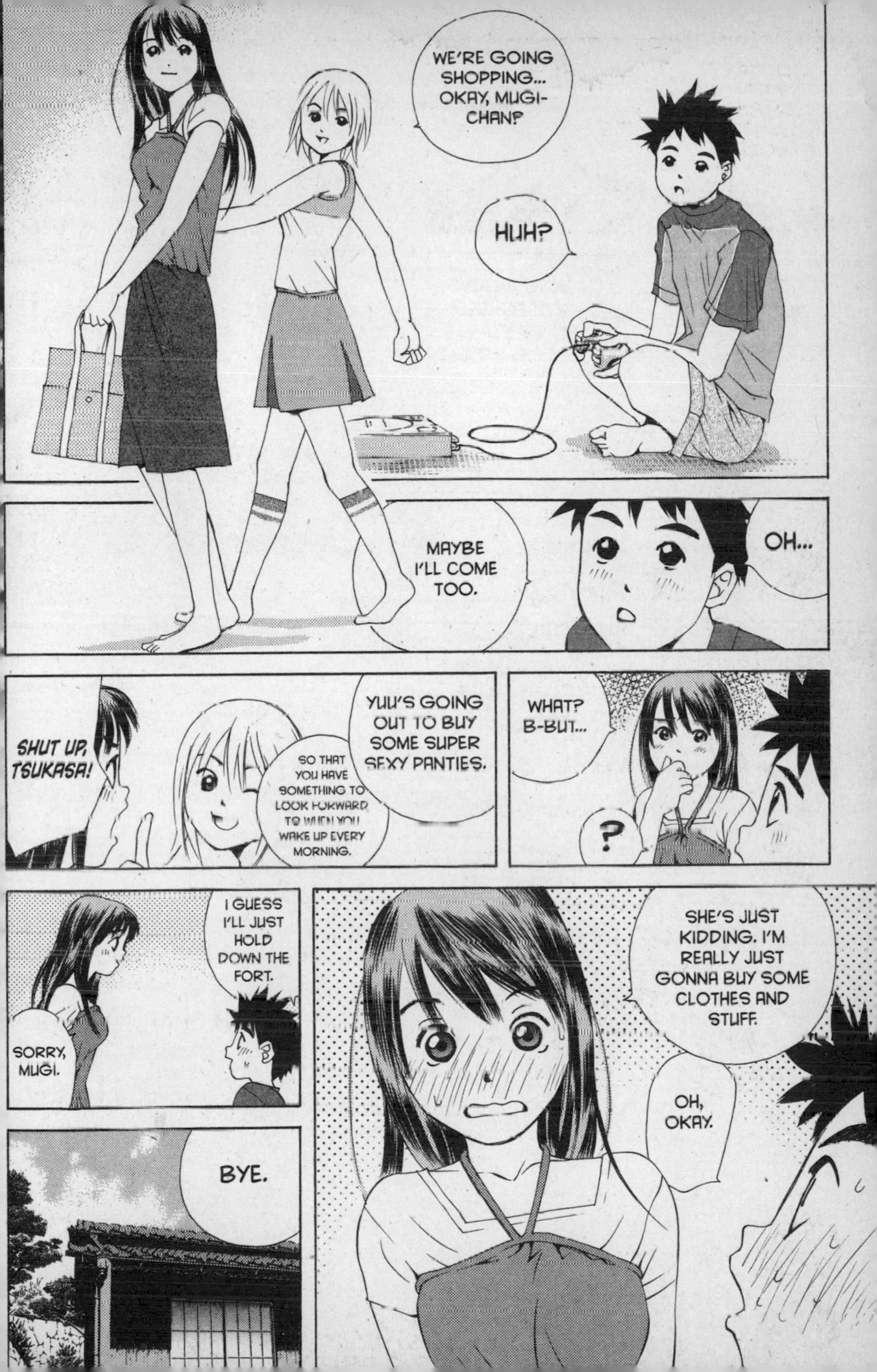
WE'RE GOING SHOPPING... OKAY, MUGI-CHAN?
HUH?
OH...
MAYBE I'LL COME TOO.
WHAT? B-BUT...
?
YUU'S GOING OUT TO BUY SOME SUPER SEXY PANTIES.
SO THAT YOU HAVE SOMETHING TO LOOK FORWARD TO WHEN YOU WAKE UP EVERY MORNING.
SHUT UP, TSUKASA!
SHE'S JUST KIDDING. I'M REALLY JUST GONNA BUY SOME CLOTHES AND STUFF.
OH, OKAY.
I GUESS I'LL JUST HOLD DOWN THE FORT.
SORRY, MUGI.
BYE.

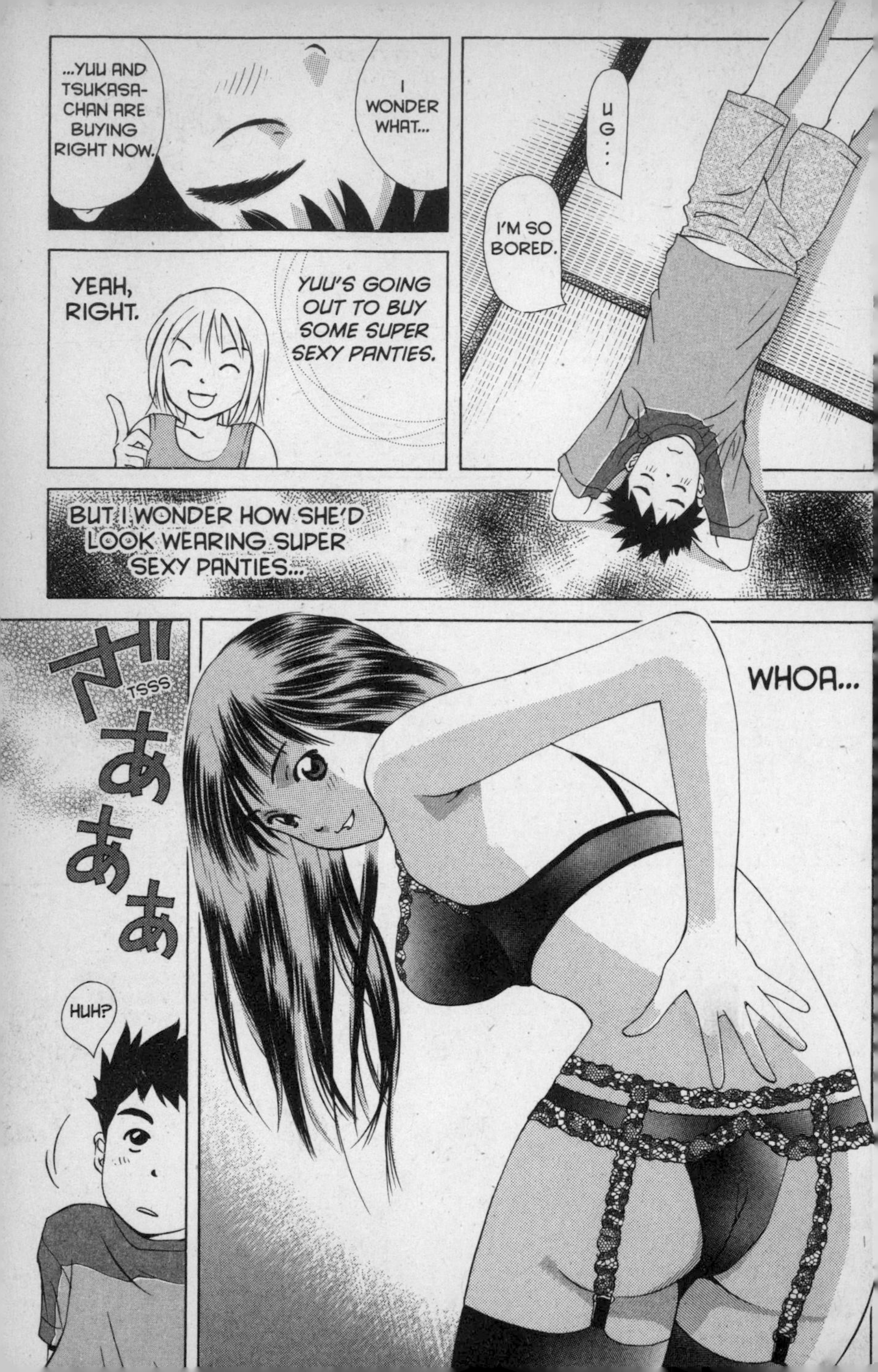
UG...
I'M SO BORED.
I WONDER WHAT...
...YUU AND TSUKASA-CHAN ARE BUYING RIGHT NOW.
YUU'S GOING OUT TO BUY SOME SUPER SEXY PANTIES.
YEAH, RIGHT.
BUT I WONDER HOW SHE'D LOOK WEARING SUPER SEXY PANTIES...
WHOA...
ざあああ
TSSS
HUH?

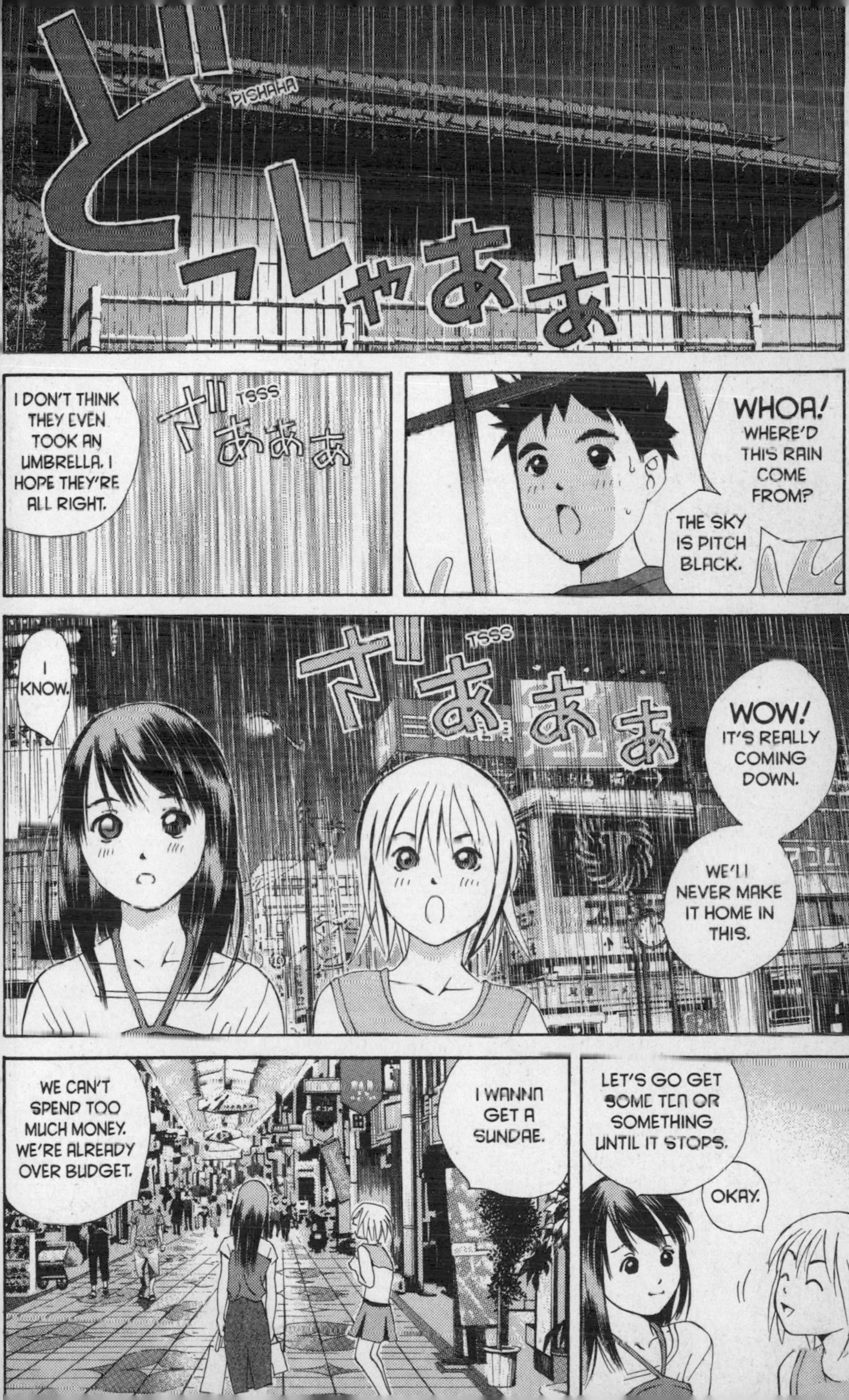
どっしゃあぁ
PISHAHA
WHOA! WHERE'D THIS RAIN COME FROM?
THE SKY IS PITCH BLACK.
ざああぁ
TSSS
I DON'T THINK THEY EVEN TOOK AN UMBRELLA. I HOPE THEY'RE ALL RIGHT.
ざああぁ
TSSS
WOW! IT'S REALLY COMING DOWN.
WE'LL NEVER MAKE IT HOME IN THIS.
I KNOW.
LET'S GO GET SOME TEA OR SOMETHING UNTIL IT STOPS.
OKAY.
I WANNA GET A SUNDAE.
WE CAN'T SPEND TOO MUCH MONEY. WE'RE ALREADY OVER BUDGET.

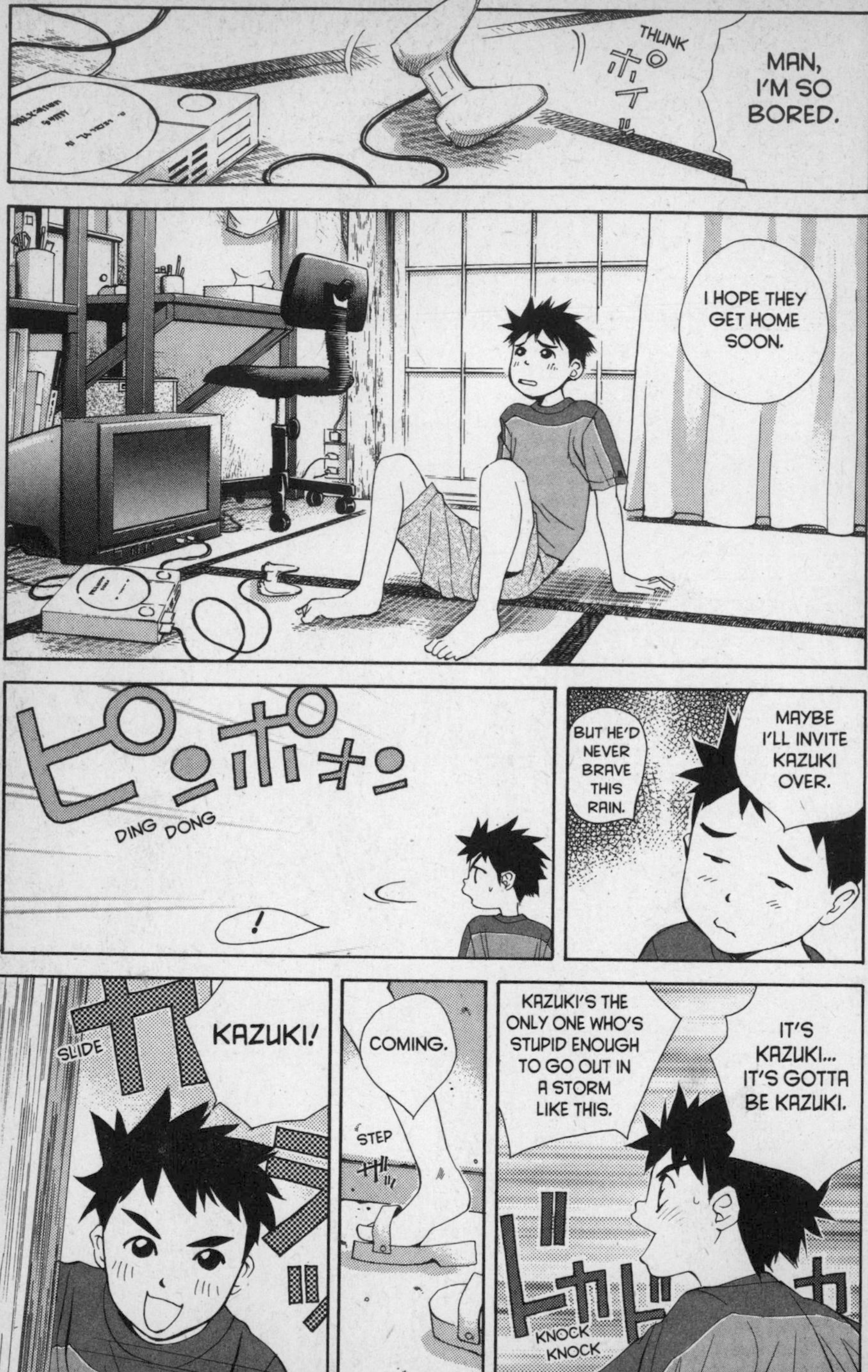
THUNK
MAN, I'M SO BORED.
I HOPE THEY GET HOME SOON.
MAYBE I'LL INVITE KAZUKI OVER.
BUT HE'D NEVER BRAVE THIS RAIN.
DING DONG
!
IT'S KAZUKI... IT'S GOTTA BE KAZUKI.
KAZUKI'S THE ONLY ONE WHO'S STUPID ENOUGH TO GO OUT IN A STORM LIKE THIS.
KNOCK KNOCK
COMING.
STEP
SLIDE
KAZUKI!

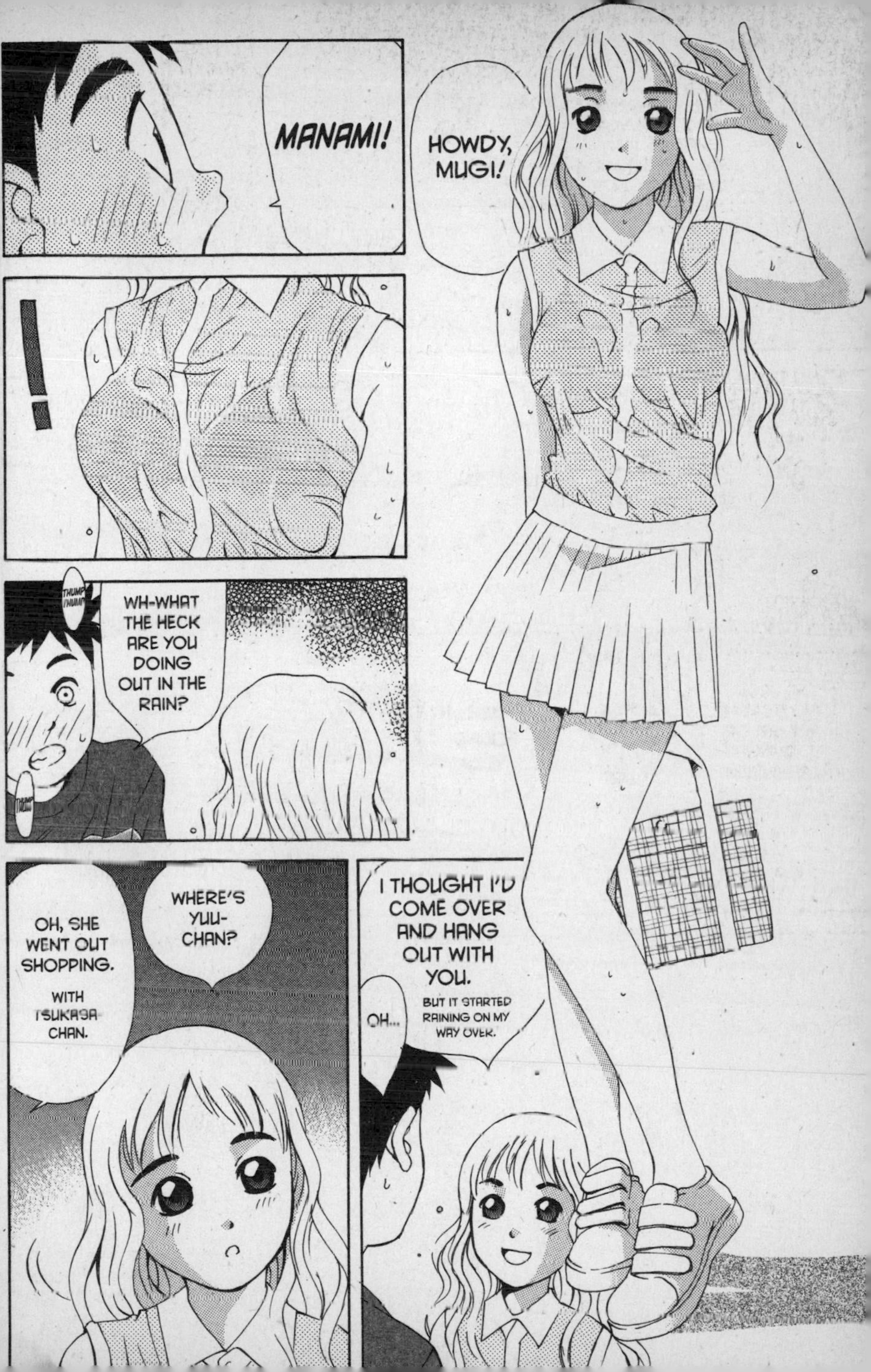
HOWDY, MUGI!
MANAMI!
!
THUMP THUMP
WH-WHAT THE HECK ARE YOU DOING OUT IN THE RAIN?
THUMP
I THOUGHT I'D COME OVER AND HANG OUT WITH YOU.
BUT IT STARTED RAINING ON MY WAY OVER.
OH...
WHERE'S YUU-CHAN?
OH, SHE WENT OUT SHOPPING.
WITH TSUKASA-CHAN.

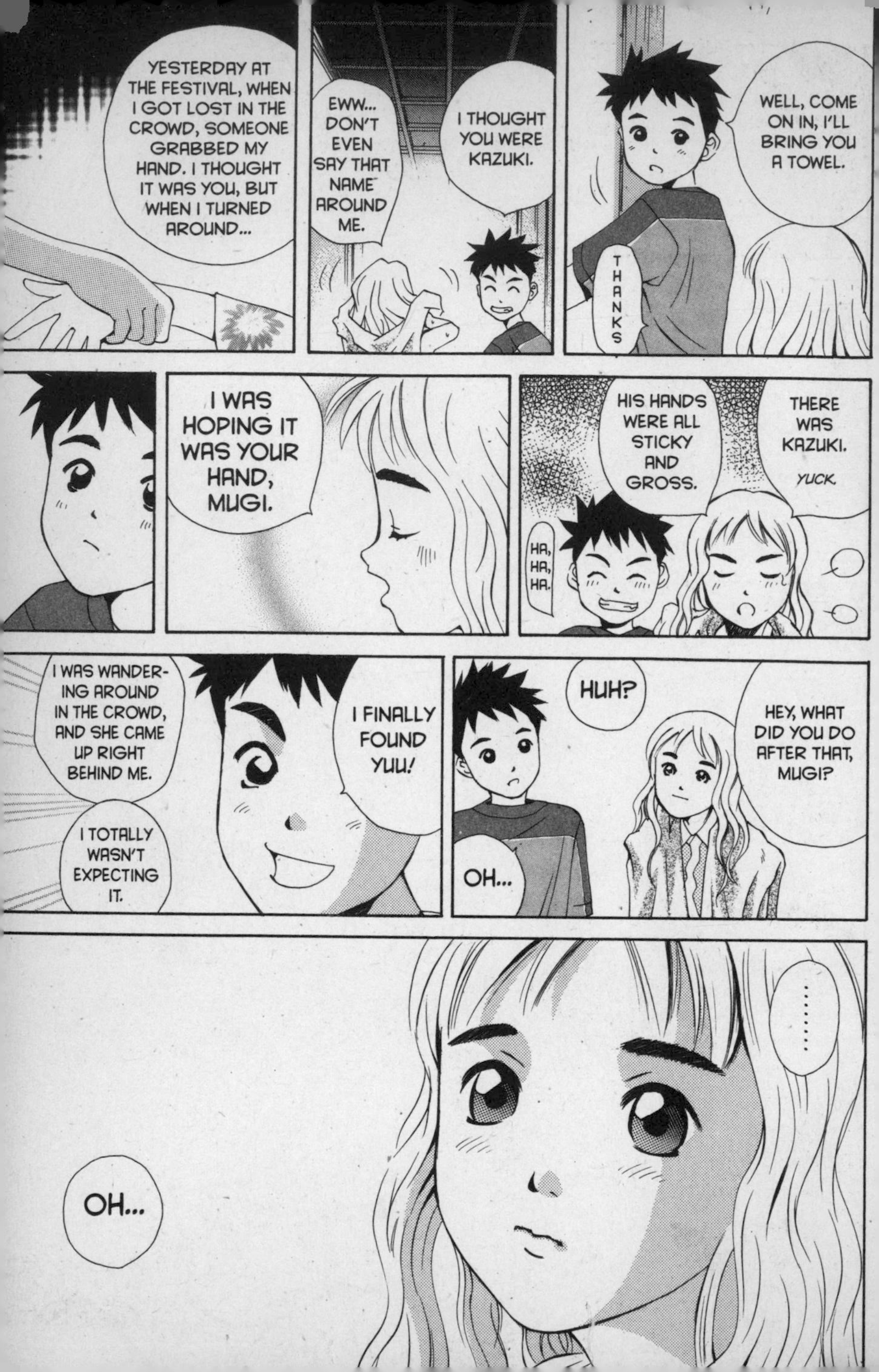
WELL, COME ON IN, I'LL BRING YOU A TOWEL.
THANKS
I THOUGHT YOU WERE KAZUKI.
EWW... DON'T EVEN SAY THAT NAME AROUND ME.
YESTERDAY AT THE FESTIVAL, WHEN I GOT LOST IN THE CROWD, SOMEONE GRABBED MY HAND. I THOUGHT IT WAS YOU, BUT WHEN I TURNED AROUND...
THERE WAS KAZUKI.
YUCK.
HIS HANDS WERE ALL STICKY AND GROSS.
HA, HA, HA.
I WAS HOPING IT WAS YOUR HAND, MUGI.
HEY, WHAT DID YOU DO AFTER THAT, MUGI?
HUH?
OH...
I FINALLY FOUND YUU!
I WAS WANDER-ING AROUND IN THE CROWD, AND SHE CAME UP RIGHT BEHIND ME.
I TOTALLY WASN'T EXPECTING IT.
......
OH...

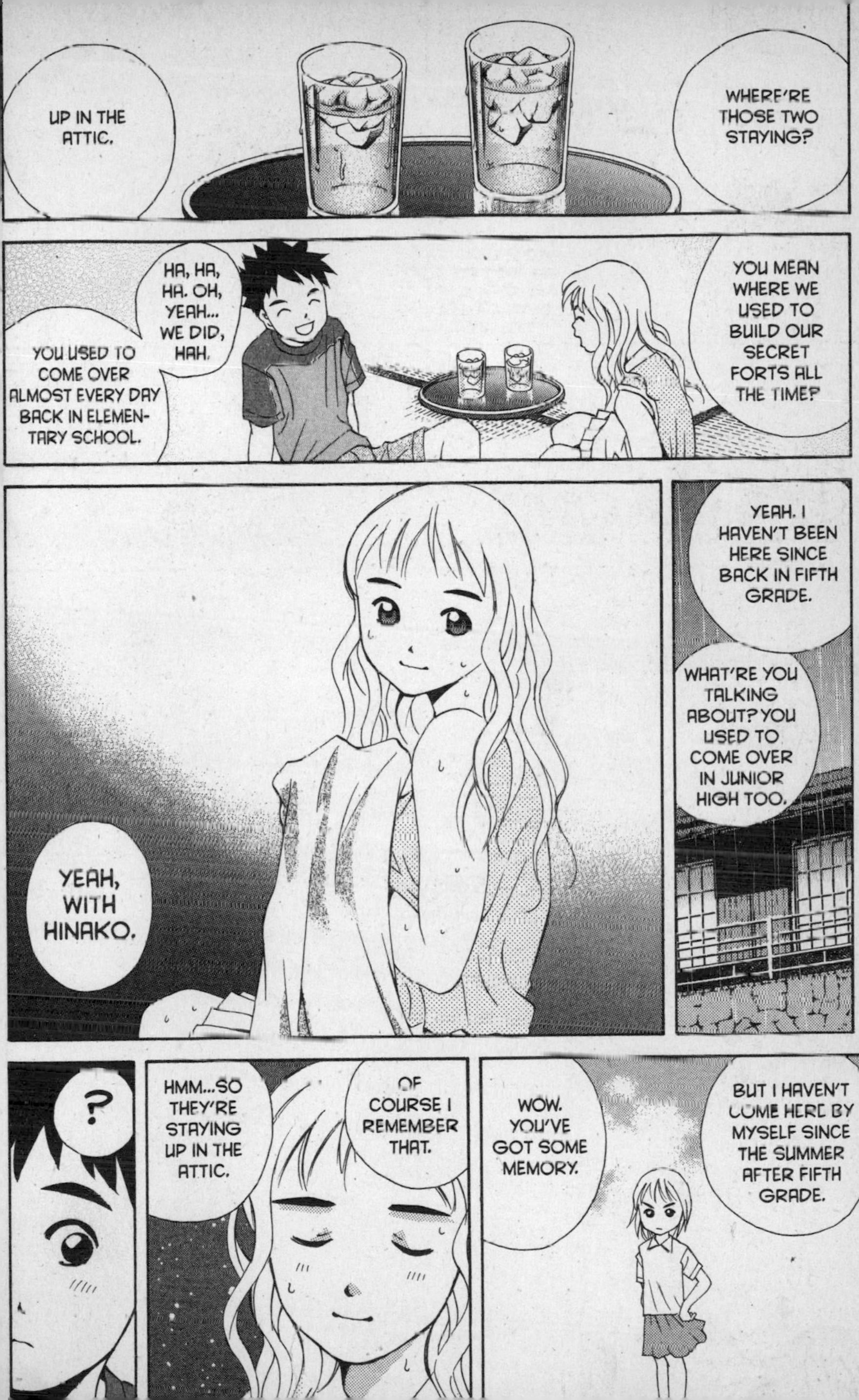
WHERE'RE THOSE TWO STAYING?
UP IN THE ATTIC.
YOU MEAN WHERE WE USED TO BUILD OUR SECRET FORTS ALL THE TIME?
HA, HA, HA. OH, YEAH... WE DID, HAH.
YOU USED TO COME OVER ALMOST EVERY DAY BACK IN ELEMENTARY SCHOOL.
YEAH. I HAVEN'T BEEN HERE SINCE BACK IN FIFTH GRADE.
WHAT'RE YOU TALKING ABOUT? YOU USED TO COME OVER IN JUNIOR HIGH TOO.
YEAH, WITH HINAKO.
BUT I HAVEN'T COME HERE BY MYSELF SINCE THE SUMMER AFTER FIFTH GRADE.
WOW. YOU'VE GOT SOME MEMORY.
OF COURSE I REMEMBER THAT.
HMM...SO THEY'RE STAYING UP IN THE ATTIC.
?

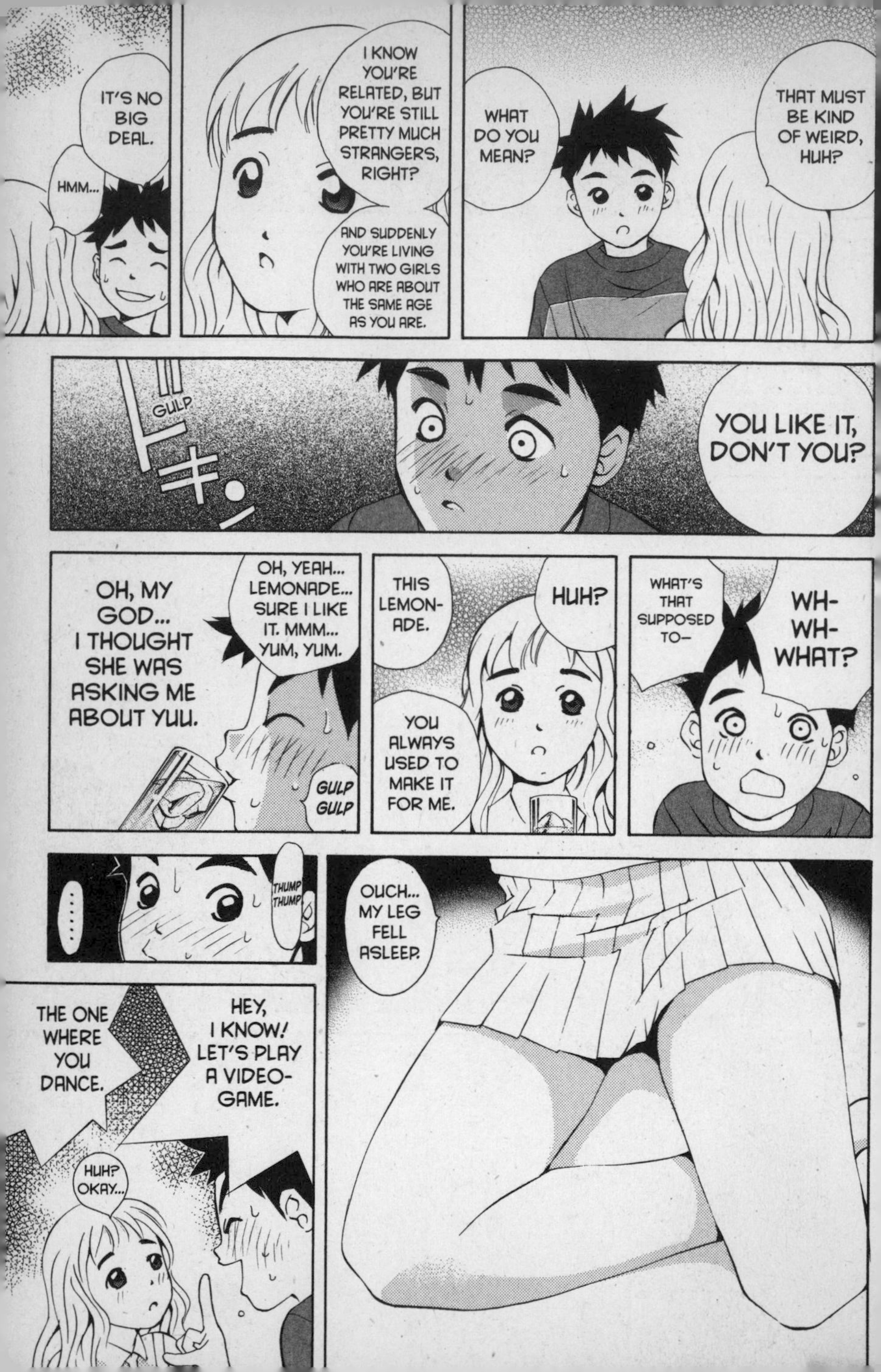
THAT MUST BE KIND OF WEIRD, HUH?
WHAT DO YOU MEAN?
I KNOW YOU'RE RELATED, BUT YOU'RE STILL PRETTY MUCH STRANGERS, RIGHT?
AND SUDDENLY YOU'RE LIVING WITH TWO GIRLS WHO ARE ABOUT THE SAME AGE AS YOU ARE.
IT'S NO BIG DEAL.
HMM...
YOU LIKE IT, DON'T YOU?
GULP
WH-WH-WHAT?
WHAT'S THAT SUPPOSED TO—
HUH?
THIS LEMONADE.
YOU ALWAYS USED TO MAKE IT FOR ME.
OH, YEAH... LEMONADE... SURE I LIKE IT. MMM... YUM, YUM.
OH, MY GOD... I THOUGHT SHE WAS ASKING ME ABOUT YUU.
GULP GULP
OUCH... MY LEG FELL ASLEEP.
THUMP THUMP
......
HEY, I KNOW! LET'S PLAY A VIDEO-GAME.
THE ONE WHERE YOU DANCE.
HUH? OKAY...

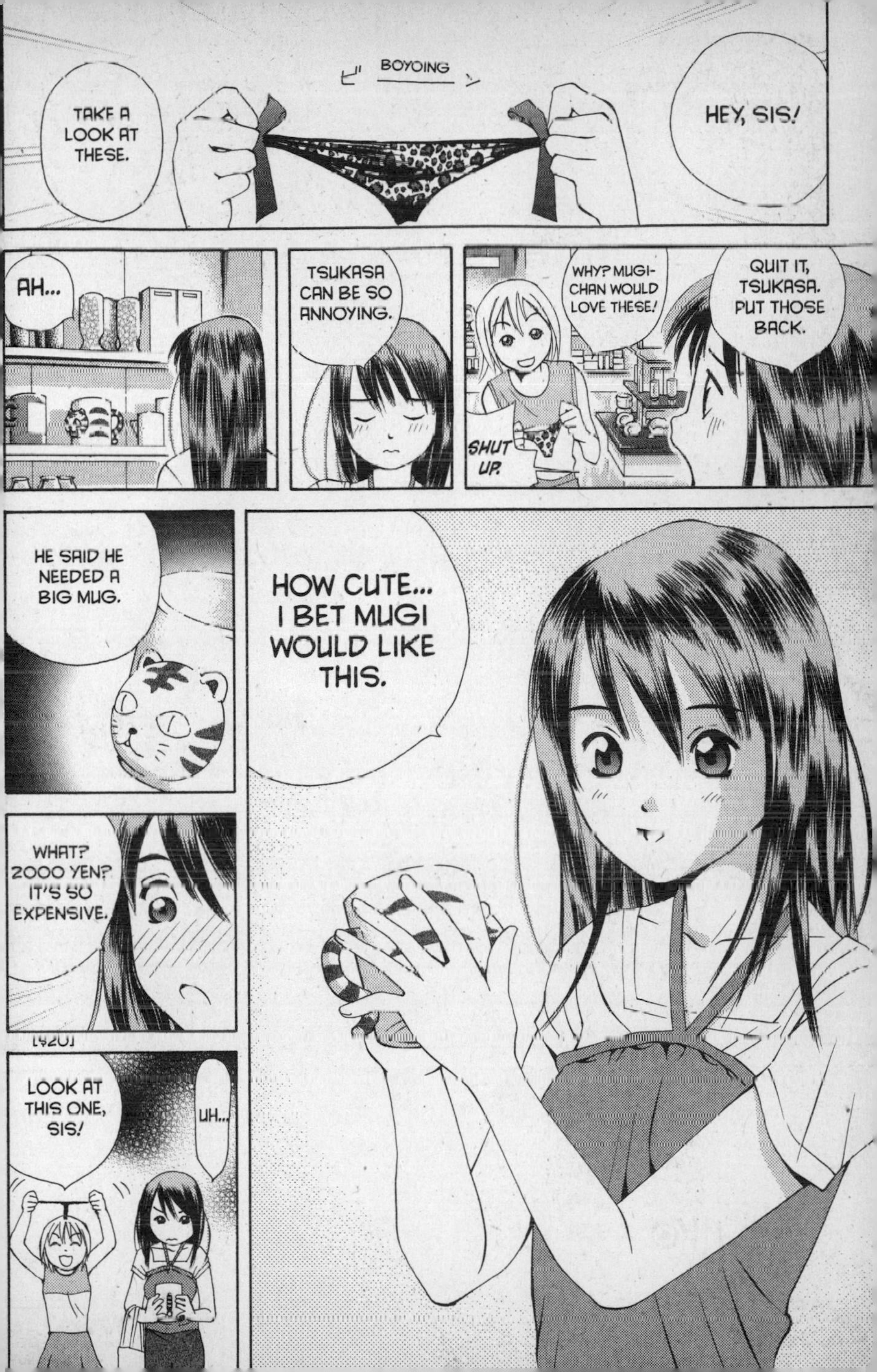
HEY, SIS!
ビ BOYOING
TAKE A LOOK AT THESE.
QUIT IT, TSUKASA. PUT THOSE BACK.
WHY? MUGI-CHAN WOULD LOVE THESE!
SHUT UP.
TSUKASA CAN BE SO ANNOYING.
AH...
HOW CUTE... I BET MUGI WOULD LIKE THIS.
HE SAID HE NEEDED A BIG MUG.
WHAT? 2000 YEN? IT'S SO EXPENSIVE.
UH...
LOOK AT THIS ONE, SIS!

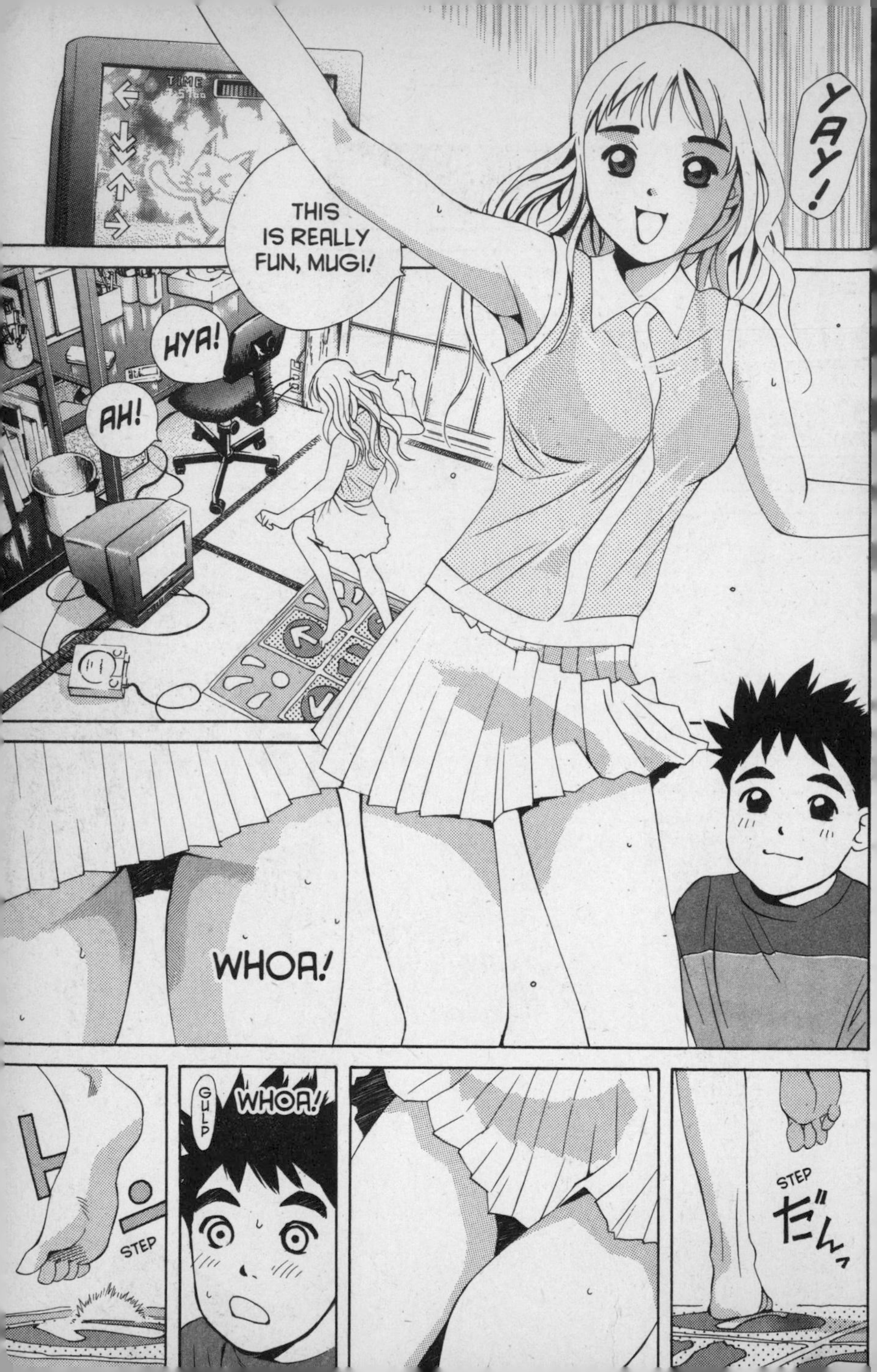
YAY!
THIS IS REALLY FUN, MUGI!
HYA!
AH!
WHOA!
STEP
だん
GULP
WHOA!
STEP

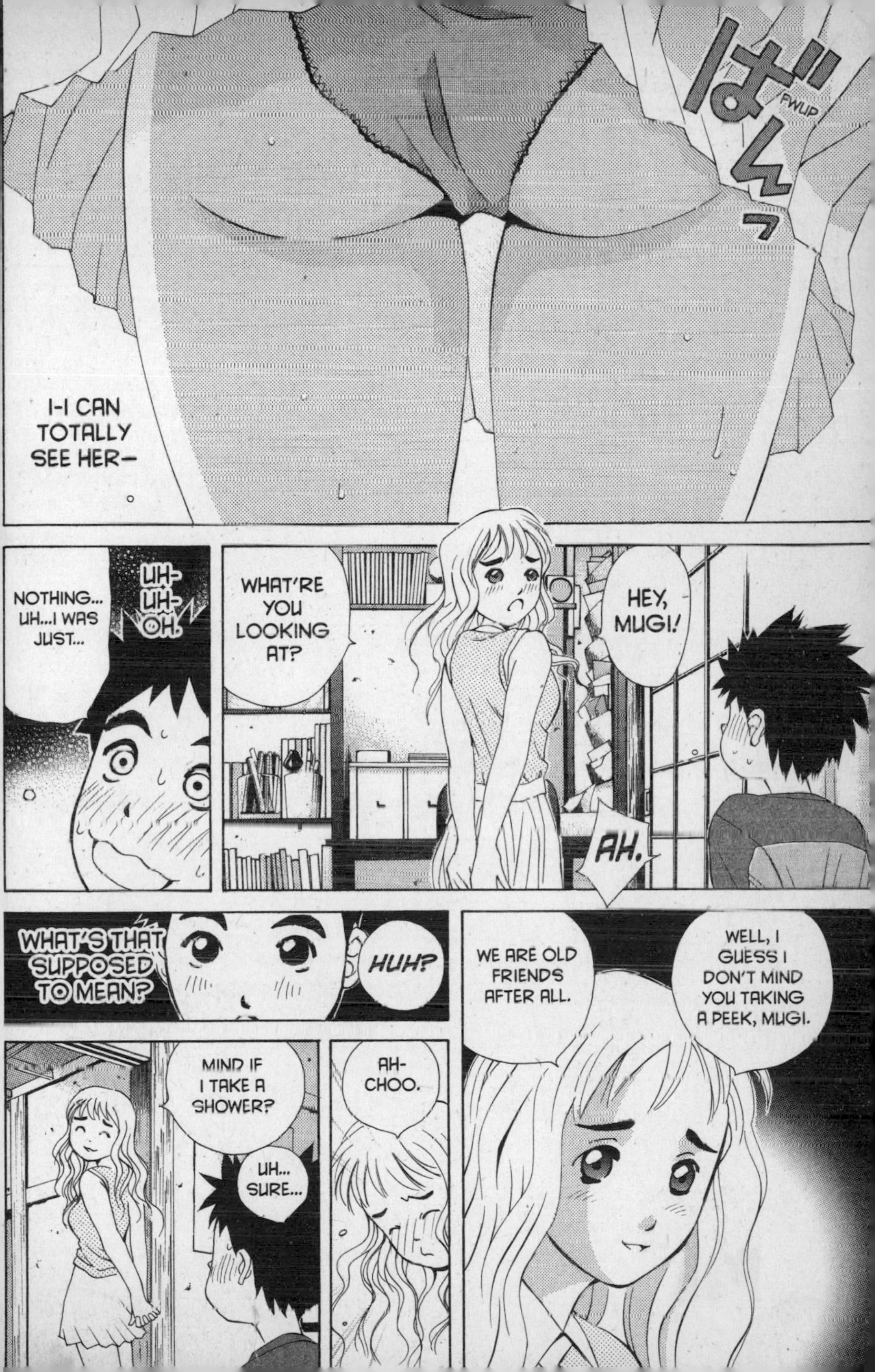
ばん
FWUP
I-I CAN TOTALLY SEE HER—
HEY, MUGI!
AH.
WHAT'RE YOU LOOKING AT?
UH-UH-OH.
NOTHING... UH...I WAS JUST...
WELL, I GUESS I DON'T MIND YOU TAKING A PEEK, MUGI.
WE ARE OLD FRIENDS AFTER ALL.
HUH?
WHAT'S THAT SUPPOSED TO MEAN?
AH-CHOO.
MIND IF I TAKE A SHOWER?
UH... SURE...

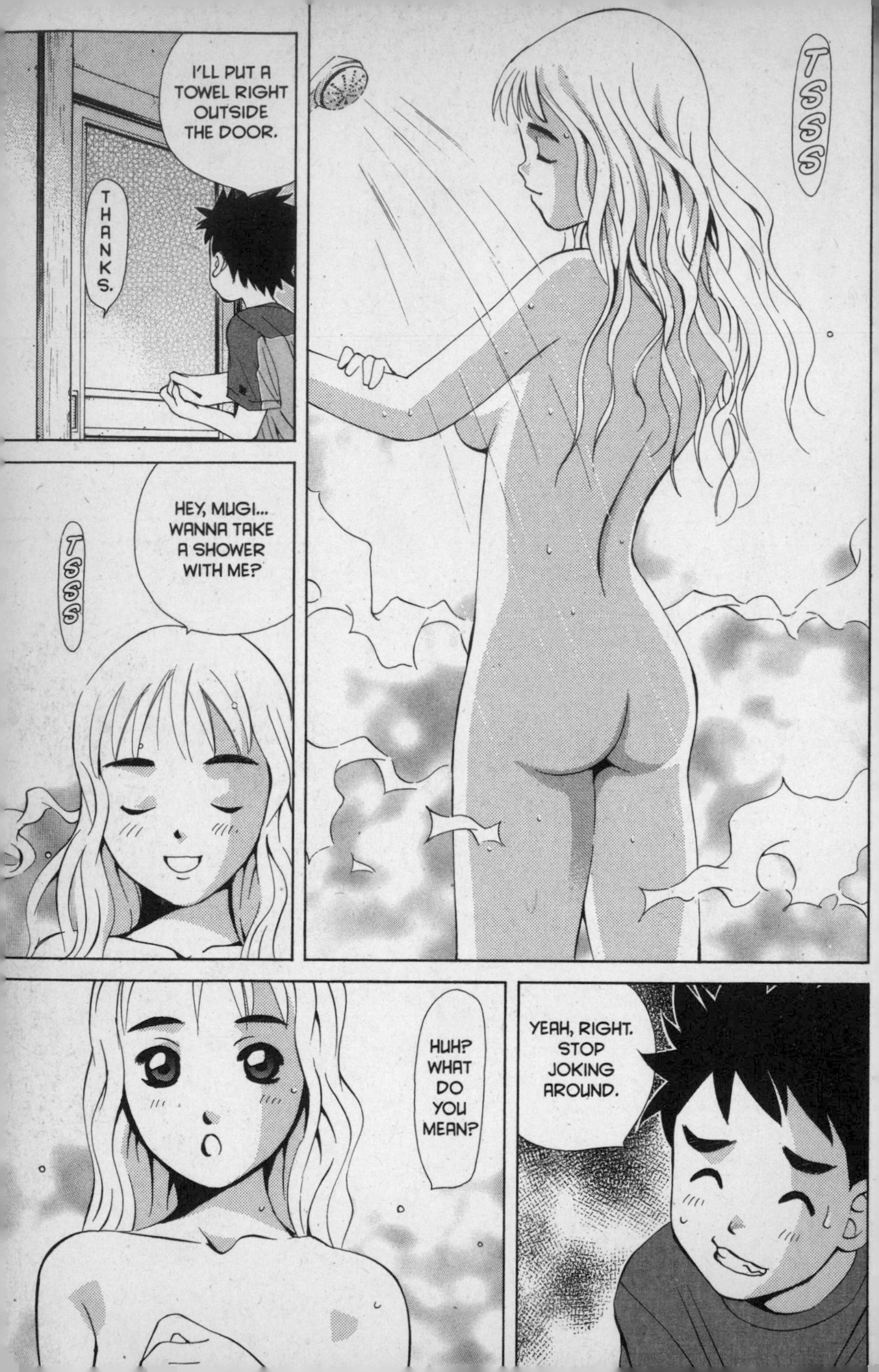
TSSS
I'LL PUT A TOWEL RIGHT OUTSIDE THE DOOR.
THANKS.
HEY, MUGI... WANNA TAKE A SHOWER WITH ME?
TSSS
YEAH, RIGHT. STOP JOKING AROUND.
HUH? WHAT DO YOU MEAN?

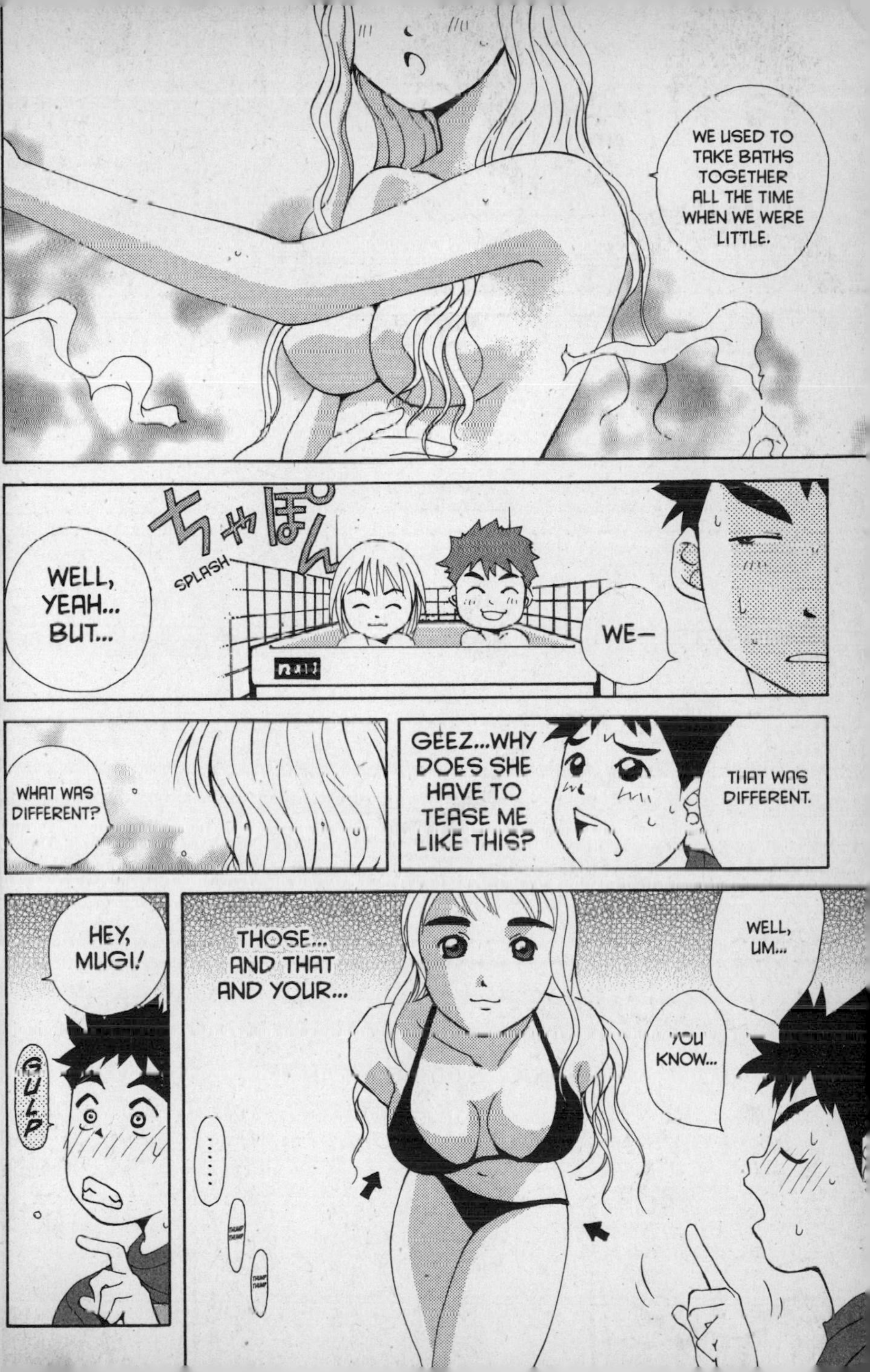
WE USED TO TAKE BATHS TOGETHER ALL THE TIME WHEN WE WERE LITTLE.
WE—
ちゃぽん
SPLASH
WELL, YEAH... BUT...
THAT WAS DIFFERENT.
GEEZ...WHY DOES SHE HAVE TO TEASE ME LIKE THIS?
WHAT WAS DIFFERENT?
WELL, UM...
YOU KNOW...
THOSE... AND THAT AND YOUR...
......
THUMP THUMP
THUMP THUMP
HEY, MUGI!
GULP

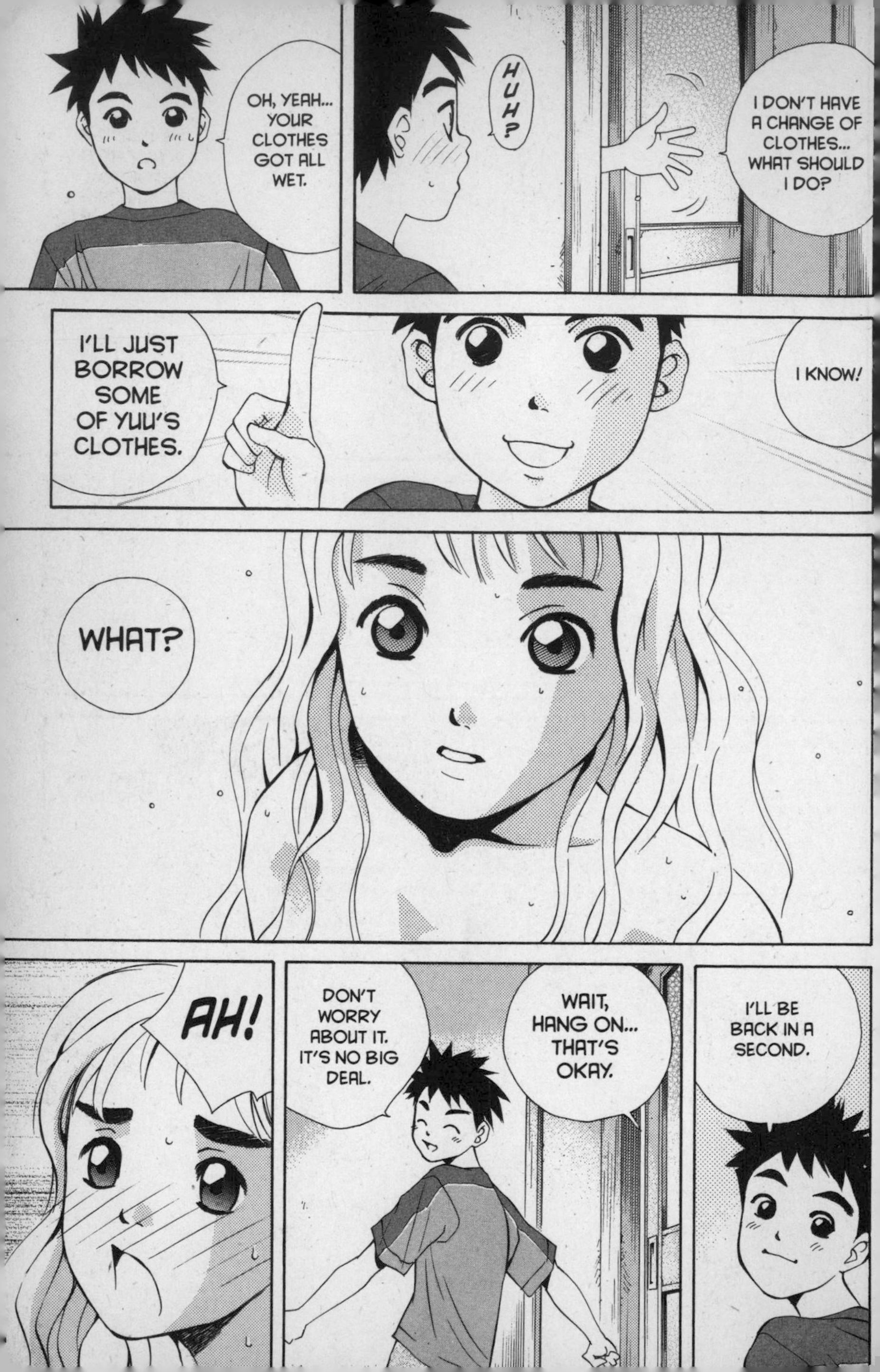
I DON'T HAVE A CHANGE OF CLOTHES... WHAT SHOULD I DO?
HUH?
OH, YEAH... YOUR CLOTHES GOT ALL WET.
I KNOW!
I'LL JUST BORROW SOME OF YUU'S CLOTHES.
WHAT?
I'LL BE BACK IN A SECOND.
WAIT, HANG ON... THAT'S OKAY.
DON'T WORRY ABOUT IT. IT'S NO BIG DEAL.
AH!

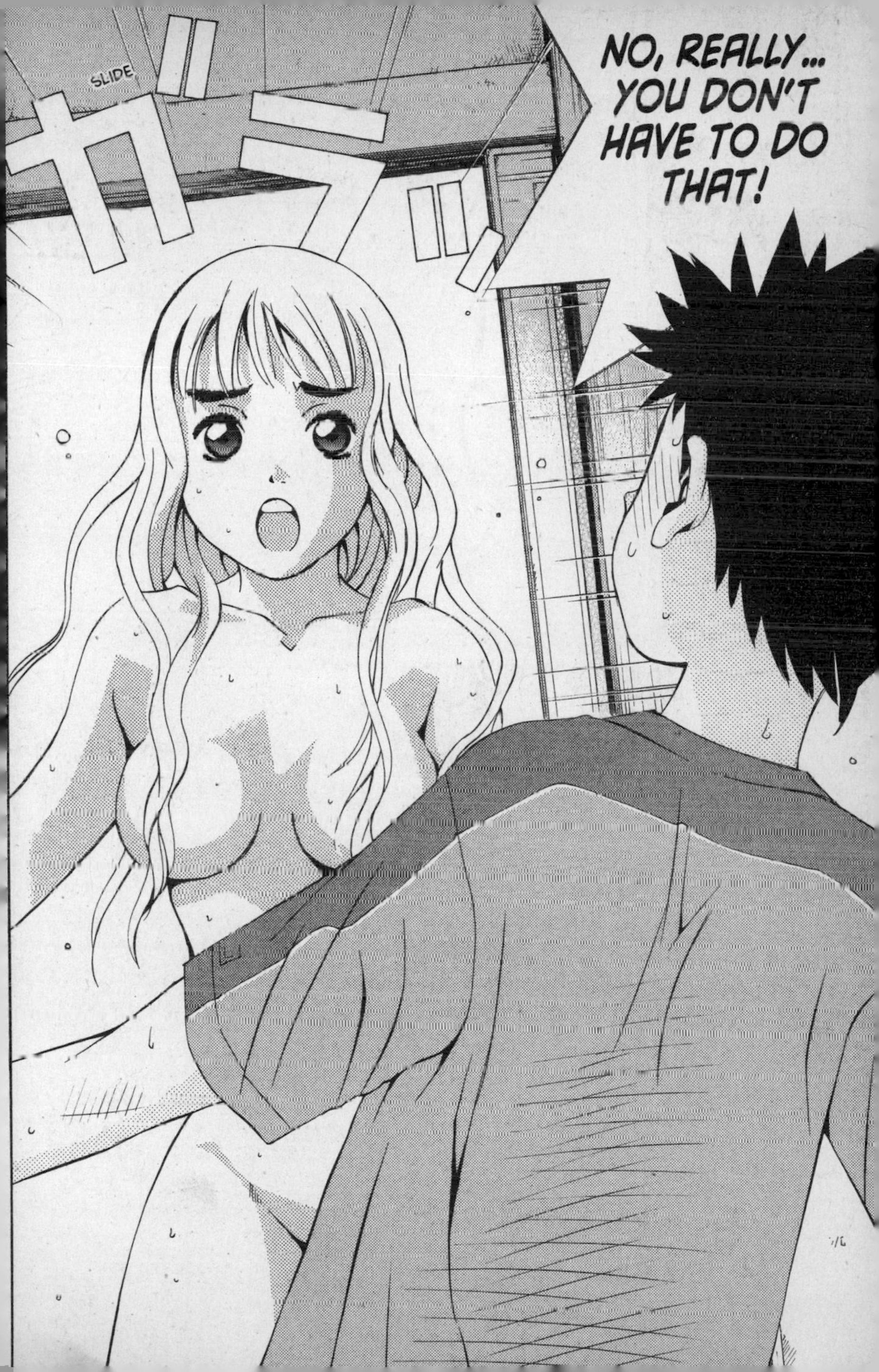
NO, REALLY... YOU DON'T HAVE TO DO THAT!
SLIDE

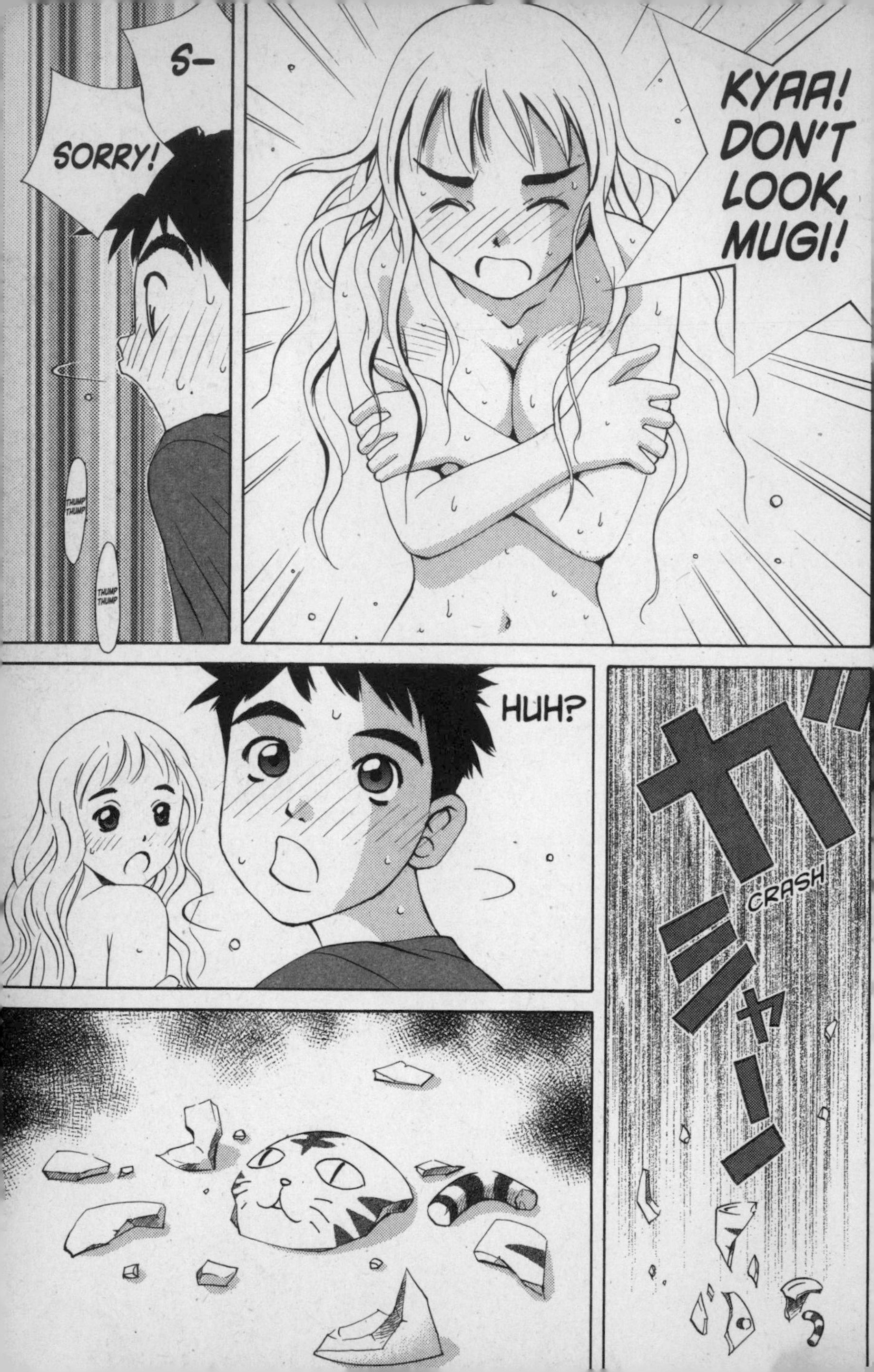
KYAA! DON'T LOOK, MUGI!
S—
SORRY!
THUMP THUMP
THUMP THUMP
CRASH
HUH?

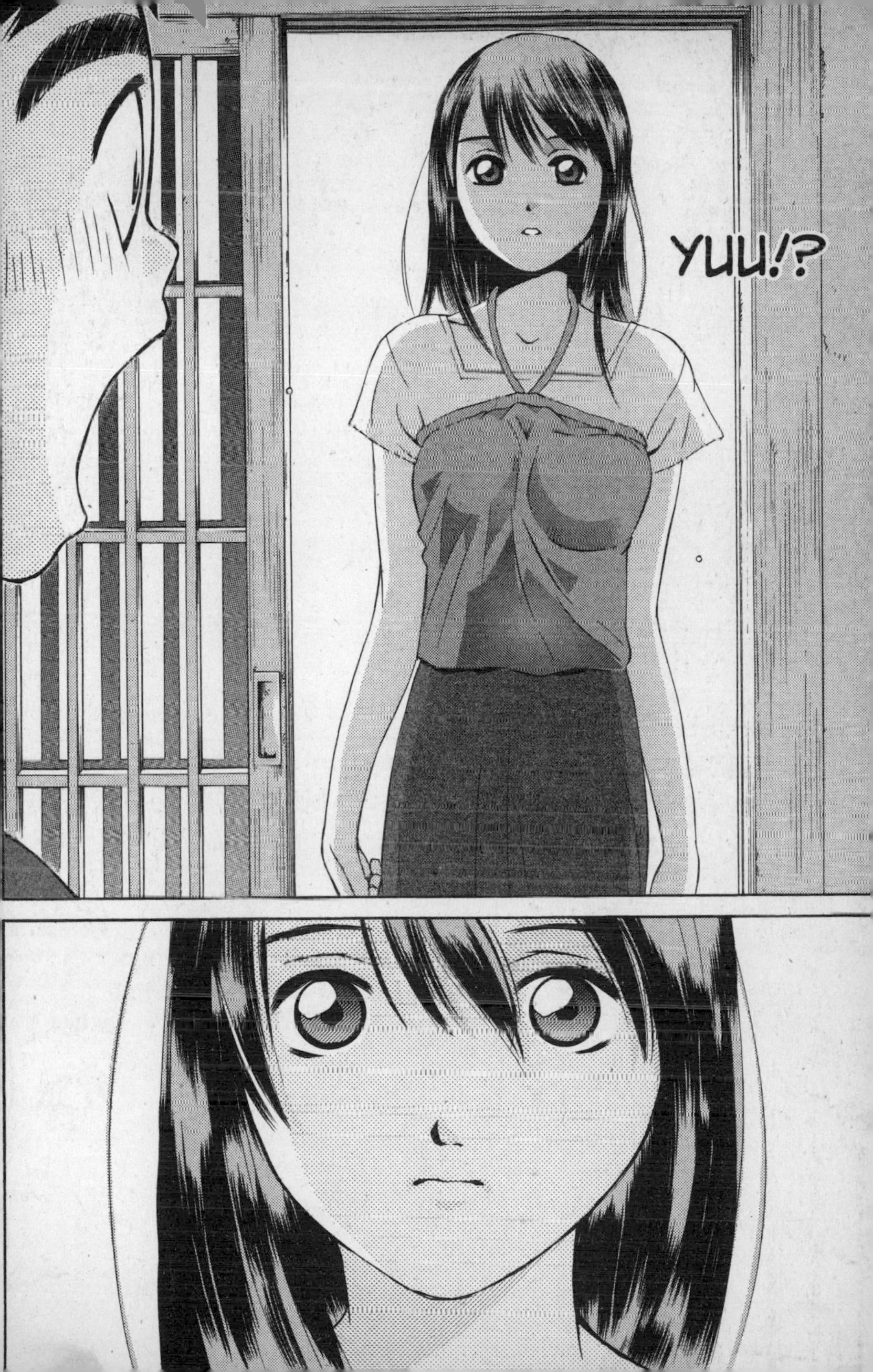
YUU!?

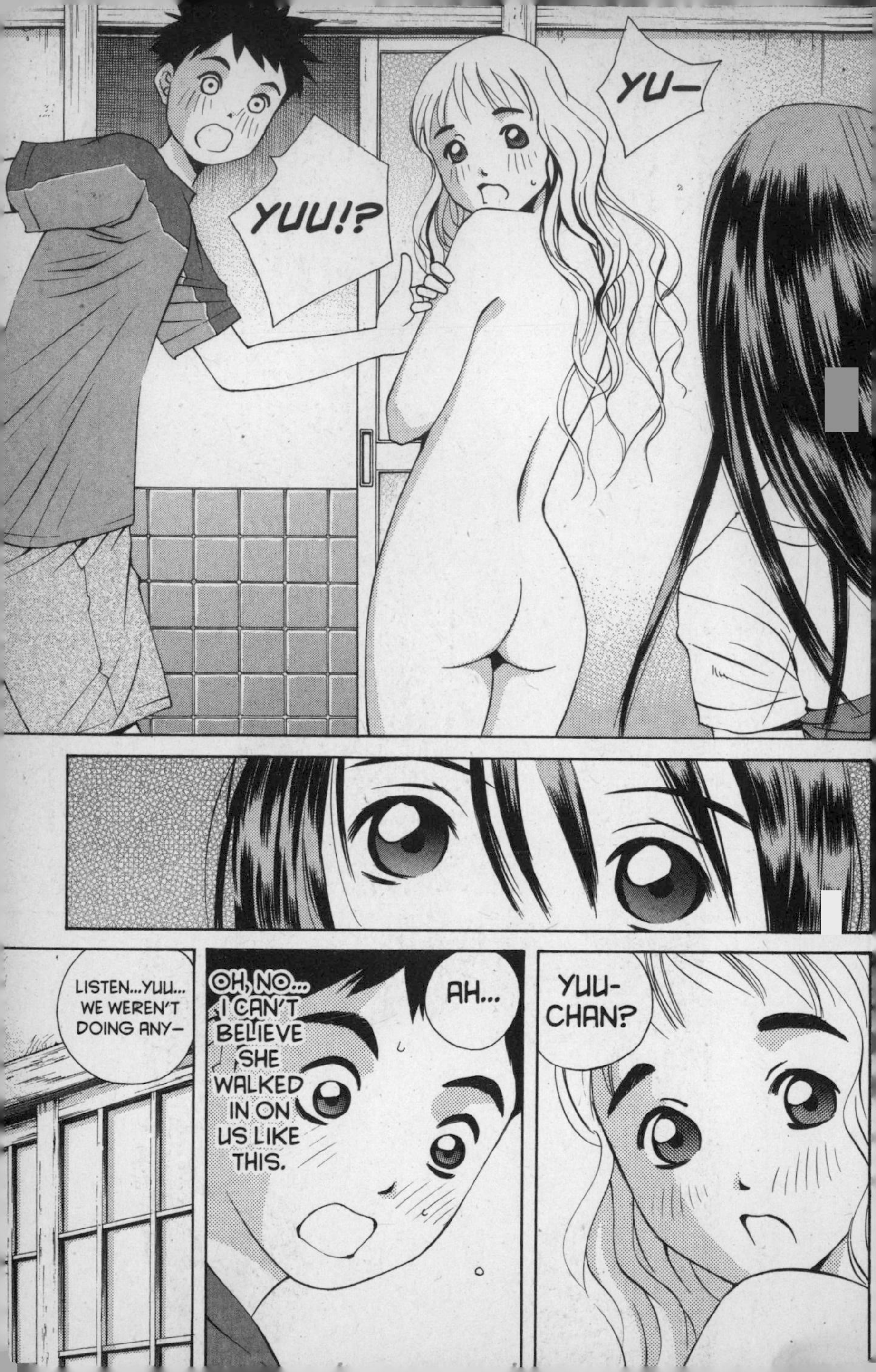
YU—
YUU!?
YUU-CHAN?
AH...
OH, NO... I CAN'T BELIEVE SHE WALKED IN ON US LIKE THIS.
LISTEN...YUU... WE WEREN'T DOING ANY—

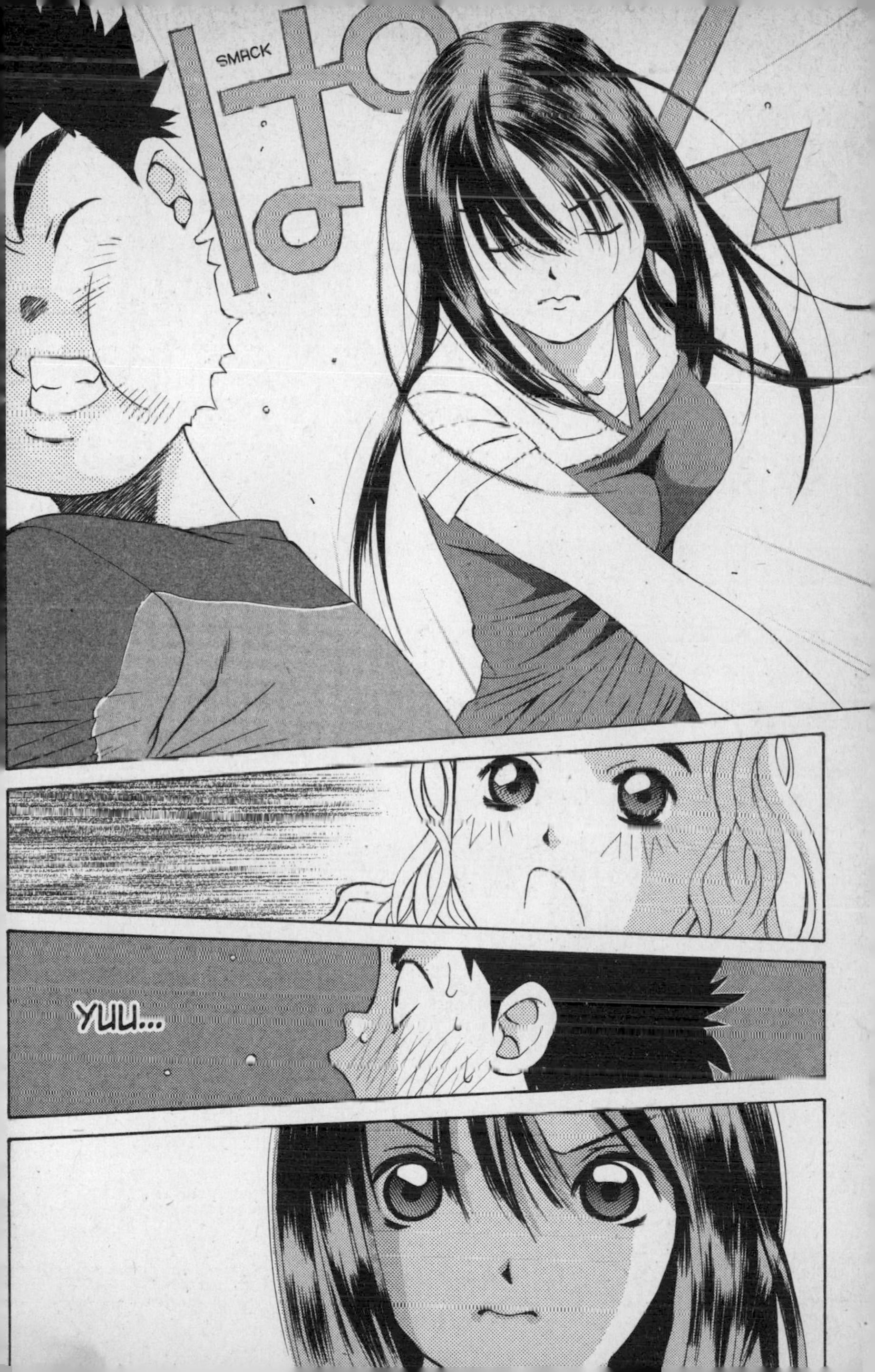
ぱし
SMACK
YUU...

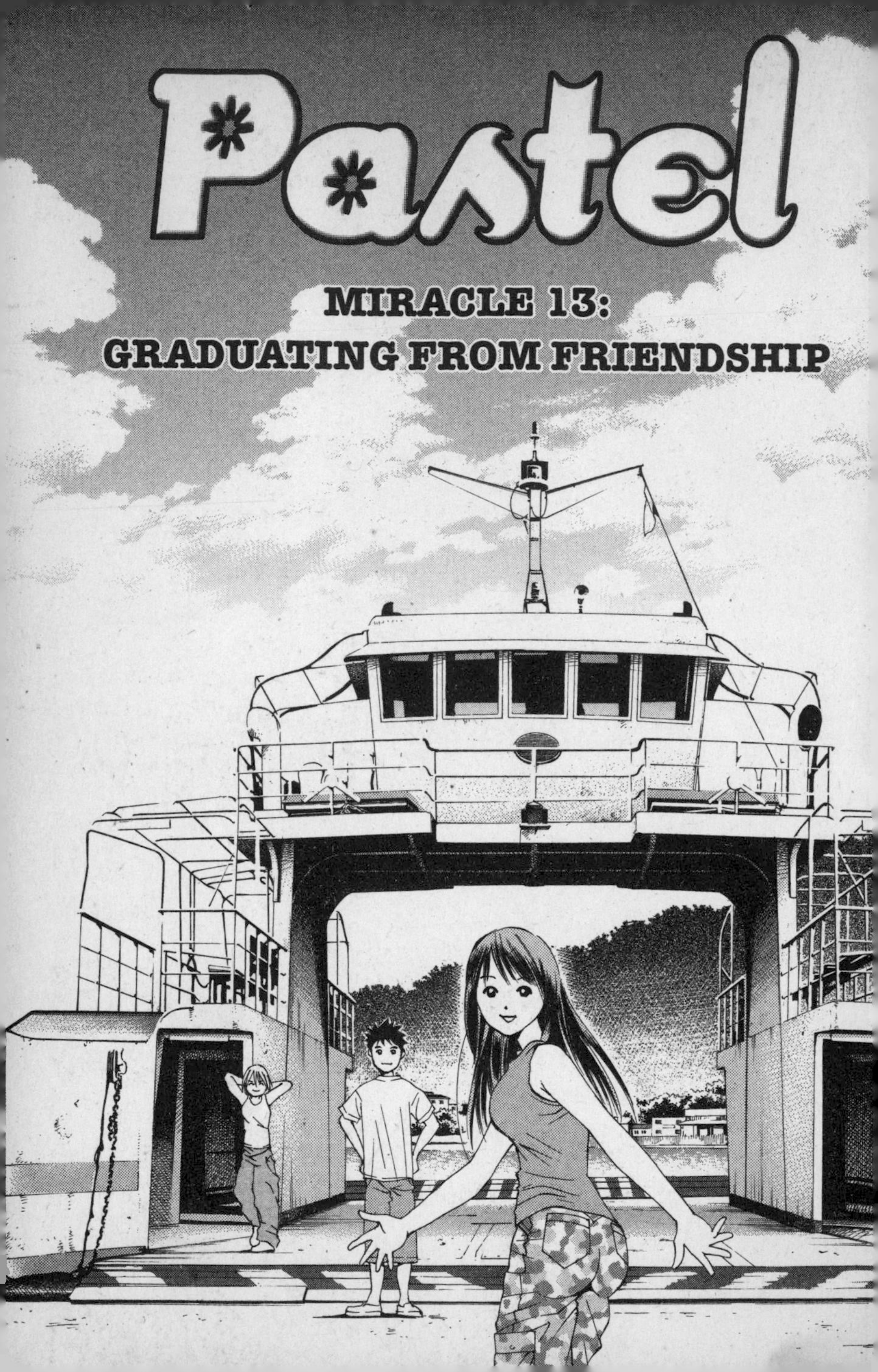
Pastel
MIRACLE 13:
GRADUATING FROM FRIENDSHIP

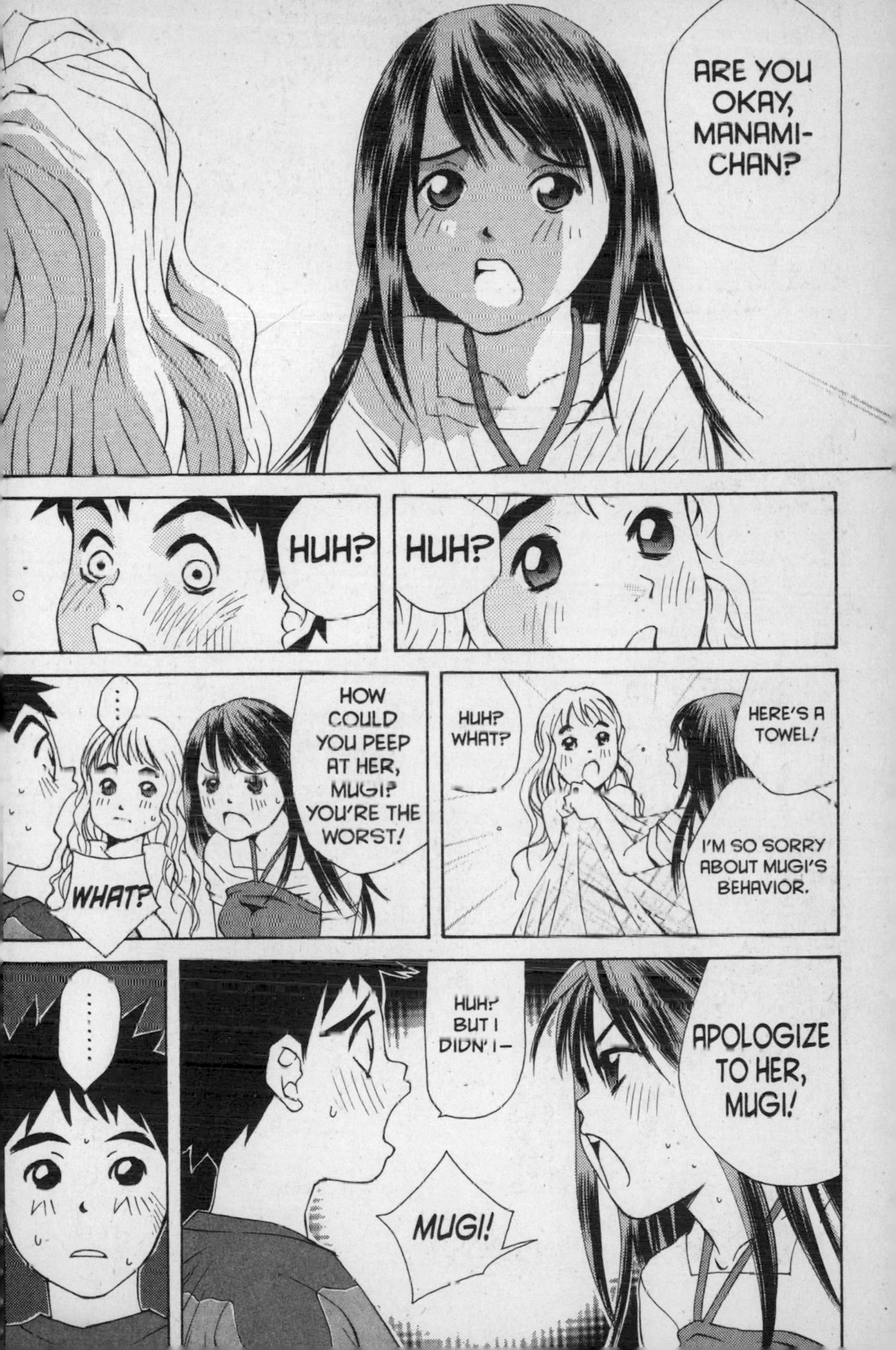
ARE YOU OKAY, MANAMI-CHAN?
HUH?
HUH?
HERE'S A TOWEL!
HUH? WHAT?
I'M SO SORRY ABOUT MUGI'S BEHAVIOR.
HOW COULD YOU PEEP AT HER, MUGI? YOU'RE THE WORST!
...
WHAT?
APOLOGIZE TO HER, MUGI!
HUH? BUT I DIDN'T—
MUGI!
....

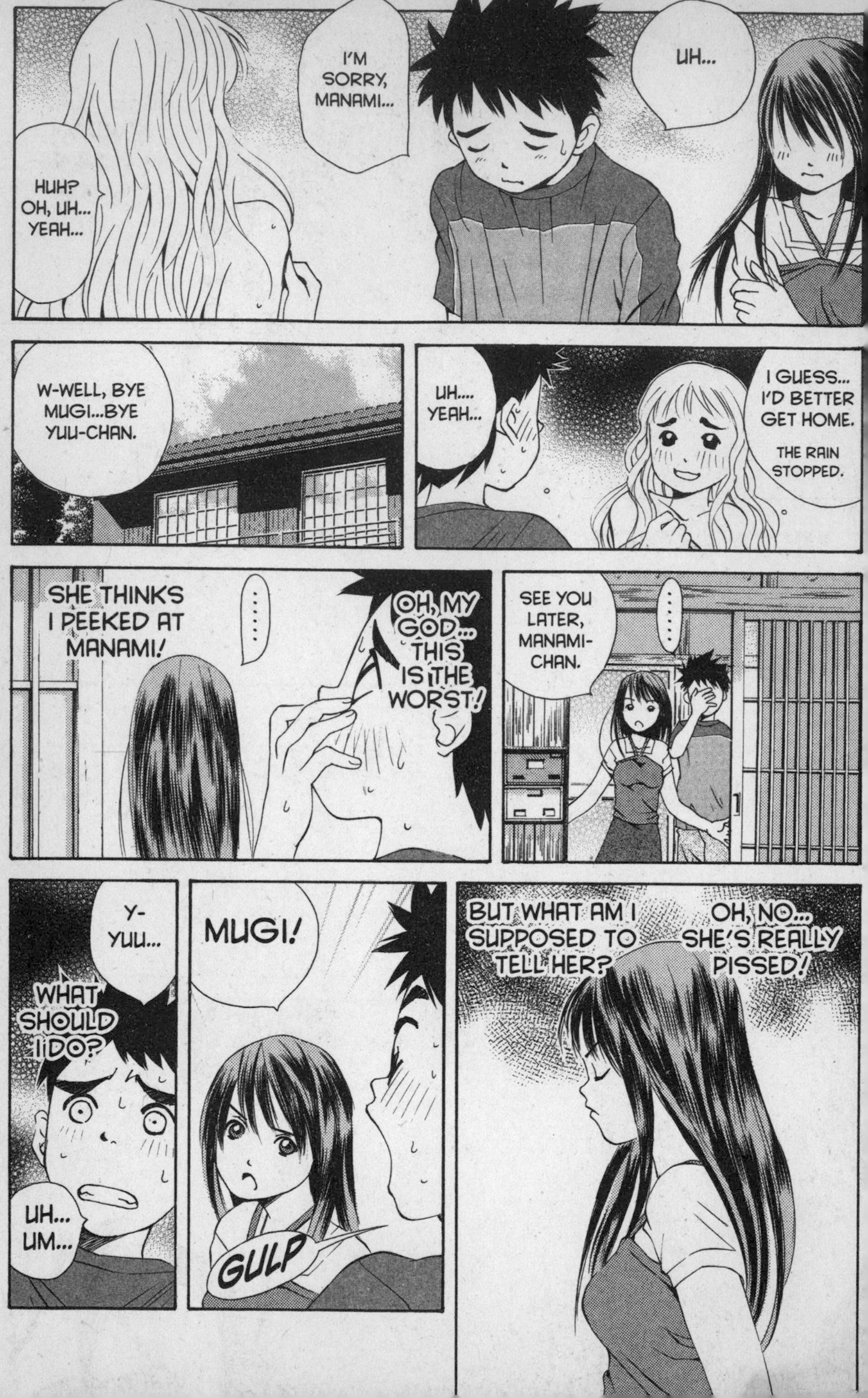
UH...
I'M SORRY, MANAMI...
HUH? OH, UH... YEAH...
I GUESS... I'D BETTER GET HOME.
THE RAIN STOPPED.
UH.... YEAH...
W-WELL, BYE MUGI...BYE YUU-CHAN.
......
SEE YOU LATER, MANAMI-CHAN.
OH, MY GOD... THIS IS THE WORST!
......
SHE THINKS I PEEKED AT MANAMI!
OH, NO... SHE'S REALLY PISSED!
BUT WHAT AM I SUPPOSED TO TELL HER?
MUGI!
GULP
Y-YUU...
WHAT SHOULD I DO?
UH... UM...

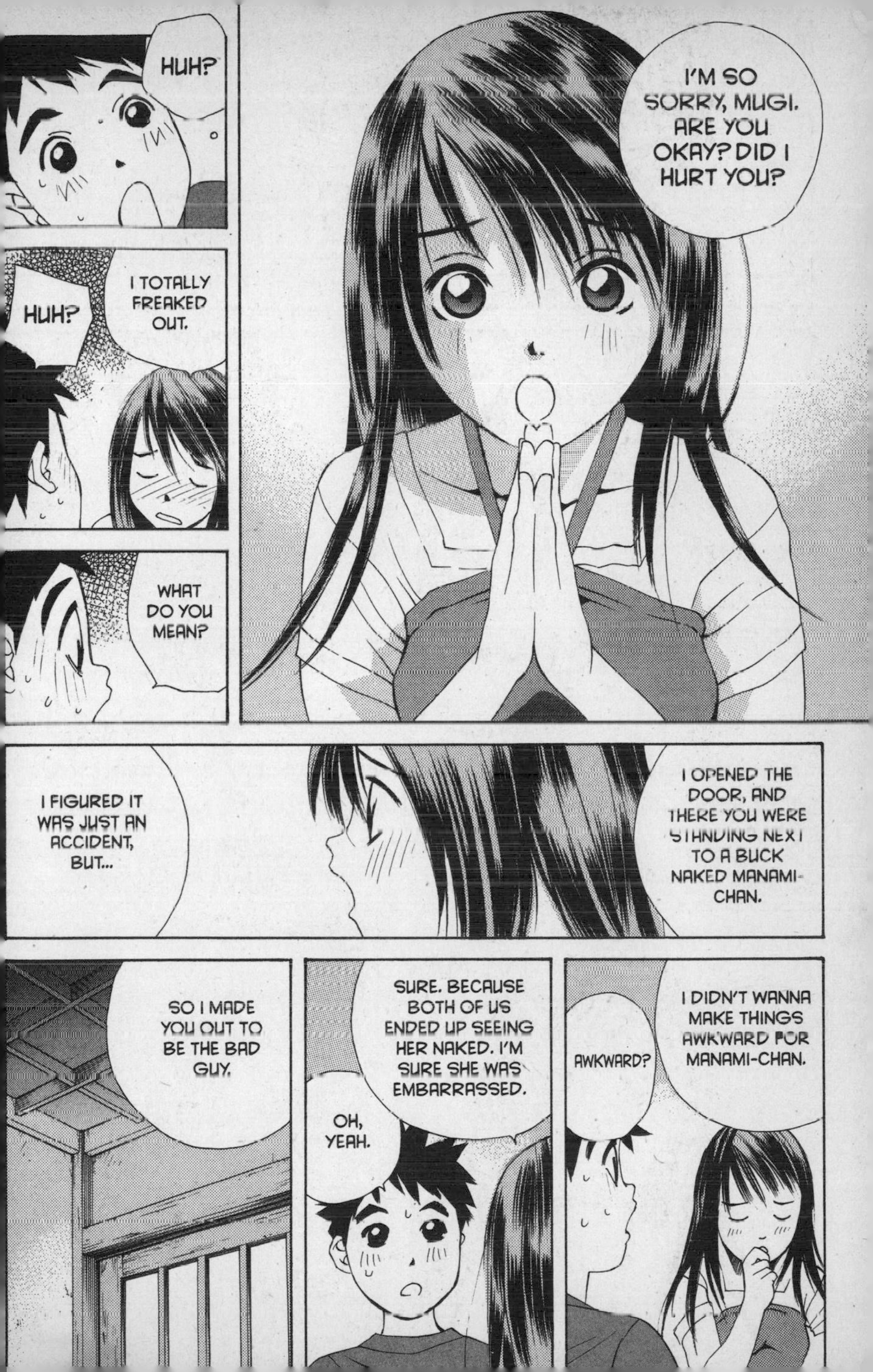
I'M SO SORRY, MUGI. ARE YOU OKAY? DID I HURT YOU?
HUH?
I TOTALLY FREAKED OUT.
HUH?
WHAT DO YOU MEAN?
I OPENED THE DOOR, AND THERE YOU WERE STANDING NEXT TO A BUCK NAKED MANAMI-CHAN.
I FIGURED IT WAS JUST AN ACCIDENT, BUT...
I DIDN'T WANNA MAKE THINGS AWKWARD FOR MANAMI-CHAN.
AWKWARD?
SURE. BECAUSE BOTH OF US ENDED UP SEEING HER NAKED. I'M SURE SHE WAS EMBARRASSED.
OH, YEAH.
SO I MADE YOU OUT TO BE THE BAD GUY.

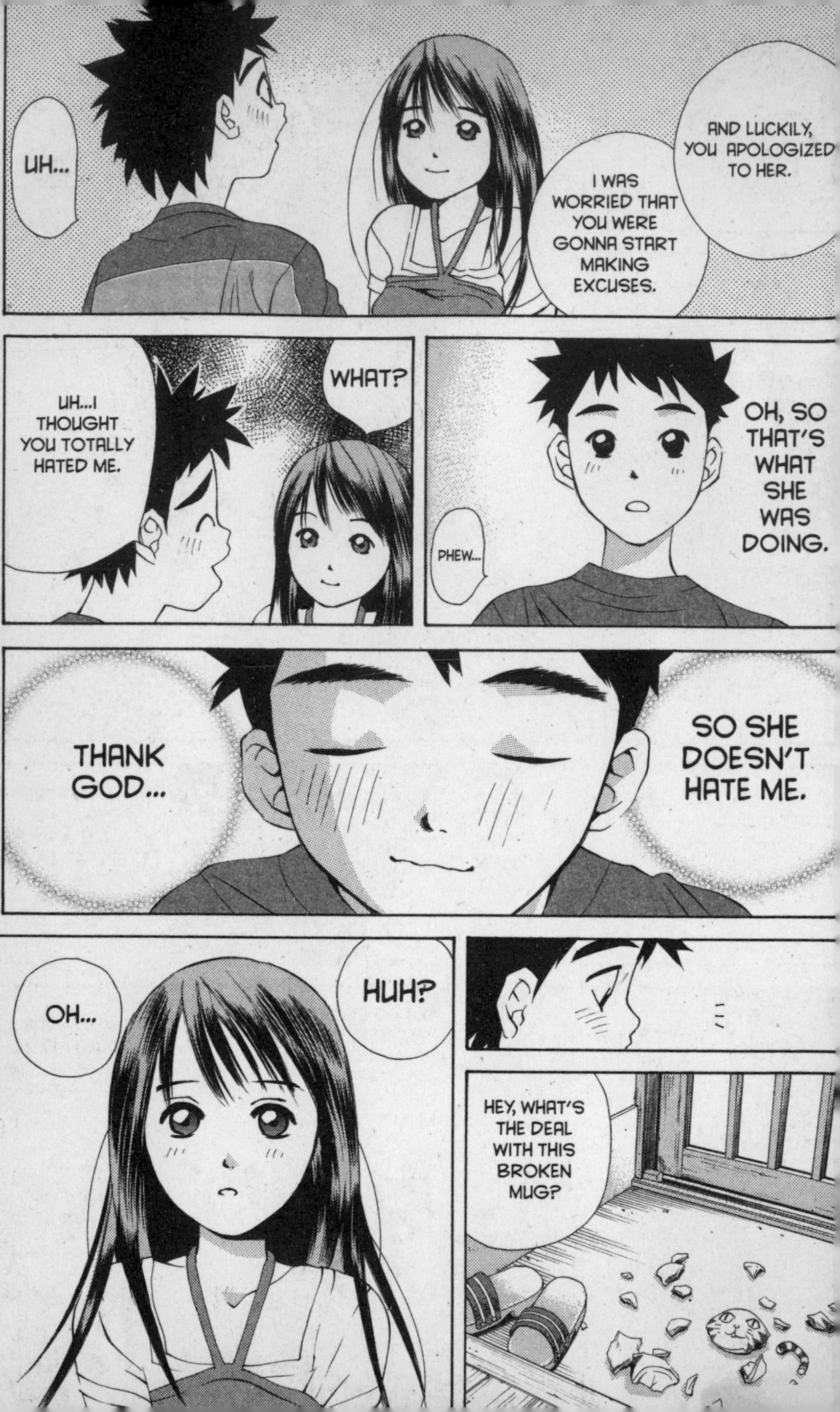
AND LUCKILY, YOU APOLOGIZED TO HER.
I WAS WORRIED THAT YOU WERE GONNA START MAKING EXCUSES.
UH...
OH, SO THAT'S WHAT SHE WAS DOING.
PHEW...
WHAT?
UH...I THOUGHT YOU TOTALLY HATED ME.
SO SHE DOESN'T HATE ME.
THANK GOD...
HEY, WHAT'S THE DEAL WITH THIS BROKEN MUG?
HUH?
OH...

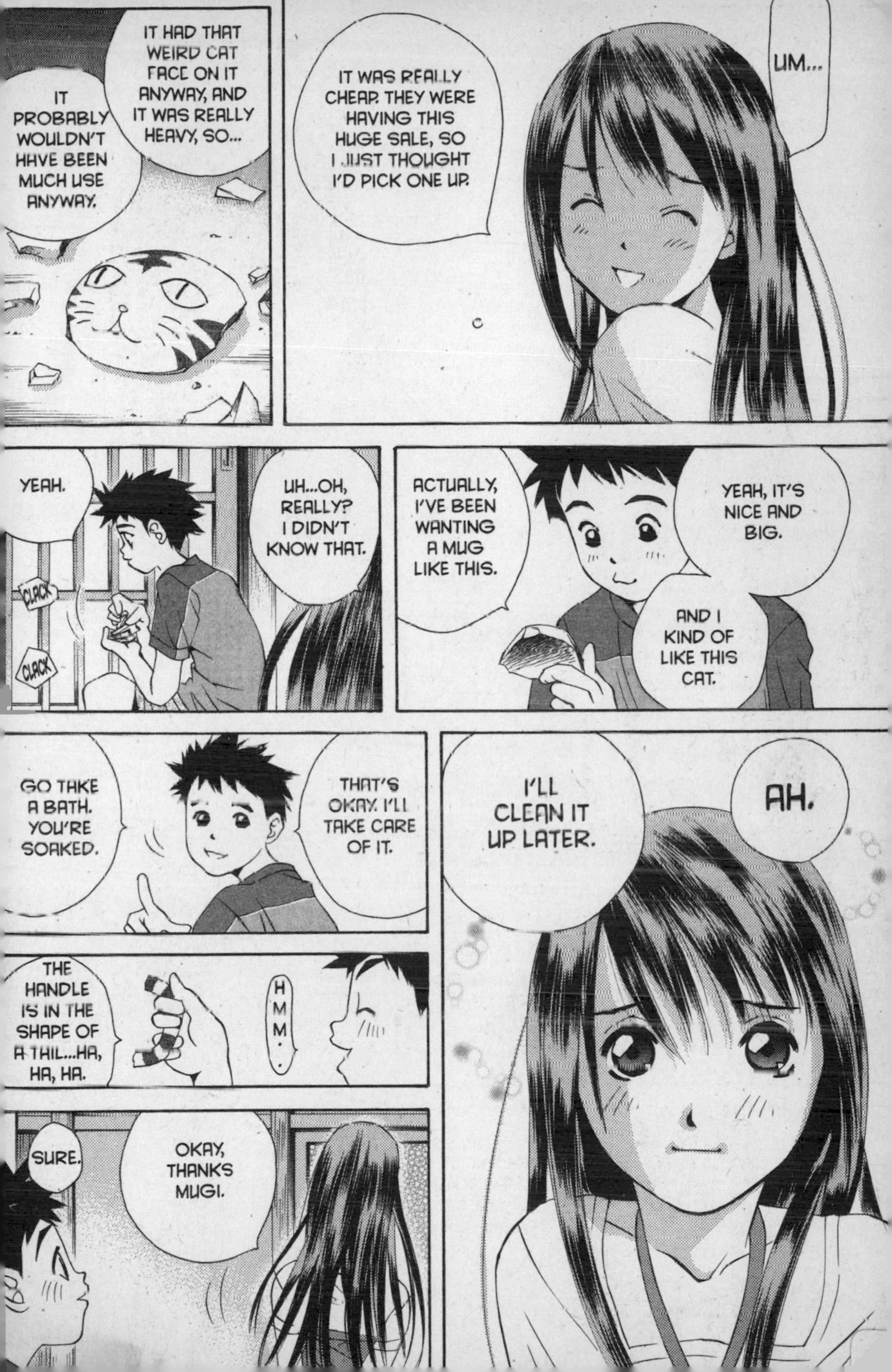
UM...
IT WAS REALLY CHEAP. THEY WERE HAVING THIS HUGE SALE, SO I JUST THOUGHT I'D PICK ONE UP.
IT HAD THAT WEIRD CAT FACE ON IT ANYWAY, AND IT WAS REALLY HEAVY, SO...
IT PROBABLY WOULDN'T HAVE BEEN MUCH USE ANYWAY.
YEAH, IT'S NICE AND BIG.
ACTUALLY, I'VE BEEN WANTING A MUG LIKE THIS.
AND I KIND OF LIKE THIS CAT.
UH...OH, REALLY? I DIDN'T KNOW THAT.
YEAH.
CLACK
CLACK
AH.
I'LL CLEAN IT UP LATER.
THAT'S OKAY. I'LL TAKE CARE OF IT.
GO TAKE A BATH. YOU'RE SOAKED.
HMM...
THE HANDLE IS IN THE SHAPE OF A TAIL...HA, HA, HA.
OKAY, THANKS MUGI.
SURE.

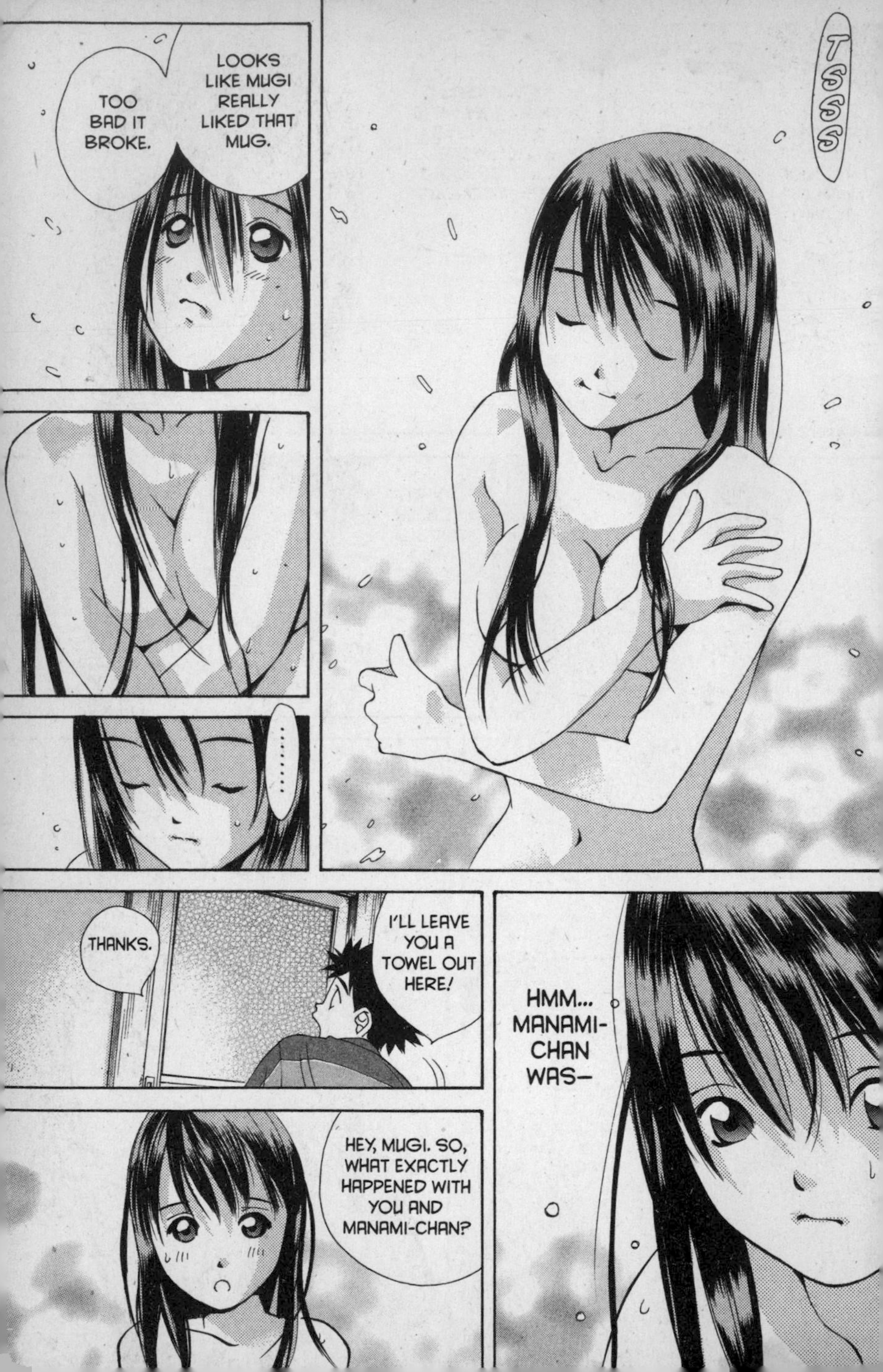
TSSS
LOOKS LIKE MUGI REALLY LIKED THAT MUG.
TOO BAD IT BROKE.
......
HMM... MANAMI-CHAN WAS—
I'LL LEAVE YOU A TOWEL OUT HERE!
THANKS.
HEY, MUGI. SO, WHAT EXACTLY HAPPENED WITH YOU AND MANAMI-CHAN?

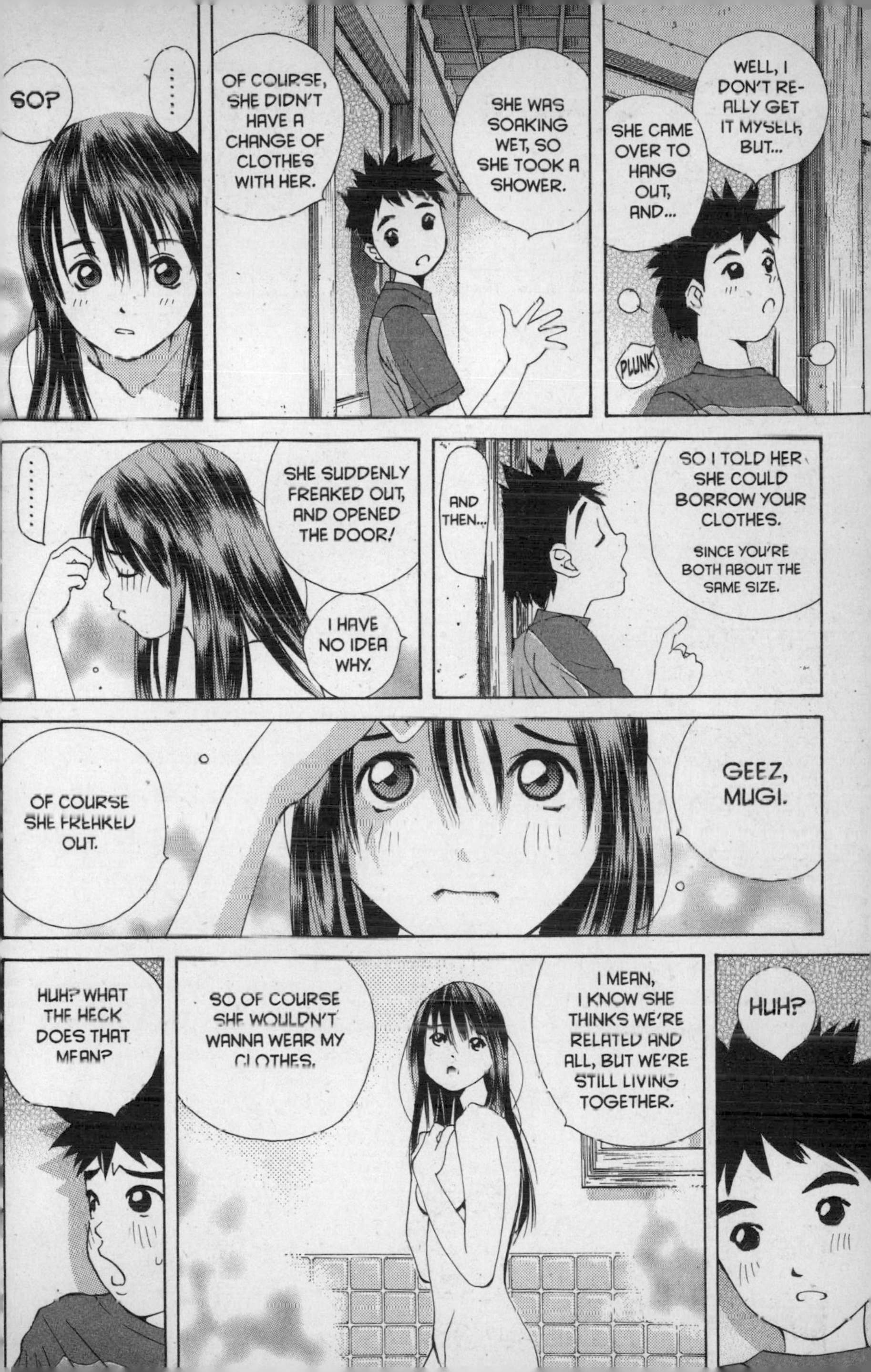
WELL, I DON'T RE-ALLY GET IT MYSELF, BUT...
SHE CAME OVER TO HANG OUT, AND...
PLUNK
SHE WAS SOAKING WET, SO SHE TOOK A SHOWER.
OF COURSE, SHE DIDN'T HAVE A CHANGE OF CLOTHES WITH HER.
......
SO?
SO I TOLD HER SHE COULD BORROW YOUR CLOTHES.
SINCE YOU'RE BOTH ABOUT THE SAME SIZE.
AND THEN...
SHE SUDDENLY FREAKED OUT, AND OPENED THE DOOR!
I HAVE NO IDEA WHY.
....
GEEZ, MUGI.
OF COURSE SHE FREAKED OUT.
HUH?
I MEAN, I KNOW SHE THINKS WE'RE RELATED AND ALL, BUT WE'RE STILL LIVING TOGETHER.
SO OF COURSE SHE WOULDN'T WANNA WEAR MY CLOTHES.
HUH? WHAT THE HECK DOES THAT MEAN?

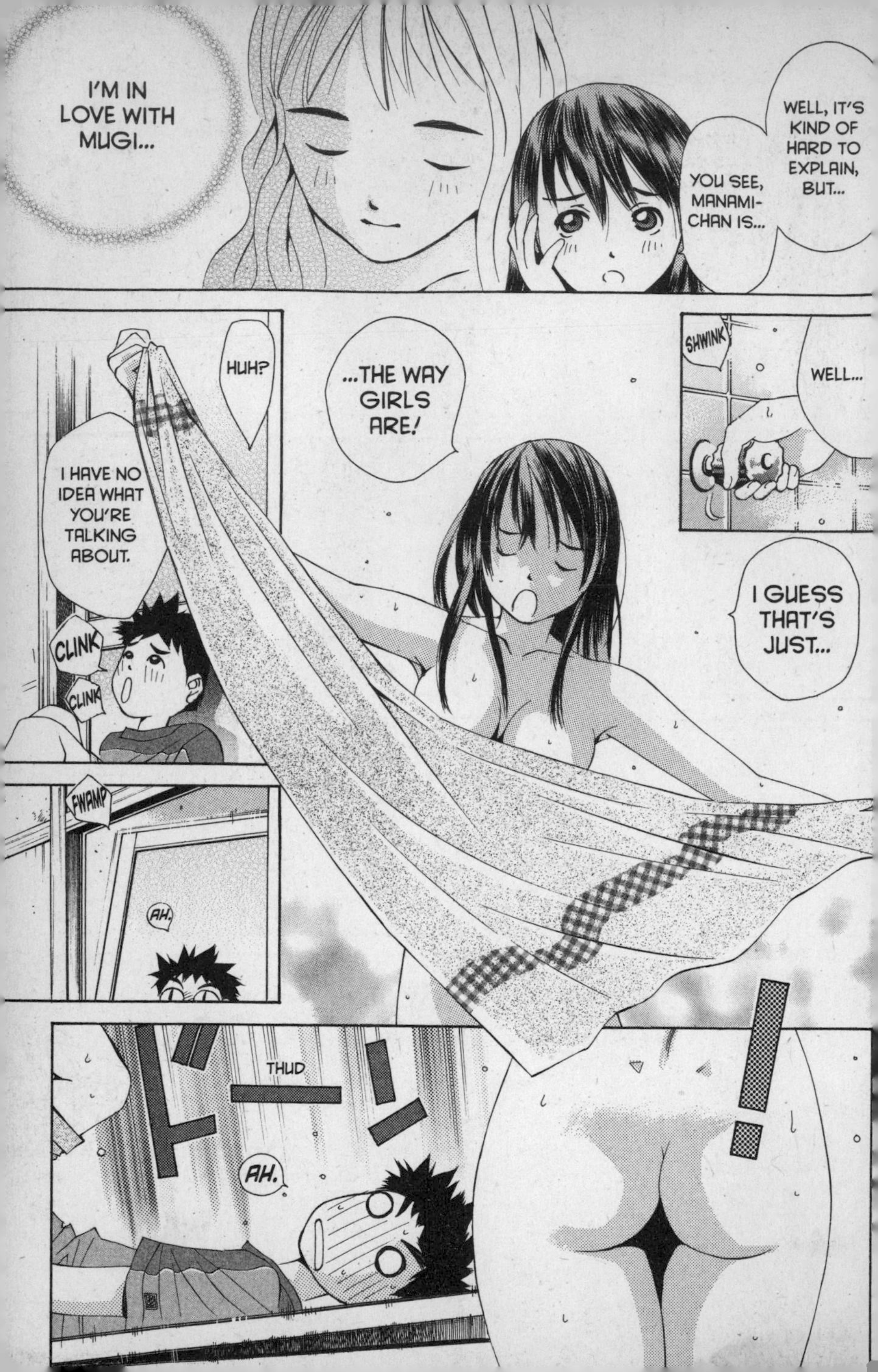

WELL, IT'S KIND OF HARD TO EXPLAIN, BUT...
YOU SEE, MANAMI-CHAN IS...
I'M IN LOVE WITH MUGI...
SHWINK
WELL...
I GUESS THAT'S JUST...
...THE WAY GIRLS ARE!
HUH?
I HAVE NO IDEA WHAT YOU'RE TALKING ABOUT.
CLINK
CLINK
FWAMP
AH.
!!
THUD
AH.

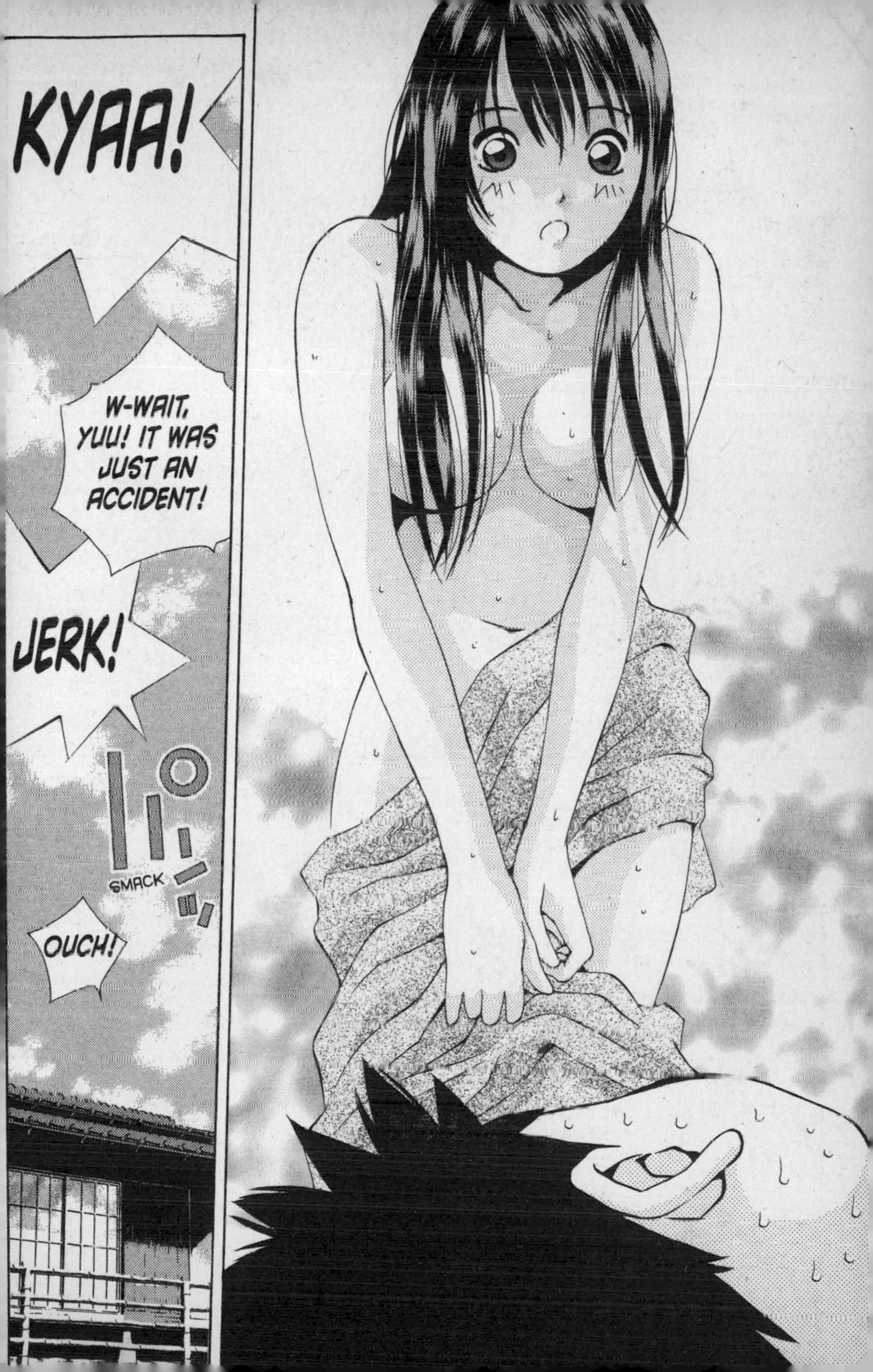
KYAA!
W-WAIT, YUU! IT WAS JUST AN ACCIDENT!
JERK!
SMACK
OUCH!

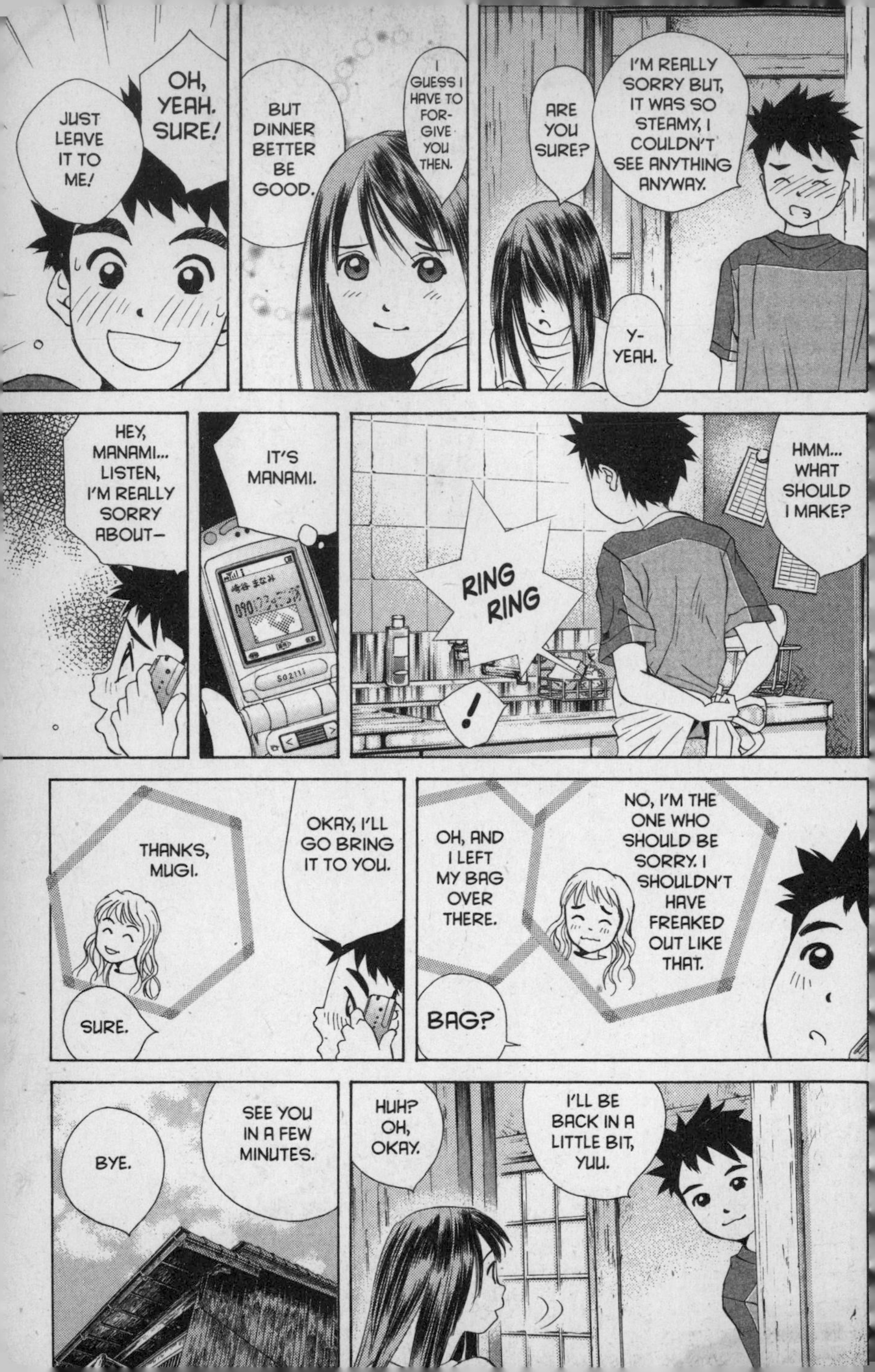
I'M REALLY SORRY BUT, IT WAS SO STEAMY, I COULDN'T SEE ANYTHING ANYWAY.
ARE YOU SURE?
Y-YEAH.
I GUESS I HAVE TO FOR-GIVE YOU THEN.
BUT DINNER BETTER BE GOOD.
OH, YEAH. SURE!
JUST LEAVE IT TO ME!
HMM... WHAT SHOULD I MAKE?
RING RING
!
IT'S MANAMI.
HEY, MANAMI... LISTEN, I'M REALLY SORRY ABOUT—
NO, I'M THE ONE WHO SHOULD BE SORRY. I SHOULDN'T HAVE FREAKED OUT LIKE THAT.
OH, AND I LEFT MY BAG OVER THERE.
BAG?
OKAY, I'LL GO BRING IT TO YOU.
THANKS, MUGI.
SURE.
I'LL BE BACK IN A LITTLE BIT, YUU.
HUH? OH, OKAY.
SEE YOU IN A FEW MINUTES.
BYE.

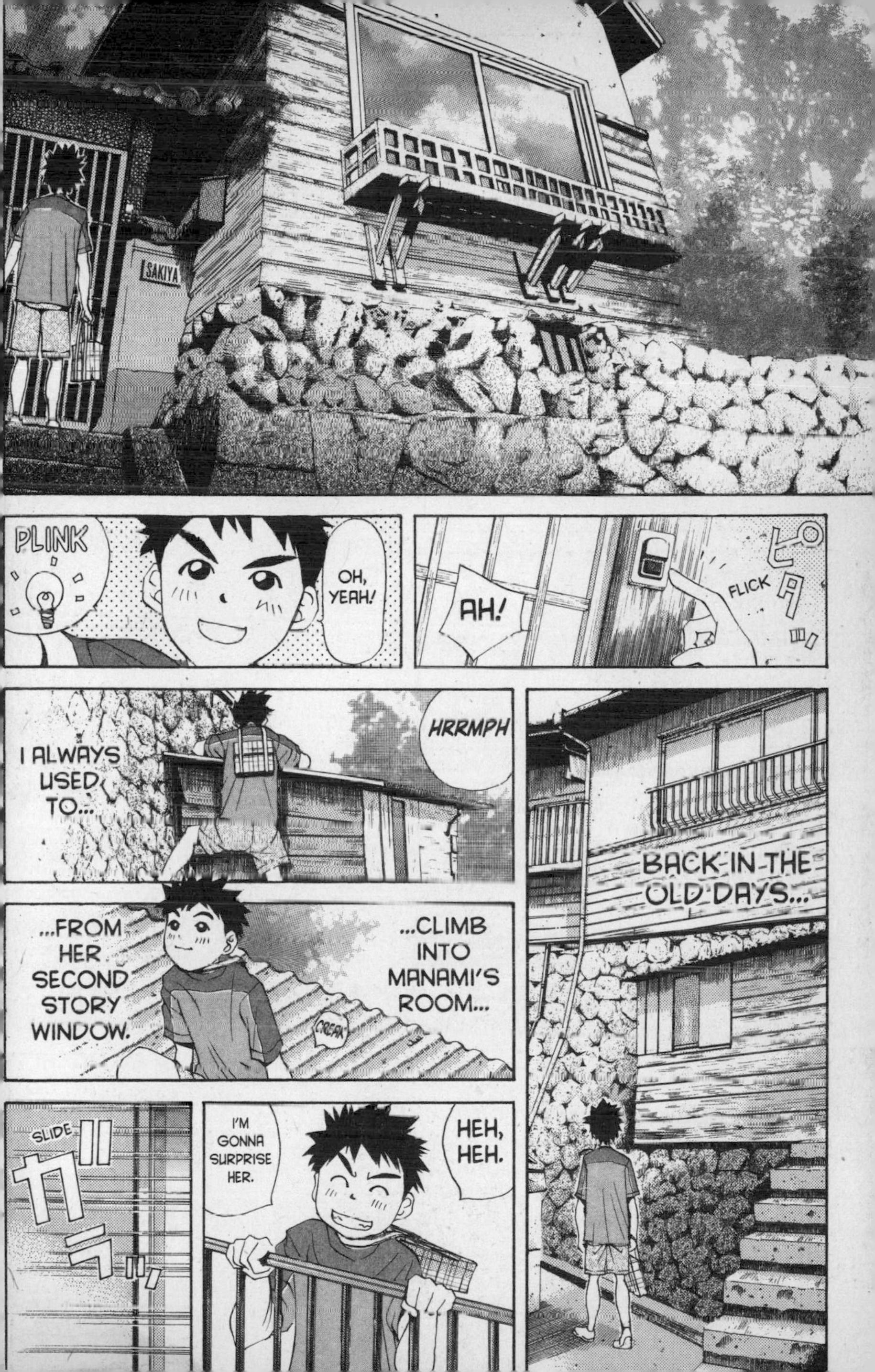
SAKIYA
AH!
FLICK
PLINK
OH, YEAH!
BACK IN THE OLD DAYS...
HRRMPH
I ALWAYS USED TO...
...CLIMB INTO MANAMI'S ROOM...
...FROM HER SECOND STORY WINDOW.
CREAK
HEH, HEH.
I'M GONNA SURPRISE HER.
SLIDE

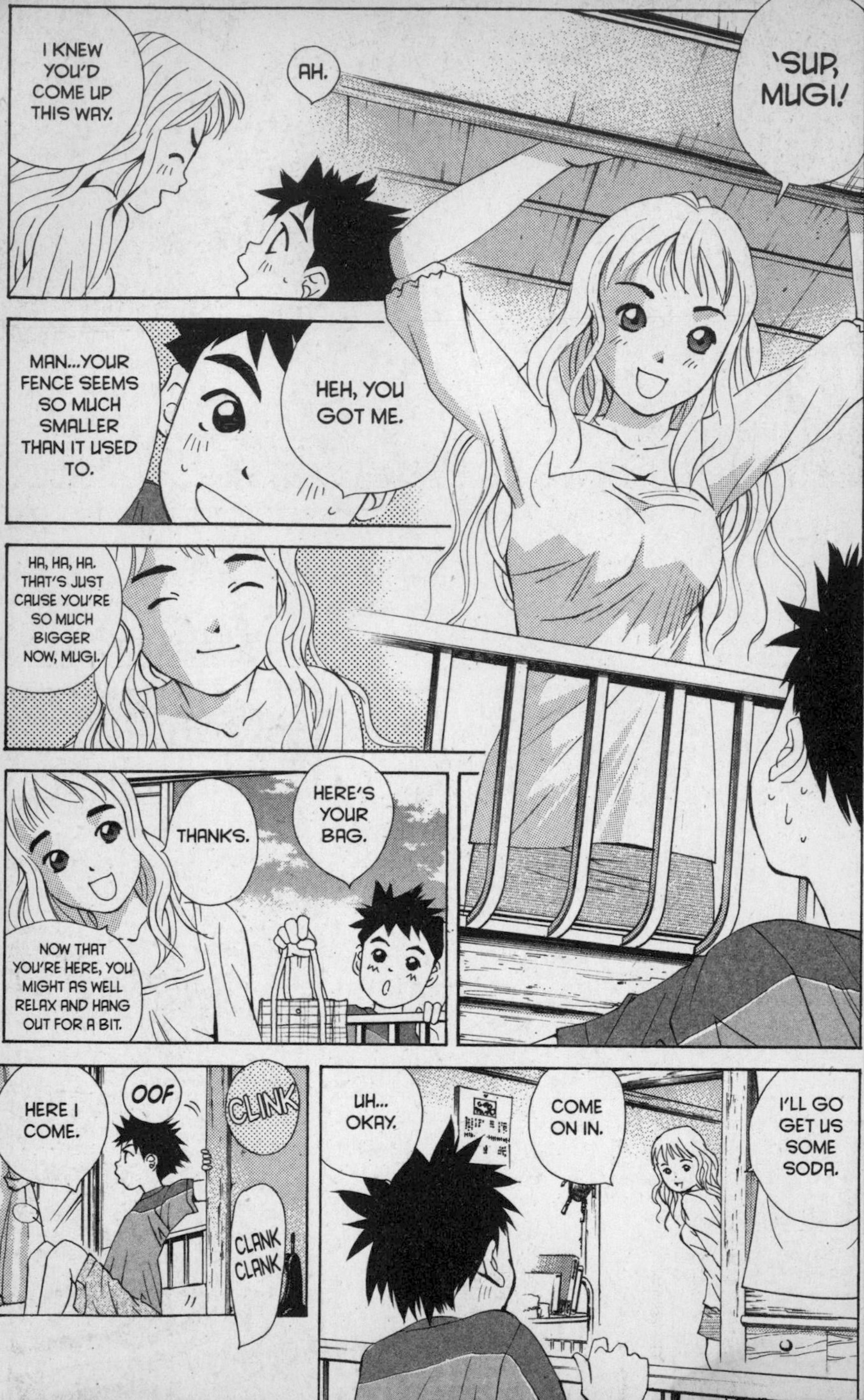
'SUP, MUGI!
AH.
I KNEW YOU'D COME UP THIS WAY.
HEH, YOU GOT ME.
MAN...YOUR FENCE SEEMS SO MUCH SMALLER THAN IT USED TO.
HA, HA, HA. THAT'S JUST CAUSE YOU'RE SO MUCH BIGGER NOW, MUGI.
HERE'S YOUR BAG.
THANKS.
NOW THAT YOU'RE HERE, YOU MIGHT AS WELL RELAX AND HANG OUT FOR A BIT.
I'LL GO GET US SOME SODA.
COME ON IN.
UH... OKAY.
CLINK
OOF
HERE I COME.
CLANK CLANK

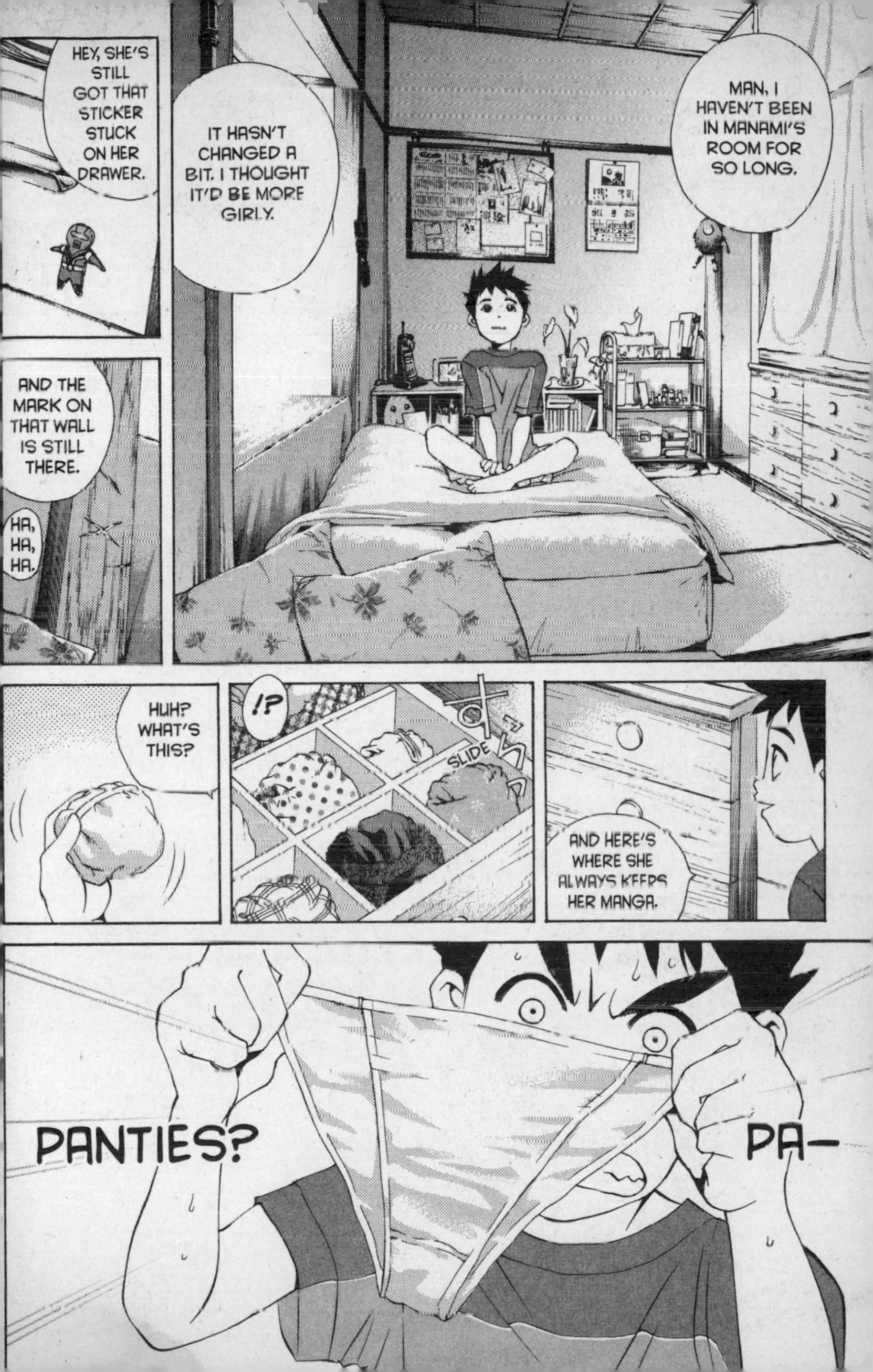
MAN, I HAVEN'T BEEN IN MANAMI'S ROOM FOR SO LONG.
IT HASN'T CHANGED A BIT. I THOUGHT IT'D BE MORE GIRLY.
HEY, SHE'S STILL GOT THAT STICKER STUCK ON HER DRAWER.
AND THE MARK ON THAT WALL IS STILL THERE.
HA, HA, HA.
AND HERE'S WHERE SHE ALWAYS KEEPS HER MANGA.
!?
SLIDE
HUH? WHAT'S THIS?
PA—
PANTIES?

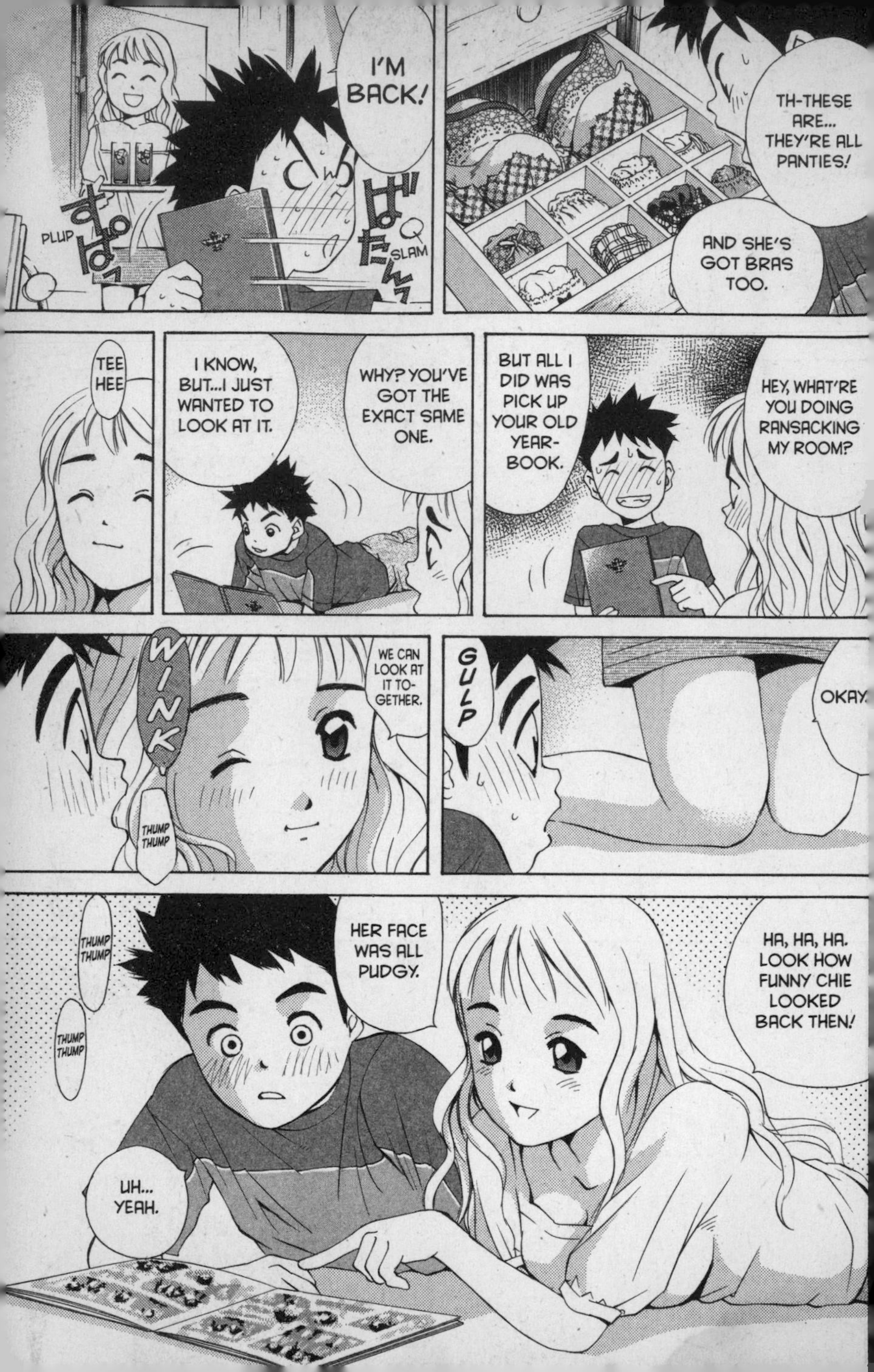
TH-THESE ARE... THEY'RE ALL PANTIES!
AND SHE'S GOT BRAS TOO.
I'M BACK!
ばたんっ
SLAM
すぽっ
PLUP
HEY, WHAT'RE YOU DOING RANSACKING MY ROOM?
BUT ALL I DID WAS PICK UP YOUR OLD YEAR-BOOK.
WHY? YOU'VE GOT THE EXACT SAME ONE.
I KNOW, BUT...I JUST WANTED TO LOOK AT IT.
TEE HEE
OKAY.
GULP
WE CAN LOOK AT IT TO-GETHER.
WINK
THUMP THUMP
HA, HA, HA. LOOK HOW FUNNY CHIE LOOKED BACK THEN!
HER FACE WAS ALL PUDGY.
THUMP THUMP
THUMP THUMP
UH... YEAH.

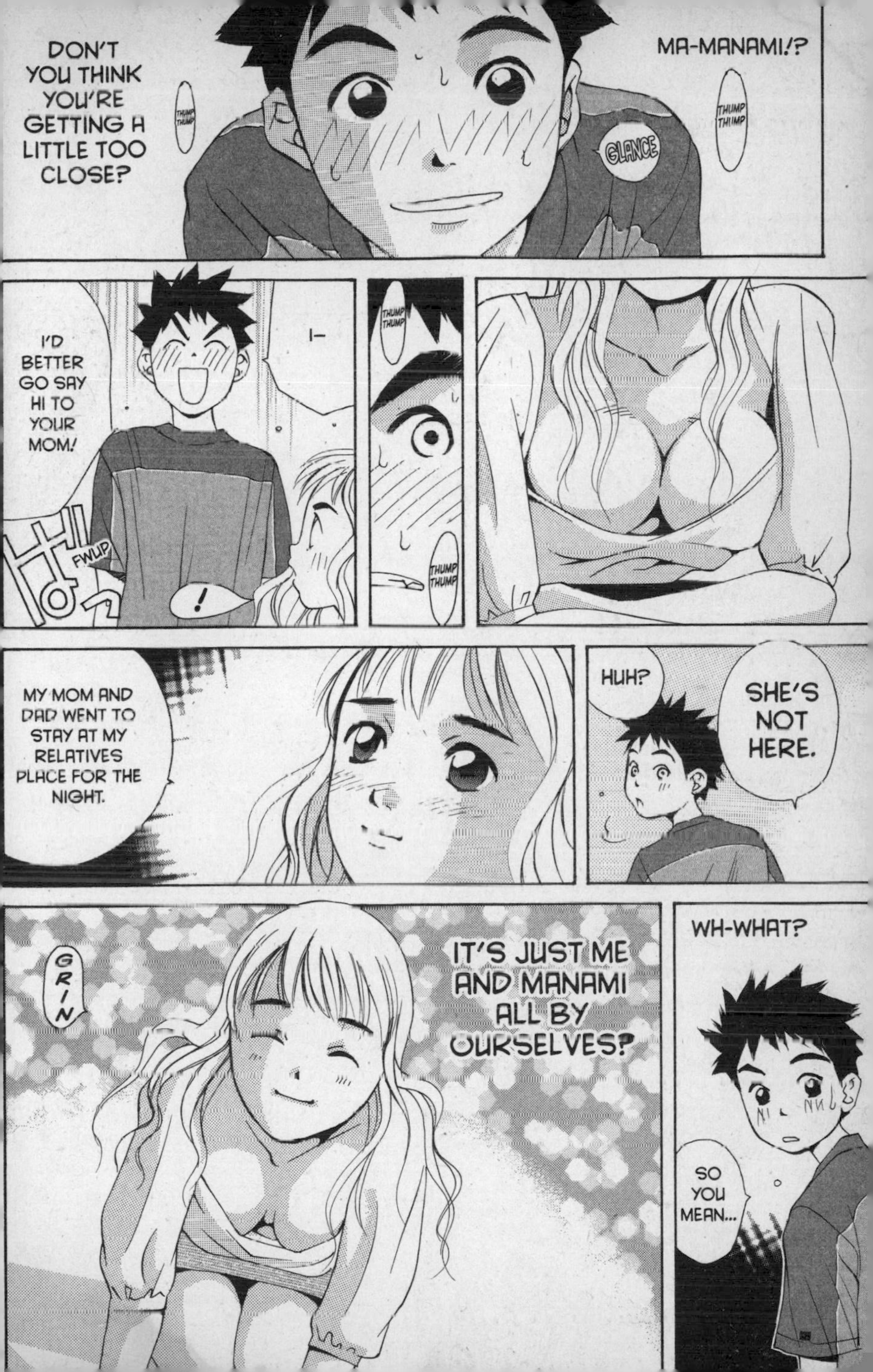
MA-MANAMI!?
THUMP THUMP
GLANCE
THUMP THUMP
DON'T YOU THINK YOU'RE GETTING A LITTLE TOO CLOSE?
THUMP THUMP
THUMP THUMP
I–
I'D BETTER GO SAY HI TO YOUR MOM!
FWUP
!
SHE'S NOT HERE.
HUH?
MY MOM AND DAD WENT TO STAY AT MY RELATIVES PLACE FOR THE NIGHT.
WH-WHAT?
SO YOU MEAN...
IT'S JUST ME AND MANAMI ALL BY OURSELVES?
GRIN

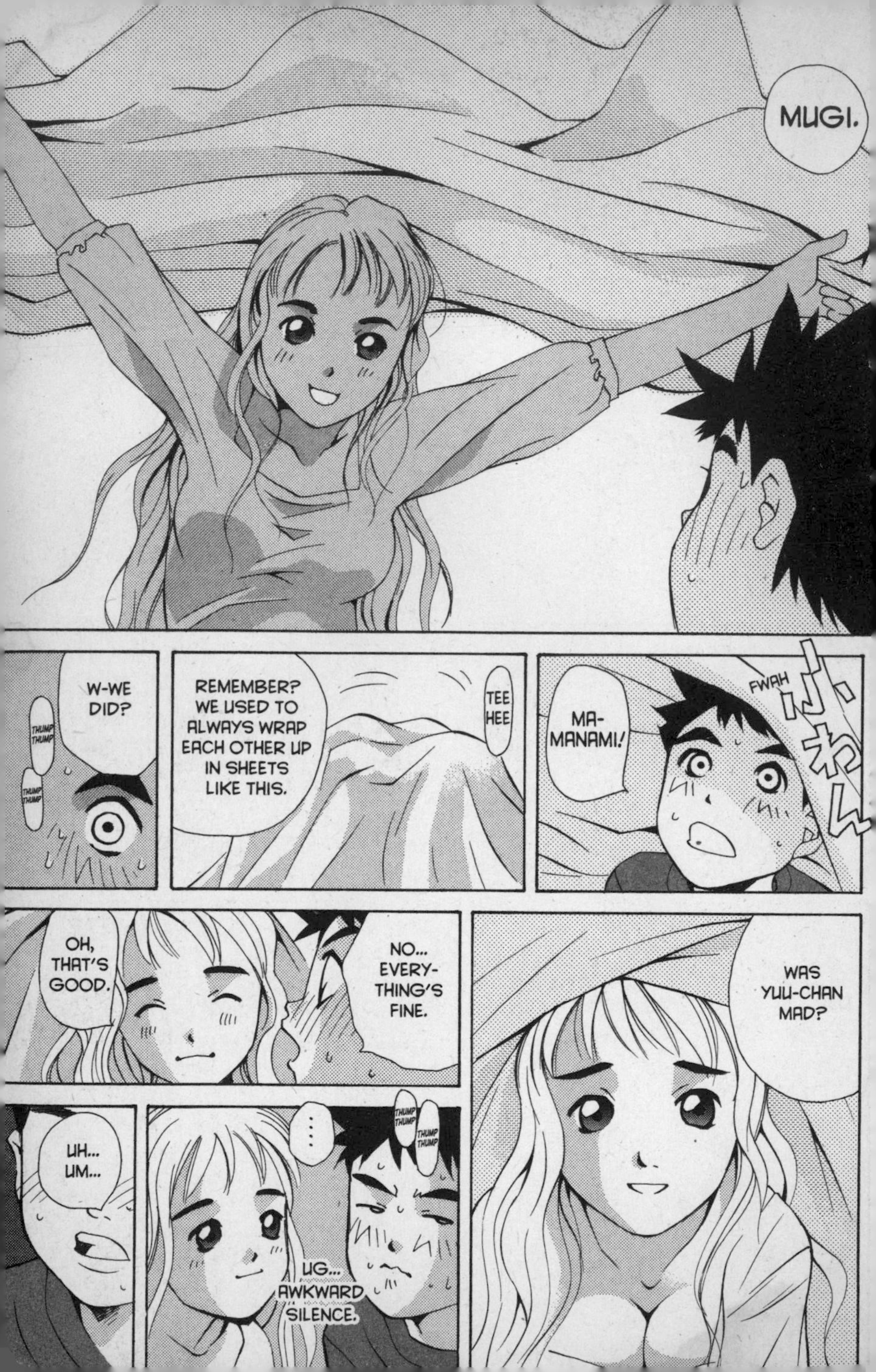
MUGI.
FWAH
MA-MANAMI!
TEE HEE
REMEMBER? WE USED TO ALWAYS WRAP EACH OTHER UP IN SHEETS LIKE THIS.
W-WE DID?
THUMP THUMP
THUMP THUMP
WAS YUU-CHAN MAD?
NO... EVERY-THING'S FINE.
OH, THAT'S GOOD.
THUMP THUMP
THUMP THUMP
....
UG... AWKWARD SILENCE.
UH... UM...

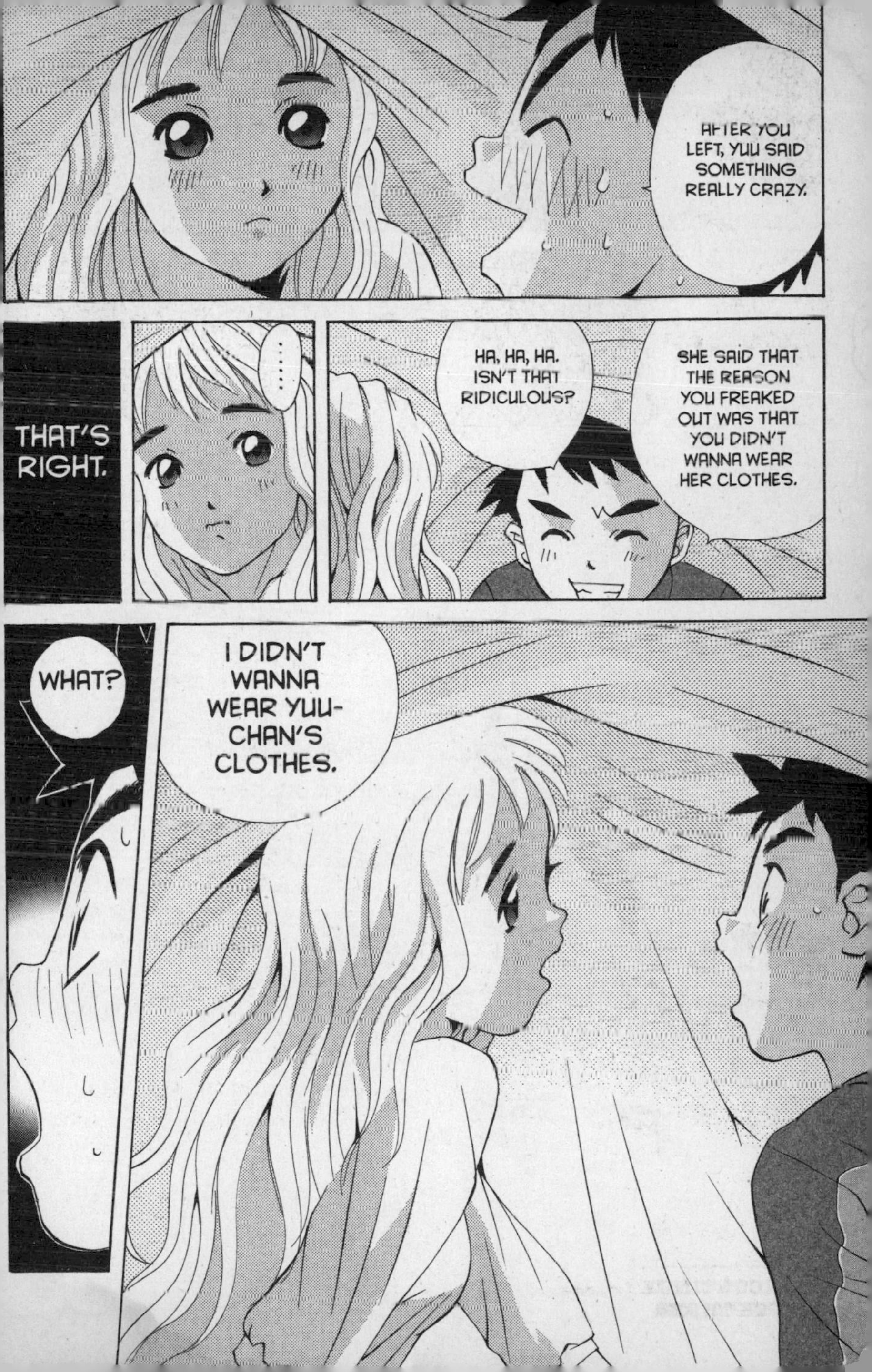
AFTER YOU LEFT, YUU SAID SOMETHING REALLY CRAZY.
SHE SAID THAT THE REASON YOU FREAKED OUT WAS THAT YOU DIDN'T WANNA WEAR HER CLOTHES.
HA, HA, HA. ISN'T THAT RIDICULOUS?
......
THAT'S RIGHT.
I DIDN'T WANNA WEAR YUU-CHAN'S CLOTHES.
WHAT?

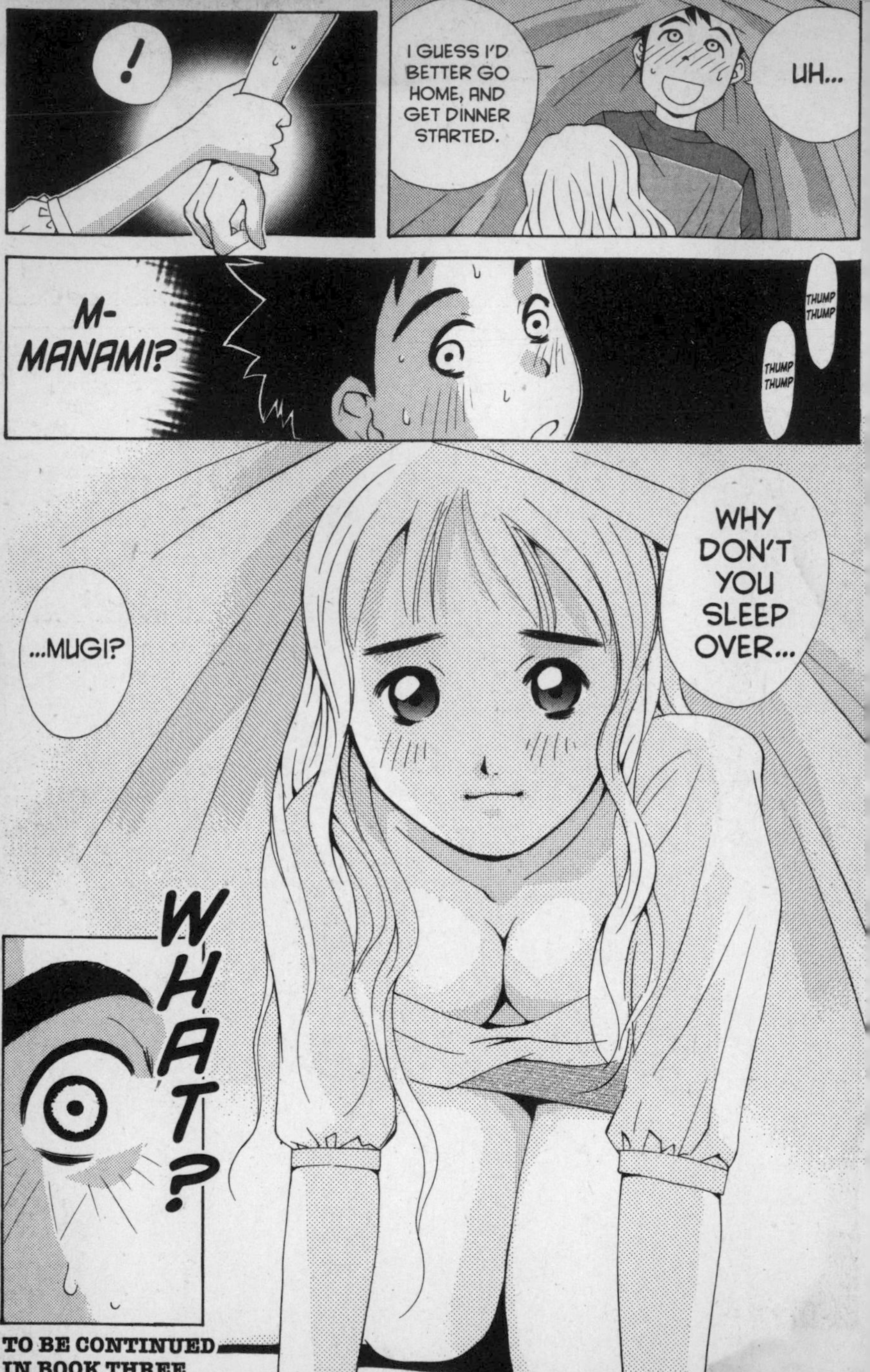
UH...
I GUESS I'D BETTER GO HOME, AND GET DINNER STARTED.
!
THUMP THUMP
THUMP THUMP
M-MANAMI?
WHY DON'T YOU SLEEP OVER...
...MUGI?
WHAT?
TO BE CONTINUED IN BOOK THREE

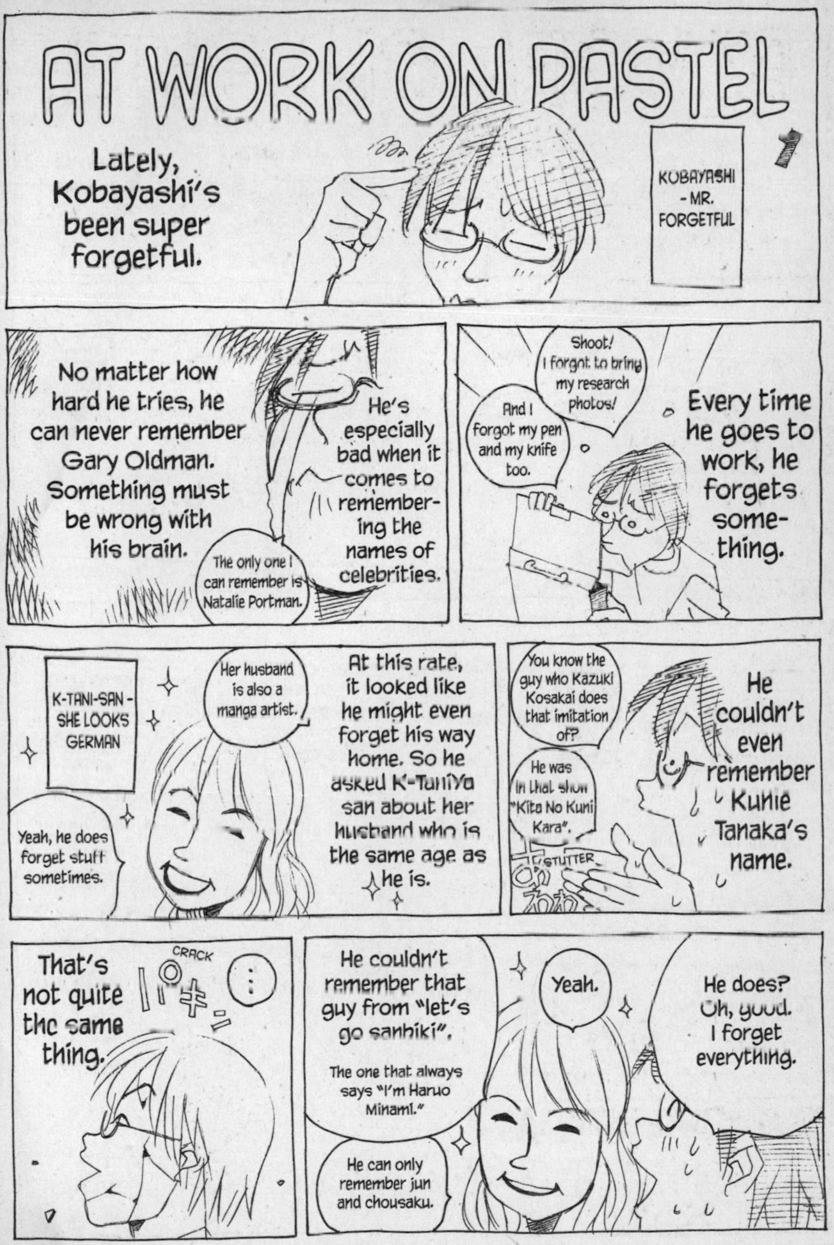
AT WORK ON PASTEL
KOBAYASHI - MR. FORGETFUL
1
Lately, Kobayashi's been super forgetful.
Every time he goes to work, he forgets something.
Shoot! I forgot to bring my research photos!
And I forgot my pen and my knife too.
He's especially bad when it comes to remembering the names of celebrities.
No matter how hard he tries, he can never remember Gary Oldman. Something must be wrong with his brain.
The only one I can remember is Natalie Portman.
He couldn't even remember Kunie Tanaka's name.
You know the guy who Kazuki Kosakai does that imitation of?
He was in that show "Kita No Kuni Kara".
STUTTER
At this rate, it looked like he might even forget his way home. So he asked K-TaniYa san about her husband who is the same age as he is.
Her husband is also a manga artist.
K-TANI-SAN - SHE LOOKS GERMAN
Yeah, he does forget stuff sometimes.
He does? Oh, good. I forget everything.
Yeah.
He couldn't remember that guy from "let's go sanbiki".
The one that always says "I'm Haruo Minami."
He can only remember jun and chousaku.
CRACK
That's not quite the same thing.

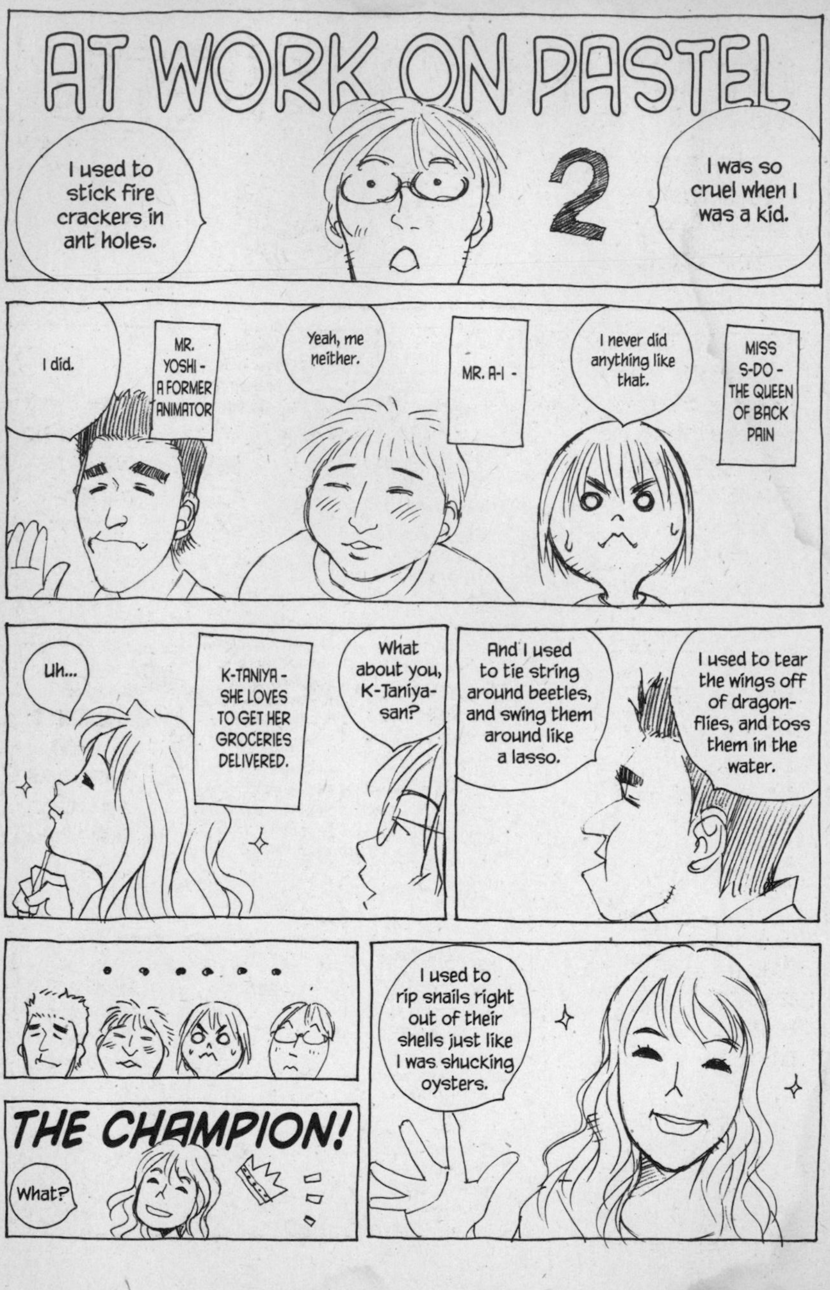
AT WORK ON PASTEL 2
I was so cruel when I was a kid.
I used to stick fire crackers in ant holes.
MISS S-DO - THE QUEEN OF BACK PAIN
I never did anything like that.
MR. A-I -
Yeah, me neither.
MR. YOSHI - A FORMER ANIMATOR
I did.
I used to tear the wings off of dragon-flies, and toss them in the water.
And I used to tie string around beetles, and swing them around like a lasso.
What about you, K-Taniya-san?
K-TANIYA - SHE LOVES TO GET HER GROCERIES DELIVERED.
Uh...
I used to rip snails right out of their shells just like I was shucking oysters.
THE CHAMPION!
What?

TOSHIHIKO KOBAYASHI

Born in Mihara city in Hiroshima. Birthday is February 25.
In 1995, "Half Coat" was serialized in "Magazine Special" from No.1 to
No.11. After the serial publication of "Parallel" in "Magazine Special"
from No.8 in 2000 to No.1 in 2002, "Pastel" was serialized in "Weekly
Shonen Magazine" from the 32nd issue in 2002 to the 33rd issue in
2003. And now "Pastel" has been running as a serial ever since
"Magazine Special" No.10 in 2003.

Favorites
Fruits
Sleeping
Hot green tea

Dislikes
Being scolded
Excessive expectations
Cigarette smoke

Translation Notes

Japanese is a tricky language for most Westerners, and translation is often more art than science. For your edification and reading pleasure, here are notes on some of the places where we could have gone in a different direction in our translation of the work, or where a Japanese cultural reference is used.

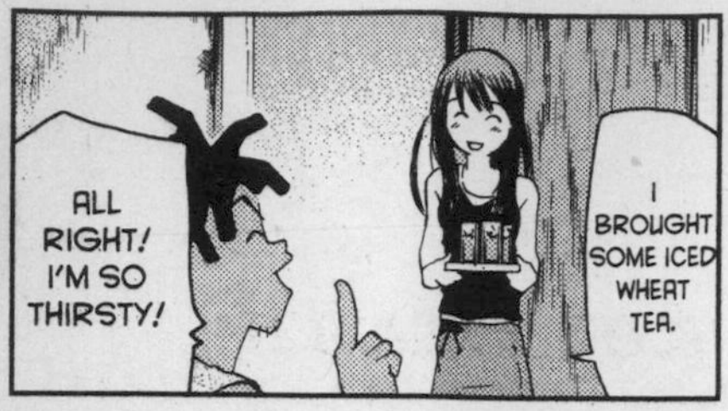
I BROUGHT SOME ICED WHEAT TEA.
ALL RIGHT! I'M SO THIRSTY!

Mugi Cha, page 39

The iced tea that Yuu-Chan brings in is called "Mugi Cha." It's a popular summer time beverage.

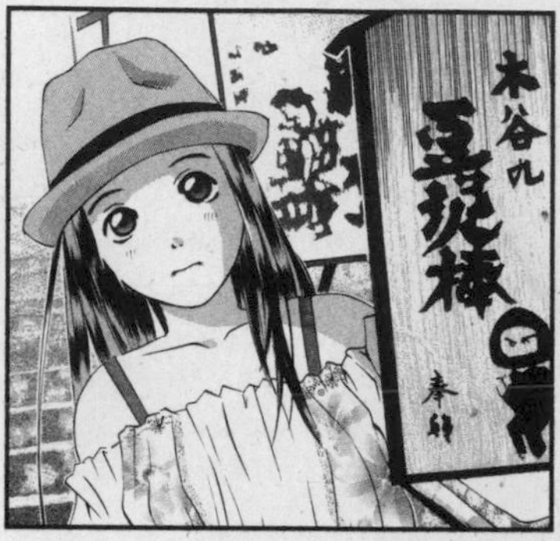

Signs, page 75

Signs, like the one pictured here, are commonly found on stairs leading up to temples and shrines. Vendors or citizens donate money and in turn get a sign with their business's name on it. This particular sign says "bean robber," which is likely the name of a store or business.

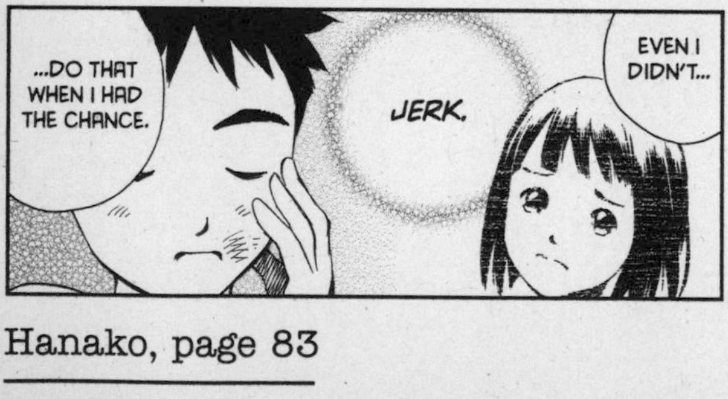
EVEN I DIDN'T...
JERK.
...DO THAT WHEN I HAD THE CHANCE.

Hanako, page 83

This is a flashback of Mugi's girlfriend from Book 1. She moved away, and they broke up.

Guu, page 93

Kazuki is saying, "Guu" which is the Japanese interpretation of the word "Good."

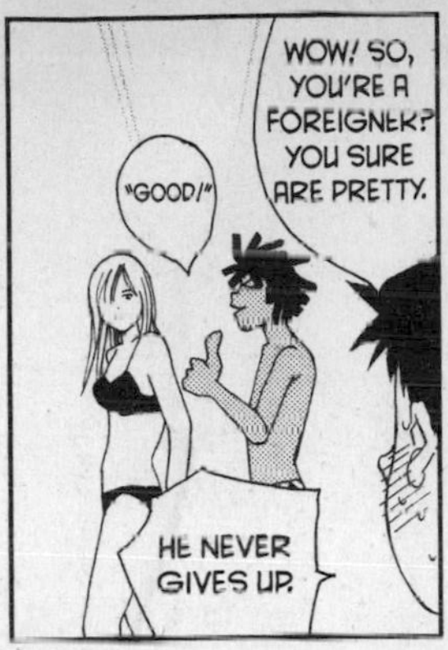
WOW! SO, YOU'RE A FOREIGNER? YOU SURE ARE PRETTY.
"GOOD!"
HE NEVER GIVES UP.

Japanese festivals, page 133

Just like an American carnival, Japanese festivals are full of games. "Goldfish scooping" is a game in which you try to scoop up a goldfish with a paper spoon before the spoon breaks.

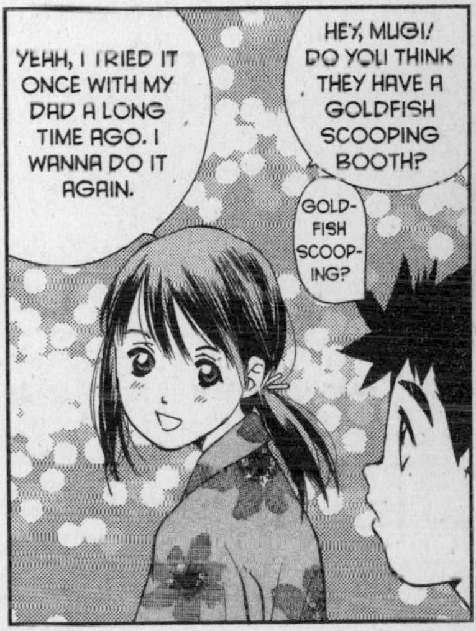
HEY, MUGI! DO YOU THINK THEY HAVE A GOLDFISH SCOOPING BOOTH?
GOLDFISH SCOOPING?
YEAH, I TRIED IT ONCE WITH MY DAD A LONG TIME AGO. I WANNA DO IT AGAIN.

Natto, page 150

"Natto," or fermented soy beans, is a popular breakfast dish, known for its sticky consistency and strong smell

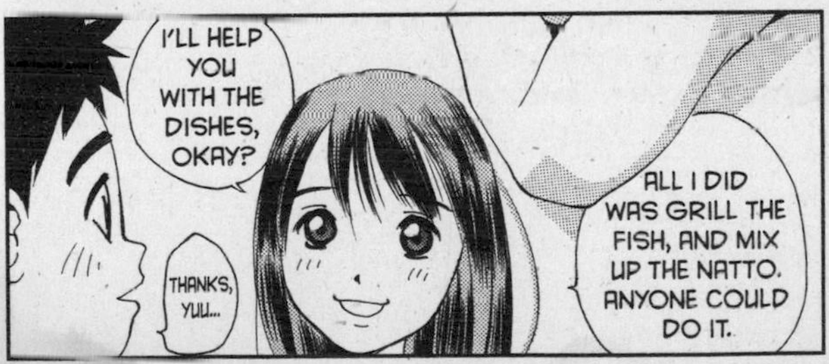
ALL I DID WAS GRILL THE FISH, AND MIX UP THE NATTO. ANYONE COULD DO IT.
I'LL HELP YOU WITH THE DISHES, OKAY?
THANKS, YUU...

Kunie Tanaka, page 190

Kunie Tanaka is a famous Japanese actor who starred in the popular long-running drama “Kita no Kuni Kara.”

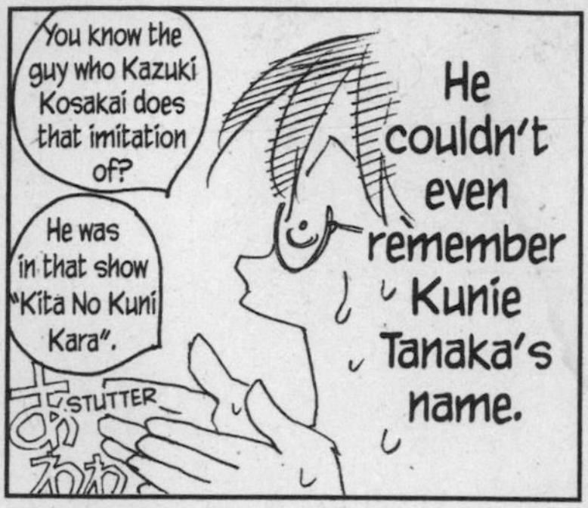
He couldn't even remember Kunie Tanaka's name.
You know the guy who Kazuki Kosakai does that imitation of?
He was in that show "Kita No Kuni Kara".
STUTTER

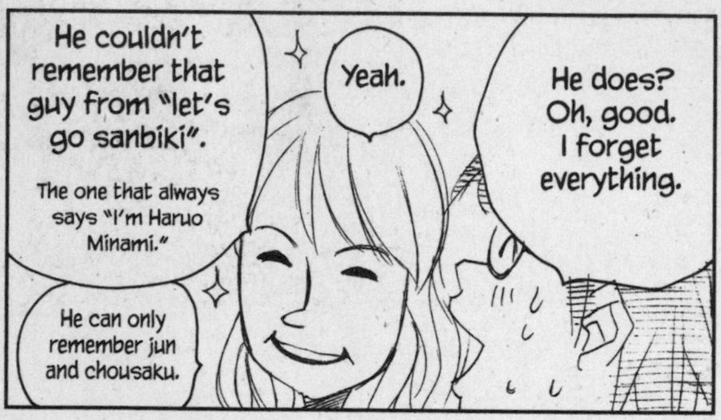
He does? Oh, good. I forget everything.
Yeah.
He couldn't remember that guy from "let's go sanbiki".
The one that always says "I'm Haruo Minami."
He can only remember jun and chousaku.

Let’s go Sanbiki, page 190

“Let’s go sanbiki” is an obscure comedy troupe from the 70s, that’s why Kobayashi is not very reassured when he hears that K-tani’s husband forgets the names of the troupe members.

Preview of Volume 3

We're pleased to present you
a preview from Volume 3.
This volume will be available
in English on June 27, 2006,
but for now you'll have to
make do with Japanese!

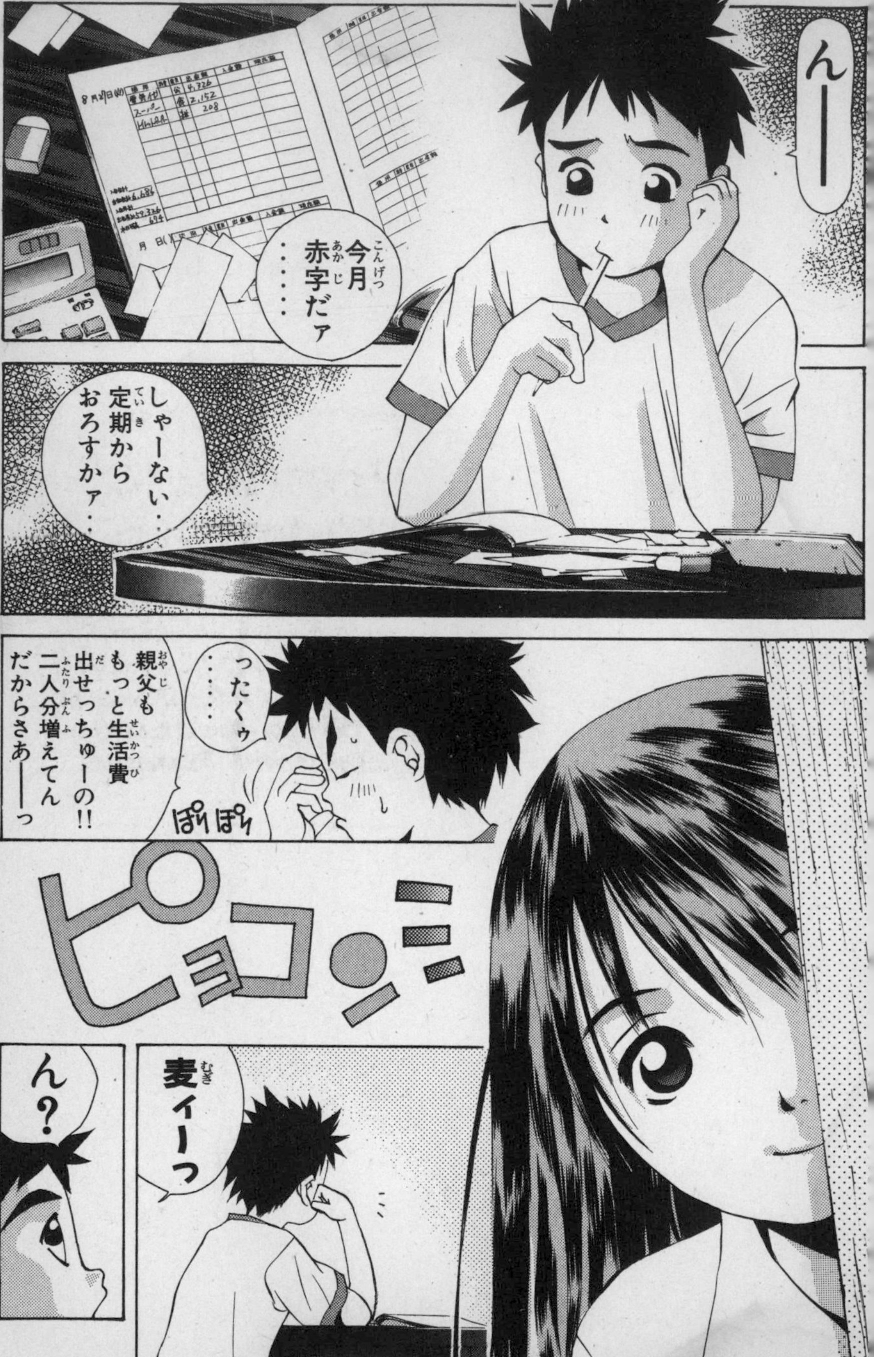
ん——
今月赤字だァ……
しゃーない…定期からおろすかァ…
ピョコン
ったくぅ……
親父ももっと生活費出せっちゅーの!! 二人分増えてんだからさあ——っ
ぽりぽり
麦ィーっ
ん？

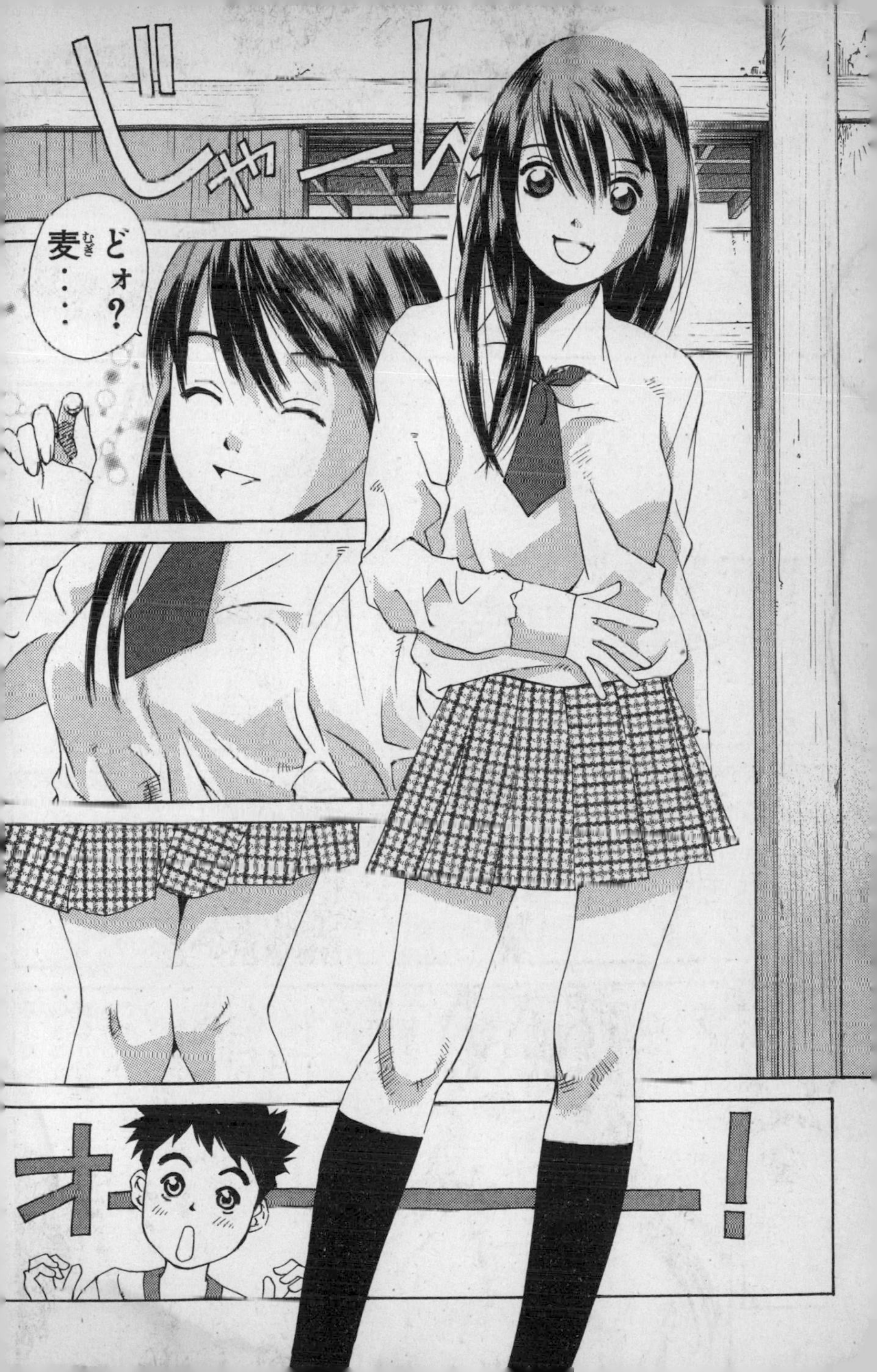
じゃーん
どォ？麦・・・・
オーーー！

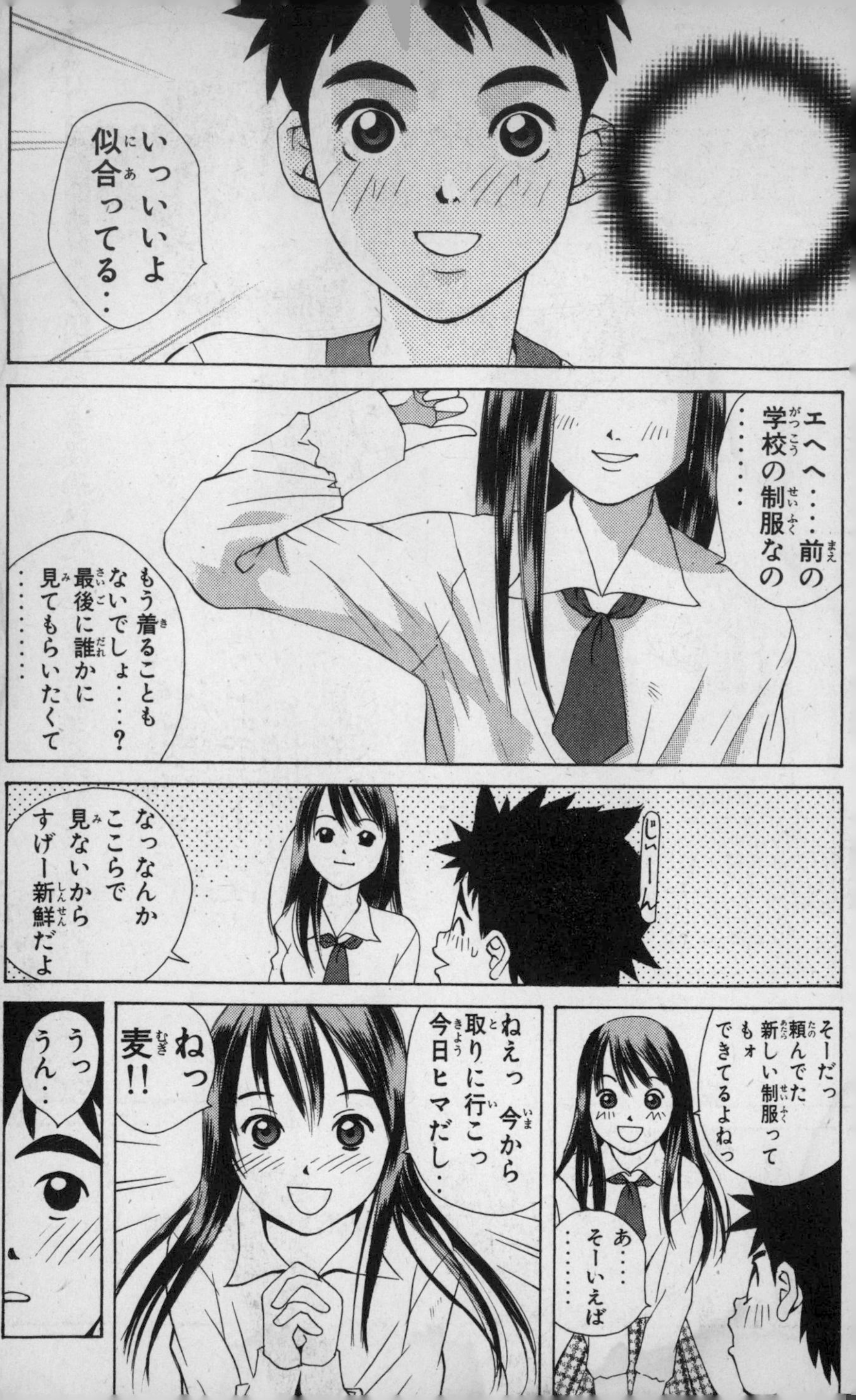
いっいいよ 似合ってる・・
エへへ・・・前の学校の制服なの・・・・・・
もう着ることもないでしょ・・・・？ 最後に誰かに見てもらいたくて・・・・・・・
じぃーーん
なっなんか ここらで見ないから すげー新鮮だよ
そーだっ 頼んでた 新しい制服って もォ できてるよねっ
あ・・・・ そーいえば・・・・・・・
ねえっ 今から 取りに行こっ 今日ヒマだし・・
ねっ 麦!!
うっ うん・・

Gacha Gacha

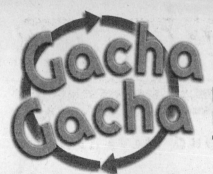

By Hiroyuki Tamakoshi

Gacha Gacha
1
HIROYUKI TAMAKOSHI

Kouhei is your typical Japanese high school student—he's usually late, he loves beef bowls, he pals around with his buddies, and he's got his first-ever crush on his childhood friend Kurara. Before he can express his feelings, however, Kurara heads off to Hawaii with her mother for summer vacation. When she returns, she seems like a totally different person . . . and that's because she is! While she was away, Kurara somehow developed an alternate personality: Arisa! And where Kurara has no time for boys, Arisa isn't interested in much else. Now Kouhei must help protect his friend's secret, and make sure that Arisa doesn't do anything Kurara would regret!

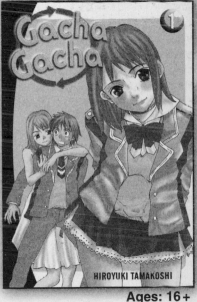

Ages: 16+

Special extras in each volume! Read them all!

DEL REY

VISIT WWW.DELREYMANGA.COM TO:

- View release date calendars for upcoming volumes
- Sign up for Del Rey's free manga e-newsletter
- Find out the latest about new Del Rey Manga series

THE wallflower
YAMATONADESHIKO SHICHIHENGE

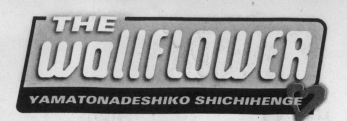

BY TOMOKO HAYAKAWA

It's a beautiful, expansive mansion, and four handsome, fifteen-year-old friends are allowed to live in it for free! But there is one condition—within three years the young men must take the owner's niece and transform her into a proper lady befitting the palace in which they all live! How hard can it be?

Enter Sunako Nakahara, the horror-movie-loving, pock-faced, frizzy-haired, fashion-illiterate hermit who has a tendency to break into explosive nosebleeds whenever she sees anyone attractive. This project is going to take far more than our four heroes ever expected; it needs a miracle!

1
THE wallflower
YAMATONADESHIKO SHICHIHENGE
TOMOKO HAYAKAWA

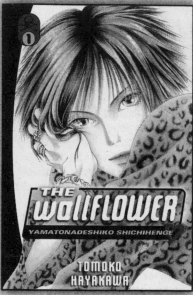

Ages: 16 +

Special extras in each volume! Read them all!

DEL REY

VISIT WWW.DELREYMANGA.COM TO:
- View release date calendars for upcoming volumes
- Sign up for Del Rey's free manga e-newsletter
- Find out the latest about new Del Rey Manga series

TOMARE!

(STOP!)

YOU'RE GOING THE WRONG WAY!

MANGA IS A COMPLETELY DIFFERENT TYPE
OF READING EXPERIENCE.

TO START AT THE BEGINNING, GO TO THE END!

THAT'S RIGHT! JUL 0 8 2008

AUTHENTIC MANGA IS READ THE TRADITIONAL
JAPANESE WAY—FROM RIGHT TO LEFT. EXACTLY THE OPPOSITE
OF HOW AMERICAN BOOKS ARE READ. IT'S EASY TO FOLLOW:
JUST GO TO THE OTHER END OF THE BOOK, AND READ EACH PAGE
—AND EACH PANEL—FROM RIGHT SIDE TO LEFT SIDE,
STARTING AT THE TOP RIGHT. NOW YOU'RE EXPERIENCING
MANGA AS IT WAS MEANT TO BE.